CW01425528

Reinsurance in Practice

British Library Cataloguing in Publication data
Kiln, Robert — Kiln, Stephen
Reinsurance in Practice — 4th ed.
1. Insurance
1. Title
368.0122

ISBN 1 85609 179 1

While the principles discussed and the details given in this book are the product of careful study, the author and publisher cannot in any way guarantee the suitability of recommendations made in this book for individual problems, and they shall not be under any legal liability of any kind in respect of or arising out of the form or contents of this book or any error therein, or the reliance of any person thereon.

REINSURANCE IN PRACTICE

Fourth Edition

by
Robert Kiln and Stephen Kiln

LONDON
WITHERBY & CO LTD
32-36 Aylesbury Street
London EC1R 0ET

Published 1981
1st Edition 1981
2nd Edition 1986
3rd Edition 1991
4th Edition 2001

ISBN 13: 978 1 85609 179 4
ISBN 10: 1 85609 179 1

Published and Printed by:
Witherby & Co. Ltd
32-36 Aylesbury Street
London EC1R 0ET

Tel: (0)20 7251 5341
Fax: (0)20 7251 1296
International Tel: +44 (0)20 7251 5341
International Fax: +44 (0)20 7251 1296
E-mail: books@witherbys.co.uk
Website: www.witherbys.com

FOREWORD TO THE 2001 EDITION

It was only when I became intimately concerned with the workings of the Lloyd's market that I came to realise just how perceptive Bob Kiln had been.

He established and led his own business with an outlook and standards which should have been a model for others. He sought audience for his views, but too often he was rebuffed by the establishment. Throughout his working life his professionalism and originality of approach inspired his own team.

I am delighted that this book has been updated and republished. I hope a new generation of readers will gain knowledge and inspiration from it.

Sir David Rowland
March 2001

FOREWORD TO THE 1991 EDITION

If there is a single business essential to the economic welfare of the world it is the insurance business, without which the investments necessary to enable the great progress made in areas ranging from medicine to space would have been impossible. At the same time, insurance would not have been able to play its role without reinsurance. Therefore, it is only fitting for this important, but relatively unknown, reinsurance business to have such a valuable text as "REINSURANCE IN PRACTICE".

I personally have had the privilege of knowing and working with Bob Kiln for over 40 years and he is universally respected by clients, Insurance and Reinsurance Brokers and competing Underwriters throughout the world. He has been able to draw upon his exceptional experience as one of the leading and most successful Reinsurance Underwriters in the history of Lloyd's to set out his interpretations of reinsurance practice which combine technical expertise, practical common sense and commercial awareness.

This text should be required reading not only for those interested in becoming involved in the reinsurance business but also those who are active reinsurance practitioners. It can also provide insurance professionals with a better understanding of the inter-relationships between insurance and reinsurance.

Bob Kiln is regarded as the "professional's professional" by those in the reinsurance business and is acknowledged by them for his many contributions to our business, of which "REINSURANCE IN PRACTICE" is one of the most important.

Robert J. Newhouse
March 1991

FOREWORD TO THE 1986 EDITION

The insurance industry, though worldwide in scope, is a small fraternity, and its leaders are known worldwide. Some of them are recognized because they head a particular company or organization; others are acclaimed for their skill and for the outstanding contributions they have made to our business. Bob Kiln is one of those.

I had the good fortune to meet Bob at Lloyd's, early in my career. He was a lead underwriter and was universally accepted by the market as an outstanding underwriter to have on any slip.

A great underwriter has many interests and abilities. Bob Kiln, who is well known as an amateur archaeologist, has demonstrated further versatility by authoring this important reinsurance text.

Clearly written, and interwoven with many anecdotes of his personal experience at Lloyd's, *Reinsurance in Practice* is the work of a professional who has spent many years on the firing line. A skillful blend of reinsurance theory and practice, it will be a welcome addition to insurance libraries as well as a useful tool for professionals and students alike.

Maurice R. Greenberg
President and Chief Executive Officer,
American International Group Inc.

PREFACE TO FIRST EDITION

This book is dedicated to the late Sir Matthew Drysdale, who brought me into insurance, and Mr. L. A. Durham, who taught me reinsurance, or some of it!

This work arises from a promise I made to the late Dr. Golding that one day I would write a book on reinsurance that would complement his own. I only regret that I could not keep that promise during his lifetime. Dr. Golding's book, alas now out of print, can still be read as a basic book on reinsurance.

My intention is to produce a practical introduction to non-marine reinsurance and reinsurance problems for those who have some insurance knowledge. Hopefully it will be found readable to many who practice reinsurance and will be useful to students and others starting in the business. My own experience of 30 years as a leading Reinsurance Underwriter, mainly in property reinsurance, colours the whole book of course. The opinions expressed are mine and mine alone. I have confined this book deliberately to the practical side of placing reinsurance and touched upon the legal aspects very lightly, if at all. Neither have I touched upon the various reinsurance markets nor attempted to deal with life, marine or aviation reinsurance but many of the problems and principles dealt with in this book are common to all classes of reinsurance.

In using mathematics I have tried to use very simple examples in the form of basic mathematics which my generation can understand. I have left such matters as law to the lawyers and theory to the academics. This book is intended for those who make their living by reinsuring or being reinsured.

In making acknowledgements I am conscious of the many people who have given me their support whilst working on this project — my wife, Letty, for bearing with me whilst I did the writing and re-writing; my colleagues in R. J. Kiln & Co. Limited for their encouragement and for allowing me time off!; to Len Durham for his anecdotes and humour, to Brian Harber, and many Brokers, for help with wordings, my son Stephen Kiln and Phillippa Ross (nee King) for reading the draft and improving upon it and, above all, Betty Levine for all her work and forebearance in producing the final version for the publishers, and generally to my old friend Hank Greenberg for taking the time in such a full and successful life to read this and to write a foreword.

Robert Kiln
Hertford, 1981

PREFACE TO SECOND EDITION

I am very happy that this book seems to read well after four years and the reader will find little change in the basic Chapters I to XIII, except some considerable amplification of Chapter VII dealing with deposits of Reserves and Letters of Credits and I have extended Chapter XIV on solvency and reserving.

I have included a new Chapter XV dealing with such matters as Rollers and Bankers. My treatment is very much, I hope, a logical and a philosophical approach because I feel the industry needs to look afresh at itself in these matters.

My thanks are due to Margaret Archer for the typing and retyping of this second edition.

This book was written to teach the younger generations some of the practical ethics and practical problems of our business and in 1985 I think this is necessary as I still believe that our problems will only be cured by commonsense based on sound practice and this does not change.

Robert Kiln
Hertford, 1986

PREFACE TO THIRD EDITION

I am still happy that the basic text reads well after ten years, or so I am told! This new edition contains a number of revisions and some new material to deal with the problems of the 1990s. I am particularly grateful to Mr. Chris Ventiroso of the Harvey Bowring syndicate for discussing in such an authoritative way the early history and source of the problems posed to the Reinsurance Market by Asbestos Related Claims and also for critically reading this edition and suggesting a number of improvements. I am also indebted to my old friend Charles Skey and to his Syndicate R. A. Edwards and others for valuable contributions on Asbestos & Pollution.

I am grateful also to my old friend Robert Newhouse who retired in early 1990 after a long and distinguished career with Guy Carpenter and Marsh McLennan for undertaking to write the Foreword to this edition. It is right that he should do so for Guy Carpenter and Robert Newhouse and his colleagues have formulated and contributed much to the development of reinsurance.

My thanks are due once again to Margaret Archer for the typing and retyping and to my cheerful publisher Alan Witherby. I would also like to thank my son Stephen Kiln and many others for their helpful suggestions.

Since compiling the second edition in 1985 much of my time has been taken up as a consultant or expert witness or arbitrator and I have now handled nearly 100 such disputes. Many of these have arisen from the stupidity or greed of reinsurers and many from reassureds or their brokers taking innocent reinsurers for a ride. In such cases, good faith between the parties does not and never did exist. Our industry was built on "Good Faith" and until all our contracts are placed and honoured in accordance with "Utmost Good Faith" we do not deserve the reputation of an honourable profession.

Robert Kiln
Hertford, 1990

PREFACE TO FOURTH EDITION

This edition is very much of a joint effort between Robert and myself. We had decided that the new edition needed substantial revisions and Robert did much of this work shortly before his untimely death. He also wrote a completely new chapter entitled "Law and Reinsurance", which was inspired by his work as an expert witness and arbitrator. I have written a completely new chapter on Retrocession which was not the type of business Robert would normally have written but even he might have been tempted with the transparency and terms available. I have done substantial rewriting to chapters X, XI and XIV but the early chapters and the stop loss chapter still read well and are almost unchanged.

I am grateful to many people for helping with this edition and for those not mentioned here. Firstly I would like to thank Sir David Rowland for his kind foreword. I would like to thank Michael Mendelowitz of Barlow Lyde and Gilbert for his help on reviewing the law chapter and his colleagues Colin Croly and John Butler for other contributions. I would like to thank my ex-colleague Ray Hunter for his personal views on Professional Indemnity and Valerie Fogleman also of Barlows for her section on pollution. I would like also to thank Thomas J Quinn of Mendes and Mount in New York for his article on the development of asbestos litigation.

I would also like to thank Bob Rundle of Guy Carpenter for all his help on wordings and for Jim Bannister for letting me use some of his ideas and material from "Alternative Risk Financing". I thank also John Cavanagh of R.K.Carvill for their ideas on claims-made contracts and Hugh Thompson and Ken Louw for their material and help on the law chapter. I am grateful for Alan Rees of Aon for his suggestions on Insurance regulation. Thank you also to Bill Rendall of Kilns for his input.

Finally I would also like to thank Margaret Archer and Liz Rudderham for their typing and Alan Witherby for his patience!

I have tried to keep this book, where I have made changes, in the spirit of the earlier editions. Some sections are a little old fashioned but I have left them often unaltered as it gives an historical perspective and I have just added later comments. I include one of the many letters he received about the book together with a typical response, which I apologise for not implementing. I would finally like to dedicate this book to Robert for his help and encouragement over the years and his plain common-sense advice which I miss.

I have included one of the many obituaries written about him which will give the readers some idea of the wide range of activities he got up to other than writing Reinsurance text books.

Steve Kiln
Hertford 2001

A message from the Publisher

Readers may find some of the text to be written in a particular style and the syntax not as Professors of English would teach!

Robert Kiln had all but finished the revision of this fourth edition before his untimely death. I took a view, as did his son Steve Kiln, who has brought the edition to completion, that the text should remain the same and not be edited.

I make no apologies for continuing to publish this excellent work, by one of the pioneers of many aspects of reinsurance, without change.

Alan Witherby
September 2001

ROBERT KILN

Lloyd's Underwriter and Sponsor of Achaeological Projects

Robert Kiln, who has died aged 77, was a Lloyd's underwriter and a former chairman of Lloyd's Life Insurance; he was also a respected archaeologist.

Robert John Kiln, the son of a marine underwriter was born in Middlesex on May 14 1920 and educated at Merchant Taylors'. After school he joined Sir Matthew Drysdale's non-marine box at Lloyd's in 1938.

On the outbreak of the Second World War, Kiln was posted from his Territorial regiment, the Honourable Artillery Company, to the Hertfordshire Yeomanry.

In 1944 his unit, the 86th Field Regiment RA, provided close support to the D-Day landings, shelling the defences behind Gold Beach near the village of La Rivière.

A more detailed analysis and critique of the landing and the subsequent campaign — *D-Day to Arnhem* — was published in 1993. This is the personal story of Kiln and four other fighting soldiers, extracts from whose diaries, together with detailed maps and photographs, provide an intimate picture of front-line experiences.

Kiln's war ended when he was hit by shell burst near Antwerp; he suffered gangrene, losing a leg and much of his hearing.

He returned to the Drysdale syndicate at Lloyd's in 1946, badly disabled but with his underwriting skills unimpaired. He possessed a quick mathematical mind and was always ready to help a broker if this could be done profitably. He built up his reputation as a specialist in excess of loss reinsurance.

Kiln was fiercely independent and in 1962 decided to form his own underwriting agency and syndicate. R. J. Kiln & Co. opened for the 1963 account, though the syndicate lost money for the next three years. Fortunately, Kiln retained the loyalty of underwriting Names and agents, and from 1968 onwards R. J. Kiln enjoyed profitable growth.

By 1995 nine syndicates were under management covering all markets; business was underwritten in every continent, with particular emphasis on America and the Commonwealth, and with special support being given to newly created national companies. Premium capacity had grown from £1 million to £500 million.

Robert Kiln wrote his first pamphlet, "Whither Lloyd's?", in 1968. In this he stated that "the Committee of Lloyd's has a special responsibility to Names", and that "some agents have not given their Names the absolute priority they should receive".

He advocated a strong initiative to boost the life insurance business, prophesied that corporate members would be needed in the future, and urged that the market should substantially increase the recruitment of high quality graduates, including women.

His reputation in the life insurance market led to his appointment to succeed Sir Henry Mance as chairman of Lloyd's Life Insurance in 1979. During Kiln's chairmanship, Lloyd's Life grew rapidly and profitably, but was sold, to Kiln's great disappointment, by the Council of Lloyd's to the Royal Insurance Company in 1986.

Whereas Kiln's commercial initiatives were influential and popular, his radical and critical views of the government and practices of Lloyd's inevitably met with opposition. He was elected with a strong popular vote, to the Committee of Lloyd's three times between 1970 and 1980, but resigned at the end of 1981, exasperated by the lack of response to his criticisms.

His contribution to the industry and to the reputation of London grew as he published his two books, *Reinsurance in Practice* (1981) and *Reinsurance Underwriting* (1985). These remain standard reading for reinsurance students.

Robert Kiln remained an active underwriter until 1975 and chairman of R. J. Kiln & Co. until his retirement in 1985. He left behind him a reputation for integrity, and a dislike of pretentiousness and pomposity. He gave encouragement to the young, explaining the complexities of the business to his juniors with patience and clarity.

Kiln's generous nature led him to spread R. J. Kiln's shares widely among directors and employees. The fashion for financial service organisations to surrender their independence did not appeal to Kiln, and he approved of the steps taken by his successors to convert R. J. Kiln & Co. into an employee trust, the purpose being to achieve independence and financial reward for the executives in the middle and longer term.

In retirement he remained in touch with the international market, and was in demand as a lecturer, arbitrator and expert witness.

In the early 1960s Kiln obtained a post-graduate diploma in Archaeology from London University, winning the prize as the outstanding student of his year. He subsequently lectured on archaeology at Durham University, was awarded an honorary Doctorate of Letters by Sheffield University in 1990, and became a Fellow of the Society of Antiquaries.

He published many pamphlets, particularly relating to archaeological work in Hertfordshire. With Clive Partidge he co-wrote the book *Ware and Hertford.*

Kiln also set up and funded the Kiln Charitable Trust, which has distributed more than £1 million, concentrating on conservation, archaeology, music and education. With Magnus Magnusson he established the British Archaeology Awards, and he privately sponsored the Pitt Rivers Award for independent archaeologists.

Robert Kiln married his first wife, Daphne, a doctor and distinguished amateur violinist, in 1949; they had three sons and three daughters. She died in 1976, and he married his second wife, Letty, in 1978.

February 19, 1997

Dear Mr. Kiln:

Assuming that you have not succumbed to one or another of the diseases that often accompany a misspent life, I would like to request that your next edition of Reinsurance in Practice does not contain references to wife-swapping and the conduct of the "best" prostitutes. Such references are not only disappointing when discussing honorable undertakings among "gentlemen", but also overlook the fact that reinsurance is no longer an "old boys club".

Under such circumstances, I, for one, am very disinclined to reference or quote your otherwise useful discussion of the limits of catastrophe covers.
Here's hoping for a truly updated edition.

Very truly yours

March 17, 1997

Dear Ms

Reinsurance in Practice

Your letter of February 19th has been forwarded on me from Witherby & Company, London. I am glad you found some of the book useful.

I can assure you that I have not succumbed yet to any of the diseases you are thinking about and my wife tells me I am in good health and well behaved. I can quite see that reference to wife swapping may be out of date as I expect as many wives swap husbands these days as husbands swap wives. Would you think therefore that we should make a reference to 'spouse' rather than wife, or perhaps even that is out of date, and should use the word 'partner'?

With regard to prostitutes, again you are probably right and that the wording of that should not refer to 'wallet' but perhaps 'purse' would be better, or may be just refer to money.
I would be grateful for your suggestions as I am just redoing the Fourth Edition, so it would be a good time to make any changes. Your advice on this and any other things in the book would be more than welcome.

I entirely agree with you that Reinsurance is no longer an 'old boys club' and in this I think my credentials are fairly good as I was the person who altered the Lloyd's ruling in the 70s to allow women to work in that Market. Also, I was the first reinsurance organization, as far as I know, on this side of the Atlantic to employ a woman Underwriter in the mid 70s and a woman Claims Settler.

With regard to your last few words, I am very glad indeed that you are not quoting from my book as it was not intended for that purpose. I wrote it for people to read and enjoy.

Yours sincerely,

Robert J. Kiln

CONTENTS

CHAPTER I

INTRODUCTION

Let us start with a simple question. What is Reinsurance? Insuring Insurers is a short and as good a description as any. That is to say, it is:

(1) The business of insuring an insurance company or Underwriter against suffering too great a loss from their insurance operations; and

(2) Allowing an insurance company or Underwriter to lay off or pass on part of their liability to another Insurer on a given insurance which they have accepted.

These two functions of Reinsurance — the laying off or passing on of liability on an insurance and the protection of an insurance account — should be remembered. They overlap at times but are nevertheless the two fundamental and distinct functions of all reinsurances.

An insurance company or Underwriter who takes out Reinsurance is known as a Reinsured or Reassured, the company or Underwriter accepting the Reinsurance as a Reinsurer. To eliminate confusion I will use the terms "Reassured" rather than "Reinsured" and "Reinsurer" for the company or Underwriter accepting the Reinsurance.

There are two types of Reinsurance — firstly, **contributing or proportional Reinsurance** and, secondly, **non-contributary or non-proportional Reinsurance**. Contributing or proportional Reinsurance is where the Reassured passes on a proportion of his liability on an individual risk or a number of risks and pays to the Reinsurer the same proportion of the original insurance premium for that risk or risks. In return, should claims arise, the Reinsurer will reimburse the Reassured for the same proportion of those claims.

To take a simple example, "A" accepts an insurance for £100,000 on a shop. "A" passes on, or cedes, to "B" £70,000 or 70% of the £100,000. "B", the Reinsurer, accepts 70% of the liability. He receives 70% of the original premium on the risk and if a claim of, say £1,000 arises "B" will pay to "A" his 70% share or £700.

An example of non-proportional Reinsurance on the same shop valued at £100,000 — "A" takes out a Reinsurance with "B" to reinsure himself should the shop suffer a loss exceeding £30,000, up to the value of the shop of £100,000. "B" assumes a liability of up to £70,000 in excess of £30,000 any one loss in respect of that shop. In the event of a claim of £30,000 or less, "B" reimburses "A" for the amount of loss in excess of £30,000 up to a further £70,000 — e.g. "B"'s share of an original loss of £40,000 will be £10,000, the amount excess of £30,000. "A" will not pay "B" 70% of the original premium but a lesser amount.

Although "B" takes on 70% of the total policy liability he does not contribute proportionally to all losses and will not receive a proportionate share of the premium. Such a non-proportional Reinsurance is called an excess of loss contract because "B"'s liability only commences in excess of a loss of a certain defined amount.

Now, to turn to methods of effecting Reinsurance, we have three basic methods by which resinsurance is done. Firstly, **facultatively**. Here each Reinsurance is effected individually. The Reassured, if he so elects, offers to a Reinsurer each Reinsurance individually and the Reinsured is free to accept such an offer or reject it. The essential point about facultative Reinsurance is that both parties are free to accept or decline, or to negotiate the terms of the Reinsurance. There is no obligation on the Reassured to reinsure and no obligation on the Resinsurer to accept. Both of the foregoing are examples of facultative Reinsurance on a shop insured for £100,000.

The second main method of Reinsurance is by an **obligatory treaty**. Here a formal agreement is drawn up between the Reassured and the Reinsurer. Under such an agreement the Reassured enters into an obligation to cede liability on individual risks to its Reinsurer and the Reinsurer is obliged to accept each cession. The formal agreement, or obligatory treaty, will stipulate the type of business to be ceded, the amounts to be ceded and the terms and conditions under which cessions are to be made. It can be a fairly lengthy legal document which will be agreed and signed by the two contracting parties. The wording of such an agreement naturally requires careful drafting and scrutinising by both parties.

A simple example of an obligatory treaty might be where "A" is insuring shops and instead of reinsuring each one facultatively he enters into an obligatory treaty arrangement with "B" under which "A" agrees to cede, i.e. to pass on to "B" 70% of his liability on *all* the shops insured for £10,000 or less which he underwrites, and to pass on 70% of all premiums he receives. "B" agrees to accept 70% of the liability on all the shops and to pay 70% of all claims which may arise. Such a treaty is known as a quota share treaty.

The third main method of Reinsurance is by a **contract** or **policy of indemnity**. Let us pursue our little shop account. "A" has entered into an obligatory quota share treaty with "B" to reinsure 70% of all his shops up to a maximum of 70% of £100,000 any one shop. "A" will retain for himself 30% of all the shops he insures up to a maximum of £30,000 any one shop. On a small shop valued at £20,000 the line retained by "A" will be £6,000, i.e. 30% of £20,000. Now, "A" may decide that he is concerned that a conflagration, or some similar disaster, could occur which might destroy a number of shops and his loss on his retained lines of 30% might be considerable. He wishes to limit his loss from any such disaster to, say, £50,000, leaving himself with a net loss of £50,000 in any such disaster. He buys a Reinsurance with "C" to reinsure him for any loss he may suffer in excess of £50,000 in any one disaster involving more than one shop. Such a Reinsurance is a contract of indemnity for which "A" will pay a premium to "C" to be indemnified against a disaster costing "A" more than £50,000.

We can take our example a stage further. Let us assume that Underwriter "A" is offered the insurance of a shop with a value of £150,000. He has an obligatory quota share treaty with his Reinsurer, "B", to take 70% of all insurances up to a capacity of £100,000 on any one shop. He has a catastrophe contract to protect him in the event of a disaster costing him more than £50,000 in respect of his retained lines of up to £30,000 on any one shop. He is now offered a shop with a value of £150,000. What are his options assuming he does not want to increase his own retained line of £30,000? He can either limit his acceptance to £100,000, part of £150,000, and allow another Insurer to take up the balance of £50,000, or he can accept a gross line of £150,000 and cede away £50,000, part of £150,000, by way of facultative Reinsurance.

We have, therefore, an example of the three methods of insurance used to perform the two functions of Reinsurance:

(1) A facultative resinsurance for £50,000, part of £150,000, on one large shop which reduces Underwriter "A"'s liability on that shop, or risk, to £100,000.

(2) An obligatory Reinsurance treaty which automatically takes 70% of Underwriter "A"'s liability on all shops up to a liability of £100,000 any one shop.

(3) A contract of indemnity which limits Underwriter "A"'s loss in the event of a disaster to £50,000.

Please note that (1) and (2) are contributing or proportional reinsurances and that (3) is a non-contributing Reinsurance.

We will carry our example (1) one stage further. Let us assume that Underwriter "A" finds that he is consistently asked to insure shops valued between £100,000 and £200,000. He still wishes to retain a net line for himself of not exceeding £30,000. He could, of course, increase his quota share to 85% of up to £200,000 on any one shop, thus leaving himself with a maximum net line of 15% of £200,000 or £30,000. However, this would mean that he would reduce his share of all shops valued at £100,000 or less and his own net retained share of the premium income would drop considerably. He can continue with individual facultative reinsurances, which has the disadvantange of being time consuming and expensive, and also he cannot accept an insurance valued at over £100,000 until he has had time to place the facultative Reinsurance.

His other alternative is to place another obligatory contributing treaty in addition to his 70% quota share treaty. This treaty would be an agreement under which "A" can cede to "D" all amounts surplus to £100,000 up to a further £100,000 on any one shop. "A" would agree to cede to such a surplus treaty all amounts surplus to £100,000 any one shop and Reinsurer "D" will agree automatically to accept all such surplus amounts up to a further £100,000 any one shop. Thus, "A" knows that "D"'s liability attaches automatically with his and he can accept an insurance of up to £200,000 on a shop knowing his liability is automatically ceded to "D".

Such an obligatory contributing treaty is known as a surplus treaty. The quota share treaty and the surplus treaty are the two types of contributing treaties.

Please note that if Underwriter "A" is now asked to insure a shop for the value of £250,000 he may do a facultative contributing Reinsurance for £50,000, part of £250,000, on this shop, then cede

£100,000, part of £250,000, to his surplus treaty and then cede 70% of £100,000 to his 70% quota share treaty. His retained line on that shop would be £30,000, part of £250,000. In the event of any loss on the risk all would contribute proportionately to that loss.

e.g. a loss of £100,000:

Facultative Reinsurance contributes	£20,000 — 20%
Surplus treaty contributes	$30,000 — 40%
Quota share treaty contributes	£28,000 — 28%
"A"'s retained loss is	£12,000 — 12%

To continue the little saga of our shop account let us assume that Underwriter "A", our Reassured, builds up a substantial book of shop business and it represents a sizeable block of premium income. He may feel that if in any one financial year his shop account turned "sour" it would adversely upset the whole balance of profit and loss on his insurance account. He could, of course, simply reduce his business and bring his shop account into balance in relation to his entire operation. he may be reluctant to do this on a profitable line of insurance.

As an alternative he may seek a contract of indemnity to reimburse him if in any one year's operation the losses on his net retained account are excessive, i.e. if his aggregation of losses after collecting from his reinsurances, his surplus treaty, his quota share treaty and his catastrophe excess of loss exceed a certain figure. Such a contract would stop his annual net losses at a certain pre-determined amount. It is a contract of indemnity known as a stop loss or excess aggregate Reinsurance. The amount at which his losses are stopped can be either a monetary figure or, more often, is expressed as a ratio of his annual retained premium income from his shop account. The retained premium income is his gross premium income after deduction of premiums ceded to his facultative reinsurances, his surplus treaty, his quota share treaty and premiums paid for his catastrophe or disaster excess of loss contract.

Example: Let us assume "A" anticipates a retained premium income of £100,000 per annum and he wishes to limit his aggregation of losses in any one year to £150,000. He would buy a stop loss excess of £150,000 in the aggregate per annum of excess of 150% of his annual retained premium income.

Underwriter "A" has now used all the types of Reinsurance and all methods. The rest of this book is merely verbiage elaborating on problems and variations. Before we proceed let us just tabulate these essentials:

(1) Facultative Reinsurance reinsures individual large risks or exposures.

(2) A contributing surplus treaty automatically takes all risks over a certain size.

(3) A contributing quota share treaty takes a fixed proportion of all risks.

(4) An excess of loss *contract* protects against an unfortunate disaster.

(5) A stop loss *contract* protects against an unfortunate aggregation of losses during a period of time.

The order of reinsurances as set out is the order in which they operate. Thus:

- facultative Reinsurance reduces a peak exposure.
- first surplus further reduces individual exposures.
- the quota share further reduces all exposures.
- the excess of loss protects the remaining accumulations.
- the stop loss protects the residual net exposures against an adverse experience.

Another way to put it is that the stop loss has the benefit of all the other reinsurances, i.e. they inure to its benefit as any losses collected under (1) to (4) are deducted before calculating the loss under the stop loss.

We have in this example the two distinct functions of Reinsurance mentioned at the start of this chapter. The traditional one of passing on or part of the original insurance policy by contributing Reinsurance under 1, 2, 3 above and the more modern development of the protection of the Insurer's account by non-contributing (Excess of loss) reinsurances under 4 and 5 above. These two functions should be distinguished. Under the first, the Reinsurer tracks the original policy; in the second, function, the individual policy is lost and Reinsurers are really insuring the Insurer against a contingency happening on his insurance account.

It is perhaps a pity that we use the term "Reinsurance" for both functions. This has led to confusion in that the case law has traditionally been concerned with passing on an original policy and that law does not necessarily apply to the second function of protecting an insurance operation. Some modern developments of the latter are more fully dealt with under Financial Reinsurances in Chapter XIV and the reader can judge when he gets that far how very different they are in concept to a facultative contributing Reinsurance.

CHAPTER II

FACULTATIVE PROPORTIONAL INSURANCE

Introduction — The policy — Net retention and how to broke — Ceding Commission — Net rate basis— The full reinsurance clause — Uses and characteristics — A fairy story — Slip and schedule

Introduction

The earliest method of reinsurance used, and the most obvious, is simply to offer another Insurer a portion of an individual risk where the amount you have accepted is too large for your own requirements. If the offer is accepted a simple reinsurance policy is issued between the two parties.

Note the essential element of the facultative method; the offer of part of the risk and its acceptance or rejection. There is no obligation to make the offer and no obligation to accept it. Each reinsurance is offered and accepted or rejected individually. The accepting or rejecting Reinsurer must make his own judgement of each individual risk in much the same way that he would if he were offered the same risk as a direct insurance. Therefore he may require very full underwriting information before he can underwrite the offered reinsurance.

However, there is one great difference which is that the original Insurer has exercised his underwriting judgement and accepted the insurance in the first place. This means that provided the Reinsurer respects and trusts the underwriting expertise and judgement of the Reassured, and provided the Reassured is keeping for himself a reasonable proportion of the risk, the Reinsurer may feel that he can follow the fortunes of the Reassured and not require full underwriting information himself. This will, of course, be modified if the motive of the Reassured in doing a facultative reinsurance is to get rid of a piece of junk. Motives are difficult to discover purely by paper transactions but a good facultative reinsurance Underwriter will be able to sense junk from the information about the risk itself, the amount the Reassured is retaining for himself and his knowledge of the character of the Reassured and how much he can trust him.

We have here the first two essential lessons in reinsurance; first, the necessity to develop trust between the Reassured and Reinsurer and, secondly, the fact that reinsurance underwriting is as much the art of underwriting people (i.e. assessing the quality of your Reassured) as the science of underwriting facts.

The Reinsurance Policy

To turn to the essential details of a facultative reinsurance it will state the details of the risk being reinsured. That is to say, the name and address of the original Assured, the interest or property insured, the period of the risk, the perils insured, the premium or rate and the total sum insured. Study any facultative slip schedule, or the example at the end of this chapter, and you will see that they contain the essential details of the original insurance policy.

Stage two in a facultative reinsurance is the involvement and interest of the Reassured and the terms of the deal between the Reassured and the Reinsurer. The first part of this information is the size of the line accepted by the Reassured and how much of that original acceptance he is reinsuring and, most important of all, how much he is keeping or retaining for himself, i.e. his net retention. Here I would like to give a word of warning; it used to be an essential part of a facultative reinsurance to state this net retention, that is to say, the actual net amount that the Reassured, or the Ceding Company, retained for their own account after deducting any amounts ceded to pro rata treaties and any amount reinsured on an excess of loss basis.

Modern practice often shows a retention which includes cessions to obligatory treaties, or includes amounts protected by excess of loss contracts. In my opinion this is a bastardisation of facultative reinsurance, as it does not allow a facultative Reinsurer to estimate the Reassured's true judgement of the risk in question, unless, of course, he knows the Reassured's reinsurance arrangements and can, therefore, estimate the actual net retention. To my mind, if one does not know the net retention of the Reassured on a facultative reinsurance, then *"uberrima fides"*, or utmost good faith, goes out of the window and is replaced by *"caveat emptor"*, or let the buyer beware! In other words, if a retention shown on a facultative reinsurance is qualified by words such as "subject to treaty reinsurance" or "subject to excess of loss reinsurance", then beware and find out a lot more about the actual risk you are writing as you cannot necessarily rely upon the Reassured's assessment of the risk.

In more recent years some reinsurances have shown a "gross retention" i.e. a retention which includes the cession made to a treaty and/or a retention protected by excess of loss reinsurance(s). This gross retention being unqualified on the presumed assumption that a "retention" can be held to mean a retention with treaty or with excess protection. In my view such an interpretation is mistaken as "retention" in any reasonable language must mean "that which is retained". However, to be safe it is now probably prudent to qualify the word "retention" with the word "net" and to refer to "net retention" and "gross retention" when you mean a "retention" with treaty or excess protection.

Net Retention and How to Broke

This book is undoubtedly due to run on in an undisciplined manner and I will now pause and tell a story about facultative reinsurance and net retentions. It concerns two great characters of the past in the Lloyd's market.

Firstly, Charlie Gould, a small sharp cockney, who started his working life as a carpenter's apprentice in Houndsditch, close to the City, and became a great expert at making Welsh dresser reproductions, as they were called at the upper end of the trade and bloody fakes at the lower end. He turned to insurance broking and was a delight to that profession, ending up as the revered Chairman of a great firm of brokers. A great man and a great and lovely character.

The other actor in this story is Matthew Watt Drysdale — a great facultative Underwriter, probably one of the best ever. A large man of impressive mien, he himself had known poverty but was one of Lloyd's great Underwriters. He became Chairman of Lloyd's many times and was justly knighted. Matthew Drysdale had previously underwritten to Charlie Gould's broking firm a facultative reinsurance of a well known U.S. insurance company where the insurance company had a net retention of U.S. $20,000 and Matthew had accepted a similar line of $20,000. In fact, he "led" the facultative reinsurance with this line. Charlie had the difficult task of telling Matthew that the U.S. Reassured had decided to halve its net retention from $20,000 to $10,000. The problem was how to get Matthew to agree this reduction without halving his line and thus prejudicing Charlie's whole slip. The answer is set out below:

> On a certain sunny afternoon Matthew Drysdale is sitting at his Box and is approached by a young insurance broker from Charlie Gould's firm. He places in front of Matthew Drysdale a facultative reinsurance of a U.S. company where the net retention of the Reassured is shown as $30,000, and on which Matthew Drysdale has also written $30,000. He then informs Matthew that the Reassured has increased the net retention from $30,000 to $50,000 and therefore will Matthew please increase his line from $30,000 to $50,000 to allow him to finish his slip. A pregnant silence which is broken by Matthew Drysdale's words, "Young man, I based my line on my own assessment of a risk and I am not the slightest bit influenced by the fact that the company I am reinsuring has decided to retain more. I wrote $30,000 and I am certainly not going to increase it. Good afternoon!"
>
> The young man retires to be replaced by the next man in the queue — Charles Gould. Conversation ... "I couldn't help overhearing what you were saying to your last customer; how right you are. We need Underwriters such as you who base their decisions on their own judgements and not on the judgement of others. I am glad you stuck to your point. By the way, there is a little thing here which you might initial, where the Ceding Company on this magnificent sawmill has reduced its net retention from $20,000 to $10,000. Obviously it will make no difference to your line of $20,000."
>
> No reply is recorded from Matthew Drysdale except perhaps the scratching of his pen.

Now, what lesson does one learn from this interchange? It seems there are two in fact. If you want to be a good insurance broker first learn how to be a carpenter. If you want to succeed as an Underwriter look and see who is next in the queue! Apart from this, however, the story does illustrate the importance or otherwise of a net retention.

We have probably spent enough time discussing the importance of retentions, and particularly net retentions, on facultative reinsurances. Let us now turn to the terms of a facultative reinsurance as regards rates and commission.

Ceding Commission

As the Reinsurer is sharing in the original risk, he will expect and will normally receive, a share in the original premium proportional to his share in the risk. However, the Reassured has incurred certain expenses in accepting the original risk. Also, he will naturally have overheads to meet. Whilst the Underwriter is underwriting, the Chairman's chauffeur will be incurring parking fees for the Mercedes, the Managing Director's secretary will have made twenty-four cups of coffee and the Investment Manager will have telephoned his mistress six times and got five wrong numbers. Such overheads are not specific to any risk but are "necessarily incurred" in the general running of a successful insurance company. Certain expenses are specific. For example, the cost of the paper and ink of a policy is specific to that policy and is not incurred if the policy is not produced. The agent's commission is specific; a tax or levy made on premium income or Stamp Duty paid on a policy is specific. All these charges are specifically incurred to acquire an original insurance and they are called "acquisition costs". They are costs which would not be incurred if the policy had not been written.

On a facultative reinsurance it is fair and reasonable for the Reinsurer to pay his share of such acquisition costs. This is done by allowing the Reassured a ceding commission, i.e. a commission for ceding the business, which covers the acquisition cost of that particular insurance. It is shown as a deduction from the gross original premium (g.o.p.) or original gross rate (o.g.r.), less 30% ceding commission.

Occasionally some of the Reassured's overheads might be regarded as acquisition costs. For example, if the Reassured maintains an efficient inspection team and they have inspected a particular risk, then a share of such costs might well be added to the specific charges and allowed for in the ceding commission, but the general rule on facultative reinsurance is to allow specific acquisition costs only and not company overheads. Another word of warning; a ceding commission is allowed off the gross original rate, or premium received by the Reassured, and is clearly stated in the facultative reinsurance.

Net Rate Basis

Modern practice often results in a facultative reinsurance being placed on an "original net rate" basis. If this o.n.r., or original net rate, basis is to be used, then it should be carefully defined, for example — as o.g.r. less 25% or o.g.r. less premium tax and original commission to agents, not exceeding 25% in all. If expressed as a figure the figure should not exceed the actual acquisition costs of the policy.

Any extra commission given for overheads should be shown and deducted from the "o.n.r." — e.g. o.n.r. less 5%. The 5% is an extra commission beyond the acquisition cost. It is usually called an overriding commission or overrider.

In a competitive world, of course, the ideals, or the theories, get blurred by sheer greed or, in more polite parlance, by "economic competition". A Ceding Underwriter, with profitable facultative reinsurance, or a first class reputation, may well be able to command a facultative reinsurance commission which is well in excess of his true acquisition costs. No-one begrudges a skilled workman the rewards of his skill but every good Facultative Reinsurer should know and calculate why he is paying more than pure acquisition costs for any risk or any block of facultative reinsurance.

The Full Reinsurance Clause

An essential part of the facultative reinsurance policy is indicated in the following words ... "Being a reinsurance of and warranted same gross rate terms and conditions as and to follow the settlements of the company" — known as the full reinsurance clause. This binds a Reinsurer to follow the fortunes of his Reassured. Minor changes in the risk, which do not affect the terms of the reinsurance policy, or do not worsen the information upon which the policy was based, would not invalidate the policy. But there is always a danger here and a Reassured is well advised to obtain Reinsurer's agreement to any change in the original policy if such a change might have influenced the Reinsurer's judgement of the risk.

The clause also obliges the Reinsurer to follow the settlements made by the Reassured. This word "settlement" is often replaced by "loss settlement" in facultative reinsurance. This ties the Reassured to settlements where liability for a loss exists. It would not extend to *"ex gratia"* or similar claims settlements where a "loss" has not occurred, i.e. where liability is not admitted. On some treaties and many excess contracts the words "claims settlements" is used, thus making the Reassured liable to follow *"ex gratia"* and other settlements where no "loss" is admitted.

I have already dwelt on the importance of the retention but it is necessary to revert to it. The retention is warranted in the facultative reinsurance policy and is normally warranted to be on identical interest. This means that a Reassured cannot keep a retention on the buildings of a warehouse and cede the contents. The retention and the cession must be on identical interest unless, of course, both parties specifically agree otherwise.

If a net retention turns out to be overstated in the facultative reinsurance, then when a loss happens the retention is less than that stated on the policy. Technically one might argue that the reinsurance is invalid; practically, the Reinsurer would follow the fortune of the Reassured and be liable for a reduced share of the loss, in proportion to the reduction of the retention from that originally stated.

Uses and Characteristics

The uses of facultative reinsurance and its advantages and disadvantages are as follows:

Firstly Facultative reinsurance is time consuming and expensive. Each risk has to be dealt with individually. This is a disadvantage to both Reassured and Reinsurer.

Secondly An original Underwriter has to arrange his facultative reinsurance before he comes on risk and very often may have to arrange it before he can commit himself to accepting his line on an original insurance, and sometimes even before he can quote for a risk. There is no simultaneous cover for the Reassured, which can be a very serious disadvantage to him.

Thirdly The onus of underwriting a facultative reinsurance is upon the Reinsurer. If results go wrong, blame should not attach to the Reassured. The Reinsurer has freely accepted the reinsurance and it is his decision. When we turn to treaty reinsurances we will see that the reverse is true. Under a treaty the Reassured accepts prime responsibility for the risks he cedes to his treaty and the Reinsurer has no option but to accept them. For this reason facultative reinsurance can be a very real advantage to a Ceding Underwriter if, for example, he does not wish to commit a hazardous risk to his treaty. Also, where a Reassured has an unusual risk on which he needs advice, or the advantage of someone else's underwriting advice, facultative reinsurance is a very good way of obtaining it. It is much better than just asking for advice because the advice will be much more reliable if the person giving it is himself sharing in the risk with you. The old theory of backing your advice with hard brass is better than any highfalutin theory from an uninterested expert.

Fourthly Where a maximum line is required from a Reinsurer, or

Reinsurers, on a particular risk, facultative reinsurance is the best way of obtaining it. The Facultative Reinsurer is assessing and underwriting the risk himself and is far more likely to back his own judgement with a good line. A very important point often overlooked is that such a Reinsurer is balancing his line against his entire premium income, whereas under a treaty the size of the line ceded to a treaty is balanced against the volume of that one treaty.

It follows, therefore, that facultative reinsurance is best used to deal with:

(1) Large risks with or without cessions to treaties.

(2) Unusual risks.

(3) Hazardous risks.

It is not the best method of dealing with the normal everyday risk because of the cost involved and the non-concurrence of attachment date. There was a time in the 1950s when, because of the expense, the gradual demise of facultative reinsurance was predicted. However, there is little doubt that the 1960s and 1970s have seen a revival.

In the late 1980s and 1990s the capacity each Reinsurer has for facultative reinsurance has increased greatly and now more and more facultative reinsurance is done with a single Reinsurer.

This is due to a number of factors. Firstly, Ceding Companies have become increasingly conscious of underwriting their own outward reinsurance treaties to make sure they are profitable and balanced (i.e. that cessions on a single risk are reasonable in relation to the premium volume of the treaty). Secondly, the increase in the size of industrial risks, both liability and property, necessitates more facultative reinsurance. Thirdly, the increasing complexity of industrial processes leads to greater need of consultation between Insurers and their Reinsurers. Fourthly, the increase of nationalism in insurance. Governments have increasingly taken the view that the benefits of a free insurance market for their own industry and commerce should be replaced by protection of their own national insurance companies. One effect of this is, of course, to make their own industry and commerce less efficient; the other effect is to greatly increase the amount of reinsurance those companies require.

This political factor and the points above have led, and are contributing, to a considerable use of facultative reinsurance. Undoubtedly very large risks, or potentially hazardous risks, will always require to be facultatively reinsured, not just because of their size but because such risks do need the wisdom of a number of Insurers and Reinsurers. Such risks will require to be underwritten with full information by Facultative Reinsurers.

A large volume of facultative reinsurance may be dealt with in a more routine fashion. Many insurance companies, geographically close together, have systemised their placing of facultative reinsurance by the use of a simple request note containing the details of the risk and facultative reinsurance desired. The accepting company simply accepts by inserting its line and signature on the duplicate and returning it. The placing of a facultative reinsurance slip is a similar process.

Modern methods of communication are already profoundly affecting the placing of facultative reinsurance. The "slip" is being increasingly replaced by the fax or e-mail and facultative reinsurances will be increasingly handled on a standardised basis of information directly between the Ceding Company and a clearing house intermediary, who will be either a Broker or a large Facultative Reinsurer or an agent who is acting for a number of Facultative Reinsurers.

Such methods should improve the speed of placing facultative reinsurance and make it possible to accept facultative reinsurance without having an office presence in a particular market. Hopefully, they should cut costs but this remains to be proven. However, such methods may be self-defeating if they lead to poorer underwriting by Facultative Reinsurers. Speed and volume are admirable but no underwriting operation can exist for long if the methods do not result in profitable business.

Bulk handling of a Reassured's facultative reinsurances are often done by a facultative obligatory treaty. This is an agreement entered into by a Reassured and his Facultative Reinsurers under which the Reassured can choose whether or not he cedes a facultative reinsurance. If he chooses to do so then his Reinsurers are obliged to accept all such cessions made within the terms and limits of the agreement. A facultative obligatory treaty is not, however, facultative reinsurance, but it is essentially a surplus treaty between two contracting parties and is included, therefore, in following chapters.

A fairy story

Let us now revert to a little fairy story to lead us on to Chapter V where we discuss surplus treaties:

Once upon a time there was an insurance company in Strasbourg whose Underwriter — a Mr. Traminer — specialised in fire insurance. When he had to insure a risk which was too large for his company he would write or call on three friendly companies, run by a Mr. Munch, Mr. Schweiz and Mr. Waters, and he would offer them his facultative reinsurances, surplus to his own line or retention.

This went on for a year or more and he found that after a time each of his three friends trusted him. They found the business profitable and each one of them would base their acceptances on Mr. Traminer's net retention. One day in 1860 Mr. Munch said, "Instead of sending me a letter every time, why don't you make a record of each facultative insurance you want and I will agree to take the same line as you? Each month make a list of all the cessions you make to me, add up my share of the premium and send me a cheque". Mr. Schweiz agreed but as his company was larger he said. "I always take 1½ times your retention". Mr. Waters, who was smaller, took half a retention. Mr. Traminer drew up an agreement, which his three friends signed, which said that he would cede to them all his fire business surplus to his own retention and which would never be less than £1,000 on any policy. They each agreed to take a proportionate share of the surpluses up to three retentions, or three lines, with a maximum cession for the three lines of £30,000 — Mr. Munch taking 1 line or 33⅓%, Mr. Schweiz taking 1½ lines or 50% and Mr. Waters taking ½ line or 16⅔%. Thus, the first surplus fire treaty was born in Central Europe.

Now, Mr. Munch, Mr. Schweiz and Mr. Waters, inspired by their idea, developed and sold it to other companies. They did so well that they gave up writing insurance direct themselves and established the three first professional reinsurance companies in Munich, Zurich and Cologne respectively and, of course, their names are enshrined in the names of our oldest and most respected reinsurance companies — the Münchener Rück, the Schweizer Rück and the Kölnische Rück.

My profound apologies and respect to three of the world's most respected reinsurance companies for this fairy story and I trust all three will forgive me for a flight of fantasy, but the development of the surplus treaty did take place in just this way in Europe in the 19th Century.

POLICY

We, Underwriting Members of the syndicates whose definitive numbers and proportions are shown in the Table attached hereto (hereinafter referred to as "the Underwriters") hereby agree, in consideration of the premium charged and subject to the terms and conditions of this Policy as set out herein, to reinsure the Reinsured's interest in payments made within the terms and conditions of the original policy.

The Reinsured, unless otherwise stated herein:

(i) shall retain during the period of this Policy at least the retention(s), subject to any proportional and/or excess of loss treaty reinsurance, on the identical subject matter and perils and in identically the same proportion(s) as stated herein. In the event of the retention(s) and/or proportion(s) being less, the Underwriters' liability will be correspondingly proportionately reduced.

(ii) warrants that the premium paid to the Underwriters for this Policy is calculated at the same gross rate as the original policy for the identical subject matter and perils and in the proportions reinsured.

In the event of inconsistencies between the original policy and this Policy, this Policy shall prevail.

If the Reinsured shall make a claim knowing the same to be false or fraudulent as regards amount or otherwise, this Policy shall become void and all claims hereunder shall be forfeited.

The Underwriters hereby bind themselves severally and not jointly, each for his own part and not one for another and therefore each of the Underwriters (his Executors and Administrators) shall be liable only for his own share of this syndicate's proportion of any loss payable under this Policy. The identity of each of the Underwriters and the amount of his share may be ascertained by the Reinsured or the Reinsured's representative on application to Lloyd's Policy Signing Office, quoting the Lloyd's Policy Signing Office number and date shown in the Table.

SCHEDULE

Policy No:

The Reinsured:

The Original Assured:

The Premium:

The Retention(s):

The Sum Reinsured hereunder:

The Period of Reinsurance:

from to
commencing and expiring at the hour expressed in the original policy, and for such further period or periods as may be mutually agreed upon.

The Subject Matter and Perils Reinsured hereunder:

Endorsements, if any:

Dated in London, the

CHAPTER III

FACULTATIVE EXCESS OF LOSS REINSURANCE

Introduction — Claims co-operation — Uses and characteristics — A typical example analysed — Underwriting property excess facultative reinsurances — Third party facultative excess reinsurances — Facultative excess liability — Wording and schedule

Introduction

The use of this method of reinsurance retains all the elements of the facultative method, i.e. the free option for either party to cede or accept. The onus of underwriting is on the Reinsuring Underwriter not the Ceding Company.

However, instead of a contributing reinsurance with a pro rata sharing of premium, liability, losses and expenses, the Reassured keeps a deductible or first loss amount on the policy reinsured and the Reinsurer agrees to pay the amount by which any loss to the policy exceeds this deductible up to a limit. Normally the retention or deductible and the limit are expressed in monetary amounts but can be expressed in percentage amounts of the original policy, although this is unusual.

The Reassured will keep 100% of all the smaller losses which do not exceed his retention or deductible. On losses which do exceed his retention the Reassured's share will be limited to the amount of his retention, the Reinsurer normally paying 100% of the excess amount. This is the essence of non-proportional reinsurance and the Reinsurer is not following the fortunes of the Reassured on a proportional basis as he is on a contributing or pro rata reinsurance. Therefore, we have a situation where the Reassured may wish to be consulted fully on any claim which is likely to exceed the deductible.

Claims Co-operation and Claim Control

A facultative excess of loss reinsurance may well contain a "claims co-operation" clause, which means that the Reassured will advise any possible claims exceeding the deductible and will advise and consult the excess Reinsurers over its settlement. On some types of business the Reassured is required to obtain Reinsurers' consent to any settlement. In these cases the Reassured will control the claims settlement through, and in conjunction with, the direct Insurer. We will revert to some of the problems relating to claims control clauses later in this chapter. They are particularly relevant to aviation and third party excess of loss reinsurances whether on a facultative or contract basis.

As the excess of loss Reinsurer is not going to pay for claims within the deductible, the premium he will receive normally will be less than a pro rata share of the original premium. This premium will be negotiated between the parties at inception and may be a fixed monetary premium or adjustable at an agreed percentage of the total policy premium.

Uses and Characteristics

The use of facultative excess of loss insurance has grown considerably in the past decades on many types of business and, before considering an example of this method, it is perhaps valid to discuss some of the advantages and disadvantages in a broad sense.

(1) The use of this method normally allows the Reassured to retain a much larger proportion of the original policy premium.

(2) The Reassured keeps all claims within the deductible for himself. These can be the "normal" run of claims which are particularly responsive to good housekeeping or loss prevention schemes. Thus, a direct writing company working closely with its direct insured, can enjoy for its net account the full benefit of any reduction in "run of the mill" losses obtained by good loss prevention.

(3) The use of excess of loss facultative reinsurance may well produce increased reinsurance capacity on a large risk.

The insurance and reinsurance markets of the world are philosophically divided into two types of operation:

Those who deal in a large volume operation of basically small sums insured. Here a wide spread of business with low limits should produce a stable loss ratio and thus a stable profit or loss. Such operations, e.g. life, private car business, householders, commercial and industrial property insurance and third party in the small and medium range, tend to be subject to rating controls or rating tariffs which produce a comparatively low level of percentage profit. In some countries, in many years, such profit may be non-existent. However, the investment side of handling a large premium volume provides additional income to the Insurer. Such an insurance operation is that which is carried out by most normal Insurance Companies and can be confined to one country or a limited geographical area.

There is another type of operation where the rates and terms of any insurance or reinsurance are negotiated individually. Here the spread of such risks (basically unusual risks, large exposures, catastrophic business) is much less. In fact, within some countries it is so limited that very little spread can be obtained.

With this type of business Underwriters are less able to pursue a long term investment policy and need to assess each risk accepted to produce a margin of "profit" to take care of a greater fluctuation of experience. Essentially this type of insurance or reinsurance operator tends to prefer the excess loss approach to that of sharing in a contributing reinsurance where he (the Reassured) has no control in establishing the rate.

Now, such Underwriters normally work on an international basis as they need an international spread of business to arrive at a balanced book. This market, specialising as it does, provides additional capacity on much excess of loss facultative business, which may not necessarily be available on a pro rata basis.

The work of a good Facultative Broker or intermediary is to utilise the expertise and capacity of both types of reinsurance markets to the best effect.

(4) As has been implied above, a great amount of insurance business is subject to rating regulation, tariffs or market rates and at times

Reinsurers may consider a rate on a particular risk inadequate. Tariff rating has reduced considerably worldwide, particularly in Europe, due to competition laws and also now in Japan. Therefore, such Reinsurers may not be a market for contributing reinsurance. However, they may be a market for excess of loss reinsurance where the terms do not follow the terms for the original insurance.

(5) There can be a great saving in time by using the excess of loss approach. The excess Reinsurer is only concerned with those exposures which penetrate his layer. He therefore only needs limited underwriting information, i.e. that relating to those particular exposures. For example, if a company wanted to reinsure a motor/fire/theft/collision and accidental damage account on a fleet of buses excess of the value of two single vehicles, then the facultative excess Reinsurer is hardly concerned with theft/collision or accidental damage, but with fire risk at the garage, and may only require information relating to such exposures.

(6) There are some whole areas of insurance which are best handled on an excess basis. A company with a large liability policy or a professional indemnity can place a facultative contributing insurance, but what it often needs is a facultative reinsurance against suffering too large a loss from that policy on its net account, and this is best handled on the excess of loss basis.

(7) At times Insurers may have, or may wish, to take on insurances which others consider unknown, unsound or underrated, and on which it is impossible to place pro rata reinsurance. In these cases the excess of loss basis may be the only possible method of reinsurance.

The disadvantage of excess loss facultative reinsurance is, of course, that many direct and pro rata Reinsurers do not always provide a market. The Reassured has to make sure that he retains enough premium to pay the losses within his retention and this can be a difficult judgement. Pro rata facultative reinsurance pays a ceding commission and a possible overrider. Excess insurance is normally quoted without a ceding commission. This has to be taken into account in judging the cost effectiveness of each.

A typical example:

Let us examine some of the problems with an actual example:

"M" is writing a construction or builder's risk policy on a building contract. He wishes to do a facultative reinsurance. The contract is for 24 months. Total contract value: D.Mks. 10,000,000. Maximum completed value on largest building: D.Mks. 4,000,000.

The policy covers all risks on site, plus transit coverage of D.Mks. 400,000 any one sending, plus third party coverage of D.Mks. 5,000,000. The original premium is D.Mks. 200,000 and "M"'s acquisition costs are 25%. Now, "M" would normally retain a fire line of D.Mks. 300,000 on one building and would wish to retain this amount on the maximum building value of D.Mks. 4,000,000.

Method 1

(a) Fac. proportional R/I for 92½% of the whole risk at 25% ceding commission (i.e. covering acquisition cost only) leaving "M" with:

D.Mks. 750,000 on contract value
D.Mks. 300,000 on the maximum building
D.Mks. 375,000 third party
D.Mks. 30,000 any one sending

"M" retains premium of:	D.Mks. 15,000
– 25%	3,750
Net:	D.Mks. 11,250

(b) Fac. proportional R/I as above with ceding commission 40%:

"M" retains premium of:	D.Mks. 11,250
plus a 15% overrider on D.Mks. 185,000	= 27,750
Total	D.Mks. 39,000

Method 2

"M" places a facultative reinsurance in two excess of loss layers:

Layer 1: D.Mks. 4,500,000 × 500,000 each and every loss
Layer 2: D.Mks. 5,000,000 × 5,000,000 each and every loss
To arrive at some idea of how such a policy might be rated let us think aloud and consider Layer 2 first.

Layer 2 is not exposed on one building; it is not exposed on a third party loss on its own. It could only pay when the site values exceed D.Mks. 5,000,000 and then only for some catastrophic risk, or possible a combination of physical and third party damage at the end of the contract period when the maximum value is at risk.

Let us assume that the value on the site will only reach D.Mks. 5,000,000 after 15 months. Therefore we have 9 months exposure with average exposure of D.Mks. 2,500,000 in excess of D.Mks. 5,000,000. Let us assume that for perils which might cause a total loss to site values — earthquake, flood or conflagation — a rate of .05% per annum is reasonable:

$\frac{9}{12} \times$ D.Mks. 2,500,000 $\times$ 0.05	= D.Mks. 940
then let us add for combination of third party and property loss	– D.Mks. 500
Total premium	– D.Mks. 1,440
or say,	– D.Mks. 1,500

Turning to:

Layer 1 — firstly, transits are eliminated by the deductible and that is worth 15% of the original premium. Consider next the fire and all risks exposure on the site. The top building value will be D.Mks. 4,000,000 when completed. For the first 6 months the exposure will probably not exceed D.Mks. 500,000 and then average D.Mks. 1,600,000 × 500,000 for 18 months. On the balance of the total contract price of D.Mks. 6,000,000 the value at risk will probably not exceed D.Mks. 500,000 until 12 months and will then average D.Mks. 2,000,000 for final 12 months. Third party coverage excess D.Mks. 500,000 is not too serious on this risk.

In addition we will have a "catastrophic" site exposure on the contract price of D.Mk. 10 million and this will be particularly exposed in the later period of the work.

Therefore, we might assess the premium for D.Mks 4,500,000 × D.Mks. 500,000 e.e. loss as follows:

Fire and all risks on site exposures:		
Top building 16,000,000 × 0.1%	=	16,000
Other buildings 2,000,000 × 0.3%	=	6,000
Third party premium 15% of D.Mks. 20,000	=	3,000
Catastrophe site exposures — average site values 6,000,000	say	10,000
Transit premium — nil		—
plus contingency for combination of third party and property and/or transit	=	5,000
Total		40,000

Therefore, we come up with a proposition:

For 1st layer: 4,500,000 × 500,000 R/I Prem.	40,000
2nd layer: 5,000,000 × 5,000,000 R/I Prem.	1,500
Leaving for first 500,000 1st loss deductible	158,500
Total	– 200,000

Now, 2nd layer Reinsurers are most unlikely to want to write 5,000,000 of liability for 1,500 premium so we will have to pay them, say, a minimum of D.Mks. 3,000 but we might persuade 1st layer to go at 37,000.

Therefore we have:

1st layer 37,000
2nd layer 3,000
Leaving – 160,000
Less costs of 25% on total premium of
D.Mks. 200,000: 50,000
Leaving a net premium of D.MKS/ 110,000

Compare Method 1 and Method 2 from the point of view of "M", the Reassured:

Method 1(a)		*Method 2*	
Net lines 750,000 contract value plus 375,000 third party		Maximum 1st loss — Net line	D.Mks. 500,000
Net premium	11,250	Net premium	D.Mks. 110,000
Method 1(b)			
Net premium	39,562		

Method 2, even though the Reassured has to pay all losses in full up to D.Mks. 500,000, allows him to retain a high proportion of his premium and, hopefully, his profit. However Method 1(b) will be his best if he can find some generous Reinsurer to pay a 40% ceding commission on costs of 25%.

These figures are illustrative only but they do show the type of approach between the two methods. In dealing with package policies of this type the Reassured may well be better off to purchase a facultative excess loss and keep a large part of the premium and pay all the small losses (which he may well be able to control) than to leave himself a very small net premium for a small net contributing line.

However, if he can obtain a substantial overrider from pro rata Reinsurers, then excess of loss may not be of great interest, but then, of course, he is acting more as a Broker than an Underwriter.

Property Excess Facultative Reinsurance

The Reassured will decide the deductible and limit he requires. The Reinsurer will have to decide the premium he requires for the excess reinsurance. This calculation will vary with each Reinsurer; that is the essence of free enterprise.

Let us take a simple example of a factory consisting of one building divided into two halves, making the probable maximum loss on the building 50% of the value. The values and original rates on these buildings are:

A total of £1,000,000 Rate: 0.30% Premium: £3,000.

Let us further assume that a facultative excess reinsurance is required for £800,000 excess of £200,000 each and every loss.

A potential Reinsurer may think like this:

"The original rate is adequate. On a value basis I am asked to reinsure 80% of the value excess of 20% for this I want 40% of the original premium. However, this risk is not fully exposed; on the basis of the probable maximum loss of £500,000. Viewing it as 2 risks of £500,000 each, my exposure is £300,000 × £200,000 on each or 60% × 40% and for this 30% of the original premium would be adequate.

I can average these two, i.e. 40% and 30% and charge 35% of the total premium. This I should discount by the original acquisition costs, of say, 20% to produce a net premium of 28% of the original gross premium.

Therefore, I quote:

£800,000 x £200,000

28% of £3,000 — which equals £840.

Does this look reasonable? It produces a rate on my exposure to the value of 105% and a rate on my exposure to maximum probable loss of £840 for £300,000 or 28% (N.B. the original net rate is 30% — 20% or 24%).

This looks not unreasonable and if I am convinced that the fireproof wall is really sound I could reduce the premium a little."

Third Party Facultative Excess Reinsurances

This method of reinsurance is the usual method where facultative reinsurance is required on third party business. A typical third party wording is at the end of this chapter. It is fairly simple wording and I have omitted certain clauses for brevity. The insuring clause is as follows:

> *Reinsurers hereby agree to indemnify the Company for their interest in the Policy stipulated in the Schedule attached hereto for that portion of their ultimate net loss in excess of the deductible stated in the Schedule in respect of each and every accident occurring during the period of this Policy, as shown in the Schedule, up to the amount of Reinsurers' limit each and every accident stated in the Schedule.*

The use of a schedule means that a standard wording can be used with the variables set out in the schedule attached to the individual policy.

Definition (a)

ACCIDENT. The word "accident" shall be understood to mean an accident or series of accidents arising out of one event.

It will be seen that the limit and deductible of this facultative reinsurance is on the basis of each and every accident rather than each and every loss and it covers accidents occurring during the policy period.

In the United States liability policies normally have separate limits for personal injury any one accident, for property damage and possibly also for products liability where the limit will be on an aggregate basis. Facultative reinsurances of such policies may also have separate limits and deductibles for each of these sections and the insuring clause and the schedule will set these out.

One accident is here defined as a series of accidents arising out of one event. We will discuss the definition of one event further in Chapter XI.

Definition (b)

ULTIMATE NET LOSS. The words "ultimate net loss" shall be understood to mean the amount actually paid in settlement of the liability of the Company after making deductions for all recoveries and for other valid and collectible reinsurances, excepting however any reinsurances protecting the Company as set out in the Schedule, and shall exclude all expenses Costs. Note *It will be seen that this clause limits the Reinsurer's liability to* "actually paid *in settlement of* liability*".*

Definition (c)

COST. The word "Costs" shall be understood to mean interest accruing after entry of judgement, investigation, adjustment and legal expenses (excluding, however, all office expenses of the Company, all expenses for salaried employees of the Company and general retainer fees for counsel normally paid by the Company).

Conditions

1. INCURRING OF COSTS. In the event of claim or claims arising which appear likely to exceed the Primary Limit(s) no Costs shall be incurred without the written consent of Reinsurers.

2. APPORTIONMENT OF COSTS. Costs incurred with the written consent of Reinsurers shall be apportioned as follows:

(a) Should any claim or claims become adjustable prior to the commencement of trial for not more than the deductible, then no Costs shall be payable by Reinsurer.

(b) Should, however, the amount for which the said claim or claims may be so adjustable exceed the deductible then Reinsurers, if they consent to the proceedings continuing, shall contribute to the Costs in the ratio that their proportion of the ultimate net loss as finally adjusted bears to the whole amount of such ultimate loss.

(c) In the event that the Company elects not to appeal a judgement in excess of the deductible Reinsurers may elect to conduct such appeal at their own cost and expense and shall be liable for the taxable court costs and interest incidental thereto, but in no event shall the total liability exceed their limit(s) of liability as provided for herein, plus the expenses of such appeal.

One of the main differences in the insurance wording between a property damage excess and a third party excess lies in the definition "ultimate net loss". On property "loss" includes loss expenses. On third party business the loss is normally confined to the amount of the loss itself and the loss does not include either litigation costs or any interest awarded in the judgement or paid as part of a settlement. These litigation costs and interest are proportioned, however, between the Reassured and Reinsurers in proportion to the loss itself.

Let us assume a facultative excess reinsurance for:

U.S. \$2,000,000 xs U.S. \$1,000,000 e.e. accident with a costs clause.

A judgement is made against the Reassured for \$1,200,000 + \$240,000 interest, and litigation cost is U.S. \$60,000 — a total loss of \$1,500,000. Reinsurers' liability for this loss, with the normal ultimate loss clause used on a physical damage excess, would be for \$500,000 × \$1,000,000.

With a cost clause the Reinsurers' liability is:

\$200,000 xs \$1,000,000 for the claim
1/6th × \$240,000 + \$60,000
or an extra \$50,000.
The total loss paid by Reinsurers is \$250,000.

Outside the U.S.A. and Canada the costs are often included as part of the loss, leaving only the interest on judgements to be pro rated. In this case settlement would have been:

Loss \$260,000 xs \$1,000,000
plus $\frac{26}{126} \times \$240,000 = \$49,524$
making a total of \$309,524 to be paid by excess Reinsurers.

On occasions third party excess Reinsurers do agree to include costs and interest as part of the loss but this is normally only done if all loss settlements are agreed and controlled by the excess Reinsurers. The excess Reinsurers then virtually stand in with the Reassured on all loss settlements. This can mean serious difficulty for the Reassured in tying their hands and causing delays.

Should such delays occur, and should they give rise to punitive or similar special damages against the Reassured, then Reinsurers might also have such damages made against them, jointly or severally. It would seem to be better either to stick to a costs clause or to have some other form of co-reinsurance.

Facultative excess reinsurances are often taken out in excess of the Reassured's normal excess of loss contract. For example, a Reassured has a general third party reinsurance for £900,000 in excess of £100,000 e.e. accident.

If a Reassured accepts a policy for £2,000,000 he may require a facultative reinsurance on that acceptance for £1,000,000 xs £1,000,000 e.e. accident. In such cases it is vital that the facultative reinsurance tracks the primary contract wording, particularly as regards "one accident" and the definition of loss and costs apportionment. A muddle will ensue if the primary contract wording includes costs in the loss and the facultative excess does not.

It should be noted that with a costs clause the limit of the Reinsurers' policy may not be the limit of their loss as their share of costs will be an addition. However, where costs are included in the loss a Reassured should be careful to buy a limit to his reinsurance in excess of his total original policy limit to cover costs, or in the USA to cover against punitive damages or ECO's.

Calculating Premiums

There are several ways by which Reinsurers and Reassureds calculate premiums — we illustrate a few.

(1) A premium rate on the R/I amount. Really this is a calculation of a minimum premium for writing the policy and would apply where the exposure to risk is very slight. For example, an excess reinsurance of £ 1,000,000 xs £ 1,000,000 for an original policy issued to the owner of residential flats for £2,000,000, might command a premium based on the £1,000,000 limit, £200, £500 or £1,000 in full. This premium might bear little relation to the original policy premium.

(2) The premium for the R/I can be set at a percentage of the original policy premium, the reinsurance premium being automatically adjusted at a certain percentage or being so calculated in advance and stipulated at a fixed premium. For example, our property owner's policy for £2,000,000 has a premium of £2,500. The reinsurance of £1,000,000 xs £1,000,000 might be rated at 20% of the policy premium subject to a minimum premium of £500.

(3) In many parts of the world third party and similar business is rated by direct Insurers by layers. For example, a primary policy of \$500.000 costs X and to increase to a \$1,000,000 costs, say, 15% of X i.e. \$500,000 × \$500,000: cost $\frac{15}{100} \times X$.

There are tables of excess limits premiums for various limits and deductibles and for various classes. In the United States these manual increase tables, or M.I.T., are often used by excess Reinsurers in determining the premium for the excess layer. These manual increases are premiums charged by direct writers for increasing the original limit from, say, $500,000 to $1,000,000. They are commonly called increased limit factors.

(4) Where an Insurer has a primary liability policy for, say, $500,000, and is required to increase it to $1,000,000, and buys facultative reinsurance, his R/I premium is often based on a percentage of the primary premium. The original premium will, of course, vary with the hazard of the original policy. The proportion of the primary premium charged for the excess reinsurance will vary with the chance of that policy having large losses.

This has become a common method of rating with automatic excess liability cession treaties. These are really obligatory or facultative obligatory excess ceding treaties and we will discuss them in the Risk Excess — Chapter X.

Where the deductible of a facultative excess is within the normal anticipated loss range then usually a premium related to the original policy premium is used. However, with high excesses a pure judgment premium is called for and the excess Reinsurer will have to anticipate the frequency and size of a loss penetrating the deductible. Normally this will be due to three types of loss:

(a) The disaster — for example, an explosion injuring many and damaging the property of others. Any Underwriter should be able to assess the excess premium for these eventualities.

(b) The large single loss to an individual which produces a delayed court award out of line with others or with past awards.

An excess third party Reinsurer has to calculate this eventuality very carefully bearing in mind past settlements and present and future trends and inflation. If a premium is calculated on the basis that the deductible is in excess of any possible single person award and this assumption proves incorrect in the passage of time between occurrence and settlement, then the excess Reinsurer's results will be disastrous.

(c) The "products" or environmental type of loss which may be very delayed in its advice and may affect many persons and will increase in size due to future inflation and changing social attitudes.

The successful excess third party Underwriter will have to assess (b) and (c), often with very little definitive information. Therefore it is vital that the Underwriter at least uses simple statistics to promulgate the chances of such losses reaching the policy deductible on the assumption of future inflation of awards and estimated delays in settlement.

A compound growth rate of 20% per annum in rate of awards would have turned a loss of, say, $300,000 in the late 1950s to one of $10,000,000 in the late 1970s. A loss estimated to settle in 1980 at $5,000,000 will cost $40,000,000 in 1992 and $160,000,000 in 2000 A.D. A single person award over $300,000 was very rare in the 1950s and a single person award over $10,000,000 was also very rare in the late 1970s.

If liability awards were to reach a 30% compound increase in the 1980's, and impaired lives continue to be prolonged by medical advances, then a claim of $5,000,000 in 1980 will reach $160,000,000 by 1992 and, perhaps what is more significant, $25,000,000 by 1986. Figures such as this make one's hair curl but so do the "run off" statistics of excess liability Reinsurers of the 1950s and 1960s!

Even if you discount or disbelieve these rates of "social" inflation, a 10% compound rate after 5 years will increase a $2,000,000 loss to $3,200,000 and if you write an excess reinsurance excess of $1,000,000 expecting a $1,000,000 loss to you, you will end up with a loss of $2,200,000 — an increase of 220%. So watch out — or, better still, do not wait to watch but find an excess Reinsurer for your own excess liability account at the lowest fixed deductible you can get, or, even better than that, a stop loss reinsurance, or both. Then get your premiums in quickly and get a good investment programme going to roll up at 15% compound free of tax.

One hesitates to predict the future. My underwriting life from 1945–1975 was an era of galloping awards due to material inflation caused by increasing scarcity of cheap raw materials at a time of increasing expectation of life and living standards. There are signs that societies are beginning to see that this cannot continue indefinitely and a slowing down of material standards of living and national outputs may be with us. It could lead to a better quality of life and it may lead to a slowing down in the rate of increase of liability awards, in which case the next 20 years will be easier than the last 20 years.

However, it must be pointed out that material inflation in the 1950s and 1960s was at a much slower rate than that of the late 1970s. Certainly, any reasonable Underwriter of liability excess reinsurance must anticipate a longer tail than in the past due to the lengthening of court awards and changing attitudes over conservation and products and the enormous prolongation of life due to medical advances.

The above words were written in the late 1970s. Looking back on them in the mid-1990s they were not too far out as a prediction. Certainly Court awards have not reached a 30% Compound increase per annum but they have certainly exceeded 10% Compound per annum in many countries. What has happened has of course been the vast opening up of the longer tail claims into areas of asbestos, pollution, which my last paragraph warned about. However, the escalation in these areas in the 1980s and 1990s has been far beyond my predictions of the 1970s.

Writing in 1997 there seems no slowing down either in the frequency or escalation in size of third party awards. Quite the reverse is true. Looking forward to, say, 2010 A.D. these awards could well increase at an annual compound rate of 20%.

DRAFT THIRD PARTY WORDING

EXCESS PUBLIC LIABILITY
(Facultative Reinsurance)

....

Reinsurers hereby agree to indemnify the Company for their interest in the Policy stipulated in the Schedule attached hereto for that portion of their ultimate net loss in excess of the deductible stated in the Schedule in respect of each and every accident occurring during the period of this Policy, as shown in the Schedule, up to the amount of Reinsurers' limit each and every accident stated in the Schedule.

DEFINITIONS

(a) ACCIDENT. The word "accident" shall be understood to mean an accident or series of accidents arising out of one event.

(b) ULTIMATE NET LOSS. The words "ultimate net loss" shall be understood to mean the amount actually paid in cash in settlement of the liability of the Company after making deductions for all recoveries and for other valid and collectible reinsurances,

excepting however any reinsurances protecting the Company as set out in the Schedule, and shall exclude all expenses and Costs.

(c) *COSTS. The word "Costs" shall be understood to mean interest accruing after entry of judgement, investigation, adjustment and legal expenses (excluding, however, all office expenses of the Company, all expenses for salaried employees of the Company and general retainer fees for counsel normally paid by the Company).*

CONDITIONS

1. *INCURRING OF COSTS. In the event of claim or claims arising which appear likely to exceed the Primary Limit(s) no Costs shall be incurred without the written consent of Reinsurers.*

2. *APPORTIONMENT OF COSTS. Costs incurred with the written consent of Reinsurers shall be apportioned as follows:*

   (a) *Should any claim or claims become adjustable prior to the commencement of trial for not more than the deductible, then no Costs shall be payable by Reinsurers.*

   (b) *Should, however, the amount for which the said claim or claims may be so adjustable exceed the deductible then Reinsurers, if they consent to the proceedings continuing, shall contribute to the Costs in the ratio that their proportion of the ultimate net loss as finally adjusted bears to the whole amount of such ultimate loss.*

   (c) *In the event that the Company elects not to appeal a judgement in excess of the deductible Reinsurers may elect to conduct such appeal at their own cost and expense and shall be liable for the taxable court costs and interest incidental thereto, but in no event shall the total liability exceed their limit(s) of liability as provided for herein, plus the expenses of such appeal.*

3. *APPLICATION OF RECOVERIES. All recoveries or payments recovered or received subsequent to a loss settlement under this Policy shall be applied as if recovered or received prior to such settlement and all necessary adjustments shall then be made between the Company and Reinsurers, provided always that nothing in this Policy shall be construed to mean that losses under this Policy are not payable until the Company's ultimate net loss has been finally ascertained.*

4. *PREMIUM COMPUTATION AND ADJUSTMENT. The premium for this Reinsurance shall be computed on the basis set forth herein and the Company agrees to pay and Reinsurers agree to return such additional or return premium as it becomes due.*

7. *NOTIFICATION OF CLAIMS. The Company upon knowledge of any occurrence likely to give rise to a claim hereunder shall give immediate written advice thereof.*

SCHEDULE

1. Policy Number.
2. Reassured.
3. Original Policy Number.
4. Assured.
5. Hazards Covered.
6. Limit of Original Policy.
7. Period of Reinsurance.
8. Premium of Original Policy.
9. Premium for Reinsurance.
10. Deductible of Reinsurance.
11. Limit of Reinsurance.
12. Underlying Reinsurances (if any).

CHAPTER IV

QUOTA SHARE REINSURANCE TREATIES

Introduction — The treaty wording — Accounts on written premium basis — Uses and characteristics of the quota share — Underwriting factors — Calculation of ceding commissions — Profit commissions — Underwriting a typical quota share treaty — The surplus relief quota share — The variable quota share — specimen wording

Introduction

The quota share treaty is an obligatory ceding treaty; that is, a formal agreement entered into between two parties — the Reassured and the Reinsurer under which the Reassured is obliged to cede a fixed percentage of all business covered by the treaty and the Reinsurer is obliged to accept all cessions so made. Under a quota share the cessions are fixed in advance at an agreed percentage of each risk. All cessions are automatically made for this agreed percentage subject to the monetary limits laid down in the agreement.

In concept, and in its execution, a quota share treaty is a very simple form of treaty:

'A' says to 'B' — "I propose to write a number of insurances covering personal accident business in the U.K. up to a maximum of £100,000 a.o. person. I want to keep 40% on each insurance for myself. Will you take the balance of 60% from me?" If 'B' says, "Yes" we have a quota share treaty in being, with 'A' the Reassured and 'B' the Reinsurer.

(*Note:* In essence a quota share treaty is not a contract of insurance or reinsurance but merely an agreement under which reinsurance may be made. If 'A' writes no personal accident business, then no reinsurance takes place.)

In practice, of course, 'B' will want to know a considerable amount of information before he can feel able to say, "Yes"', and an agreement will have to be reached on a number of details relating to the operation of the quota share treaty and the terms under which cessions will be made.

The Treaty Wording

The terms and details, once agreed between the two contracting parties, will be drawn up in a treaty wording which will be signed by the two contracting parties. Each wording will be peculiar to that quota share but we will consider a typical wording which is contained at the end of this chapter. I must warn the reader that there are wide variations in the way such wordings are drawn up but we will, firstly, consider and comment upon the one contained at the end of this chapter.

Preamble — This will set out the names and addresses of the two contracting parties.

ARTICLE 1

Term

This Agreement shall commence at on and shall continue until terminated by either party giving the other at least 3 months notice to terminate at the 31 st December of any year.

ARTICLE 1

A quota share treaty may be for a fixed term or period corresponding to the business ceded. For example, a crop hail quota share may protect a season's account and will refer to the 1980 season without a specific period. However, most treaties, whether quota share or surplus, are continuous agreements which can only be terminated once a year by the giving of the required notice by one party to the other. Ninety days or 3 months notice is normal. With such annual notice each party will review the progress and results of the treaty well before the notice date (normally Ist October each year). In certain cases protective or provisional notice may be given by one party or both if the results or information are not available by that date, or if one party or the other contemplates changes which cannot be resolved before notice has to be given. In that event, the giving of provisional notice by one party does not prevent the other party from giving definite notice and, of course, provisional notice, once given, can be made definitive after the notice date has been passed.

If the parties do not wish to give or accept even protective notice, then they may mutually agree to reduce the notice period for that year to 60 days or a lesser period, so that negotiations may proceed without one party or the other being under "pressure" of notice.

ARTICLES 2, 3 and 4

Articles 2, 3 and 4 deal with territory, classes of business and exclusions. These are self explanatory.

ARTICLE 5

Insuring clause

> *The company binds itself to cede and the Reinsurer agrees to accept a fixed proportion of 70% of all business falling within the terms of this a agreement up to a limit of .*
> *The company agrees to retain for its own account the balance of 30% of all business subject to the benefit of excess of loss catastrophe reinsurance. It is agreed that the liability of the Reinsurer shall commence and cease simultaneously with that of the company. The Reinsurer shall be subject to the same conditions as the original policies and shall follow, subject to the terms of this agreement, the fortunes of the company in respect of all business ceded hereunder. The company may reinsure elsewhere any risk or part of any risk should it consider it in the interest of both parties.*

Article 5 clearly sets out the obligatory nature of the agreement. Normally a schedule of limits might well be contained in this Article or attached in a schedule which would be referred to in this Article. Should the Reassured's retention, in this case 30%, not be retained net, then it must be stipulated. The importance of this net retention cannot be overstressed. The Reinsurer is entering into a partnership with the Reassured and agrees to follow the fortunes of the Reassured primarily because the Reassured has the stipulated retention on all business and is a true partner. Certain aspects of this partnership are here set out:

(a) Automatic and simultaneous attachment of liability. This is, of course, one vital advantage of an obligatory treaty as compared to the facultative method of conducting reinsurance.

(b) The Reinsurers are subject to all conditions of the original policies and follow the Reassured's fortunes in relation to the business ceded.

Quota share wordings often have a variety of phraseology emphasising the true partnership of the agreement. Permission to reinsure elsewhere is a very sensible agreement as it allows the Reassured to protect itself and the Reinsurers if it is felt, for example, that the quota share treaty has too much liability on a class of business, or too much on an individual exposure, or that certain types of business, e.g. accommodation lines, are best reinsured facultatively.

ARTICLE 6

Premium clause

The Reinsurer shall receive 70% of the gross premiums received by the company in respect of business hereunder, without any deductions. The Reinsurers shall allow the company a ceding commission of 40% of the premiums so ceded.

This is a straightforward clause. The Reinsurers are entitled to receive the full gross premiums without deductions of taxes, commissions or other costs. To cover the costs of the Reassured the Reinsurers will allow a ceding commission, which is deducted from the gross premium and kept by the Reassured.

It is not uncommon for quota share treaties to be written on a net premium basis. If this is done then the net premium should be defined, or example, as gross premium less original commissions, premium taxes (i.e. acquisition costs) plus overhead expenses of 10%. With such a contribution to overheads of 10% there would normally be no additional commission allowable to the Reassured.

An alternative would be to define original net rate (o.n.r.) as original gross rate (o.g.r.) less acquisition costs (not exceeding 30% on an individual cession) and then to allow the Reassured an overrider off the o.n.r. for example:

o.n.r. (as defined) — 12½%

There is no correct or right way in this matter. If an o.n.r. basis is used, a clear definition of o.n.r. is desirable. Often Reinsurers would desire to put an overall limit on the deduction from the gross rate on any single cession, as indicated above.

When considering the calculation of ceding commission it is at once apparent that a quota share contract is a partnership over either a Reassured's whole account or a part of it. Therefore, the quota share Reinsurer must expect to contribute to the whole expense of the operation and not just the acquisition expenses of the individual risk. For example, a quota share of a Reassured's department would be expected to allow a ceding commission sufficient to cover commissions, premium taxes, inspection costs, cost of policy, underwriting expenses and the expenses of that department. This contrasts completely with a facultative reinsurance. Of course, the exact amount of the ceding commission will be a matter of negotiation and we will consider it later in this chapter.

ARTICLE 7

Claims settlements

> *The Reinsurer will be liable for its proportion of all claims and claims expenses paid by the company. The Reinsurers agree to follow the claims settlements of the company, including settlement made on a compromise or ex gratia basis.*

This again is an expression of partnership. Claims expenses are normally included as part of the claim settlement. Normally, on a quota share partnership the Reinsurer will agree to follow the Reassured in his settlements of claims, even if these take the form of compromises or *ex gratia* payments where the Reassured does not admit liability for the claims. A claim settlement is wider that a loss settlement. The latter presumes liability. Again, this is in contrast to the position on facultative reinsurance where normally a Reinsurer would only commit himself to follow settlements within the conditions of the original policies.

ARTICLE 8

Cession register

> *The company shall keep a register of each and every risk ceded hereunder showing the period, amount and premium on that risk.*

It was normally common practice for a quota share treaty to require bordereaux of all cessions to be sent by the Reassured to the Reinsurer. These bordereaux would contain full details of the original risk, e.g. name, address, perils covered, interest, amount, rate and premium.

However, as a quota share is a fixed percentage of all business, unlike a surplus, there is no need for bordereaux to be kept for premium purposes. The only reason for bordereaux would be to pass on information of the details of individual risks ceded. This might be required by a Reinsurer to find out the type of business being ceded. However, bordereaux are very rarely found on quota share treaties. Some form of cession register of risks falling under the treaty normally will be used, or some coding on companies' files or. of course, these days, a specific computer reference so that premiums and claims are automatically coded and accounted.

The use of a coded quota share with each code representing a different quota share percentage is now coming more into vogue as it combines the simplicity of the quota share with some of the flexibility of the surplus treaty. Such a treaty is described at the end of this chapter.

ARTICLE 9

Accounts

The company shall submit within 60 days of the close of each quarter an account showing the total of gross premium ceded (including additional premium and return premium) during the quarter, the ceding commission due, claims and claims expenses paid during the quarter less any salvages or recoveries. With each quarterly account the company will advise the total of losses outstanding at the close of the quarter.

The balance of the account shall be paid by the debtor to the creditor within 90 days of the close of the quarter. Should the accounts submitted not be agreed by the Reinsurers at this time, then payment shall be made on the basis of accounts submitted by the company and adjusted between the parties in the next quarter's accounts. If not so settled the balance shall carry interest at 1% per month until settlement is made.

Most treaties are accounted quarterly, the accounts being taken from totals shown in the Reassured's register or a print-off from his computer. Normally the premiums total will have additional premiums shown separately and return premiums also identified as a separate total.

On the debit side the total claims paid will be shown with salvage and recoveries as a separate item. Most treaties include a provision for the special collection of large individual losses in between quarterly settlements to enable the Reassured to recoup the Reinsurers' share should it feel necessary to do so.

In addition, there is often a requirement for large individual claims settled in a quarterly account to be separately identified so that Reinsurers may pick them out for possible loss collections under their own retrocession protection. Some quota share treaties might call for complete claims bordereaux where all claims are individually specified by name and amount.

A Reinsurer often wants to identify claims arising from major losses such as a catastrophe for his own statistical records and, again, for his own possible reinsurance recoveries. In the United States, for example, major or catastrophic losses are serially numbered on a national basis. A quota share treaty might well contain provision for any individual loss under the treaty to be identfied by its national number.

Normally quarterly accounts are required to be submitted within a reasonable period after the close of the quarter. A period of 60 days should usually be sufficient with a quota share treaty but a period of 90 days is frequently used. If, on receipt of the accounts, the Reinsurer does not agree them, then he should notify the Reassured at once.

It is important to realise that a treaty accounted on a written premiums basis, as is the one we are considering, will have quarterly accounts for each annual period, which will continue until such time as all the business ceded under any one annual period is finalised, that is until all the losses are paid. This may take several years.

To make the point clear a treaty commencing on the 1st January 1999, and continuing for 2000 and 2001, will have accounts submitted for the calendar quarter ending 30th March 2001 as follows:

9th Quarter	1999	Year
5th Quarter	2000	Year
1st Quarter	2001	Year

The basis of settlement is by payment of the balance by one party to the other. In practice long delays can occur between receipt of the accounts by Reinsurers and payment. In fact, long delays can occur before Reinsurers agree the accounts.

The parties may agree various periods of making settlement, for example:

> "Within 15 days of agreement of the accounts by Reinsurers", or it may be normal for the Reassured to make payment of the balance with the account. Of course, if the balance is due from Reinsurers, the Reassured would expect immediate payment of that balance.

The clause suggested here calls for settlement within 90 days of the close of quarter. If accounts are not agreed by then, a provisional settlement should be made with any adjustment in the next quarter's account.

I feel strongly that whatever system is adopted a settlement date of 90 days after the close of a quarter is long enough and therefore if the deadline is not made, then the aggrieved party is entitled to interest, and 1% per month seems to me to be sufficiently severe to expedite settlement.

The idea of interest on overdue payments on reinsurance treaties is not, however, universally welcomed. Nevertheless, it is a discipline imposed on us all by other businesses, i.e. Banks and Tax Collectors. I see no reason why the same normal trade penalties should not be applied in reinsurance transactions and it might be a very salutary lesson if they were.

The wording calls for quarterly advices of outstanding losses. These do not fall for settlement but are for advice only and are advised quarterly with the actual cash accounts. Some treaties may call for a full outstanding loss advice borderaux with its name, date of loss, period, amount of policy and estimate of loss.

This treaty is accounted on a written premium basis and settlement is made quarterly of the balance between written premiums and paid losses. Outstanding losses are merely advised and not paid or advanced and form no part of that settlement.

A quota share, or a surplus treaty, can be accounted on a written basis or on an earned premium basis, or on a written basis with a transfer of unearned premium portfolio from one annual period to another. Alternatively, a treaty can be accounted on a written basis with the Reinsurers, in addition, depositing with the company their share of any premium and loss reserves that the company is required to establish for solvency purposes.

In this chapter we have confined our discussions to a treaty on a written basis without either depositing of reserves or transfer of unearned premium reserves. It must be emphasised that no one method of accounting is used for a quota share treaty. They can be accounted on a variety of bases. For further discussions on treaty accounts and reserves please read Chapter VII.

ARTICLE 10

Profit commission

The Reinsurers agree to pay to the company a profit commission of 20% of the final net ascertained profit on each annual period this agreement is in force. A calculation shall be made at the end of the second year, or eighth quarter, of each account on the results as then known. Further calculations shall be made annually thereafter until all losses and other transactions are finalised. The profit commission due, or any adjustment required to a previous payment, shall be paid by the debtor to the creditor as soon as the profit commission statement is agreed by Reinsurers.

Income	*Outgo*
(1) Gross premium income paid less returns for all quarters to date.	*(2) Ceding commission paid.*
	(3) Claims and claims expenses paid to date.
	(4) Amount of outstanding losses (if any).
	(5) Reinsurers' expenses at 5% of item (1).
	(6) Deficit (if any) carried forward from previous profit commission statement.

The excess of income over outgo shall be considered the profit or provisional, profit as applicable. However, should the outgo exceed the income then such deficit shall be carried forward as an outgo to the following year's profit commission.

A participation in the profits made under a treaty is a standard reward for the Reassured. Not only that, but it is a very great incentive for the Reassured to preserve the quality of the business to produce the maximum profit. Therefore, most Reinsurers welcome a reasonable profit commission and much prefer it to an inflated ceding commission.

We have seen that the accounting of any year will continue until all claims are paid. Article 10 provides that the profit commission is calculated at the end of the 8th quarter or one year after the close of ,each annual period on the results as then known. If the final result is not known, (for example, there may be losses not yet settled or recoveries due from third parties on claims already paid) then further calculations and adjustments will be made annually until final settlement is achieved.

Sometimes the two parties may agree to commute outstanding losses, particularly if the amount is small, to prevent small adjustments having to be made year after year. Such commutation would then be accepted by both parties as a final settlement of the year of account in question and would allow the profit commission to be finalised at the same time.

The items making up the profit commission statement need little comment. Item (4) — the outstanding losses will only appear until losses are all settled and will not appear in the final profit commission statement. Item (5) — it is normal and sensible for an expense factor for Reinsurers' expenses to be included. The Reinsurer will not make a profit until his expenses are cleared. A figure of 5% is very common. However, the exact percentage is a matter for negotiation. An expenses factor of less than 2½% or more than 10% is unusual. Item (6) — The deficit from the previous year is a normal provision. It is sensible when a loss is incurred in one year, that that loss is recouped before future profit commissions become payable. Should there be very large deficit in any year, then it is possible that it may take several years of profitability before such a deficit is eliminated.

Such an unlimited deficit clause may not be desirable as the Reassured may feel that a future profit commission can never be earned and may feel tempted to start a new treaty or find new Reinsurers who have not suffered the deficit and who would not, therefore, require the deficit to be carried forward.

Therefore, very frequently the carry forward of a deficit is limited to three years. A deficit from Year 1 is carried to Year 2 and any deficit left is carried to Year 3; any deficit then left is carried to Year 4 but would not be carried to Year 5.

ARTICLE 11

Books and records

The Reinsurers, or their authorised representatives, shall, during normal office hours, have access to all the company's books and records relating to this agreement.

This gives the Reinsurer the right to examine the company's books and records to satisfy himself that the treaty is being handled correctly, premiums are correctly accounted and losses correctly settled and accounted.

Such examination is paid for by the Reinsurer and can be expensive. Therefore it is not generally carried out unless a Reinsurer feels that the treaty is not being accounted properly and cannot resolve the problem by normal enquiries.

ARTICLE 12

Errors, omissions and alterations

Accidental errors or omissions shall not prejudice the rights of either party hereunder but shall be rectified as soon as possible.

All alterations, provided they are agreed by both parties, whether recorded by addendum or correspondence, shall be binding on the parties.

It is standard practice that an accidental or inadvertent error or omission shall not prejudice the treaty itself. The error or omission will be corrected and the necessary adjustments made.

ARTICLE 13

Arbitration

Disputes between the parties are referred to arbitration. There is normal practice on both proportional treaties and non-proportional reinsurance contracts.

ARTICLE 14

Intermediary clause

Messrs .... are recognised as the intermediaries negotiating this contract through whom all correspondence shall be passed. However, settlements between the two parties shall be made direct.

An intermediary clause will be inserted where there is a Broker negotiating the contract between the two parties.

This particular clause is unusual in that the Brokers are recognised as the intermediaries for all correspondence except that settlements are made *direct* between the parties I prefer this clause and, in saying so, I realise I may be upsetting some of my Broker friends.

A more normal clause would state that all correspondence, accounts and settlements are made to the intermediary. The whole subject of intermediaries receiving money passing between clients is contentious but personally I believe that the two contracting principals should have the right to make such settlements direct in the treaty wording, even though, in practice, they may not always do so.

Quota Share Treaties

Characteristics and uses

The quota share treaty has certain characteristics as a method of reinsurance which, to a great extent, determine how and when it is used in preference to other methods.

Firstly, it is the only method of reinsurance when the Reassured and the Reinsurer are true partners in a portfolio of business. Secondly, it is simple to operate and account. Sometimes it is virtually the only method of reinsurance which can be used. Thirdly, the volume of premium ceded is high in relation to the capacity or the liability ceded on an individual exposure or risk. Fourthly, it is inflexible.

We will consider these characteristics.

(1) Partnership

As a true partnership it is often used on new accounts or a new class of business where the two parties want to share in the deal, for better or for worse.

I remember a typical example in 1956 when Morocco was just about to achieve its independance from France. At that time the major French insurance companies had a monopoly of all the fire and allied perils business in Morocco. They decided that the risk of riot and malicious damage and arson losses made such business uninsurable. They therefore unilaterally refused to give any cover for riots and malicious damage and also excluded any fire losses arising from those perils.

There was one small local Moroccan company who did not agree and thought that the coverage could be provided. They came to London and I agreed to lead a QS Treaty up to £1,000,000 any one risk for them. We agreed a scale of rates for riot cover varying with the type of risk. The Moroccan company kept 2% net and I led a 98% Quota Share in the London and World Market excluding the French!

It was successful as a joint partnership and the Quota Share income reached £500,000 in a year and had few losses. A Quota Share reinsurance was the only way by which insurance cover could have been provided for these Moroccan risks.

The same argument may apply to unusual classes of business. The confidence given to the Reinsurer when he knows he is a partner and cannot be selected against, can be very necessary. There have been many occasions when an existing reinsurance arrangement has been unprofitable, for example a first surplus treaty, and it may be impossible for Reinsurers to find any terms for its continuation. Sometimes, on such occasions, the Reassured's net account has been profitable and the gross account on the business may also be satisfactory. The solution may be to replace the first surplus or to replace part of the first surplus with a quota share treaty.

Another alternative adopted when surplus treaties are unprofitable and the company's net account is profitable, is for the Reassured to offer a quota share of the net account to its surplus Reinsurers to give them a better chance of profit overall, and also to given them a better balance of premiums against liability.

(2) Simplicity

The great beauty of a quota share treaty is its simplicity. There are some classes of business which are difficult to reinsure on either an excess of loss or a surplus method. These are usually classes where the definition of one loss is extremely difficult or where the definition of a single risk or exposure is difficult. Obvious examples are crop insurance against hail or weather, insurance of standing timber against fire, disease insurance such as foot and mouth in cattle or medical insurance on human beings.

Here, the quota share or the stop loss method may be the only practical method. The simplicity of the quota share method is now being used on more conventional classes in place of the surplus method by use of a variable quota share. We discuss this a little later on.

(3) Volume reinsurance

When compared to other methods the premium volume ceded to a quota share treaty is large compared to the capacity ceded on a single exposure. The quota share is, therefore, an ideal reinsurance treaty where the ceding away of a volume of premium is the object.

One of the main uses of a quota share treaty is in this field. Consider an insurance company whose capitalisation or surplus does not support the premium income it is writing. The long term remedy is, of course, to raise more capital, but this takes time and may not, in any case, be easy or possible.

Alternatively, the company may reduce its volume of acceptances or cancel some business. Again, this takes time and it may be undesirable; no Underwriter will want to cancel or reduce on profitable business. No company will wish to alienate its client's Agents, Brokers or Assureds by so doing.

Very often the best way out of the problem is to effect a quota share reinsurance for that proportion of the account as is necessary to reduce the total premium income to the desired level. Such quota share treaties are often called "surplus relief" quota share treaties. Their purpose is really financial and not an underwriting one. They will often be judged more as premium volume propositions with a fairly low margin of percentage profit, which may well be supplemented by the Reinsurer being able to make some investment gain on the balance of funds, which he may hold. Surplus relief quota share treaties often will be of a temporary nature. They will be reduced or discontinued once the Reassured's financial position improves.

(4) In force accounts

Another major use of the quota share reinsurance is to cede away a whole portfolio of "in force" business. Because of its simplicity the quota share method can easily apply not just to new business as it is written or accepted, but can be simply applied to business already written for the run-off or the unexpired portion of those risks. Say, for example, that an insurance company has to cease its underwriting in a particular country from Ist July. From that date they will cease to accept new business but on that date they will have a portfolio of business in force until the original policies expire or are cancelled. The company may decide that it wishes to reduce this liability drastically so as not to expose itself to a loss in a country where there is no way of balancing that possible loss with continuing business. The answer will be to obtain a quota share reinsurance of all business in force at 1st July.

(5) Run-off accounts

Probably the largest use of the quota share method has been to take a 100% quota share of the running off of a portfolio of business often when all business has expired. The reinsurance then covers the running off of outstanding liabilities. The normal Lloyd's Reinsurance to Close is such a contract, and 100% quota share run-offs have been a feature of the 1980s and the 1990s. The Equitas Quota Share Reinsurance of all Lloyd's

Syndicates' Run Offs is undoubtedly the biggest group of quota shares ever written.

Run Off accounts are included under Chapter XIV.

However, reinsurance is more normally required to provide maximum capacity on individual exposures in comparison with premium ceded, or, in other words, reinsurance is normally sought to enable a direct writing company to balance its book by retaining a certain sized retention on each risk or exposure. The Ceding Company wishes to retain for itself up to 100% of its small risks or exposures and to purchase a considerable amount of reinsurance on larger risks and very large amounts on its peak risks or exposures. The company seeks to achieve the retention of as much premium income as is possible with a balanced "book". This means that quota share reinsurance is very rarely used as the main underwriting reinsurance vehicle. This role is better fulfilled by either a surplus treaty for first party business and excess of loss insurance for third party business or by various combinations of facultative reinsurance surplus reinsurance and excess of loss reinsurance. However, some flexibility can be achieved by the use of a variable quota share and such a contract may be used in place of a surplus treaty as the main reinsurance vehicle.

We could, therefore, summarise the main uses of the quota share treaty as follows:

(1) For new or unusual types of business.

(2) To replace existing reinsurance methods when these have proved impossible.

(3) To give Reinsurers a share in the net account to support other reinsurance programmes.

(4) To reinsure classes or types of business which cannot, or cannot easily, be reinsured by other methods.

(5) The ceding away of premium volume for security or financial reasons.

(6) The ceding away of portfolios of "in force" business.

(7) The use of a variable quota share treaty in place of a surplus treaty.

(8) To cover Run Off business.

Underwriting Considerations

General

Let us now turn our thoughts to the placing and underwriting of quota share contracts. As such treaties are usually taken out for special reasons, and not as the main underwriting protection, it is important to establish these reasons and for both parties to be frank and open as to the purpose of the contract. Most of the clauses and terms in a quota share contract are straight forward; the variable features are the percentage of quota share ceded, the net retention of the Reassured, the ceding commission and the profit commission.

The percentage cession

The percentage cession will be decided by the Reassured and he will determine this by the size of the retention he wishes to keep. The size of the retention often will be determined more by the volume of business to be kept rather than the size of the individual risk exposure. A Reinsurer will normally determine his acceptance share using the same criteria.

The ceding commission

The fixing of the ceding commission is, of course, the major underwriting factor. As a quota share is a partnership a Reassured will expect to be reimbursed for his acquisition costs and his overheads incurred on the subject matter of the business ceded. In practice, ceding commissions tend to be determined to produce an anticipated margin between gross premiums and losses. The margin will be a matter of judgement. A large balanced treaty, i.e. a treaty with a small exposure per risk and little catastrophic exposure and a large premium volume, will be written at a much smaller margin than a treaty with a large risk exposure or an exposure to catastrophic losses or exposure to wide loss fluctuations — e.g. where one is dealing with weather insurance on crops or epidemics in animals. The margin required will need to take care of these exposure fluctuations and to allow a reasonable profit in addition.

It is therefore of importance for a Reassured, if he is to obtain the maximum commission from his Reinsurers, to achieve this balance and to take steps to avoid, as far as possible, the quota share treaty being exposed to major fluctuations. The elimination of peak risk exposures is often best done by facultative reinsurance on a contributing basis to reduce these exposures to such a level that a total loss will not unduly affect the loss ratio of the quota share treaty.

Catastrophe exposures of all kinds are best protected by either the purchase of excess of loss reinsurance for joint account, i.e. a catastrophe excess of loss, which protects each partner in proportion and to which each pays the premium in proportion. Alternatively, a special excess of loss can be purchased for the quota share Reinsurers on their own. The cost of such reinsurances normally will be debited to quota share Reinsurers in the treaties' quarterly accounts. On occasions the Reassured may pay for this quota share protection, particularly where he is anxious to preserve his ceding commission or his profit commission, but this is unusually altruistic.

In dealing with large volume treaties, the investment element of the premium balances to be held by Reinsurers is a prime consideration. Where written premiums are paid, then Reinsurers may expect to have the benefit of substantial sums to invest. This benefit may enable Reinsurers to underwrite such business with very little anticipation of underwriting profit, if any. This type of underwriting, however, can be extremely short sighted unless the treaties are of proven reliability and not subject to experience fluctuations. It is particularly noticeable that very often real exposures exist which are ignored, because in the past these exposures have never produced losses to affect the past experience of that particular treaty.

A well balanced fire treaty may include, say, 20% of its premium for allied perils, windstorm and earthquake. If the anticipated loss ratio based on past experience is, say, 45%, then a Reinsurer might be tempted to pay 50% ceding commission to achieve a 5% profit. However, this is not a "real" profit in years when earthquakes and windstorms do not occur. It is important to ascertain whether the past experience, on which future anticipated loss ratio is calculated, does contain allied peril losses and how much. If they are non existent, then the true fire loss ratio is not 45% but $\frac{45}{80}$ or 56%, and 50% ceding commission will mean that a Reinsurer is writing the fire business at a loss of 6% and relying for his profit on part of the allied peril income. A thoroughly unsound proposition.

Again, a personal accident treaty must incorporate an extra margin for the catastrophic risk of several Assureds being killed in the same aircraft or bus.

In my opinion many crop hail quota share treaties consistently underestimate the very real cataclysmic possibility of the forces of nature. A hail quota share will, after a "normal" run of experience, be placed with ceding commission allowing a margin which would be very acceptable on a less volatile class of risk but can be a fool's paradise on

TABLE 4-1: Triangle 1

Treaty Year of Account	Percentage of losses settled to gross premiums written at end of:								
	Year 1	Year 2	Year 3	Year 4	Year 5	Year 6	Year 7	Year 8	Year 9
1990	35	45	54	64	68	70	70	71	71
1991	40	49	55	63	66	66	67	68	
1992	50	60	66	70	72	74	75		
1993	53	65	70	73	75	77			
1994	48	58	65	68	69				
1995	49	60	67	65					
1996	47	57	63						
1997	44	55							
1998	50								

TABLE 4-2: Triangle 2

Treaty Year of Account	Percentage of losses incurred (paid plus outstanding) at end of each year to gross premiums written at end of:									Our Estimated Final L.R. from above
	Year 1	Year 2	Year 3	Year 4	Year 5	Year 6	Year 7	Year 8	Year 9	
1990	58	68	71	74	72	71	71	71	71	71
1991	60	69	72	73	72	71	70	70		69
1992	63	79	84	84	80	78	78			77
1993	75	80	80	82	81	80				80
1994	60	70	72	74	76					74
1995	65	74	76	74						74
1996	60	70	70							71
1997	55	68								78
1998	65									80

(3) Changes in personnel, particularly in ownership or underwriting staff, or even agency network, may radically alter past experience for better or for worse.

(4) The entry into new territories or new classes of business may well change future experience.

(5) Quota share treaties are often taken out covering a Reassured's net account, i.e. where the quota share Reinsurers are protected or benefit from the Reassured's other reinsurances. These may be excess of loss protections or treaties, or facultative reinsurances.

In all these cases it is very important to ensure that such reinsurances are continuing and that past experience reflects both the future cost of such reinsurances and the future protection afforded.

(6) It is important that the figures provided are on the same basis as the future treaty. If the treaty is to be on an earned premium basis, the past figures should be the same. If past figures are on a written premium basis then the last year's written premium will have to be discounted by the net unearned premium at the close of that year and if this figure is not available then an estimation will have to be made. Where brokerage is paid this should be shown in past figures as an additional debit item.

(7) Losses should be clearly set out each year showing losses paid in respect of each year, including loss expenses. In addition, known outstandings for each year should be set out and allowance will have to be made for unknown loss or incurred but not reported claims or losses. In dealing with long tail business the progression of losses must be a fundamental consideration.

(8) On long tail business likely changes in settlement patterns must be assessed. For example, will outstanding claims in the future be delayed in settlement?

It is very essential that both parties and their intermediaries, if any, should see that past figures are clearly set out and the basis (i.e. written, earned, paid losses, incurred losses) is clearly stated.

It all sounds simple and commonsense but even with the simplest quota share treaty, people still assume that written premiums are earned or they forget to deduct brokerage or, more often, Reinsurers are completely misled as to the long tail nature of the account and its late advice of losses.

The first major factor in determining the ceding commission on a quota share treaty therefore will be the estimated future margin between claims and commission. Reliable past figures of that business play a major role in this. Of course, where no past figures exist, then recourse may be made to other people's results on similar business, but these will at best be a poor substitute for the track record of the Reassured.

The second major factor in determining ceding commission will be the costs of the Reassured. An Underwriter, or a company, will not normally wish to cede away a partnership on its business without receiving in return a ceding commission equal to its total costs on that business. The exception will be where the Reassured is prepared to accept a loss on the business by bearing part of the cost. This exception may be the result of necessity to cede volume on an undesirable class or because the Reassured is forced to shed volume. Unless the Reassured has a special reason to accept a loss he will rightly expect his quota share partners to allow him a ceding commission which meets his acquisition cost plus his overheads on the business ceded. This means that the ceding commission on a quota share is normally higher than it would be on a surplus treaty on the same business and considerably higher than on a facultative reinsurance.

The third factor is common to all reinsurance negotiations — competition. As regards quota share treaties, these are often large volume reinsurances and therefore, when there is an excess of reinsurance capacity, a ready market exists for quota share treaties. This is because a large premium income can be underwritten by the Reinsurer for a minimum of expense, i.e. the cost of the original negotiations and the setting up of a fairly simple accounting system. However, in times of capacity shortage, the taking on of a large volume of premium for a small underwriting profit may not be possible, the reason being that Reinsurers may be limited by their own lack of capital or lack of surplus funds to finance a large premium volume.

One can say that when reinsurance markets are easy and Reinsurers are chasing volume to acquire a premium income for investment or otherwise, then the placing of quota share treaties, with slim or non-existent margins of underwriting profits, becomes — alas — a normal theme.

However, when the cycle turns and capacity becomes tight, then a

Reassured will be lucky to find reinsurance unless he can show a real and definite margin to attract Reinsurers. This may well mean that he has to cede a quota share at a ceding commission which does not cover his costs.

Therefore, the four major factors in determining ceding commission are:

(1) Future margin required to cover profit, experience fluctuations and claims development.

(2) The Reassured's costs on the business.

(3) Competition.

(4) The investment value put on the holding of premium balances.

Profit Commissions

The amount of profit commission is the third main negotiated variable in the terms of a quota share treaty. The basic idea of a participation in profits by the producer of the business is sound. From his point of view it gives him a reward in addition to his own net account profit if the business goes well. Any Reinsurer, too, will normally welcome giving a reasonable profit commission as an added incentive to the Reassured to produce good results. However, we should realise that with a quota share treaty the results and interests of the two parties are already the same. They share proportionally in good and bad experience without any profit commission.

With a surplus treaty the situation is different. Here it is more important for the Reassured to receive a profit commission on the treaty as his own net results may be entirely different. The Reassured is in a position to control the results of the surplus materially, without sharing those results. With a quota share, however, the profit commission can only be an added incentive or reward. Certainly, where ceding commissions are high, or where the type of business is very volatile, it may be sensible to have no profit commission or a small one of, say, 10%. Normally profit commissions under a quota share contract would not exceed 20%.

We have discussed at length the necessity for a margin to cover large exposures or catastrophic fluctuations in experience and also, of course, a Reinsurer will have his own expenses. It is important, therefore, to decide at what point a Reinsurer can be said to make a real profit.

Dealing first with Reinsurers' expenses, these will tend to be constant whatever the size of premium income to the quota share. It costs very little more to deal with a quota share volume of, say, $1,000,000 than it does with a volume of $1,000. Of course, where brokerage is paid, this will be expressed as a percentage and the amount will vary with volume. It is common to allow 2½% or 5% of the gross ceded premiums as an expense item, and this will vary with the brokerage and the volume of the treaty. There is a necessity to include a fluctuation margin as well as the normal 2½% or 5% expense item, the size of any such margin will vary according to the catastrophe and large risk exposures, and to the "balance" of the treaty.

A large volume treaty with little catastrophic or large risk exposure may need no extra margin, but often a high exposure, small volume treaty may need, in theory, a considerable extra fluctuation margin. In practice such a margin is extremely difficult to obtain from a Reassured and however unbalanced a treaty, an extra margin of 10% is very unusual. Normally the best one can hope to achieve is to keep the amount of profit commission itself fairly low and include a total expense factor of 10%, which could be 5% for expenses +5% for fluctuation.

If a fluctuation margin is used, then what happens after a major loss? i.e. when the fluctuation has happened and results in no profit commission for many years ahead. The answer is, of course, that most quota shares will contain a limited deficit clause in their profit commission clause and the large loss will only be a debit to future profit commission in the year it occurs and the two following years.

It is also not uncommon for the two parties to exclude from any profit commission calculation the amount of any large loss in excess of an agreed figure in return for an increased expense item or fluctuation margin. Assume a quota share treaty with an annual volume of $1,000,000 for example. The profit commission statement will have an expense item of 10% instead of a normal 5% expenses; the amount of any loss in excess of $200,000 to the treaty being ignored for all purposes of calculating the profit commission. In a year when the big loss happens only the first $200,000 counts, but in all years an extra $50,000 expenses goes in the debit side of the profit commission. It is my belief that parties to treaties should negotiate some such arrangement, especially those treaties with potential or actual large exposures.

Of course, where the quota share treaty is actually protected by an excess of loss reinsurance, much the same effect is produced with the excess of loss premium being debited to the profit commission statement and recoveries from it being credited. On many treaties in potentially hazardous areas, e.g. fire and windstorm in Florida, the purchase of excess of loss protection gives the treaty a much better balance; it protects both quota share Reinsurers and the profit commission of the Reassured. As such, a treaty may be very profitable in a non-hurricane year and the cost may easily be borne against this profit.

Very good care must be taken with profit commissions on long tail treaties. It will be seen, with our example of a quota share motor account, that our progression triangles show that any estimate of "profit" after one year is impossible. It is only after 2 years that estimates are reasonable. With longer tail business, for example, on employers' liability or third party business, it may be four or more years before the result can be reasonably estimated.

It is sensible then for calculation of profit commission to wait until the experience can be properly estimated and then for annual adjustments to be made until losses are finalised or, of course, the outstanding losses are commuted or liability for them is transferred to a future treaty year.

An alternative method frequently used on long tail quota share treaties is for the profit commission to be finalised after, say, 3 years on the basis of estimated outstandings at that time. Any future variations from these outstandings being carried forward to the profit commission calculations for future years as a debit or credit item in those future statements.

However, this method may well result in an overpayment of profit commission which can never be rectified if, for example, the treaty is cancelled or the future years are unprofitable themselves. The best solution is either not to allow profit commission at all on long tail quota shares or only allow them after a period of at *least* three years, and then only if both parties can agree to commute the losses themselves at the same moment. The profit commission is then paid on the same basis as the final settlement between the two parties.

A Typical Example of a Quota Share Treaty

We might consider an Underwriter who decides to issue a personal accident scheme through a credit card agency. Assume that the scheme is for personal accident cover for £5,000 per person, and all credit card holders will be issued with the cover at a premium of £5 per head, i.e. at the rate of 1‰. There are 50,000 credit card holders and the scheme will produce an annual premium of £250,000. Now, the original writing insurance company is concerned with these problems:

(1) The venture is a new one with no experience and until the record is proven he wants some protection.

(2) The volume is large and he would be satisfied with a net volume of £100,000 — at least for the first year or so.

(3) He is concerned about the possible catastrophic loss in an aircraft or similar disaster.

A suggested reinsurance programme might be to buy, firstly, a 60% quota share reinsurance on the scheme and, secondly, to buy a catastrophe excess of loss protection in excess of, say, 4 lives i.e. £20,000 on the gross account — the excess of loss will protect his net account and his 60% quota share Reinsurers.

We will not go into the factors which determine the excess of loss premium at this point, but let us assume that the 100% account can be protected for 100% of £280,000 × £20,000 each and every loss for a rate of 2% of the gross premium income, or an excess of loss premium of £5,000 per annum. Let us also assume that the original writing company's costs are 30% to the travel agency and extra head office expenses of 7½%. Here we have an example of a classical use of a quota share treaty:

(1) The Reassured wants a partner to share in a new venture. He may well select that partner because the partner has considerable experience in similar ventures and will help the direct writing company with the original business or will, at least, confirm that he considers the venture to be sensibly conceived.

(2) Quota share reinsurance is probably the only way this business can be reinsured. The problem is not one of large individual exposures which could be facultatively reinsured or reinsured by the surplus method. Reinsurance is needed to cede volume and to reduce exposure to the Reassured if things go wrong, i.e. if his original rates prove inadequate or if he has misjudged his exposure or is just plumb unlucky.

Now, what sort of information should the Reassured give and what will the Reinsurer want to know? We will tabulate some of these probable questions:

(1) What experience has the Reassured in this class and who will handle the account for them?

(2) How has the original 1‰ premium rate been arrived at? What statistical evidence is there and are there comparable schemes with an experience record?

(3) Exactly what coverage is given under the original policy, i.e. 24hour cover? Travel only? What is coverage for disablement? Are medical expenses covered? What are the exclusions?

(4) Can the 30% costs be justified?

(5) Are the credit card holders a special class of people? For example, are any of them mountaineers or deep sea divers? Are they geographically well spread?

(6) How will accounting be done by the travel agent and who will settle claims?

Having established the validity of the original business the Reassured will now try and establish the future experience. In all probability'the direct writing company will have arrived at the 1‰ rate on these lines:

Anticipated claims	45‰
Agency costs	30‰
Overheads	075‰
Profit and margin	17½‰

If the Reassured feels that this is viable he, or his Brokers, might draft a proposition as follows:

To take a 60% quota share of all personal accident policies issued to XYZ credit card holders — maximum 60% of £5,000 any one person:

1/1/95 subject to 90 days notice to any anniversary.

Terms: G.O.R. less 42½% ceding commission

Brokerage 2½%

Profit commission 20% (5% expenses. 3 years deficit clause.)

Warranted that protection for joint account at joint expense is taken out for £280,000 e.e. loss × £20,000 at 2%.gross premium income, or as mutually agreed.

Quarterly accounts on a written premium basis.

Quarterly settlements within 90 days.

The 42½% ceding commission allows the Reassured his full expenses plus a good overrider (i.e. 30% cost to agents, 7½% overhead expenses and 5% overrider). He will also enjoy a share of 20% in the profits, if any.

The Reinsurer has this prospect:

42½%	ceding commission
2½%	brokerage
45 %	estimated loss ratio
2 %	excess of loss cost
92 %	
8 %	margin

In addition, if he makes an 8% margin he hands back 20% of 5½% (i.e. 8% less 2½% expenses) or an additional 1%. On a new class a margin of 7% is meagre; assuming the Reinsurer has 3% expenses, he is down to a profit of 4% on his volume of 60% of £250,000 premium. This equals £6,000 or his exposure on two persons. If I were in that position I would say, "Not on your nelly!" "Give me a chance." "Make the ceding commission 40% and profit commission expenses 7½%".

Consider the Broker's position. He has had a nice easy negotiation and will have a very simple accounting job to do and will receive 2½% of £150,000 or £3,750 per annum. If anyone has to give any more it should be the Broker: 1½% brokerage on the gross, or 2½% on the nett, is not a bad intermediary's charge on a medium or large volume quota share, whatever my broker friends argue. A quota,share does not warrant as large a brokerage as a surplus treaty. As a Reinsurer we might suggest:

40 %	commission
1½%	brokerage
45 %	estimated losses
2 %	excess of loss cost
88½%	
11½%	margin
100%	

This margin is reduced by 20% profit commission on only 5%, an extra 1% making the net margin approximately 10.50% against 7%. Assuming the Reinsurer's expense is 3%, he will be left with a 7.5% profit or £11,550. This allows 4 extra lives above the normal expectancy, to be lost per annum before Reinsurers lose money.

The Surplus Relief Quota Share

Let us turn away our thoughts from underwriting and consider one of the major uses of a quota share, that of premium relief or, i.e. ceding away a volume of premium to comply with solvency requirements.

Now, almost all regulatory authorities, whether they be State Commissioners in the U.S.A., the Council of Lloyd's or the Department of Trade and Industry relate premium income to surplus or free assets or capital as a test of future solvency. The theory is that liability taken on by an Insurer, measured by premium income, should have relation to that Insurer's freely available assets. In the United States these assets are the company's surplus, i.e. assets which are surplus to other commitments, not earmarked for debts, unearned premiums or outstanding losses. In Lloyd's a Name's premium income limit is related to his readily available assets. The Lloyd's test is now based on gross premium income with no allowance for reinsurance. Therefore, premium relief reinsurances for Lloyd's Syndicates cannot now be used to reduce a Syndicate's income for solvency purposes. However, Lloyd's allowed for the late 1980s Qualifying Quota Shares which allowed syndicates who were short of capital (Names) to buy a Qualifying Quota Share (up to 25% of capacity). This percentage was reduced quite sensibly in later years as the market softened.

Therefore, when an insurance company reaches his permitted premium income limit he has to shed income or shut up shop. The quickest and most effective method to avoid the latter option is to effect a quota share reinsurance on business in force, i.e. a quota share of the portfolio of business already written and/or a reinsurance of new business. The quota share method will shed liability in proportion to the premium ceded, or it should so do. Provided the regulatory authority accepts the security of the quota share Reinsurer, then the original overwriter has corrected the position and he, the regulator, will be satisfied. The quota share method of reinsurance is really the only method by which an immediate reduction in income can be achieved.

It should be noted here that the use of premium income as a solvency test is open to question. Certainly,the relationship of premium income to liability can be very variable according to the class of business, for example, its exposure to fluctuations or the length of settlement of losses.

However, no-one has yet come up with an easier and better method. Certainly, one could devise better methods but they would be both complicated and time consuming to apply. Therefore, the use of the yardstick of premium volume as a guide to exposure is generally accepted by both regulatory authorities and the industry as a whole. In dealing with a particular case, an Insurer will often feel that he, or his company, presents no real security problem. He knows and has confidence in his account and its profitability.

Such a "successful" Insurer will not want to shed off or pass on to others his "profitable" business; he will want to keep not only his income but also his future profit for himself. The word "successful", has to be extended in this context to include all those who think themselves successful, which includes an awful lot of Underwriters. If such a person has to cede away volume he will obviously negotiate the best possible ceding commission with his Reinsurers, which is fair enough. On top of that he will negotiate the best possible share in the profits of his business, which is also fair enough.

However, in order to obtain the highest possible share in profits he may agree to reduce his ceding commission very considerably if his business turns out to be unprofitable. Believing that his business will be profitable he is quite prepared to accept a very small ceding commission if things go wrong in return for a very big commission if things go well.

In other words, he will accept a scale of commission which slides according to results. In Chapter V, I deal more fully with sliding scales of commission so let us here take a very simple and exaggerated scale which has been used for surplus relief treaties. Instead of a flat ceding commission of 40% there is introduced a provisional commission of 40% adjustable as follows:

L.R. 0% — Ceding commission 95%
then for each rise in loss ratio the ceding commission reduces 1% for 1% to L.R. 95% — Ceding commission 0%

The effect of this is that the Reassured has ceded away his volume as required by the regulatory authority, but has he shed liability commensurate with that volume? Clearly — no! Effectively the Reassured has guaranteed his Reinsurer a profit whatever the loss ratio is until it reaches 100%. The protection he has bought only benefits him if his L.R. exceeds 100%. Clearly such a "guaranteed profit" quota share should not be permitted by the regulatory authority.

To be strictly correct, the thinking reader will have quickly realised that such a quota share is really a stop loss reinsurance for unlimited liability × 95% loss ratio for a premium of 5% and the regulatory authority should allow a premium relief of 5% of ceded premiums only.

To turn from the case of the successful Underwriter in premium income trouble to the poor so-and-so who is in premium income trouble and has an unprofitable business, and who cannot place a quota share at a normal commission term. In order to obtain reinsurance he may he forced into a similar guaranteed profit quota share.

In his case the scale may go even further:

0% L.R.	ceding commission 95%
150% L.R.	ceding commission –55%

Of course, possibly one is using an absurd example. You cannot have a minus ceding commission, or even if you can it does not look good, so a little dressing up is done.

The quota share treaty is placed on a scale which at a loss ratio of 30% pays a ceding commission of 63%. That looks a bit better and anyway everyone knows that it is impossible for the loss ratio to be as low as 30%. To repeat, L.R. 30%, ceding commission 63%, then for each 1% rise in L.R. the ceding commission is reduced by 1% to a L.R. of 90%, where the minimum ceding commission is 3%. Then the Ceding Company (our Reassured) agrees to write a stop loss reinsurance of his own quota share Reinsurers for unlimited liability in excess of 90% loss ratio for a premium rate of 2%. What is the effect of this? At a loss ratio of 150% the quota share Reinsurers will pay the Reassured the minimum commission of 3% and will have a loss of 53%. Under the reciprocal stop loss they will have paid the Reassured 2% of the premium and have recovered 60% × 90%. The Reinsurer's position is credit 60%, debit (53% + 2%) = 55%. On balance a 5% profit. The Reassured, having taken out a quota share to relieve his solvency situation, has in fact made it worse. The ceding away of a volume of reinsurance and then buying back by stop loss reinsurance, or other devices, is, and can only be, a deliberate attempt to evade insurance regulations and should be treated equally as seriously as other methods of deliberate evasion of regulations.

Most regulatory authorities do not allow credit for reinsurance purposes for sliding scale guaranteed profit quota shares, and quite rightly so. However, the protection given back by the Reassured on his own quota share relief treaty is sometimes very difficult to establish. It can be a separate reinsurance transaction not easily traced, particularly if the stop loss protection is issued by a third party to the quota share Reinsurer, and then the third party is in his turn held harmless or reinsured 100% by the original Reassured.

The only way to discover such illicit deals is by careful examination of individual acceptances, which is not easy to do in time. The only answer really is to enforce severe penalties if such misdemeanours are discovered. Luckily most of us are honest and such lapses are the exception rather than the rule. However, we are all at times too inclined to turn a blind eye to immorality and are tempted to write such deals, even if we might shudder at placing them ourselves.

These remarks do not in any way detract from the valid use of a quota share treaty to relieve the financial strains of a company. The quota share method is the most effective and quickest method. It is perfectly proper and correct provided that (1) the liability ceded is not reduced by a large reduction in ceding commission if experience is adverse and (2) the Reassured does not protect back or assume back his liability in some other way.

Putting morality to one side, and coming down to the placing and underwriting of surplus relief treaties, or premium shedding quota shares, obviously the percentage quota share will be determined by the Reassured and will be calculated to shed the volume of premium necessary. The Reassured will, of course, be very concerned with the future viability, i.e. solvency, of his Reinsurers and will wish to effect the cession of premium at a minimum cost to himself. That is to say, he will want to obtain a ceding commission which covers all his costs and a very sizeable share in the future profits. He will be helped in this by the fact that such a quota share will often be ceded on a written premium basis (to get rid of the premium) and may, therefore, have a substantial investment element for the Reinsurer who will have a balance of premium in hand until losses become payable.

A surplus relief quota share often may be taken out in the middle or towards the end of the Reassured's annual accounting period. Often the need to effect the quota share is not known until then. In addition, immediate relief is needed and this can be achieved best by either backdating the cession date to the start of the annual account or backdating it to some convenient date, e.g. the start of the previous quarter, or by ceding the in force business. Back-dating can have advantages in that it is often simpler and will get rid of a large volume.

Although it may sound unethical in that the results are already known, it is not always so. A volume of seasonable business may have to be back-dated. An account with a heavy seasonal risk, e.g. hurricane or typhoon exposure, ceded in August might be impossible to place without back-dating it to the first of the year. A cession of long tail business could easily take place a year after it has started as results will not be known at that time. Normally however, the quota share will commence when it is placed. In order to give immediate relief the portfolio of business in force will be ceded along with new and renewal business.

When considering taking out such a quota share a Reassured will have a number of other decisions to make. We will not go into them all in details because they are self-explanatory and will be variable case by case.

(1) Will the quota share be on his net account? Normally this will be so and the Reassured will have prepared his past statistics on this basis and future protection will be stated in the quota share treaty.

Not only should the future protections be stated in the Quota Share Treaty, but is best to warrant them and also to make sure that any recoveries due thereunder are deducted whether collected or not. It is necessary to spell out that recoveries not collected, due say to insolvency of other Reinsurers, are not paid by the Quota Share Reinsurer but any such non-collections remain with the Reassured. After all, he chose those Reinsurers!

Dealing with "run off" reinsurances the reverse may be true and the Reinsurer may take over responsibility for such non-recoveries.

(2) The Reassured may decide to cede the quota share on his entire account, across the book. Alternatively, it may be sensible and easier to confine the quota share to one department or class of business. Here he will have to consider whether the reinsurance will be easier to place confined to one class. Often this will be the case; at least the amount of information to be provided will be less. In addition, as the duration of the quota share may be temporary, for example, until fresh capital is raised, the inclusion of long term business such as employers' liability, third party or motor business may not be desirable because claims, and thus the accounts, may continue long after the quota share itself has been terminated.

(3) The Reassured may be able to solve his premium income problems by ceding his in force business and not take out a quota share for his new and renewal business. This can be reduced by cutting back on the volume of new business by eliminating unprofitable risks or classes.

(4) He must seriously consider the ceding commission. If it does not meet his costs on the business ceded he may incur a severe financial strain on his expenses and if this strain is too great he may find it better to cut his original business and cut his own expenses.

The Variable Quota Scheme

One of the great merits of the quota share is its simplicity in accounting. Even with the most sophisticated computers there is a considerable saving in performing one mathematical calculation thousands of times over than performing a thousand different calculations once. The surplus treaty does involve a large number of individual calculations of cession premiums whereas with a quota share the cession percentage can be applied *en bloc*. The disadvantage of the quota share for ceding normal underwriting exposures is that it is too inflexible. The use of a variable quota share introduces a flexibility whilst retaining this simplicity of accounting.

The concept is quite simple — a quota share is taken out which is variable in percentages at the choice of the Reassured for each risk ceded. Let us assume a simple example with four options:

Col. 1 *Numerical code*	*Col. 2* *Percentage cession*	*Col. 3* *Percentage retention*	*Col. 4* *No. of lines of cession*
A	50 % Quota share	50 %	1 line
B	66⅔% Quota share	33⅓%	2 lines
C	80 % Quota share	20 %	4 lines
D	90 % Quota share	10 %	9 lines

Each time a risk is written the Reassured codes it A, B, C or D — or if he wants no reinsurance he uses no code or a code X or 0. Once the coding is made, accounting of premium and losses is done in bulk per code. However, whilst the accounting side is easy the operation of such a treaty, as compared to, say, a 10 line surplus, is more difficult due to the lack of flexibility. Take a Reassured whose normal net retention is £10,000 on a brick-built house:

Value £25,000

On a first surplus he keeps £10,000 — cedes £ 15,000 (1½ lines)
On this ceded quota share he can classify the risk A.
He then keeps £ 12,500 and cedes £ 12,500 (1 line) or he can code it B. He then keeps £8,333 and cedes £16,666 (2 lines).

Of course, the number of options or codes can be increased to the infinite number of options available under a first surplus but then you might as well have a surplus. With a variable quota share of, say, 10 options:

A	33⅓%	½ line
B	50 %	1 line
C	60 %	1½ lines
D	66⅔%	2 lines
E	75 %	3 lines
F	80 %	4 lines
G	83.33%	5 lines
H	85.73%	6 lines
J	88.88%	8 lines
K	91 %	10 lines

You can have a pretty flexible treaty but there will still be cases where net lines cannot be fixed at a pre-determined figure. However, you now have virtually an animal which you can call a coded quota share or a coded surplus. Such coded quota shares or surplus are of considerable use to those Underwriters who can select easily the gross line they can write, as happens in Lloyd's or in the London market, or a bourse or similar market place. Here the use of a coded share of, say, a few variables allows the Underwriter to write his normal net line and then to increase that by a definite percentage and to cede that increase to his treaty. e.g.:

Codes A	33⅓%
B	50 %
C	66⅔%

the multiple of the net line to arrive at gross line is

A	1½ times or 150%
B	twice or 200%
C	three times or 300%

So an Underwriter normally writing a £10,000 net line simply uses his treaty and writes:

either	£10,000 No code
or	£15,000 Coded A
or	£20,000 Coded B
or	£30,000 Coded C

The reader can play around with this idea but in practical terms the use of such a method in place of the surplus method takes a little getting used to and is really not advised for smaller or medium sized companies which are used to thc surplus method and which, in any case, do not have the ability to select the size of their gross acceptances.

SPECIMEN QUOTA SHARE TREATY

Agreement between — X — (hereinafter called the Company) and — Y — (hereinafter called the Reinsurer)

ARTICLE 1

Term

This agreement shall commence at on
and shall continue until terminated by either party giving the other at least 3 months notice to terminate at the 31st December of any year.

ARTICLE 2

Territory

This agreement shall be limited to business emanating from

ARTICLE 3

Classes

This agreement shall apply to all classes written in the company's department

ARTICLE 4

Exclusive

This agreement does not cover any of the following:
(1)

ARTICLE 5

Insuring clause

The company binds itself to cede and the Reinsurer agrees to accept a fixed proportion of 70% of all business falling within the terms of this agreement up to a limit of

The company agrees to retain for its own account the balance of 30% of all business subject to the benefit of excess of loss catastrophe reinsurance. It is agreed that the liability of the Reinsurer shall commence and cease simultaneously with that of the company.

The Reinsurer shall be subject to the same conditions as the original policies and shall follow, subject to the terms of this agreement, the fortunes of the company in respect of all business ceded hereunder. The company may reinsure elsewhere any risk or part of any risk should it consider it in the interest of both parties.

ARTICLE 6

Premium clause

The Reinsurer shall receive 70% of the gross premiums received by the company in respect of business hereunder, without any deductions. The Reinsurers shall allow the company a ceding commission of 40% of the premiums so ceded.

ARTICLE 7

Claims settlements

The Reinsurer will be liable for its proportion of all claims and claims expenses paid by the company. The Reinsurers agree to follow the claims settlements of the company, including settlements made on a compromise or *ex gratia* basis.

ARTICLE 8

Cession register

The company shall keep a register of each and every risk ceded hereunder showing the period, amount and premium on that risk.

ARTICLE 9

Accounts

The company shall submit within 60 days of the close of each quarter an account showing the total of gross premium ceded (including additional premium and return premium) during the quarter, the ceding commission due, claims and claims expenses paid during the quarter less any salvages or recoveries.

With each quarterly account the company will advise the total of losses outstanding at the close of the quarter.

The balance of the account shall be paid by the debtor to the creditor within 90 days of the close of the quarter. Should the accounts submitted not be agreed by Reinsurers at this time, then payment shall be made on the basis of accounts submitted by the company and adjusted between the parties in the next quarter's accounts. If not so settled the balance shall carry interest at 1% per month until settlement is made.

ARTICLE 10

The Reinsurers agree to pay to the company a profit commission of 20% of the final net ascertained profit on each annual period this agrement is in force. A calculation shall be made at the end of the second year, or eighth quarter, of each account on the results as then known. Further calculations shall be made annually thereafter until all losses and other transactions are finalised. The profit commission due, or any adjustment required to a previous payment, shall be paid by the debtor to the creditor as soon as the profit commission statement is agreed by Reinsurers.

Income	*Outgo*
(1) Gross premium income paid less returns for all quarters to date.	(2) Ceding commission paid.
	(3) Claims and claims expenses paid to date.
	(4) Amount of outstanding losses (if any).
	(5) Reinsurers' expenses at 5% of item (1).
	(6) Deficit (if any) carried forward from previous profit commission statement.

The excess of income over outgo shall be considered the profit or provisional, profit as applicable. However, should the outgo exceed the income then such deficit shall be carried forward as an outgo to the following year's profit commission.

ARTICLE 11

Books and records

The Reinsurers, or their authorised representatives, shall, during normal office hours, have access to all the company's books and records relating to this agreement.

ARTICLE 12

Errors, omissions and alterations

Accidental errors or omissions shall not prejudice the rights of either party hereunder but shall be rectified as soon as possible.

All alterations, provided they are agreed by both parties, whether recorded by addendum or correspondence, shall be binding on the parties.

ARTICLE 13

Arbitration

ARTICLE 14

Intermediary clause

Messrs. are recognised as the intermediaries negotiating this contract through whom all correspondence shall be passed. However, settlements between the two parties shall be made direct.

CHAPTER V

SURPLUS TREATIES

Introduction — The treaty wording — Term and period — Basis of cessions — Loss reports — Earned premium basis — Sliding scale of commission — Currency — Loss reserves and letters of credit

Introduction

We come now to discuss the method of reinsurance which accounted for the majority of reinsurance premiums in the world in the 1970s but now has been replaced more by excess of loss treaties.

Like a quota share treaty a surplus treaty is an agreement between the Reassured and his Reinsurer(s) to cede reinsurance from the former to the latter. Unlike the quota share, where a fixed percentage is agreed in advance, the Reassured agrees to cede only that part of any individual insurance policy which is surplus to its net retention. Therefore, as the net retention may vary risk by risk, the percentage cession may vary risk by risk, each cession requiring to be noted and the reinsurance premium being calculated individually.

Most surplus treaties are obligatory, i.e. obligatory on the Reassured to cede all surpluses and on the Reinsured to accept all cessions up to the agreed limits of the treaty. The obligatory surplus treaty is thus a flexible instrument which allows a direct writing company to handle its business in a way it can best serve the public. The obligatory nature of a surplus treaty obliges the Reinsurer to accept all cessions made automatically. This obligatory nature means that the attachment of the treaty Reinsurer on a risk is automatic once the Reassured has decided the net retention, as this decision automatically triggers the cession to the obligatory surplus Reinsurer.

It is this obligatory feature on both sides, plus the automatic attachment, which makes the obligatory. surplus so much more efficient than the facultative method when handling the large numbers of risks and large and varied values and types of risks for which modern industry and commerce needs insurance protection.

The Treaty Wording

Let us pursue our usual method — a plough through a surplus treaty wording. I must, however, say that I have yet to see a standard treaty wording. Perhaps it is time that one was promulgated, but each treaty is really unique and perhaps one could only achieve unification of certain clauses. The particular wording I have selected is one which might have been in use in the late 1970s between a major U.S. company group and its London and world-wide Reinsurers. It is a practical wording between a Reassured and Reinsurers who have known and dealt with each other for many years and have developed a considerable trust between themselves based upon a long and valuable connection. I have omitted certain complications from the wording and certain standard clauses, notably the exclusions.

The preamble is simple and sets out the names of the two contracting parties. Please note that the contract is numbered for reference. Large modern treaties, such as this one, will be placed with, or underwritten by, many Reinsurers; a "line" being equal to the Reassured's retention on any policy. Customarily, treaty limits are expressed as so many "lines" — see Article 5 Para. 3. Many years ago, and sometimes even today on smaller treaties, Reinsurers expressed their acceptance share in lines, e.g. 2 lines, 1 line, ½ line and so on. More normally Reinsurers express their lines as a percentage of the whole treaty. Thus, in this case, with a treaty of 5 lines, a percentage line of 10% would represent half a line. Often Reinsurers sign for their shares on the wording itself but a schedule attached to the wording is common practice.

Term and Period

ARTICLE 1

TERM

This Contract shall apply to all cessions declared on and after 1st April 1977 (except as regards reporting form and similar types of policies to which this Contract shall apply in respect to all reports for periods commencing 1st April 1977) and shall remain in force for an indefinite period but may be terminated on the last day of March in any year by either party giving to the other 90 days' notice of cancellation.

In the event of cancellation the Reinsurers shall continue to participate in all insurances and/or reinsurances coming within the terms of this Contract during the said period of 90 days and the Reassured shall have the option of:

(a) continuing cessions in respect of all business in force at the date of cancellation until their expiry or renewal of the original policy or for a period of one year following the effective date of cancellation, whichever is the earlier.

(b) relieving Reinsurers of all liability at date of cancellation.

Surplus treaties are normally entered into for an unlimited period subject to cancellation by either party giving notice to an annual anniversary date, in this case 1st April. The period of notice most frequently used is 90 days or three months, and unless either party gives notice, then the treaty continues. Any review of the treaty's progress should be completed before this 90-day period. This means that the statistics and results are reviewed and any required amendments to the terms are discussed and agreed before this date.

In practice it sometimes happens that this is not possible, or a Reassured may wish to alter participations in the treaty within the 90-day period. In this case provisional notice to cancel may be given by one party to the other, or, alternatively, the two parties may mutually agree to reduce the notice period for that year only from 90 days to a lesser period. Of course, the giving and receiving of provisional notice creates considerable extra work for all parties and at a later date the provisional notice has to be either withdrawn or made definite. If this is left until near the anniversary date it can cause considerable concern to a company which needs to know that its treaty is placed well before the anniversary date.

Therefore, the giving of provisional notice should not be done by either party unless circumstances are unusual. There are still some Reinsurers and some Reassured's who have the nasty habit of sending out provisional notice far too freely.

Should Reinsurers wish to give notice, then the onus is on them to do so. As regards non-marine treaties placed in Lloyd's and other Broker markets, it is a customary market practice for Reinsurers to require Brokers to present an agreement to continue on each treaty prior to the notice date. Actually, this is more of an agreement not to give notice. It signifies that the Underwriters or companies have been shown the treaty results and reviewed the terms and their lines or commitments and are happy not to give either provisional or definite notice. However, it must be emphasised that should a non-marine reinsurance Broker fail to show such "an agreement to continue" then any Reinsurer who has not given notice is obliged to continue.

It has become a practice in some markets, notably London, for Reinsurers when they write or renew a treaty to insert against their line at the time of writing "Notice to cancel at anniversary date given" Some Reinsurers have adopted the nasty habit of incorporating the initials "N.C.A.D." in their stamp!

This in my view is an unacceptable practice as effectively it attempts to make a continuous treaty into an annual contract. No reinsurance Broker or ceding company should accept a line on this basis. Far better to place a treaty for a year at a time. The practice leads to disputes as often the Broker does not tell his client, the Reassured, that lines are qualified in this way.

Most treaties have anniversary dates at 1st January, with the exception of Australia where the normal date is 1st July. This, of course, means that September is a busy month for the treaty Underwriter. The use of the date of 1st April is unusual but has the great advantage of avoiding the normal "rush hour".

This particular wording. deals with reporting form policies in a somewhat unusual way. Under such policies the insurance company receives its premium monthly or quarterly, based on values reported for that month or quarter, and does not receive premium at inception of the insurance policy. In this case cessions are made to this treaty on the first reporting date after 1st April, not the first renewal date.

Normally, when a treaty is cancelled by either party, all cessions continue to be made during the period of notice. On the date of termination no new cessions can be made. However, all existing cessions will continue in force until their natural expiry date or their renewal dates. This is the natural order of things unless the parties agree otherwise. Where the normal course is pursued and cessions run to their expiry or renewal dates, then certain problems can arise:

Firstly — an original policy can be continuous, and therefore have no renewal or termination date. It may be for a period of years — 3 years or 5 years. In such cases the treaty will normally call for termination of the cession at the first anniversary date of the policy after the termination of the treaty.

Secondly — an original policy may be for a long period for a specific job. For example, a construction or builders' risk. Here it is extremely difficult for such a cession to be terminated at the anniversary date of the original policy. An anniversary date on such a policy is a purely artificial date as the original policy is written for an indivisible premium. In such cases cessions will have to continue until their full term unless special arrangements are made to calculate fairly the amount of the premium for the cession period if it is terminated artifically at an "anniversary" date.

The reader will see that where a Reinsurer, or several Reinsurers, cancel their share of a treaty, then accounts will have to be rendered to them for at least a further year and often for longer. The Ceding Company will have replaced the cancelled part with new Reinsurers and accounts will be sent to them for the new and renewal business.

This process can become extremely burdensome administratively and therefore on most treaties the Ceding Company (or the Reassured) has the option to "take back" the in force business or reassume the portfolio of business in force. This means that the cancelling Reinsurer's liability on all cessions in force at the termination date stops on that date. He is "off risk" on that date, not only for new cessions but for existing cessions.

Where a treaty is on a written basis, such a Reinsurer will hand back or be debited with the premium for all such unexpired cessions. That is, unearned premium at termination date is returned to the Ceding Company. The Reinsurer "takes back the portfolio" of business, and receives back the premium for it.

Please note that the cancelling Reinsurer still remains liable to pay losses which occurred prior to termination date, whenever they are settled, but can have no liability for losses occurring after that date. We will return to this in the next chapter so if you are lost, have patience or read that chapter now!

Let us return to our particular wording. Under this wording the Reassured has two options — the second option (b) is to relieve Reinsurers of all liability at the date of cancellation, i.e. the Reassured takes back all the business in force at that date, exactly as we have discussed above. However, this treaty is on an earned basis and Reinsurers have never received the premium for this unexpired business and therefore no unearned premium is due back to the Reassured. Option (a) which is unusual in that cessions are continued until the natural expiry date or renewal date, or for a full 12 months period, whichever comes first.

This means that a policy expiring in the June following cancellation of the treaty in April will terminate then, whether such a policy is renewed or not. Continuous or long term policies with longer than 12 months to run will continue to run off, under the cancelled treaty, for a full 12 months period. This procedure is somewhat unusual in that normally with U.S.A. treaties 3-year and 5-year fire and extended coverage business is often terminated at the first anniversary date. In other words, the anniversary date of the original policy is treated for this purpose as if it were a renewal date.

Basis of Cessions

Articles 2, 3 and 4 deal respectively with the type of business to be ceded, the territory covered and the exclusions. As regards type of business, it is now common for a treaty to cover the business of a department or departments of a company's operation rather than to specify the actual perils.

As regards territory, whilst this is defined as the U.S.A. and Canada, the words "and/or as original" widen the territorial scope to include a cession which might extend beyond these limits. Actually, "and/or as original" are words which reinsurance Brokers carry on their shirt cuffs for use on every possible occasion. They achieve a very comprehensive sweeping up operation and can be used with cunning to make a Reinsurer liable for almost anything. Here, however, the use may be justified, provided the two parties understand what this means.

In my view the words "and/or as original" are too vague. Do they mean that the Reassured can cede a risk which is entirely located outside the USA or Canada. If so, when and how often? Do they apply to a risk located outside USA underwritten in the USA or Canada? And what about transits abroad from the USA and Canada? The territorial clause should read somewhat as follows: "This reinsurance only covers individual risks located in the USA and Canada except where an original policy covering such risks includes incidental coverage or transits outside the USA and Canada."

ARTICLE 5

TREATY DETAIL

In many treaty wordings Article 5 would be broken down into a number of different Articles but I rather like the following set-out which concentrates the treaty details into one Article of ten clauses:

TREATY DETAIL

> *1. The Reassured agrees to cede and the Reinsurers agree to accept 100% of every surplus amount or amounts (within the limits hereinafter prescribed) after the retention of the Reassured on all risks underwritten by the Reassured.*

This is the essential insuring clause of the treaty. It is uncompromisingly obligatory on both sides — "agrees to cede", "agree to accept", "every surplus amount". This statement summarises in straightforward and simple language exactly what a first surplus treaty is. I commend it to you.

> *2. The Reassured are however permitted at their discretion to effect other reinsurance before using this Treaty; to effect reinsurance for the joint account and at the joint expense of themselves and Reinsurers; to restrict allotments on some risks in such a manner that the liability of the Reinsurers thereon shall be less than the maximum provided herein; provided, however, that said rights shall be used only when it appears to be beneficial to the Reinsurers.*

This is an essential clause which allows the Reassured to "underwrite" the treaty and to protect it where he considers it to be in the Reinsurer's interest. Firstly, he need not cede a heavy exposure or bad risk to the treaty but can use a facultative reinsurance instead. Secondly, he can take out a joint account reinsurance to protect the treaty and his net account. For example, a large cession could be protected by a facultative excess of loss on that cession or a block of business, or the whole treaty protected by catastrophe excess of loss protection. However, should the latter course, i.e. protection of the whole treaty, be considered desirable, I would imagine that Reinsurers would be consulted before such a protection was placed. In addition, the Reassured may restrict the amount of cession which allows them another right to "underwrite" the treaty.

3. *The surplus amounts ceded to the Reinsurers on any one risk shall in no case exceed 5 times the Reassured's net retention up to a maximum limit of $5,000,000 Probable Maximum Loss (PML) but not exceeding $15,000,000 irrespective of the PML. The Reassured shall be the sole judge of what constitutes one risk and of the PML, of any risk.*

Here the limits of the treaty are clearly set out using the normal modern technique of expressing the limit on any one risk, both on a PML basis and on a sum insured basis. The surplus amounts are also limited to 5 times the Reassured's net retention. This treaty is a 5-line treaty with limits per line of $3,000,000 sum insured and $1,000,000 PML. Thus, for a risk of $20,000,000 with PML of $12,000,000 or 60% and a net retention of $2,000,000 sum insured and $1,200,000 PML, the cession is 5 × $2,000,000 = $10,000,000 sum insured with PML of $6,000,000 (N.B. PML is too much). Therefore cession must be reduced to $8,333,333 sum insured to comply with maximum PML limit of $5m.

However, as we discussed in the preamble, with a large modern treaty of this size, Reinsurers will not be thinking on a line basis but rather basing their acceptances on percentages of the limits per risk and, of course, the premium income generated. The Reassured is the sole judge of the PML on any risk and this again is normal practice.

4. *The minimum net retention of the Reassured shall be $200,000 any one risk.*

Here the minimum retention is stated simply on a sum insured basis. A PML minimum retention is not necessary. In any case, minimum retention risks would probably be 100% PML.

5. *The liability of the Reinsurers shall commence simultaneously with the liability of the Reassured on all risks and shall be subject to all the general and special conditions, clauses, stipulations and endorsements of the original insurances and/or reinsurances. If a loss should occur after the Reassured has become liable on a risk but prior to the time the Reassured, in the regular course of business, has had an opportunity to make a cession hereunder the Reassured shall fix their net retention according to their usual practice and shall cede the surplus just as if no loss had occurred.*

This is the second major insuring clause of a surplus treaty. We have seen that under a quota share treaty the liability of Reinsurers attaches automatically and simultaneously with the Reassured. Once the Reassured accepts a risk then Reinsurers are "on risk" for their predetermined percentage. With a first surplus treaty this does not happen and cannot happen until the Reassured has determined and recorded the net retention on that risk.

Simultaneous attachment can be of vital importance. No Reassured can run the risk of a major loss happening before a net retention is established. On occasions this can take time. For example, the decision on net retention may have to be referred from an agent or branch office to head office. Therefore, this clause states that there is simultaneous attachment and the second half of the clause states what happens if a loss occurs on that risk before the Reassured has been able to fix the net retention and to actually make and record the treaty cession.

Of course, this procedure will only be successful if both parties trust each other and, in particular, if Reinsurers have complete faith in the fairness of the Reassured to act after a loss in the way they would have acted if no loss had happened. Apart from simultaneous commencement of Reinsurers' liability, this clause also binds them to follow the conditions of the original policies.

> *6. In respect of Builders' Risks and policies issued on a reporting form basis, cessions made hitherto shall be a fixed percentage or fraction of the maximum liability at the location, the intention being that this Contract shall protect the actual amounts at risk in the proportion that the cession bears to the limit of liability at the location.*

Reporting form policies, stock policies and any policy issued for a limit of liabdity, where the actual values at risk either fluctuate or gradually build up, can create problems. Obviously it would be very burdensome to cede and recede such policies as the reported values changed. Therefore the net retention and the surplus cessions, and, if necessary, any other reinsurances, are based on the policy limits. Once so ceded, any future values, premiums and losses are apportioned to the original cessions. In other words, the reinsurance on that policy becomes a quota share reinsurance with the 1st surplus taking a fixed percentage of that particular policy.

> *7. Cessions hereunder shall be based on the Reassured's retention for the key peril or key section of any original policy and shall include a proportionate cession of all other perils or sections of that policy.*

Much the same philosophy applies to individual perils. The Reassured may base his retention on a key peril but once that retention and the treaty cession is established for that key peril, then the same percentage is applied to all other perils. This treatment is also used for multiple section policies. For example, a shop-keeper's comprehensive policy covering: stock for fire and burglary, stock in transit, cash in transit, third party liability. The retention and cession would be established on the key peril or key section — let us say the fire peril on stock. Then all other perils and sections would be ceded in the same proportion as the fire peril. Of course, on occasions, specific sections of composite or multi-peril policies may be ceded individually but this is unusual and would only be done if the cession were made at the specific full premium for that peril or section and with the full agreement of the Reinsurers.

> 8. *Cessions hereunder on schedule policies shall be based on the Reassured's retention on the key location and shall include a proportionate cession of all other locations. However, where the Reassured feels it will not prejudice Reinsurers, items in schedule policies, whether specific or reporting, may be ceded as in the case of single locations, provided full rates are applied to the cessions and not the schedule average rates. However, it is understood that policies issued to single or joint Assureds covering a single general location or plant complex shall be treated as one cession and items or parts cannot be ceded as single locations even if specifically rated.*

In dealing with schedule policies, where numbers of different locations are involved, the same principle is used. The retention and the cession are ceded on the basis of the value and PML of the key location and proportioned over all other locations. Again, once the cession is established, the reinsurance becomes a quota share reinsurance of all locations on that policy. However, in this treaty the Reassured may cede a specific location from a schedule as if it were a single policy, provided specific rates are applied. This concession is unusual and where it is given it should, in fairness, be used very sparingly. A Reassured who consistently uses his first surplus treaty to "dump" the heavy risks from his schedule policies, keeping the more desirable part of those schedules for himself, will not keep his Reinsurers very long. Personally, I would give such a concession only to a Reassured who I knew and trusted implicitly.

This wording specifically deals with the difficult problem of large industrial or commercial complexes and these, such as a petrochemical plant, may be spread over a very large area. This will consist of a large number of structures, some hazardous and some less hazardous. Many of these are spread out and technically a surveyor may consider them separate fire or explosion "risks". In addition, each such separate part of the complex may be rated individually.

Is it proper for a Reassured to cede different parts of one complex as if they are individual risks? Certainly, this practice of regarding individually rated parts of one large risk or complex as a separate risk has become prevalent, or at least it is not regarded as improper. It is my view that it is improper. To cede an individual plant as if it were a number of separate risks is hardly fair to surplus Reinsurers. The test must be to ask the question, "Would the Reassured have written a picked out item on that risk without a line on the whole risk?". In nearly all cases an Insured would hardly accept a line on, say, the "cat cracker" whilst foregoing a line on the unexposed administration office of the same plant. If so, it cannot be right that surplus Reinsurers are selected against in this manner. Therefore, a single plant should be ceded as one entity as a quota share of all items.

> 9. *The Reassured's retention may, at their discretion, be on building and/or contents and/or other interests on a risk and cessions hereunder may be made in any name or interest on the same risk and not necessarily in the same name or interest as their own retained lines.*

Normal treaty practice is for the Reassured's net retention and the treaty cession to be on the identical interest. It would be wrong, for example, on a flood policy for a retention to be kept on the building and for the treaty cession to be made on the contents. However, it frequently happens that a Reassured writes an additional line on the contents of a building. Assume that the Reassured has kept his full retention on the building and made a one-line cession to his treaty, and that the contents value is equal in value to half the building value. For example:

	Gross Line	Net Retention	Cession
Buildings	$1,000,000	$500,000	$500,000
Contents	$500,000	Nil	$500,000
Total	$1,500,000	$500,000	$1,000,000

This, clause gives the Reassured the discretion to cede as in this example. By having this discretion he avoids having to cancel and recede the building line.

The correct cession, of course, should be as follows:

	Gross Line	Net Retention	Cession
Buildings	$1,000,000	$333,333	$666,667
Contents	$500,000	$166,667	$333,333
Total	$1,500,000	$500,000	$1,000,000

When the original policy is re-written as a single policy, one would expect the cession to be re-made on this basis. Once again, I must emphasise that this wording is one between two parties who know each other well and the Reinsurers know that they can give this discretion to this Reassured with confidence that he will *normally cede* on identical interest and only use this concession with discretion.

> *10. The Reassured shall retain their net retention of each and every cession hereunder net for their own account subject only to the protection of their catastrophe excess of loss reinsurance. Collections under such policies shall not be considered as vitiating the Reassured's net retention.*

This clause, which warrants that the Reassured's retention is retained net, subject to catastrophe protection, needs no comment.

Loss Reports

Article 6 deals with the reporting and settlement of losses under the treaty.

ARTICLE 6

LOSSES

(1) Losses and loss expenses shall be charged in the quarterly accounts, supported by a statement showing:
- *(a) the paid losses and paid loss expenses segregated into years of occurrence;*
- *(b) particulars of every paid loss and its expenses included therein*
  - *(i) where loss to 100% of this Contract exceeds $250,000; and*
  - *(ii) in respect of those losses where Reinsurers have previously been furnished with an individual notice of loss;*

(c) *the aggregate figures of settlements made in respect of any event which is recognised by Reinsurers to be a catastrophe.*

This sets out the basis by which paid losses and paid loss expenses are settled between the parties. All losses are settled quarterly in bulk, segregated into years of occurrence. Individual details of losses are not required except for large losses over $250,000 to the treaty, or for losses which have previously been individually advised under 6.6. This is necessary so that Reinsurers may clear their records of these notified outstanding losses.

Under Para. 6.1c special advice is given of losses in respect of known catastrophes so that Reinsurers may have a note for their own records and for possible collection from their own catastrophe or excess of loss Reinsurers. The Reinsurers may request the Reassured to keep these advices on any 1oss or loss occurrence which they desire. In the U.S.A. most major catastrophic occurrences are Federally noted with a serial catastrophic number, and in most cases any such noted catastrophe would probably be separately treated for reporting under Para. 6.1c. Of course, individual treaties will vary. A small treaty may well have bordereaux of every single paid loss with its name, peril, date and amount. The basis set out here is sensible for a large treaty where greater details would achieve little and create a lot of paper.

ARTICLE 6

(2) *The term "loss expenses" shall exclude the salaries of employees or officials of the Reassured other than those employed for the express purpose of settling losses whose expenses shall be computed in accordance with the scale agreed between the Reassured and the Reinsurers and may include an allowance for salaried adjusters or other salaried officials or employees diverted from normal duties to the service of field adjustments in connection with losses hereunder.*

Loss expenses normally exclude the "in house" loss expenses of the Reassured. For example, salaries of the Reassured's own claims staff are not normally "loss expenses". A loss expense is something specific to that loss itself. Obviously an outside adjuster's fee is a loss expense. However, many, companies have found it cheaper and more efficient to have a number of adjusters on their own staff. In addition, their own claims staff may be diverted from their normal duties and put on outside adjustment work. This can often happen with a major loss or a catastrophe where field adjusters may be fully occupied and any Insurer will have to pull in all available hands to settle losses.

ARTICLE 6

> *(3) In addition the Reassured shall submit a statement showing the total losses outstanding at the end of each quarter segregated into years of occurrence.*

Apart from the statement or bordereaux of paid losses which form part of the quarterly settlement the Reassured will advise the total of outstanding losses separately for each year of occurrence with individual advices of large losses. It should be noted that Para. 6.3 just calls for advice of outstanding losses. There is no question of paying or advancing them as loss reserves. This aspect is covered in the loss reserve clause later in the wording.

ARTICLE 6

> *(4) Reinsurers shall participate pro rata to their respective interests in any sums which may be received by the Reassured either as salvage or otherwise.*

A simple clause to state Reinsurers' right to salvage or recoveries.

ARTICLE 6

> *(5) All loss settlements made by the Reassured, provided same are within the conditions of the original policies and within the terms of the present Contract, shall be unconditionally binding upon the Reinsurers and amounts falling to the share of the Reinsurers shall be payable by the Reinsurers upon reasonable evidence of the amount paid or payable on settlement of loss being given by the Reassured to the Reinsurers.*

A standard loss settlement clause. Note the wording — "All *loss* settlements", not "All *Claims* settlements", and therefore an *ex gratia* settlement of a claim which is not admitted as a loss is not binding, upon Reinsurers. Please contrast with the claims settlement clause Article 7 of the Quota Share Treaty.

My own feeling is that most major 1st Surplus treaties such as this would now have a claims settlement clause as the Quota Share and not the more restrictive loss settlement clause contained herein.

ARTICLE 6

(6) *In the event that any one loss to 100% of this Contact should equal or exceed $250,000 Reinsurers will, at the option and upon demand of the Reassured, pay their proportionate share of such loss by special remittance immediately upon receipt of a special loss account which shall be prepared by the Reassured and shall contain all relevant details in connection with the loss.*

All treaties call for a special settlement of large losses if the Reassured requires it. These settlements are made at once and the Reassured does not have to wait until the quarterly settlement for payment.

Earned Premium Basis

ARTICLE 7

PREMIUMS

The Reassured shall pay Reinsurers the earned portion of premiums at the original gross rates received by the Reassured.

When we discussed our quota share treaty we discussed a treaty on a written premium basis. This particular treaty is, however, accounted on an earned premium basis. Please do not assume that quota shares are normally on a written basis and surplus treaties on an earned basis. This is not true; all treaties can be on either basis. In practice the earned premium basis is commonly used in the U.S.A. and Canada,. the written basis more commonly used elsewhere in the world. The use of a written premium basis will often mean that Reinsurers may establish an unearned premium reserve with the Reassured, and we deal more fully with this whole matter in the next chapter.

The earned premium basis on this treaty simply means that the premium paid each quarter for each cession is the portion of premium earned by that cession during that quarter. For example, in the accounts for the quarter 1st April — 1st July 1990.

A 12-months policy which commenced on 1st March 1990 will earn $\frac{91}{365}$ths of its total annual premium in that quarter. A 24-months policy commincing 1st June 1990 will earn $\frac{30}{630}$ths of its premium.

It will be clearly seen that;

(1) The calculation of the earned premium must really be done cession by cession and is a considerable chore, lessened of course by computers.

(2) At the end of every quarter the Reinsurer holds no premiums in hand and if the treaty were cancelled at that time, with termination of all liability, no return of premium need be made to the Reassured.

(3) The Reinsurer has no premium balances to invest, only the amount held for outstanding loss and profit, if any.

However, the earned method makes it much easier to follow the true results of a treaty quarter by quarter and does away with the complications of premium reserves. It is the only method of accounting which should be used with a sliding scale of commission.

Sliding Scale of Commission

ARTICLE 8

COMMISSION

A. *The Reinsurers shall allow the Reassured a provisional commission of 37.5% upon the gross earned premiums hereunder. Such provisional commission of 37.5% shall be provisionally adjusted at the close of each Contract Year and finally adjusted twelve months after the close of each Contract Year on the following basis:*

(a) If the ratio of loss incurred to premiums earned is 65% or higher, the commission shall be 27.5%.

(b) If the ratio of losses incurred to premiums earned is less than 65% and 60% or more, the adjusted rate of commission shall be determined by adding to 27.5% one-half of the difference between the loss ratio and 65% until a rate of commission of 30% is achieved at 60% loss ratio. Thereafter, if the ratio of losses incurred to premiums earned is less than 60%, the adjusted rate of commission shall be determined by adding to 30% three-fourths of the difference between the loss ratio and 60% subject to a maximum rate of commission of 55% at 26.67% loss ratio or less.

The principle of a sliding scale is simple; instead of a fixed ceding commission of, say, 37½% you substitute a provisional commission of 37½%, which will vary up and down according to the results of the treaty. This variation of commission to loss ratio can be fixed to produce a constant margin of "profit". For example, to produce a margin of 7½% within a limited range:

> If the loss ratio is 50% or less the ceding commission is 42½%. The commission then reduces by 1% for each 1% the loss ratio rises above 50%. Thus, Loss ratio — 60% — commission 32½%

this would give a minimum commission of 32½% and a maximum commission of 42½%. The scale can be extended upwards or downwards, or both. For example:

> Loss ratio: 45% or less — commission 47½% maximum
> Decreasing 1% for 1% increase in loss ratio to:
> Loss ratio: 62½% — commission 30% minimum, or instead of the commission rising or falling 1% for each 1% change in loss ratio, it can vary ½% for each 1% change in loss ratio or any other fraction you choose.

Example

> Minimum commission: 30% at loss ratio 67½% or over — ½% rise in commission for each 1% decrease in loss ratio to commission: 35% at loss ratio 57½%, then ¾% rise in commission for each 1% decrease in loss ratio to
> commission: 40% at loss ratio 50%, then .90% rise in commission for each 1% to maximum commission of 49% at loss ratio 40%.
>
> Please note that the margins vary:
>
> at L.R. 67½% the margin is 2½%
> at L.R. 57½% the margin is 7½%
> at L.R. 50% the margin is 10%
> at L.R. 40% the margin is 11%

The sliding scale is a highly sensitive system and infinitely variable. When a treaty develops a loss ratio over the top of the scale the margin of profit will soon disappear and the Reassured will show a loss fairly quickly. In the above example, when the loss ratio is 70% the commission is 30%. At a loss ratio of 75% the Reassured has a loss of 5% plus his expenses. In many cases this deficit is carried forward to the next year's sliding scale calculation. The deficit carried forward is a monetary amount not the points of loss ratio. For example:

P.I. $100,000 Year 1 L. Ratio 75% Commission 30% Deficit 5%
P.I. $200,000 Year 2 L. Ratio 57½% Commission ?

Without the deficit coming forward the commission on Year 2 would be 35%. However, there is a deficit of 5% × $100,000 from Year 1 and the calculation of Year 2's commission is as follows:

Gross Earned Premium $200,000 Losses $115,000 + Deficit $5,000
Result: Premium $200,000 Losses + Deficit $120,000 L. Ratio 60%

At 60% L. Ratio scale commission is 33.75%. Actual results without deficit clause:

Year 1 Loss $5,000 (5% × $100,000)
Year 2 Profit $15,000

With deficit clause:

Year 1 Loss $5,000 as above
Year 2's Loss ratio is still 57.50% but commission is 33.75%

Therefore profit is: 100% less 91.25% which equals 8.75% or $17,500

Therefore — Year 1 Loss $5,000
Year 2 Profit $17,500

The deficit clause and the ½% for 1% sliding scale results in 50% of the Year 1 loss being recouped in Year 2. We have carried forward as a debit from Year 1 the deficit over 70%. Had we wished to allow Reinsurers an expense item or an extra margin for large exposures, or catastrophic potential, we could have used a loss ratio of 65%, which would have allowed Reinsurers a margin of 5% for expenses or reserve. The argument here is the same as allowing a 5% margin in a normal profit commission statement which we discussed in the chapter on quota share treaties.

One can argue that the purpose of a sliding scale is to regulate the results under a treaty so that Reinsurers make an agreed margin. If a year is so bad that the resulting loss ratio comes over the top of the scale and Reinsurers lose money, or do not make the envisaged minimum charge, then a deficit or debit carry forward is used. Conversely, it can be argued that if the loss ratio is so good that it goes below the other end of the scale, then Reinsurers are making more than was envisaged and that a credit should be carried forward to the next year's calculation. We then arrive at a sliding scale where both debits and credits are carried forward and this has the effect over the years of spreading a good or bad experience from one year forward over succeeding years.

We can now look at its effect on the sliding scale set out in Article 8. In tabular form this is as follows:

Loss Ratio	*Commission*	*Gross Margin*	*Remarks*
65%	27.50%	71%	Minimum commission
			½% for 1% to
60%	30%	10%	¾% for 1% to
26.67%	55%	18⅓%	Maximum commission

Any debits over 65% or credits under 26.67% are carried forward. This is a wide scale with a reasonable margin for Reinsurers where loss ratio is good. With a large volume treaty it is unlikely that loss ratios below 26.67% or above 65% will occur except in an occasional year.

However, one difficulty must be mentioned; should there be a continuing bad experience, or an obviously deteriorating experience, a very substantial debit could be built up. If the experience then improves this may mean that the Reassured will have to suffer a minimum commission over a period of good experience. In such circumstances the tendency is for a Reassured to cancel the treaty and start again.

The reverse is true, and can be very difficult, if a large credit is built up. This credit,may then allow the Reassured a very high commission through a series of bad years. This has a tendency to induce Reinsurers to cancel because they realise that in the short term they are going to lose money. The chance of a large credit being built up in this treaty is not great because a succession of years below 26.67% loss ratio is unlikely. With sliding scales, where the margin of profit is small within the scale, it may be wise for both parties to agree to some limitation on the debit or credit carry forwards, either in amount or in time. This is much the same philosophy as having a three-year limit on the deficit carry forward under a profit commission.

Let us now turn to Article 8 in detail. The clause calls for a provisional commission which will be used in the quarterly accounts and which will be adjusted when the results of the year are known.

ARTICLE 8

B. *(a)* *the expression "Contract Year" as used herein shall mean the period of 12 months from 1st April in each year;*

(b) *the expression "earned premiums" as used herein shall mean the premiums as declared by the Reassured in their quarterly statements of account.*

This paragaph sets out the definitions and needs no comment.

ARTICLE 8

C. *For the Contract Year 1997/98, the expression "losses incurred" shall be the net losses and loss adjustment expenses recovered hereunder during the period from 1st April 1997 to 31st March 1999 on losses occurring during the Contract Year 1997/98*

plus

the net losses and loss adjustment expenses recovered hereunder during the period from 1st April 1998 to 31st March 1999 on losses occurring during the Contract Years 1996/97 and prior

plus

the estimated unpaid loss reserve outstanding at 31st March 1999 on losses occurring during the Contract Years 1997/98 and prior

less

the estimated unpaid loss reserves outstanding hereunder at 31st March 1998 on losses occurring during the Contract Years 1996/97 and prior, and

plus or minus

any debit or credit carried forward from previous years, in accordance with Paragraph A(c) of this Article.

ARTICLE 8

D. *For each subsequent year, the expression "losses incurred" shall be defined as in the preceding paragraph except that the Contract Years mentioned therein shall be amended accordingly.*

E. *The statement of adjusted commission shall be prepared and submitted by the Reassured within three months of the close of the year next succeeding the close of the Contract*

Year under adjustment and all adjustments shall be computed and payable by applying the percentage difference in commission to the earned premiums shown in each such statement. Should this Contract be cancelled, the Reassured may submit a provisional statement of adjusted commission twelve months following the date of cancellation and covering the final Contract Year, subject to adjustment following the expiration of all cessions and the settlement of all losses under this Contract.

Paragraph C sets out in detail exactly what "losses" are to be used in this calculation. The premiums used will be the gross earned premiums ceded for the four quarters of the year. The corresponding figure will be "incurred losses", in other words the losses which occur in that year as finally settled. If we wait until those losses are finally settled, the adjustments of the sliding scale of commission may take several years. It is quite possible to calculate the sliding scale at the close of the year on the basis of losses paid during the year, plus the estimated outstanding losses at the close of the year. Obviously, if the outstanding losses turn out to be inaccurate, then the commission adjustment will be done on results or a loss ratio which is different from the actual result of the year, and sometimes this difference will be very large.

It is important to remember in this contract that the Reinsurers of 1999 are going to pay all losses that occur in 1999 whenever those losses are settled. There are two ways to overcome this problem; the first is to do a provisional adjustment of the sliding scale for each year at the close of that year on the basis of paid plus known outstandings at that time. Periodically thereafter this provisional calculation is altered, either quarterly or annually, until such time as all losses are paid. A final adjustment of the commission is then made. This may mean many years open at once and is at the best a bore.

The second way is for a definite adjustment of the sliding scale commission for each year to be made at the close of that year, using the known outstanding losses. Then for the succeeding year's — or years' — adjustments to pick up any change in these outstandings as the losses are settled. This is done by crediting it with the outstanding loss reserve debited against the previous year and debiting with any settlements made during the year for losses which occurred on prior years. An example is easier to follow. (Again, I warn the reader that this in-and-out movement of outstanding losses is only done to calculate the sliding scale.)

1999 loss ratio is calculated by applying incurred losses made up as follows:

Incurred loss = losses paid in 1979
+ losses outstanding at end of 1979
– losses outstanding at start of 1979
or paid loss + outstanding losses out
– outstanding loss in.

This calculation is exactly the same method when outstanding loss reserves are actually transferred from year to year. (See the next chapter.) It can, of course, mean that its use on a treaty, where losses remain in the year of occurrence, will still cause differences in the loss figures for the sliding scale calculations, but such differences are picked up in future years as the losses are settled, provided that the commission remains within the scale.

In a large modern treaty such as this, bordereaux or computer print-outs of cessions or XLSpreadsheet are not passed to Reinsurers. They are retained by the Reassured as evidence of the cessions and as evidence in the compilation of the treaty accounts. These are, of course, available to Reinsurers under the access to records clause. In many treaties, however, bordereaux or print-outs, or direct input from computer to computer or disc or tapes, or other devices, will pass between Reassured and Reinsurer. These will give details of the cessions and we will deal with this more fully in the next chapter.

Here the Reassured furnishes only quarterly accounts and straight payment of balance between cash items — as set out in Article 6 — is made. Please note that the balance is *payable* within two months of the close of the quarter; a very fast settlement date compared to many treaties but one which is easily possible with a well-run treaty and modern equipment.

Currency

ARTICLE 10

CURRENCY

The Dollars ($) mentioned herein shall mean United States Dollars for cessions on policies issued by the Reassured in United States Dollars and Canadian Dollars for cessions on policies issued by the Reassured in Canadian Dollars.

Under this treaty cessions and accounts are submitted in two currencies U.S. $ and Canadian $. The effect is that we really have two treaties; one for U.S. $ business and the second for Canadian $ business. Balances are paid in the original currencies and no question of conversion arises, except in making calculations of the loss ratio for adjustment of the sliding scale of commission. In many other treaties dealing with business in a number of currencies it is common practice for both premiums and losses to be accounted for at prevailing rates of exchange. Normally the rates used will be the rates the company itself uses in making exchange remittances. Alternatively, where such remittances are not made some definite date will be used, e.g. for premiums and losses in quarterly accounts, the rates of exchange ruling on the last day of that quarter and for special settlements of losses, the rate ruling when the company itself makes payment of that loss.

Loss Reserves and Letters of Credit

ARTICLE 11

LOSS RESERVES

(U.S. Dollar Reinsurers Letters of Credit)

(This Clause is only applicable to those Reinsurers who cannot qualify for credit by the State having jurisdiction over the Reassured's loss reserves.)

As regards policies or bonds issued by the Reassured coming within the scope of this Contract, the Reassured agrees that when it shall file with the Insurance Department or set up on its books reserves for losses covered hereunder which it shall be required to set up by law it will forward to the Reinsurers a statement showing the proportion of such loss reserves which is applicable to them. The Reinsurers hereby agree that they will apply for and secure delivery to the Reassured a clean irrevocable Letter of Credit issued by "X" Bank in an amount equal to Reinsurers' proportion of said loss reserves.

The Reassured undertakes to use and apply any amount which it may draw upon such Credit pursuant to the terms of the Contract under which the Letter of Credit is held, and for the following purposes only:

(a) To pay the Reinsurers' share or to reimburse the Reassured for the Reinsurers' share of any liability for loss reinsured by this Contract.
(b) To make refund of any sum which is in excess of the actual amount required to pay Reinsurers' share of any liability reinsured by this Contract.

"X" Bank shall have no responsibility whatsoever in connection with the propriety of withdrawals made by the

Reassured or the disposition of funds withdrawn, except to see that withdrawals are made only upon the order of properly authorised representatives of the Reassured.

As has been stated, this treaty is accounted on an earned premium basis. There is, therefore, no unearned premium reserve. As regards outstanding losses, a United States insurance company may, in its annual solvency returns to the various State insurance department, take credit for recoveries due from Reinsurers licensed in that State.

Where Reinsurers are "not admitted", i.e. where they are not licensed to conduct reinsurance in the various States in the United States, then the Reassured cannot take credit in the annual solvency returns to the State regulatory bodies for such Reinsurer's proportion of outstanding losses.

This clause calls for the depositing by such Reinsurers of their share of outstanding losses by way of an irrevocable Letter of Credit which the Reinsurer will arrange to be issued by a U.S. Bank acceptable to the various State insurance departments as security for such Letters of Credit. The Letter of Credit, being irrevocable, cannot be withdrawn once made and it is drawn upon by the Reassured either when the outstanding losses are settled or to refund any amount if the outstanding losses are washed out or settled below the outstanding amounts.

A fuller discussion on loss reserves and use of Letters of Credit is given in the next chapter.

The remaining Articles of this wording:

Arbitration
Insolvency
Service of Suit
Errors and Omissions
Access to Records

are clauses standard to most U.S.A. treaties and contracts.

CONTRACT OF REINSURANCE
NO. 87/101

between the

Insurance Company
(herinafter referred to as the "Reassured")

and

the subscribing Reinsurers signing the attached schedule
(hereinafter referred to as "Reinsurers")

PROPERTY FIRST SURPLUS TREATY

ARTICLE 1

TERM

This Contract shall apply to all cessions declared on and after 1st April 1987 (except as regards reporting form and similar types of policies to which this Contract shall apply in respect to all reporis for periods commencing 1st April 1987) and shall remain in force for an indefinite period but may be terminated on the last day of March in any year by either party giving to the other 90 days' notice of cancellation.

In the event of cancellation the Reinsurers shall continue to participate in all insurances and/or reinsurances coming within the terms of this Contract during the said period of 90 days and the Reassured shall have the option of:

(a) continuing cessions in respect of all business in force at the date of cancellation until their expiry or renewal of the original policy or for a period of one year following the effective date of cancellation, whichever is the earlier;
(b) relieving Reinsurers of all liability at date of cancellation.

ARTICLE 2

BUSINESS COVERED

This Contract shall apply to risks written and coded by the Reassured as PROPERTY and MULTIPLE LINE BUSINESS, as now or hereafter constituted (excluding casualty except where such business forms part of a policy which also covers other hazards which come within the scope of this Contract), as original.

ARTICLE 3

TERRITORY

This Contract shall cover interest anywhere in the United States of America (comprising the fifty States of the Union and the District of Columbia) and/or other possessions of the United States of America, and/or the Dominion of Canada and/or as original.

ARTICLE 4

EXCLUSIONS

The following risks and kinds of insurance are excluded from coverage under this Contract and no loss or losses thereon shall be recoverable hereunder.

ARTICLE 5

TREATY DETAIL

1. The Reassured agree to cede and the Reinsurers agree to accept 100% of every surplus amount or amounts (within the limits hereinafter prescribed) after the retention of the Reassured on all risks underwritten by the Reassured.

2. The Reassured are however permitted at their discretion to effect other reinsurance before using this Treaty; to effect reinsurance for the joint account and at the joint expense of themselves and Reinsurers; to restrict allotments on some risks in such a manner that the liability of the Reinsurers thereon shall be less than the maximum provided herein; provided, however, that said rights shall be used only when it appears to be beneficial to the Reinsurers.

3. The surplus amounts ceded to the Reinsurers on any one risk shall in no case exceed 5 times the Reassured's net retention up to a maximum limit of $5,000,000 Probable Maximum Loss (PML) but not exceeding $15,000,000 irrespective of the PML. The Reassured shall be the sole judge of what constitutes one risk and of the PML of any risk.

4. The minimum retention of the Reassured shall be $200,000 any one risk.

5. The liability of the Reinsurers shall commence simultaneously with the liability of the Reassured on all risks and shall be subject to all the general and special conditions, clauses, stipulations and endorsements of the original insurances and/or reinsurances. If a loss should occur after the Reassured has become liable on a risk but prior to the time the Reassured, in the regular course of business, has had an opportunity to make a cession hereunder the Reassured shall fix their net retention according to their practice and shall cede the surplus just as if no loss had occurred.

6. In respect of Builders' Risks and policies issued on a reporting form basis, cessions made hitherto shall be a fixed percentage or fraction of the maximum liability at the location, the intention being that this Contract shall protect the actual amounts at risk in the proportion that the cession bears to the limit of liability at the location.

7. *Cessions hereunder shall be based on the Reassured's retention for the key peril or key section of any original policy and shall include a proportionate cession of all other perils or sections of that policy.*

8. *Cessions hereunder on schedule policies shall be based on the Reassured's retention on the key location and shall include a proportionate cession of all other locations. However, where the Reassured feels it will not prejudice Reinsurers, items in schedule policies, whether specific or reporting, may be ceded as in the case of single locations, provided full rates are applied to the cessions and not the schedule average rates. However, it is understood that policies issued to single or joint Assureds covering a single general location or plant complex shall be treated as one cession and items or parts cannot be ceded as single locations even if specifically rated.*

9. *The Reassured's retention may, at their discretion, be on buildings and/or contents and/or other interests on a risk and cessions hereunder may be made in any name or interest on the same risk and not necessarily in the same name or interest as their own retained lines.*

10. *The Reassured shall retain their net-retention of each and every cession hereunder net for their own account subject only to the protection of their catastrophe excess of loss reinsurances. Collections under such policies shall not be considered as vitiating the Reassured's net retention.*

ARTICLE 6

LOSSES

1. *Losses and loss expenses shall be charged in the quarterly accounts, supported by a statement showing:*
   (a) the paid losses and paid loss expenses segregated into years of occurence
   (b) particulars of every paid loss and its expenses included therein
      (1.) where loss to 100% of this Contract exceeds $250,000.
      and

(2) *in respect of those losses where Reinsurers have previously been furnished with an individual notice of loss.*

(c) *the aggregate figures of settlements made in respect of any event which is recognised by Reinsurers to be a catastrophe.*

2. *The term "loss expenses" shall exclude the salaries of employees or officials of the Reassured other than those employed for the express purpose of settling losses whose expenses shall be computed in accordance with the scale agreed between the Reassured and the Reinsurers and may include an allowance for salaried adjusters or other salaried, officials or employees diverted from normal duties to the service of field adjustments in connection with losses hereunder.*

3. *In addition the Reassured shall submit a statement showing the total losses outstanding at the end of each quarter segregated into years of occurrence.*

Individual notices of loss shall be furnished to Reinsurers where loss to 100% of this Contract is reserved at $250,000 or more.

4. *Reinsurers shall participate pro rata to their respective interests in any sums which may be received by the Reassured either as salvage or otherwise.*

5. *All loss settlements made by the Reassured, provided same are within the conditions of the original policies and within the terms of the present Contract, shall be unconditionally binding upon the Reinsurers and amounts falling to the share of the Reinsurers shall be payable by the Reinsurers upon reasonable evidence of the amount paid or payable on settlement of loss being given by the Reassured to the Reinsurers.*

6. *In the event that any one loss to 100% of this Contract should equal or exceed $250,000 Reinsurers will, at the option and upon demand of the Reassured, pay their proportionate share of such loss by special remittance immediately upon receipt of a special loss account which shall be prepared by the Reassured and shall contain all relevant details in connection with the loss.*

ARTICLE 7

PREMIUMS

The Reassured shall pay Reinsurers the earned portion of premiums at the original gross rates received by the Reassured.

ARTICLE 8

COMMISSION

A. *The Reinsurers shall allow the Reassured a provisional commission of 37.5% upon the gross earned premiums hereunder. Such provisional commission of 37.5% shall be provisionally adjusted at the close of each Contract Year and finally adjusted twelve months after the close of each Contract Year on the following basis:*

   (a) *If the ratio of losses incurred to premiums earned is 65% or higher, the commission shall be 27.5%*

   (b) *If the ratio of losses incurred to premiums earned is less than 65% and 60% or more, the adjusted rate of commission shall he determined by adding to 27.5% one/half of the difference between the loss ratio and 65% until a rate of commission of 30% is achieved at 60% loss ratio. Thereafter, if the ratio of losses incurred to premiums earned is less than 60%, the adjusted rate of commission shall be determined by adding to 30% three/fourths of the difference between the loss ratio and 60% subject to a maximum rate of commission of 55% at 26.67% loss ratio or less.*

   (c) *If the ratio of losses incurred to premiums earned is less than 26.67% or more than 65% the difference in per cent shall be multiplied by the earned premiums ceded during the period and the result shall be carried forward to losses incurred as a debit or credit whichever the case may be for purposes of sliding scale computation for the following Contract Year.*

B. (a) *the expression "Contract Year" as used herein shall mean the period of 12 months from 1st April in each year.*

   (b) *the expression "earned premiums" as used herein shall mean the premiums as declared by the Reassured in their quarterly statement of account.*

C. *For the Contract Year 1997/98, the expression "losses incurred" shall be the net losses and loss adjustment expenses recovered hereunder during the period from 1st April 1997 to 31st March 1999 on losses occurring during the Contract Year 1997/98*

plus

the net losses and loss adjustment expenses recovered hereunder during the period from Ist April 1998 to 31st March 1999 on losses occurring during the Contract Years 1996/97 and prior

plus

the estimated unpaid loss reserve outstanding at 31st March 1999 on losses occurring during the Contract Years 1997/98 and prior

less

the estimated unpaid loss reserves outstanding hereunder at 31st March 1998 on losses occurring during the Contract Years 1996/97 and prior, and

plus or minus

any debit or credit carryforward from previous years, in accordance with Paragraph A (c) of this Article.

D. For each subsequent year, the expression "losses incurred" shall be defined as in the preceding paragraph except that the Contract Years mentioned therein shall be amended accordingly.

E. The statement of adjusted commission shall be prepared and submitted by the Reassured within three months of the close. of the year next succeeding the close of the Contract Year under adjustment and all adjustments shall be computed and payable by applying the percentage difference in commission to the earned premium shown in each such statement. Should this Contract be cancelled, the Reassured may submit a provisional statement of adjusted commission twelve months following the date of cancellation and covering the final Contract Year, subject to adjustment following the expiration of all cessions and the settlement of all losses under this Contract.

F. Canadian Dollar items shall, for the purposes of this clause, be converted into United States Dollars at par.

ARTICLE 9

ACCOUNTS

The Reassured shall furnish quarterly accounts, in which all premiums and other amounts due the Reinsurers shall be credited and losses, commission, etc. due from the Reinsurers shall be debited. The resulting net balance shall be payable by the debtor party within 2 months after the close of each quarter.

For the purposes of accounting this Contract, the first quarter of each year shall be deemed to end at 30th June, the second at 30th September, the third at 31st December and the fourth at 31st March.

ARTICLE 10

CURRENCY

The Dollars ($) mentioned herein shall mean United States Dollars for cessions on policies issued by the Reassured in United States Dollars and

Canadian Dollars for cessions on policies issued by the Reassured in Canadian Dollars.

ARTICLE 11

LOSS RESERVES

(U.S. Dollar Reinsurances Letters of Credit)

(This Clause is only applicable to those Reinsurers who cannot qualify for credit by the State having jurisdiction over the Reassured's loss reserves).

As regards policies or bonds issued by the Reassured coming within the scope of this Contract, the Reassured agrees that when it shall file with the Insurance Department or set up on its books reserves for losses covered hereunder which it shall be required to set up by law it will forward to the Reinsurers a statement showing the proportion of such loss reserves which is applicable to them. The Reinsurers hereby agree that they will apply for and secure delivery to the Reassured a clean irrevocable Letter of Credit issued by "X" Bank in an amount equal to Reinsurers' proportion of said loss reserves.

The Reassured undertakes to use and apply any amounts which it may draw upon such Credit pursuant to the terms of the Contract under which the Letter of Credit is held, and for the following purposes only:

(a) To pay the Reinsurers' share or to reimburse the Reassured for the Reinsurers' share of any liability for loss reinsured by this Contract.

(b) To make refund of any sum which is in excess of the actual amount required to pay Reinsurers' share of any liability reinsured by this Contract.

"X" Bank shall have no responsibility whatsoever in connection with the propriety of withdrawals made by the Reassured or the disposition of funds withdrawn, except to see that withdrawals are made only upon the order of properly authorised representatives of the Reassured.

ARTICLE 12

ARBITRATION

As a precedent to any right of action hereunder, if any dispute shall arise between the Reassured and the Reinsurers with reference to the interpretation of this Contract or the rights with respect to any transaction involved, the dispute shall be referred to two Arbitrators, one to be chosen by each party, and such Arbitrators shall choose an Umpire before entering upon the reference and in the event of said Arbitrators not agreeing the decision of said Umpire shall be final and binding upon all parties. The Arbitrators and Umpire shall interpret this Contract as an honourable engagement, and they shall make their award with a view to effecting the general purpose of this Contract in a reasonable manner rather than in accordance with a literal interpretation of the language. Each party shall bear the expense of its own Arbitrator and shall jointly and equally bear with the other the expenses of the Umpire and of the Arbitration which shall be held in the U.S.A.

ARTICLE 13

INSOLVENCY

In the event of the insolvency of the Reassured, this reinsurance shall be payable directly to the Reassured, or to its liquidator, receiver, conservator or statutory successor on the basis of the liability of the Reassured without diminution because of the insolvency of the Reassured or because the liquidator, receiver, conservator or statutory successor of the Reassured has failed to pay all or a portion of any claim. It is agreed, however, that the liquidator, receiver, conservator or statutory successor of the Reassured shall give written notice to the Reinsurers of the pendency of a claim against the Reassured indicating the policy or bond reinsured which claim would involve a possible liability on the part of the Reinsurers within a reasonable time after such claim is filed in the conservation or liquidation proceeding or in the receivership, and that during the pendency of such claim, the Reinsurers may investigate such claim and interpose, at their own expense, in the proceeding where such claim is to be adjudicated any defence or defences that they may deem available to the Reassured or its liquidator, receiver, conservator or statutory successor. The expense thus incurred by the Reinsurers shall be chargeable subject to the approval of the court, against the Reassured as part of the expense of conservation or liquidation to the extent of a pro rata share of the benefit which may accrue to the Reassured solely as a result of the defence undertaken by the Reinsurers.

ARTICLE 14

ERRORS AND OMISSIONS

Any inadvertent delay, omission or error shall not be held to relieve either party hereto from any liability which would attach to it hereunder if such delay, omission or error had not been made, provided such delay, omission or error is rectified as soon as reasonably practicable upon discovery.

ARTICLE 15

ACCESS TO RECORDS

The Reinsurers or their designated representatives shall have free access at any reasonable time to all records of the Reassured which pertain in any way to this Contract.

Secondly, a first surplus, if it is profitable, will be earning a high ceding commission, either by the use of a sliding scale or by a substantial flat commission earned from good past experience. If the treaty is disturbed by doubling its exposures, Reinsurers will be likely to reduce the ceding commission. The size of profit commission may also be affected.

Thirdly, the existing first surplus may well be ceded to Reinsurers for reciprocity or for special reasons, for example, to a parent or sister company. The use of a balanced first surplus for reciprocity is very common and the balance and profitability will determine the quality of the reciprocal business that is obtained in exchange.

Therefore, second surplus treaties are quite common; their wordings and operation are similar to first surplus treaties. They are obligatory on both parties, the Reassured being obliged to cede once the first surplus is filled.

There. are several factors here. Firstly, it must be realised that when a first surplus has an exclusion and the second surplus does not, then the second surplus becomes a first surplus for those excluded cessions. For example, the major Japanese insurance companies have first surplus fire treaties which normally exclude those risks on which earthquake is a peril. Thus, the first surplus is confined to fire business excluding earthquake. This helps the Reassured to obtain high ceding commissions and profit commission and/or good reciprocity. The second surplus treaties are second surplus for pure fire risks but first surplus for those risks which include the peril of earthquake. Obviously the second surplus/first surplus earthquake treaties have lower commission terms and may not be suitable to obtain good reciprocal business.

Secondly, although a Reassured is obliged to cede to a second surplus once the first surplus is filled, he may not always be obliged to fill the first surplus. Often the first surplus will give the Reassured the option of not ceding at all on undesirable business or of making a restricted cession if he considers it in the interest of the first surplus Reinsurers. Such risks could then be ceded to the second surplus by bypassing, or partially by-passing, the first surplus. Therefore, most second surplus treaties will have an insuring clause as follows:

> "The Reassured agrees to cede and the Reinsurers agree to accept 100% of every surplus amount or amounts, after the retention of the Reassured and after cessions to the Reassured's five line first surplus, on all risks underwritten by the Reassured.

However, no cession shall be made hereon unless at least two lines have been ceded in priority to the first surplus."

or, as an alternative to the last paragraph:

"However, the amount of cession hereon shall never exceed the amount ceded to the Reassured's first surplus."

Obviously this clause can be varied by agreement between the parties, but unless some such restriction is imposed the second surplus can become a dumping ground for risks which are not considered as suitable for the first surplus.

Thirdly, the second surplus will be less balanced than the first surplus and, the ceding commission and profit commission will normally be smaller. With a greater unbalance the use of sliding scale commissions are less frequent than on first surplus treaties. Apart from these factors the wordings will be similar.

The use of third surplus treaties is less common and these, of necessity, can become extremely unbalanced. Their wordings are similar to a second surplus.

Facultative Obligatory Treaties

Often a Reassured will operate with a first surplus for reciprocity and obligatory second surplus treaty and an additional treaty where the Reassured is not obliged to cede but the Reinsurer is obliged to accept. Such treaties are known as facultative obligatory treaties, i.e. facultative or optional on the Reassured but obligatory on Reinsurers. Such a treaty is really a method by which a Reassured obtains an automatic market for his facultative reinsurances. These facultative reinsurances may be large risks where obligatory treaties are filled, or facultative reinsurances where the Reassured wishes to limit cessions to his other treaties. Obviously, Reinsurers can have very adverse selection. Therefore, the use of a facultative obligatory treaty should impose considerable responsibility on the Reassured to cede sensibly, otherwise the arrangement will not endure.

The advantages of a facultative obligatory treaty to a Reassured are really two-fold. He obtains automatic attachment of his facultative Reinsurers, which enables him to accept business without obtaining his facultative Reinsurers' agreement. Secondly, if the facultative obligatory arrangement is successful, the Reassured may obtain a profit commission and he may obtain a higher ceding commission than he would by effecting individual facultative placings.

These are formidable advantages and a Reassured, if he is sensible, will select the business ceded to a facultative obligatory cover carefully. The bulk quarterly accounting of facultative reinsurances by use of a facultative obligatory treaty will also save a Reassured time and money.

The wordings of facultative/obligatory treaties follow normal treaties with two exceptions:

(1) The insuring clause.

(2) The claims settlement clause. Under a facultative obligatory treaty the Reinsurer would not normally follow *ex gratia* settlements of claims but would follow only settlement of losses.

The Placing and Acceptance of Surplus Treaties

The surplus treaty is such a flexible and useful arrangement that it is used as the main method of reinsuring individual property policies. A direct writing company makes use of the surplus treaty so that it can serve the insuring public in the most efficient way, e.g. by low costs, adequate capacity and fast service. It needs a treaty if it is to survive and provide that service.

It is therefore vital that any Reassured looks after, protects and underwrites his outward reinsurance treaties just as he does his inward writings. Not only does the obligatory nature of thic treaty impose this upon him, but the self-interest in retaining a treaty on favourable terms reinforces it. In addition, the ceding commission and profit commission should make a sizeable contribution to the Reassured's own expenses. Some Underwriters I have known have been so successful in this regard that they have had minus expenses ratios for some time.

Lastly, a good outwards treaty can be exchanged for good inwards business, the basis of treaty swapping or treaty reciprocal exchanges.

Therefore, the placing of treaty business should be seen as a marriage, a mutual act to produce the best possible result on the treaty to the benefit of both parties and, above all, as a long term partnership. Bearing this in mind we can turn our thoughts to the various factors which have to be negotiated:

(1) The limits both monetary and the number of lines. This will be primarily governed by the capacity desired by the Reassured in conjunction with his other facilities. A new or small company will generally strive to work on a small net retention and to want both a sizeable monetary limit and a large number of lines of reinsurance.

However, we have already discussed the importance of "balance" to a treaty. The greater. the capacity in relation to premium income developed, the less the balance and the more volatile will be the results of the treaty. A first surplus of 1.0 to 20 lines should be enough and 40 lines or more too many. Ideally, the monetary limit per risk or the P.M.L. limit should be considerably less than the annual premium volume, but this may take time to achieve.

A second surplus in its number of lines often tracks the first, and here it is unlikely that the premium volume will exceed the monetary limits. Very large Reassureds may be content with a first surplus of 5 lines generating a volume of premium several times the maximum risk exposure. The Reassured, in trying to achieve maximum capacity to serve his needs, should always remember not to overbalance his surplus treaties but to use facultative reinsurance to achieve a balance on them. Where cession limits are set on a P.M.L., M.P.L., M.F.L. or similar basis then it is vital that these terms are clearly defined and understood between the parties.

Estimated maximum loss
Probable maximum loss
Maximum probable loss
Maximum foreseeable loss
Amount subject

These terms have created as much trauma as anything else in insurance and reinsurance. It is not the task of this book to discuss them. However, two rules are vital:

(1) Wherever treaty limits are set on a P.M.L. etc. basis, then an additional limit should be set on a location or "risk" basis as well.

(2) The terms P.M.L., M.F.L., etc. must be defined and understood by Reinsurers.

Minimum Retentions

It is not reasonable for first surplus Reinsurers to receive cessions on accommodation business and a reasonable minimum retention should be set to prevent this. This also demonstrates to the Reinsurers that the treaty is to be used for its primary purpose of providing the Reassured with an automatic capacity to acquire desirable business. If problems arise one answer may be to allow a restricted number of lines to be ceded below a certain figure. For example, with the 5-line treaty, discussed in the previous Chapter, 2 lines only might be permitted where the retention was between $100,000 and $200,000, with an absolute minimum retention of $ 100,000.

Fixing the Ceding Commission

The various factors which determine the amount of ceding commission can be summarised as follows:

(A) The acquisition costs of the business.

(B) The overheads of the company on that business.

(C) The anticipated future experience based on past results.

(D) The balance of the treaty and its exposure to catastrophes or other fluctuations.

(E) The volume of the treaty.

(F) The prospects of investment gain on funds held by Reinsurers.

(G) Competition.

(H) Reciprocal considerations.

A & B

In theory a first surplus falls between a facultative reinsurance and a quota share. The ceding commission on a facultative reinsurance covers the Reassured's acquisition costs only with possibly a small overrider. The ceding commission on the quota share should cover the Reassured's total expenses on that class of business. The ceding commission on a first surplus with a large volume and good balance and results may well follow the quota share. A second or third surplus will tend to follow the facultative commission with the ceding commission covering acquisition costs only, plus a small overrider.

C

Where a treaty has been in existence for some time past results will play a predominant part in determining ceding commission. We have already discussed many of the factors in Chapter IV in dealing with quota share treaties, and these apply to all treaties. In brief, past experience is only a guide to future experience. Changing factors, such as deteriorating or improving past results, changes in territory, classes of business or rating must be taken into account. The ceding commission on many large volume established treaties with a consistent past record are set to produce a margin of 2½%, 5% or 10% and ceding commissions on such treaties will end to follow past results, very often to the exclusion of other considerations.

D & E

This margin of "profit" aimed for should itself be determined by the balance of the treaty, i.e. the risk exposures compared to the premium income. A good balance will mean a lower margin and thus a higher commission. Catastrophe exposure, e.g. earthquake or windstorm, will mean that the "margin" must be greater to cope with the greater potential loss exposure or experience fluctuations. In addition, large volume not only makes for a better balance but reduces Reinsurers' cost and therefore may be written for a smaller margin.

F

The possibility of investment gain to Reinsurers is another major factor. Here the larger volume has greater potential. A treaty on an earned basis has less investment possibilities than a treaty on a written basis. Where the basis is written with deposit of reserves the interest payable on such reserves may become an important factor in Reinsurers' overall profit.

Investment income is often an over played hand on proportional treaties as accounts are often slow and cash losses are often used to the detriment of Reinsurers. Reinsurers must be aware that on treaties which have high premium reserves and commissions, then for the first year of a treaty the Reinsurer is very often funding the ceding company despite it being a profitable treaty.

G

Competition — When everything else has been settled it is often the market price which determines ceding commissions, In times when there is a tight market., i.e. when Reinsurers are hard to find, ceding commissions decrease; in easy times they increase.

H

Reciprocity — When one surplus treaty is being exchanged for a share in another then a Reassured is obtaining something back and the two transactions often balance. Thus, ceding commissions on reciprocal exchanges tend to be lower than without reciprocity. A typical treaty commission set-up might look like the following:

Company "X" has —	*Ceding Commission*
(i) a 20% quota share against reciprocity	42½%
(ii) a 5-line 1 st surplus with reciprocity	37½%
without reciprocity	40%
(iii) a 10-line 2nd surplus no reciprocity	35%
(iv) a 10-line facultative obligatory treaty no reciprocity	30%

2001 Comment

Reciprocal Teaties are very rare as so few proportional treaties are consistently profitable. This is mainly due to the disappearance of tariff rating and competition in many countries

Profit Commissions and Sliding Scales

Many of the considerations of profit commissions were discussed in Chapter IV. On a surplus treaty the profit commission is a very vital factor. The Reassured underwrites his own surplus treaty. It is the Reassured who selects the business, who limits cessions, who places facultative reinsurance to protect the treaty. Today, particularly with computers, the Reinsurer has little or no chance to underwrite the business ceded to a treaty. In fact he will have no knowledge from cession bordereaux of the quality of business being ceded. Therefore it is vital that the Reassured is encouraged by a profit commission. On some treaties the profit commission may be 30% or 40%, or even higher, giving the Reassured a very real incentive to produce profitable business. The expense factor deducted before profit commission is due should cover Reinsurers' expenses. These will vary with the treaty volume and often range from minimums of 1% or 2% up to 5%.

It is vital that profit commissions are not paid on catastrophic perils such as earthquake. For example, in recent years many Japanese treaties do not pay profit commission on the earthquake income. In other treaties with such exposures, or with other possible inherent fluctuations, an additional "expense" allowance is made. For example, an expense allowance of 2½% plus "fluctuation" allowance of 5%, making a total deduction of 7½% to Reinsurers before a profit commission is made.

If ceding commissions are set low then often profit commissions are higher:

(a) a 35% ceding commission with 40% profit commission (2½% expenses) might well equate with

(b) a 40% ceding commission with 10% profit commission (10% expenses) at a loss ratio of 50% under (a) Reinsurers pay 35% plus 40% of 12½% or 40% under (b) 40%.

Where the L.R. is under 50% (a) will benefit the Reassured more than (b).

Sliding Scales

The operation of sliding scales has been discussed in Chapter V. They are basically an extension of profit commission. For example, a treaty with a minimum commission of 30% increasing ½% for each 1% improvement in L.R. below 65% is the same as a treaty with a 30% flat commission plus a 50% P.C. (5% expenses). The sliding scale is used to produce a "reasonable margin". Again, this margin will vary with balance, volume, fluctuation potential, investment gain and competition.

Sliding Scale Commissions with Treaties on a Written Basis

The use of a sliding scale with a treaty on an earned basis presents few major difficulties and we have discussed these in Chapter V. However, where a treaty is accounted on a written basis and the ceding commission is paid on the written premium, great care must be taken to see that the calculation of the commission adjustment under a sliding scale of commission is calculated not on the earned results but on the written results.

If the commission adjustment is to be made on written income then the calculation to produce that commission must be done on the same basis, otherwise some very queer anomalies will be produced. For example, take a year where the written income is $100,000 and the final losses on that written income are $50,000. Assume a sliding scale of commission with a minimum commission of 35% at L.R. of 55% rising 1% for each 1% fall in loss ratio to a maximum commission of 55% at L.R. of 35%. The first year's L.R. is 50% and should produce a 40%

ceding commission and a 10% margin to Reinsurers. this is the intention of both parties.

Now, if the parties agree to calculate the commission at the end of the contract year on an "earned basis", using 50% of written income for calculating the earned premium, then we may well have the following result on an "earned basis" for Year 1:

Earned premium $50,000
Year incurred losses $20,000
Earned L.R. 40% — which produces a commission of 50% under the scale. This is then applied to the written income and will produce a 50% commission for the first year on which the final losses will be 50%.

Year 2 will, of course, redress the balance as its calculation will take into account an incoming portfolio premium of $50,000 on which the losses will be $30,000. However, Year 2's own results may be such that the minimum commission under the scale may be reached and the first year's overpayment may never be rectified. Of course, the reader will soon see that if debits and credits above and below the scale are carried forward and, provided the treaty continues long enough, the situation will eventually sort itself out ... or will it?

Unfortunately, the answer is that it will very rarely do so for the following reason:

In an inflationary period the income under a treaty will normally increase every year. This means that the volume in the latter months of any year is greater than in the earlier months and thus the earned premium for a year is never as much as 50% of the written premium. The unearned premium is, on the other hand, always greater than 50%. Assume that losses fall consistently, then if a 50% basis is used, the losses on the earned 50% will always be lighter and the losses on the unearned portion always heavier than normal.

The mathematician can work out the effect using various increases in the treaty income but a modest increase of around 1% per month, or 12% a year, will produce a lowered loss ratio of about 6%, i.e. a loss ratio of 50% will be reduced to around 47% and this will produce a false increase in commission of 3% on a 1% for 1% sliding scale. This increase will be consistent every year and could in itself, without any other anomalies, virtually wipe out any profit in the treaty.

If the rate of increase in the premium income is greater then the effect is increased and it is not difficult to reach an effect of a reduction in loss ratio of around 10%, a true L.R. of 50% becoming 45%. With the following:

Scale Minimum commission 35% at L.R. 55%
40% at L.R. 50%
45% at L.R. 45%
Maximum commission 50% at L.R. 40%
Margin within scale — 10% Reinsurers' expenses, say, 4%
Profit and reserve — say, 6%
Final written L.R.: 50% True commission: 40%
False commission: 45%

each year the 6% profit and reserve is virtually wiped out *without any chance of recovery in future years whilst the treaty growth continues.*

The reader can see that with a smaller margin in the sliding scale and an increase in annual volume of 25% or more, then the treaty will consistently lose money. This is inevitable but this mathematical certainty is often ignored by Reinsurers.

The answer is that where sliding scales are used with a treaty on a written basis they must be adjusted on the written results. This does not preclude a provisional adjustment being done on an "earned" basis. The earned basis used for the provisional adjustment should be calculated not on a 50% basis but a quarterly ⅛th basis, or a monthly 1/24th basis. The best answer, of course, is that where a sliding scale is to be used then either the whole treaty should be ceded on an earned basis and not on a written basis; or the sliding scale adjustment must be calculated on written results then like is adjusted on like.

General Underwriting Considerations

When placing treaties a Reassured will not only look for the best possible terms but also for stability and continuity from his Reinsurers. A Reassured needs a Reinsurer who will not cancel when markets turn sour or his own treaty takes an occasional loss. Rather than an extra 2½% ceding commission, a Reassured needs Reinsurers who are solvent, and thus established and *profitable*; he needs Reinsurers who operate without currency or remittance problems and, above all, he will want to work with people he can trust.

Again, a Reinsurer must select his clients using similar criteria. He must obtain a territorial balance in his business., he must make sure that proper allowances are made for catastrophic risks. It is quite vital that when dealing with earthquake, flood and hurricane under property treaties that the premium from such perils are reported separately. It is also vital that the actual liabilities ceded to a treaty from, say, earthquake in any given area are recorded and known. Only by having such reports will a Reinsurer be able to aggregate and assess his own potential loss to such perils.

It has become common that as a result of the large catastrophe losses arising out of Hurricane Andrew, that certain quota share and surplus treaties in windstorm and earthquake areas have occurrence limits, c.f. Risk excess treaties — article 11, Chapter 10.

The occurrence limit is usually set as a monetary amount with a provision that it will adjust at say, 300% of the gross premium of the treaty. Sometimes as another alternative a cession limit or sum insured limit is applied to the treaty per zone. Reinsurers then know what their maximum exposure could be and can calculate their own P.M.L.s. They can also accept a size of line appropriate with the amount of catastrophe exposure they wish to accept.

Reciprocity

There are two subjects in this book about which my knowledge and experience are abysmal; one is the successful underwriting of long tail reinsurance on a large scale and, secondly, the handling of reciprocity. The reader may, of course, feel that this is a profound understatement. Reciprocity is the exchange of a share of your treaty to "X" in return for the acceptance of a share of "X"s treaty. It is a natural and obvious idea and is beneficial to both parties if results are similar each way and if the incoming and outgoing business is not the same business. There is little point in ceding away a volume of Jamaican hurricane business to receive back a similar volume belonging to someone else.

Historically, reciprocity business grew in those countries of the world with a restrictive spread of market, notably in Europe. It was easier for a French company to obtain Swedish business by ceding to a company in Sweden part of its own business in return for some Swedish business, rather than by setting up a direct operation in Sweden. This still applies even though many large companies may now write throughout Europe direct.

The underwriting of reciprocal treaties and their wordings and problems follows any other treaty, i.e. there is no difference between reciprocal and non-reciprocal treaty wordings. The underwriting considerations are similar also. However, these are modified by the underwriting relative merits or demerits of the incoming business on offer.

So far we have been discussing straight reciprocity between two direct writing companies. However, many "professional" Reinsurers will offer their direct clients reciprocity as well. This will be a share of other clients' incoming treaties, often formed into a reciprocal pool. This method of reciprocity can, of course, produce a very wide spread book of business. It will incur extra costs because the pooling and distribution will cost money. However, these overhead costs may be no more than the direct writer would have incurred if he himself had dealt with a large number of reciprocal exchanges. Such a reciprocal pool will itself have to be underwritten and balanced if it is to succeed. Obviously, if the reinsuring company is to keep some business for itself, the outward reciprocal volume to any Reassured must be less than the volume put in.

Reciprocity has a great attraction too as an earner of foreign exchange. All national economies look with disfavour on an outwards flow of reinsurance, even though the protection provided to that country may be far more valuable than the outflow. However, incoming reciprocity may straighten out the foreign exchange problem. It is for this reason more than any other that reciprocal exchanges, inefficient as they are so often, are here to stay and increase.

We have moved as well to Broker reciprocity. The large international Broker realises that "his" business can command reciprocity for him to place and obtain additional commission. However, it must be said here that brokerage, on reciprocal exchanges, if it is taken both ways, is less than the normal single brokerage.

In the U.S.A. a company in Connecticut, for example, which wanted to spread territorially into Maryland did so by direct entry into Maryland, often through a large general agency. The U.S.A., with a continental spread within itself, never had the incentive to use reciprocity in the same way as smaller countries and it still does not do so.

If successful, reciprocity achieves the following:

(1) An increase of incoming business to offset the volume of outwards reinsurance, thus helping with the Reassured's overall expense ratio, investments and rank in the premium income hierarchy.

(2) An incoming flow of profits to offset profits ceded away.

(3) A territorial spread or a diversification by type of business.

(4) A wider knowledge of other companies and their business and problems.

The disadvantages of reciprocity are:

(1) Other people's business may be less profitable than your own and it may be better to obtain higher commission or profit commission on your own account than to accept theirs.

(2) Incoming reciprocity on similar business to your own may only add to your problems during a bad cycle.

(3) The costs: reciprocity may mean expenses both ways and it may mean a large number of Reinsurers to obtain a spread.

(4) Direct reciprocity does not give you access to the expertise of the large professional Reinsurer.

Reciprocal exchanges tend to be judged on their profitability and volume. "A" cedes to "B" a similar volume with a similar profit as "B" cedes to "A", or half the volume with double the anticipated profit. The principle of reciprocity can be applied to all types of reinsurance — quota shares, a volume of facultative reinsurance, even excess of loss business, but the greatest volume is the exchange of first surplus treaties. However, as said earlier, much less reciprocity is done these days as the number of low rates Surplus Treaties has reduced and due to competition, very few Pro Rata Treaties are profitable. This makes reciprocity difficult. Who wants to swap losses!

Accounts and Claims

The great disadvantage of the surplus treaty is the high cost of administration to the Reassured and, to a lesser extent, the Reinsurer. Each risk is a separate transaction which must be recorded for:

(a) calculation of premium

(b) a cession record in case a loss occurs

(c) a cession record to see that it is within treaty terms

(d) in addition, a record may be needed by Reinsurers of cessions made for underwriting purposes.

Originally all four purposes were covered by cession bordereaux which were made out manually and showed pretty full details of every cession, e.g. name, address, period, interest, perils, amount of original policy, cession amount, net retention, total premium and cession premium.

The underwriting details were checked by Reinsurers in some detail to ensure, firstly, that they corresponded with treaty terms; secondly, to see the type and quality of business ceded and, lastly, to pick out large risks or exposures which might give Reinsurers an accumulation from a number of treaties. Many of my generation will recall that one of the first jobs one did as a junior in a reinsurance office was to go through treaty bordereaux with a large stamp marked "Treaty terms". One perused, stamped and initialled each bordereaux, then checked the premiums and totals and reconciled the premium totals carried forward to the quarterly accounts. Of course, labour was cheap; my salary in 1938 was £60 per annurn — £5 or $10 per month.

It is perhaps relevant to consider what has been lost under the modern treaty. Firstly, the establishment of the cession is achieved by a cession register, or some method by which the Reassured registers the net retention and the treaty cession. The validity of the cession can be checked automatically by computerising the treaty terms, e.g. that number of lines in not exceeded or minimum retention not breached. Secondly, the premium has to be allocated by the Reassured per cession and totalled, recorded and paid. What is lost is the underwriting checking by Reinsurers of the type of business being ceded.

This can now only be done effectively by sample checks or by close liaison between Reinsurers and the Reassured's Underwriters. Therefore, under a modern treaty we are left with a register of the cession being made by the Reassured. This is not advised to Reinsurers but is open to their inspection. Then a quarterly account of premiums and claims in bulk supported by perhaps greater detail of individual claims. If further information is required by Reinsurers it can be programmed, e.g. it might be desirable for quarterly reports to be made of the aggregation of earthquake liability ceded in Mexico. Provided the parties agree beforehand what information is necessary, then it can usually be produced by modern techniques. It is difficult and costly, however, to produce it retrospectively.

Computer accounts may be rendered in print-out or discs and

certainly this is being done increasingly by discs or by direct access, computer to computer. All this leads to greater emphasis on trust between parties and a greater responsibility on the Reassured to underwrite his treaty. It also leads to Reassureds having to review carefully the underwriting and its results at each annual review date before notice is due.

I do not propose to incorporate a typical treaty bordereaux or computer account but I do set out below one suggested sheet print-out for the review and annual underwriting of a typical treaty which would enable the Reinsurer's Underwriters to see the treaty results and treaty details in a simple and standard form at least once a year.

The past results of any treaty always have to be viewed in relation to future experience and allowance may have to be made in that experience for changes in the underwriting. However, in doing so, one must always bear in mind that a Reassured's actual record may be a better guide than an "as if" recapitulation and to end on a lighter note, I give here the verbatim report of the origin of the 'Aunt and Uncle' clause (A.A.U. Cl.).

Dialogue between leading Treaty Lloyd's Underwriter and an aggressive Broker attempting to place a Treaty with a hopelessly unfavourable past record:

Broker: "I am sure that you will be interested in this attractive Treaty which comes from the right stable and should become a very desirable piece of business."

Underwriter: *[Looking at the slip]* "Show me the figures."

Broker: "I should not take too much notice of the figures; statistics can be misleading. After all, you are being asked to underwrite the future, not the past."

Underwriter: *[Looking at the figures]* "But the past looks disastrous."

Broker: "Yes, but they can easily be explained. The losses were mainly incurred on classes of business they no longer underwrite. If we reflect the figures on the present classes of business, very different results would be made manifest."

Underwriter: "But, if their judgement was wrong then it could be wrong again?"

Broker: "Oh no, they have sacked the old Underwriter. If the present Underwriter was writing then, far better results would be shown."

Underwriter: "Can you show me some figures applying to the present classes?"

Broker: *[Diffidently]* "Yes, I am sure that you will find these interesting."

Underwriter: *[Examining new figures]* "But these figures do not reflect any profit."

Broker: "Ah, but let me enlighten you. Since then, the rates on these classes have been increased and if these classes of business had been written at the present level of rating there would show up a much more improved experience."

Underwriter: *[Wearily handing back the slip]* "And, undoubtedly, if your aunt had balls she would be your uncle."

Thus was born one of those classic little clauses which is known as the "A and U Clause" and is suitable for attachment to those treaties with doubtful past statistics.

CHAPTER VII

PREMIUM INCOME AND RESERVES

Premium income — Written — Earned — 24th system — Accounted or debited — Unearned premiums — Premium reserves — Portfolio transfers — Loss reserves — Loss portfolios — Bank guarantees — Letters of credit — O.C.A.s.

In this chapter I will discuss a number of matters relating to reinsurance accounting. Some of these matters will have already been mentioned in earlier chapters but a little repetition may not be a bad thing.

Premium Income

There are basically three types of premium income:

(1) Written premium income

(2) Earned premium income

(3) Accounted or debited premium income.

Written Premium Income

The written premium income of an Insurer in any one year is the sum total of the premiums (including additional premiums and less return premiums) for insurances which have inception or renewal dates in that year. In other words, it is the premium written for the year and not necessarily the premium physically written during the year. The premium for a policy "written" or contracted in, say, November 1980, with an attachment date in January 1981, is premium written in January 1981 not November 1980. Similarly, an additional premium put through in March 1982 on a policy running from June 1981 to June 1982, is 1981 written income not 1982 written income.

Earned Premium Income

The earned premium on any policy during a year is the proportion of the total policy premium "earned" during the year as represented by the time that the policy has run or been "on risk" during that year. Thus, a company's earned premium for any year is the aggregate sum of a fraction of the written premium of each policy written in that year and during the previous year, such fraction being calculated as follows:

$$\frac{\text{Time that the policy has run during that year}}{\text{Total term of the policy}}$$

To take the calendar year 1981 —
A 12-month policy, incepting at midnight on 15th January 1981, will run for 350 days in 1981 and its earned premium during 1981 will be:

$\frac{350}{365}$ × the written premium for that policy.

A 24-months policy, incepting on 16th December 1981, will run for 15 days in 1981 and its earned premium will be:

$\frac{15}{730}$ ths of the 24-months policy premium.

On a company's gross account, or under a treaty where accounting is done on an earned basis, this calculation can be made policy by policy, and this is the only accurate method of calculating earned premium. However, very often an approximation of earned premium is desired, for example, where a treaty is accounted on a written premium basis a calculation of the earned premium for the year is desirable to ascertain the results of that year's business at that time, or a calculation of a Reassured's net earned premium income for any year is necessary to adjust an excess of loss contract where the premium is calculated on the earned premium income.

We will now discuss methods of calculating approximations of earned premiums from written premiums on a bulk basis.

The 24th System

This is a fairly accurate approximation as it is based on the assumption that all policies commencing in a given calendar month can be given an assumed inception date of half way through that month. For example, the policies starting in, say, December will on average have run half a month before the close of 1979. Half a month is $\frac{1}{24}$th of a year. Thus the earned premium for 1979 will be $\frac{1}{24}$th. The unearned premium on such policies at 31st December 1979 will be $\frac{23}{24}$ths and the earned premium in 1980 will also be $\frac{23}{24}$ths of the December 1979 *written* income.

Note that this method assumes two things:

(1) That policies attach evently through the month. The whole accuracy will be thrown out if, for example, most policies commence on the first day of the month.

(2) All policies, or at least the average policy, are for 12 months, or if there are long term policies, e.g. 36 months, such policies have their premiums accounted or "written" on an annual basis.

Given that these two assumptions are correct, the 24th system can be used with pretty good accuracy to determine either the earned premium for any year or the unearned premium at any point in time.

In tabular form we can set out the calculation of earned premium for 1979 and the unearned premium at the close of 1979 for business written in 1978 and 1979.

With modern computers the earned premium can be worked out readily by the day and thus earned premium can be more accurate now.

Date Premium written	*Fraction earned in 1979 on 24th system*			*Freaction unearned at 31st December 1979*
January 1978	$\frac{1}{24}$ths		This total equals the unearned premium in force at 31st Dec. 1978	Nil
February 1978		$\frac{3}{24}$ths		Nil
March 1978	$\frac{5}{24}$ths			Nil
April 1978		$\frac{7}{24}$ths		Nil
May 1978	$\frac{9}{24}$ths			Nil
June 1978		$\frac{11}{24}$ths		Nil
July 1978	$\frac{13}{24}$ths			Nil
August 1978		$\frac{15}{24}$ths		Nil
September 1978	$\frac{17}{24}$ths			Nil
October 1978		$\frac{19}{24}$ths		Nil
November 1978	$\frac{21}{24}$ths			Nil
December 1978		$\frac{33}{24}$ths		Nil

January 1979	$\frac{23}{24}$ths		$\frac{1}{24}$th		or the unearned premium in force at 31st Dec. 1979
February 1979		$\frac{21}{24}$ths		$\frac{3}{24}$ths	
March 1979	$\frac{19}{24}$ths		$\frac{5}{24}$ths		
April 1979		$\frac{17}{24}$ths		$\frac{7}{24}$ths	
May 1979	$\frac{15}{24}$ths		$\frac{9}{24}$ths		
June 1979		$\frac{13}{24}$ths		$\frac{11}{24}$ths	
July 1979	$\frac{11}{24}$ths		$\frac{13}{24}$ths		
August 1979		$\frac{9}{24}$ths		$\frac{15}{24}$ths	
September 1979	$\frac{7}{24}$ths		$\frac{17}{24}$ths		
October 1979		$\frac{5}{24}$ths		$\frac{19}{24}$ths	
November 1979	$\frac{3}{24}$ths		$\frac{21}{24}$ths		
December 1979		$\frac{1}{24}$ths		$\frac{23}{24}$ths	

The 24th system is a widely used method of making approximations of earned premium income during a period and/or the unearned premium at any point in time.

Where pre-paid 3-year business is concerned, as was frequent in the U.S.A., then the system to apply to such premiums is not a 24th system but a 72nd system. In other words, a 3-year premium written in February

1979 would earn $\frac{21}{72}$nds in 1979 and would earn $\frac{24}{72}$nds in 1980, $\frac{24}{72}$nds in 1981 and $\frac{3}{72}$nds in 1982.

It must be noted:

(1) That for short term policies, e.g. travel personal accident business, no 24th system will work.

(2) That for long term business, where the exposure varies during the term of the business, no 24th or 72nd, or similar fractional method, will work.

For example, it cannot be used on construction business where the values and exposures will increase the longer the policy remains in force.

(3) That substantial A.P.'s and R.P.'s will produce anomalies in the system.

A system similar to the 24th system, but based on quarterly premiums, would be an "⅛th system". This is, of course, less accurate and is not in frequent use. An even less accurate extimate of the earned premium can be made by assuming that the average policy incepts half way though an annual period and using a "½ system". That is to say, 50% of the premium written in a year is earned in that year and 50% in the next succeeding year.

Although this method is not accurate it is a very easy and useful way of roughly estimating how much of an annual written income is earned during a year. For example, one is asked to take a quota share of an agency operation with the following figures:

	Net written premiums		*Claims paid*
1980	100,000		30,000
1981	150,000		60,000
		Losses outstanding at 31/12/81	100,000
Total premiums	$250,000	Total claims	$190,000

The difference between net premiums and losses is a plus of $60,000 which, on the face of it, might appear satisfactory.

On a quick analysis to an earned basis the figures become:

	Net written premiums		*Claims paid*
1980	50,000	(50% of 100,000)	30,000
1981	125,000	(50% of 100,000)	60,000
		(+50% of 150,000)	
		Claims outstanding	100,000
Total premiums	$175,000		$190,000

As the premium income is growing it is likely that more will be written in the last 6 months of each year than in the first 6 months and therefore the actual earned premium income for the two years is really less than $175,000.

Accounted or Debited Premium Income

The accounted premium income of a year is the premium income accounted in that year regardless of when a policy incepted. It will therefore often include premiums or additional premiums pertaining to insurance policies which incepted in earlier years and may not include late accounted premiums in respect of some policies incepting during the year. Debited premium income is a term often used as an alternative to "accounted" premium income, particularly where insurance companies are writing through Brokers or Agents. The premium of a policy written in, say January, would in a perfect world, be debited to the Broker or agent in a January account for settlement by that Broker or Agent within, say, 30 days.

However, such speed is rare and a policy incepting on the 1st January may not be processed by the Broker for some time. The particular policy may have been placed with a number of companies and Underwriters and their shares of the premium will have to be calculated and advised to each before the Broker can be debited. This can take an unconscionable long time, which can be accentuated by other factors:

(1) The Broker may, for commercial reasons, wish to give his client a period of credit before he debits that client.

(2) A Broker dealing with a sub-Broker may well account with sub-Broker quarterly and thus a premium for a January risk may not be debited by the Broker until 1st April.

(3) Even where a Broker is himself paid promptly he may well wish to hold that premium himself for a period of time and be reluctant to expedite the passing of it to the Reinsurers. The motives for this will vary between sheer avarice to obtain interest for his own benefit to a more laudable intention to build up a fund in his hand so that he can pay losses quickly to his clients without waiting for all the loss collections to come in from companies and/or Underwriters.

(4) Companies or Underwriters may, on occasions, defer debiting or receiving premiums because they wish to keep their own premium income low to avoid overwriting in relation to their assets or deposits.

However, whatever the cause, the fact is that the debited premium income may be well in arrears of the written income and can bear little relation to it. The average Lloyd's marine, aviation or non-marine Syndicate starting a new account will be lucky if their debited or accounted premium in Year 1 comes to more than 50% of their eventual written income for that year. Of course, once such a Syndicate or a company operation has been running for some time the debited or accounted years' premium income will consist of a mixture of the premium income written during that year and the immediately preceding years. The point is that such a premium income may bear little relation to either the written or earned premium for the year in question. Any Reinsurer of a Syndicate or company operating an accounted or debited premium should be aware of the delays inevitably occurring with such a method.

There is also a lesson here for regulatory authorities in that the debited or accounted premium income may be well behind the actual written premium and such debited premium will not reflect the liability assumed by a company or Underwriter. With a fast growing company the debited premium will be very much less than the written income.

Whilst debited premiums may be very delayed the accounted income of a company writing through branch offices and its own agencies should not suffer the same delays and, therefore, where a company is not writing through Brokers, and where there are no unusual accounting delays, then the difference between written and accounted income may not be very material. This is particularly so where the volume of business is fairly constant.

To refer, for a moment, to Lloyd's Syndicates and London companies, Marine, and possibly Aviation accounts, using a 3-year account basis:

Business written in, say, 1980 (that is business with inception dates in 1980) would constitute that Syndicate's or company's 1980 account.

A Lloyd's 1980 account premium income was, therefore, equivalent to a normal 1980 written premium. As the 1980 account will be kept open for 3 years, there will be no unearned premium, or very very little, after 36 months. A 3-year account does not really have an "earned premium" as all the signed or written premium is earned during the 3-year period during which that account is left open. Of course, the year of account premium will be accounted and received by Underwriters gradually over the 3-year period of the account. A typical situation for a new account starting in 1980 might be as follows:

Premiums accounted in:	*1980*	*1981*	*1982*	*1983*	*Total*
1980 Year of A/c	50	46	4		100
1981 Year of A/c		75	69	6	150
1982 Year of A/c			100	92	200 est
	50	121	173	?	

The written and earned income for each *year of account* are:

1980 — 100
1981 — 150
1982 — 200

The premiums accounted in each calendar year for all years of account are:

1980 — 50
1981 — 121
1982 — 173

Calculation of Unearned Premiums Under Pro Rata Treaties

Where a treaty is accounted on an earned premium basis the calculation of such earned premium is done accurately, normally policy by policy or, if agreed, by a 24ths system. At any time the unearned premium (which represents the premium for Reinsurers' unexpired liability on each policy) can be ascertained accurately on such a treaty by deducting the earned premium from the written premium. This unearned premium is, of course, retained by the Ceding Company and it is "reserved" by the company for future liability (i.e. for the unexpired part of each cession). This unearned premium reserve automatically remains in the hands of the Ceding Company. Of course, it will be gradually released each quarter in future quarterly accounts after it has been earned.

Therefore, this means that under an earned treaty the unearned premium reserve is automatic. Any regulatory authority concerned with the solvency reserves of a company, or of course the company's directors who are also vitally so concerned, does not have to insist on the creation of an unearned reserve for premiums under treaties accounted on an earned basis. (There is one caveat in relation to this with which I will deal in a later section of this chapter.)

Where a treaty is accounted on a written premium basis no automatic unearned premium reserve is left with the Ceding Company. In fact, the Reinsurers have been paid such unearned premiums as part of the written premiums. Should those Reinsurers go bankrupt, or be unable to pay future losses under the treaty due to any cause, for example, a Government freeze on remittances or a state of war, then this means that the Ceding Company has paid over premiums and is unable to recoup future claims which will occur. This will represent a financial loss to the company.

To safeguard against this event treaties accounted on a written basis will normally make provision for the retention by the Ceding Company of an "unearned premium reserve". Often this is insisted upon by the regulatory authorities of the countries or states in which the Ceding Company is resident or operating.

Therefore, it is often a statutory solvency requirement. Even where it is not so, most Ceding Companies with treaties on a written basis insist upon such reserves being deposited with them for their own protection. The calculation of such a premium reserve will be distinct from the cash settlements of the quarterly accounts. Normally such reserves are calculated once a year and held for twelve months and then re-calculated and the reserve adjusted. They are in fact deposited by the Reinsurer with the Ceding Company and the Reinsurer will be paid interest on them. They may, of course, be made by the Reinsurer depositing actual securities with the Ceding Company, in which case both interest and any capital appreciation or depreciation will be at the *Reinsurers'* risk.

The actual calculation can be done on a policy by policy basis and it will then be equal to the actual unearned premium on that treaty. Alternatively, such a reserve can be calculated on a 24th system. More frequently, however, an approximation is used which is based on the assumption that 50% of the annual net written premium is earned. This is the use of a "½" system.

It would appear, therefore, that a treaty accounted for on a written premium basis, with a ceding commission of 35%, should have a premium reserve of:

> 50% of the net ceded premium (i.e. 50% of 65%) or 32½% of the gross ceded premium.

However, this would be an inadequate premium reserve for the following reason. Assume that the Ceding Company cancels all its business at the close of the treaty year; in that event the Ceding Company will have to return to its policy holders 50% of its *gross* premiums. It will have paid its costs in writing and acquiring that business in advance, some of which will be irrevocable.

Let us assume that these amount to 15% of the premiums concerned, i.e. 15% of 50%. This makes a total liability to the Ceding Company of 57½% of its written premium. It has already received a 35% ceding commission on this 50%, i.e. 17½% of the gross. It therefore needs to hold 40% by way of premium reserve, or, to put it more briefly, it needs a premium reserve equal to net unearned premium of 32½% already in the hands of Reinsurers plus an additional 7½% to cover these unrecoverable expenses.

Of course, the actual figures will vary according to the ceding commission and the irretrievable costs, but the premium reserves on most treaties accounted on a written basis are normally set at around 40% of the annual gross treaty premium income. The effect on the Reinsurer in taking on a treaty can mean a considerable financial burden. The Reinsurer may be financing a treaty for some years. In other words, he will be tying up money in order to take on the business.

The setting up of such premium reserves should be a separate and distant operation from the normal treaty cash accounting which is carried out quarterly. Normally the reserve is calculated and deposited at the close of the annual period and remains so deposited with the Ceding Company for the following twelve months. Then it is released and a new reserve calculated and deposited for the new treaty year just closing.

Alternatively, the reserve can be set up quarterly alongside the cash quarterly settlements. In that case each quarterly reserve remains deposited for 12 months and is then released and a new deposit made for the current quarter. (See Page 140.)

For example:

Assume a treaty has 100,000 gross written premium income each quarter during the year. With a 40% reserve and a 35% ceding commission the position, without paying any losses, would look like this:

			METHOD A Annual Reserve held for 12 months		*METHOD B* Quarter Reserves held for 12 months	
	Cumulative Gross P.I.	Ceding Commission	Reserve Amount	Blance after Ceding Commission and Reserve	Reserve Amount	Balance after Ceding Commission and Reserve
1st Quarter	100,000	35,000	Nil	65,000	40,000	25,000
2nd Quarter	200,000	70,000	Nil	130,000	80,000	50,000
3rd Quarter	300,000	150,000	Nil	195,000	120,000	75,000
4th Quarter	400,000	140,000	160,000	100,000	160,000	100,000
5th Quarter	400,000	140,000	160,000	100,000	120,000	140,000
6th Quarter	400,000	140,000	160,000	100,000	80,000	180,000
7th Quarter	400,000	140,000	160,000	100,000	40,000	220,000
8th Quarter	400,000	140,000	Nil	260,000	Nil	260,000

This is a very simplified figure but it shows that with an annual constituted reserve held for 12 months very heavy financing occurs during the 5th to 8th Quarters, when the majority of claims are being settled, but of course no financing is done during the first 4 Quarters.

Method B, where the reserves are set up quarterly and released 12 months later — the financing starts at once, reaches a maximum at the end of the 4th Quarter and gradually decreases. This is a very simple picture as in practice some premium will come in during the 5th to the 8th Quarters.

As already explained, the method of accounting on a written basis accompanied by a premium reserve of around 40% of the gross written does mean that the Ceding Company has deposited with it the full premium reserve necessary to close up and cancel its book of business at the close of each year or each quarter. Most statutory authorities would not impose any financial burden therefore on a Ceding Company having such reserves, provided they are constituted on *written* premiums and not *debited* premiums.

However, where a treaty is accounted on an earned premium basis then a financial penalty may result to the Ceding Company. This happens because no extra reserve is made to compensate the Ceding Company for its pre-paid and irrecoverable expenses. Compare the position at the end of the 4th Quarter on a treaty as shown on the next page, with quarterly written premiums of 100,000 and a 35% ceding commission, and contrast results to the Ceding Company when accounting is on written premiums with a 40% reserve and when it is on an earned basis. (See Figure on Page 142.)

Of course, although the Ceding Company with a treaty on an earned basis may suffer this penalty of 30,000 it gains by the fact that 270,000 is held by the company in cash and earns them interest and possible capital appreciation, whereas on a written basis it would only have 140,000 to use and invest. It is a nice balance as to which is the most useful method for a Ceding Company and the method adopted will often depend on the attitude of regulatory bodies as to whether they give credit to a company's Reinsurers. From the Reinsurers' viewpoint there is no doubt that the earned basis without a premium reserve means that they have no financing to do and the treaty accounting, being on an earned basis, follows the actual results of the business more closely.

As I have said before, the earned basis is used very commonly in the U.S.A. and Canada, whilst the written basis plus premium reserve is used in Europe and most of the rest of the world.

	Ceding Commission 35%	Net Cash to Reinsurers	Ceding Reserve at 40%	Company's Retention	Net Balances
G.W.P.I. 400,000	140,000	260,000	160,000	300,000	100,000
G.E.P.I. 200,000	70,000	130,000	Nil	270,000	130,000

Portfolio Transfers

If any reader has reached this far in this chapter I applaud him; he will by now realise, I hope, that I have been simply discussing treaty cash accounting and premium reserves. We will now discuss actual transfers of liability or portfolio transfers.

Consider a treaty accounted on an earned basis. At the close of any year, or even any quarter, the Ceding Company has paid to its Reinsurers the exact earned premium for the liability they have run up to that date. The Ceding Company has in its own pocket all the premium for future liability. It could, at least arithmetically at that time. just keep this portfolio of business in force for itself. On the other hand, it could cede the portfolio of in force business to a new Reinsurer. If this is done the Ceding Company would be "transferring the portfolio". The consideration for the portfolio transfer is the amount of unearned premium in force at that date.

Thus, a treaty with a gross written premium of 100,000 per quarter, or 400,000 a year, might have an earned premium during the year and an unearned premium in force at the close of the year of 200,000 gross. The portfolio transfer is done by paying the new Reinsurer the 200,000 of "in force" premiums. The old Reinsurer is then "off risk". In a fairly short time, when claims are settled, his results will be known without waiting for all the individual policies to expire.

Treaties normally continue from one year to the next and it saves an awful lot of trouble if each year can be finalised at the close of each year and its portfolio of business in force taken over by the next succeeding year.

Viz:

Year 1

A — Gross written premiums	100,000
B — Gross earned premiums	40,000
C — Gross unearned premiums	60,000

Year 2

D — Gross written premiums	200,000
E — Gross earned premiums	80,000
F — Gross unearned premiums	120,000

Right! Year 1 transfers C — 60,000 — to Year 2, which agrees to assume that portfolio and will in its turn pass F on to Year 3. We now have this picture:

Year 1 —	Gross written premium	100,000	
	Less outgoing premium portfolio	60,000	
	Gross earned — Year 1		40,000
Year 2 —	Incoming premium portfolio from Year 1	60,000	
	Gross written premium	200,000	
	Less outgoing premium portfolio to Year 3	120,000	
	Gross earned Year 2		140,000

Note
Year 1 is responsible for all losses that occur in Year 1 on policies which incepted in Year 1.

Year 2 is responsible for all losses that occur in Year 2 on policies which incepted in Year 1 or Year 2.

Neither year is responsible for losses which occur after the year is finished, so each year can be closed and finalised once losses are settled.

How can this procedure be done on a written basis? On an earned treaty it is easy. The unearned premium is precisely known at the close of every year and no arithmetical problems arise. With a treaty accounted on a written premium basis the unearned premium may not be known accurately and we have recourse to systems such as the 24th or the 8th, or even the rather poor approximation of the half system, i.e. a transfer of 50% of the previous year's written premium.

This premium transfer for the portfolio of business in force must *not* be confused with a premium reserve; the two operations are quite distinct. A portfolio transfer does not assume that the Ceding Company has to cancel its original business. Unlike a premium reserve the portfolio transfer is done at the actual unearned premium or as close an approximation as is possible. If a 24th system is used the approximation will be good. If the 50% system is used it will be an approximation at best. However, consider a treaty as follows:

Year 1	A	Gross written premiums	100,000
	B	Unearned at close of Year 1 calculated at 50%	50,000
Year 2	C	Gross written premiums	200,000
	D	Unearned at close of Year 2 calculated at 50%	100,000

Year 1 — transfers B to Year 2
Year 2 — accepts transfer of B and transfers D to Year 3

Thus:	Year 1 — Gross earned	50,000
	Year 2 — Gross earned	150,000

But Year 1 Reinsurers have already paid the Ceding Company the ceding commission on the full written income of 100,000. Therefore it is easier to transfer on a net basis. So assume a ceding commission of 40% — the transfer could be done on a net basis and figures would look like this:

Year 1	Gross written	100,000	
	Less ceding commission @ 40%	40,000	
	Net written	60,000	
	50% transfer	30,000	
	Leaving net earned	30,000	30,000
Year 2	Year 1 net portfolio	30,000	
	Gross written	200,000	
	Ceding commission @ 40%	80,000	
	Net written	120,000	
	50% transfer	60,000	
	Year 2 net earned	60,000	60,000
	Year 1 and Year 2 net earned in Year 2 equals:		90,000

Note
If the ceding commission on the two years is different, as the transfer is done on a net basis, the new year assumes the premium transfer at the old commission terms. In this case the net transfer is 30% of the gross written, i.e. 50% (100% — 40% ceding commission).

We now arrive at a position where the transfer of the portfolio of in force business can be transferred from one treaty year to the next on a net basis at an agreed percentage of the gross writien premium for the year. This percentage figure will be a fair approximation if it is done at a figure around 30% to 35% of the gross written premium, the actual figure varying with the ceding commission. Combining this with the establishment of a premium reserve we may postulate a treaty where accounting is done on a written premium basis with the following clauses:

Portfolio transfer in and out at 32½% gross. Premium reserve at 40% gross (quarterly basis).

This is "slip" shorthand which would appear in the treaty wording somewhat as follows:

Portfolio transfer

"Reinsurers will assume liability for claims occurring on all business in force under this treaty at the start of the year and will be relieved of all liability for future claims on business in force at the close of the year. At the start of each annual period Reinsurers will be credited at inception with an amount equal to 32½% of the gross written premium for the previous year and will be debited in the 4th quarter's account with an amount equal to 32½% of the gross written premium for the current year."

Premium reserve

"The Reinsurers agree to deposit with the Ceding Company at the close of each quarter a premium reserve equal to 40% of the gross written premium during that quarter, such reserve being released to Reinsurers in the corresponding quarter's account of the next succeeding year. The Ceding Company will agree to credit the Reinsurers quarterly in arrears with interest at a rate of 6% per annum on all amounts so deposited."

Page 154 shows a simple example of a treaty on a written premium basis starting in Year 1 with a gross written premium of 40,000 for that year, which doubles to 80,000 for Year 2:

We will assume:

(a) a ceding commission of 35% for each year;

(b) portfolio transfer at 32½% gross written;

(c) premium reserve of 40% gross written;

(d) losses at 60%.

This shows an overall debit of 15,000 at the end of Year 1.

However, the first account of Year 2 will receive as a credit item the portfolio transfer of 13,000 from Year 1, so Reinsurers' position, taking the two years combined, will show cash in hand of 14,000 with reserve of 16,000, a "financing" of 3,000 as Reinsurers have "earned" the cash profit of 1,000 on Year 1. Once the 2nd Year's first quarter account is presented with the new written premiums the cash in hand should exceed the reserve amount. It will all depend on the claims side of the equation!

It will be realised that the timing of the accounts is very important. The reserve will be created by Year 1 simultaneously with the 4th quarter accounts. The portfolio transfer out of Year 1 will either be debited in the 4th quarter account, in which case it should be paid over to Year 2 at once and not left for that Year's 1st quarter accounts. Alternatively, the portfolio transfer can be debited in Year l's 5th quarter accounts and credited to Year 2 in that year's lst quarter accounts, these two accounts being settled simultaneously.

It should be noted that the premium reserve is made by Reinsurers to the Ceding Company whilst the portfolio transfer is a payment by one year's Reinsurers to the next year's Reinsurers as a consideration for the assumption of the unexpired liability.

Summary

To conclude these sections on premium reserves and portfolio transfers the purpose of each can be summarised as follows:

Firstly, reserves: the purpose of a premium reserve is to ensure that the Ceding Company suffers no financial impairment if all its original business is cancelled and it had to return a pro rata share of each original premium to its policy holders. To do this it needs to retain under its control the net unearned premiums at any date plus irrecoverable costs in respect of that business in force. Looked at another way round, it requires the gross unearned premium reserve less any expenses which are recoverable or will not be incurred if the business is cancelled.

Where a treaty is on a "written basis" a premium reserve is a normal requirement. Where a treaty is on an earned basis a premium reserve is not used, however the Ceding Company may suffer an audit penalty equal to its irrecoverable acquisition costs on the unexpired portfolio of business.

A premium portfolio transfer is made between one set of Reinsurers and another and represents a fair sum of money for the transfer of the unexpired portion of individual policies constituting a "portfolio" of continuing business. Where a treaty is on a written basis such a portfolio

At the close of the first year, Reinsurers' account will look like this:

	Year 1							
	Cash Account			Reserve Account			Overall Balance	
	Credit	Debit	Balance	Credit	Debit	Balance	Credit	Debit
Gross Written Premiums	40,000							
Ceding Commission at 35%		14,000						
Loses 60% Gross earned		12,000						
Portfolio transfer at 32½% of G.W.P.I.		13,000						
Premium reserve 40%					16,000			
Cash	40,000	39,000	1,000			–16,000		–15,000

transfer is often done at an arbitrary amount between one year's Reinsurers and the next. Where a treaty is on an earned basis the transfer of liability can be done by simple agreement without transfer of money, with the assuming Reinsurer merely being paid the future earned premium quarterly.

Loss Reserves and Outstanding Loss Portfolios

Loss reserves

A Ceding Company will receive payments from its Reinsurers for all settled or paid losses. It will have to make financial provision in its own accounts for losses which have been advised but not settled, i.e. for outstanding losses. It may have to account or reserve such outstanding losses on a gross basis until payment is received from its Reinsurers. An Auditor should disallow any such recoveries which are in dispute or where there could be undue delay in remittances due to political factors or where doubt exists over solvency of the Reinsurer.

Regulatory authorities adopt somewhat different attitudes. In the United Kingdom, generally speaking, the authorities would follow the above auditing rules but allow as a credit potential reinsurance recoveries for outstanding loss. However, in France, and for "unlicensed" reinsurance in the U.S.A., potential reinsurance recoveries are not deductible and therefore, to avoid a financial penalty, it is necessary for the Ceding Company to hold cash or securities for Reinsurers' share of outstanding losses.

It can be seen that where no credit is given for potential reinsurance recoveries in respect of outstanding losses then the Ceding Company either has to earmark the gross reserves out of its own resources or ask Reinsurers to fund their share of such outgoings. Apart from these legal requirements a Ceding Company may feel happier and more secure if it holds Reinsurers' share of outstanding loss reserves, both because it obviates a possible financial risk and, more importantly, because such reserves may be used once losses are paid to pay Reinsurers' share without the delay of collecting the loss specially.

Therefore, in many areas of the world loss reserves are an accepted part of treaty business in the same way as premium reserves. A typical clause for an outstanding loss reserve is as follows:

DEPOSIT OF RESERVES FOR LOSSES

The Reinsurer undertakes to set up in the hands of the Company reserves for outstanding losses calculated in accordance with the regulations in force, at 31st December of each year, for as long as liability exists by reason of this treaty.

Such reserves will be set up in cash or in securities, approved by the Ministry of Finance, at the Reinsurer's choice. However, it is specified that the Reinsurer must make his choice known by 30th September of each year at the latest, for the closing of accounts at the following 31st December. If he fails to do so, it will be assumed that the deposit is to be made in cash or, if the treaty was already in force the preceding year, in the manner then used.

On amounts deposited in cash, in accordance with this clause, the Company agrees to pay the Reinsurer interest at the rate of % (variable) per annum, calculated from the date when the deposit is made until the date when the loss becomes payable by the Reinsurer in accordance with this treaty. Such interest will be calculated and payable on 31st December of each year. Before such date and when applicable the Company must be in possession of the annual request for reduction of or exemption from French tax on interest (forms type RF2 and others), duly completed by the Reinsurer and endorsed by the competent authorities. If after 31st December the Reinsurer has not taken the necessary steps to send this document, he will be debited with the entire "retention at source".

If at the time when the Reinsurer makes such a deposit a sum is due to him by reason of this treaty, the Reinsurer will have the right to deduct this sum in setting up the deposit, subject however to having informed the Company thereof at least fifteen days in advance in order to permit the latter either to settle its debt separately or to accept the set-off from it.

If the Company enters into liquidation, or if a provisional administrator is appointed, the Reinsurer will be authorised to deduct from any sum becoming due to the Company by reason of this treaty, or of another treaty, or of several other reinsurance treaties, all sums which are stipulated therein as payable at a fixed rate or at a specified date and, from such time, the Reinsurer will no longer be obliged to set up additional reserves, notwithstanding any stipulations to the contrary resulting from this clause.

We must be careful to compare two things. Firstly, the statutory loss reserve situation — for example on French business — requires the establishment of a reserve for outstanding losses at the close of each year. That reserve is then held for 12 months and reconstituted twelve months later. The reserve is not used to pay settlements of the individual losses which take place in that 12 months period. The deposits of such reserves with the Ceding Company is a distinct operation additional to the payment of the claims themselves. These deposits are made either in cash or in securities, or may sometimes be made by some form of guarantee or letter of credit.

Such deposits may be made by deposit of securities by the Reinsurers with the Ceding Company, the securities being approved by the Ceding Company and its regulatory authority. If this is done then the interest and change in value of the reserve is for the benefit, or possible detriment, of the Reinsurer. Normally deposit of securities is only used where loss reserves are deposited annually as the constant changes in a quarterly reserve make it difficult to operate.

Whichever method is used ties up funds which the Reinsurer might put to better use.

Who Owns Deposit of Reserves?

Before leaving this subject I must revert back to a reserve deposit with the Ceding Company either in cash or in securities.

The wording quoted on Pages 156 and 157 clearly implies that the loss reserve becomes the property of the Ceding Company. If the Ceding Company goes bankrupt and the reserve is not used up for loss payments then it should be released back to the Reinsurer. However a liquidator may treat him as a normal creditor and thus the Reinsurer could receive back only a fraction.

Let us start with a simple case of an outstanding reserve, for a single claim. A Reinsurer deposits his share of the reserve so that the Reinsured may take credit for the deposit as an asset. In order that the asset is one which an auditor of a regulatory authority may accept as being valid it must either belong to, or be available unconditionally, to the Reinsured for settlement of the loss for which it is created, up to the monetary limit of the deposit of reserve created. There are two processes here:

(1) Agreement by the Reinsurer to set the claim which may be automatic or in any case may be implicit.

(2) Release of deposit of reserve.

Once (1) is agreed, (2) must be automatic with the Reinsurer being unable to prevent it. Where settlement is less than the deposit of reserve then the balance between the deposit and the reserve should belong to the Reinsurer and not the Ceding Company. Any interest on such deposit should belong to the Reinsurer.

If the deposit is invested or is put up in securities' increase in value then any surplus over the monetary reserve amount should belong to the Reinsurer. If the deposit investment decreases in value then the Reinsurer should be required to increase the deposit to the agreed monetary amount. If the deposit investment has increased in value and the liability has also increased, should the Ceding Company have an automatic right without Reinsurer's consent to use the increased reserve value to satisfy the increased liability? The answer to this must surely be no. The right to use the surplus should be dependent on the Reinsurer's agreement to the increased reserve.

In order to achieve this the creation of a loss reserve deposit should surely be regarded as a form of trust.

(1) Under which the trustee is empowered to release to the Ceding Company (without the Reinsurers' approval) money for settlement of a specified liability up to the monetary amount specified for that liability. Before releasing such monies the trustee should require proof of settlement and proof of Reinsurers agreement to that settlement unless of course this is automatic under the contract between the Ceding Company and the Reinsurers. NB the setting up of the deposit of reserve by Reinsurers must surely imply that the Reinsurer accepts liability for the claim up to the monetary amount of the reserve.

(2) The Trustee is required to release to the Reinsurer, without the Ceding Company's approval, any balance not so required. (This will include any interest or appreciation.)

To me a Trust seems the best way to deal with our problem as a deposit of loss reserve "belongs" exclusively to neither party. If the cash deposits are held in the name of the Ceding Company and that Ceding Company becomes insolvent then the Reinsurer has to recover his "balance" as a normal creditor. If they are held in the name of the Reinsurer, with the Ceding Company having the right to withdraw them then, if the Reinsurer goes bust, the Ceding Company may be in a position of a normal creditor. If they are held in joint names then liquidation of either could cause problems for the other, unless the joint ownership is in the form of a joint trusteeship with the rights of both parties to ownership clearly set out. *Viz*, that the Ceding Company's ownership only extends to that monetary amount of the reserve that relates to the settlement of a specified and agreed liability up to a specified monetary amount and that any balances belong to the Reinsurer.

Where securities are deposited, the same philosophy must apply. They should be held either in a trust with a third party as trustee, or in joint trustee ownership with ownership defined as above. Where a deposit of reserves in securities in a bank is in both names this surely should be construed as a joint trusteeship. And to facilitate this a trust document should be drawn up and signed by both parties. Where the securities are held in the name of the Ceding Company only, then the securities belong legally to the Ceding Company. Nevertheless, this should be a limited right. The Reinsurer should keep the loss of profit of value, interests and dividends; but how can we ensure this, in the event that the Ceding Company becomes bankrupt, without creating a trust?

When a loss is settled, securities would have to be sold or transferred to the Ceding Company for the monetary amount of the settlement (as above) with balance released to the Reinsurer. I find the idea of a joint trusteeship between a Ceding Company and it's Reinsurer a difficult one and in order to resolve disputes, a third impartial trustee or referee might have to be appointed.

Where deposit reserves are set up for a number of losses, provided these losses are specified, the same principles can apply.

I therefore conclude that all deposits of loss reserves should have trustee status. Some readers may feel that this is not necessary as laws in some countries do make ownership clear but I also believe that with the wide international character of Reinsurance it may be difficult to either establish which law applies or how it would be applied by different jurisdictions. If a legal trust is not created then at least the deposit of reserve clauses in the treaty wording should be formulated as a trust making the intentions quite clear. Even so, without a legal trust a liquidator of one party may well get his hands on the other party's money.

If we move on to a more normal practice, when deposit of outstanding loss reserves are set up with a number of outstanding losses, when individual losses may not be specified, or when a reserve includes an IBNR feature or some formula designed to cope with fluctuations in reserve, here the deposit reserve is solely created to cover both known outstanding and unknown outstanding losses which are covered by a specific treaty wording. I see no reason why the same procedures set out above should not be applied with trustees "releasing to Ceding Companies payments for settlement on all losses which have been agreed between the two parties and releasing to the Reinsurer any reduction in the reserves agreed between the two parties, and finally releasing to the Reinsurer any balances which remain when all liabilities have been settled", this might of course take several years.

To turn to the question of the deposit of Unearned Premium Reserves. 1 feel that the purpose of a deposit of an Unearned Premium must be to allow the Ceding Company to reimburse itself for future claims if its Reinsurer goes bankrupt or does not fulfil its obligation to pay such future claims. If this is so, then the same arguments apply; the Ceding Company is entitled to draw down from the deposits payment for claims or return premiums which are covered under that particular treaty, but that any balances including appreciation or interest should be paid to the Reinsurer. It is my view therefore, that logically all Premium Reserves should be held in trust in the same way as loss reserves.

In practical terms:

(1) A deposit of premium reserve should cease to be the property of the Ceding Company when the portfolio of unexpired liability has been transferred from the Reinsurer, i.e. once the Reinsurer has passed his responsibility for future claims back to the Ceding Company. The deposit of reserve then belongs to the Reinsurer.

(2) In many cases a Reinsurer might take the view that if a Ceding Company goes bankrupt then the deposit of premium reserve is going to be used up anyway, i.e. there will be no surplus left.

If this is so, then a Reinsurer might well not think a transfer worthwhile and leave the deposit of premium reserve as the property of the Ceding Company.

Bank Guarantees or Letters of Credit

As outstanding loss reserves or claims advances are not cash settlements but only financial pledges, an alternative method has been used for many years, particularly in the U.S.A., and its use in other countries is gaining ground. This method is for a guarantee to be given to the Ceding Company by an acceptable Bank, i.e. that the Bank will guarantee to find the money for the reserve when it is required. Obviously the Bank giving the guarantee will have to be financially acceptable to both the Ceding Company and its regulatory authorities as the Bank's guarantee stands in lieu of either cash or deposits of securities. Obviously, too, the Bank granting such a guarantee or a "Letter of Credit" will need to secure such credit on the assets of Reinsurers and will, as a normal matter of business course, only issue Letters of Credit if it is satisfied that Reinsurers are financially solvent for the amount of all its Letters of Credit.

Furthermore, the Bank will make a charge for such credit facilities and the amount of such charge will be fixed at a percentage of the amount of the line of credit given. This charge is variable but is usually not greater than 1%.

The use of Bank guarantees in lieu of cash or security deposits has some advantages for both the Ceding Company and, more so, for Reinsurers. The Ceding Company does not have the bother of holding securities or handling cash deposits. Reinsurers have full use of these funds and this return may be considerably greater than interest it might receive on a physical deposit even after the credit charge made.

Again, in addition, once the system is set up the use of such guarantees is simple and flexible and also obviates the risk of currency fluctuations which always exist when physical reserves are deposited in other currencies. There is little doubt in my mind that a wider use of such facilities would be beneficial and will gradually spread. Of course it can only do so provided the method is approved by regulatory authorities and acceptable Banks are prepared to quote reasonable terms.

The terms and conditions of how and who authorises encashment of such a line of credit are vital. Provided the amounts in the Guarantee are clearly identified loss by loss then the Guarantee can be irrevocable, i.e. one over which the Reinsurer has no control, the Ceding Company being empowered to draw upon it once settlements of losses have been agreed between the Ceding Company and its Reinsurers.

The Ceding Company's powers must be controlled carefully so that encashment can only be done for payments of the claims specified in the Guarantee and only up to the amounts so specified. Obviously this problem is fundamental to the greater use of Bank Guarantees. In order for the Guarantee to be a "good" asset to the Ceding Company, and to be so admitted by the regulatory authorities, then neither the Reinsurer nor the Bank can be allowed to cancel or reduce the Guarantee at will.

On the other hand, a Reinsurer can hardly be expected to make a line of credit available at his cost and his risk if it can be drawn upon without discharging his responsibility for the specified claims or liabilities for which the Guarantee was set up. Provided these conditions are met then the use of Bank Guarantees for outstanding loss reserves has much to commend it.

The extension of this idea to cover premium reserves is one which has not yet been fully utilised. This is due partly to the fact that Letters of Credit have been used primarily in the U.S.A. where treaties are normally on an earned premium basis and do not therefore carry premium reserves. Secondly, the difficulty with granting a Letter of Credit to cover premium reserves is to specify and tie down the purposes or circumstances under which the Letter of Credit may be drawn upon by the Ceding Company. With outstanding losses the losses are identified for a specified monetary amount or are indentified as losses for which a Reinsurer is liable under the treaty concerned. They can be drawn down when those losses are settled. With a premium reserve one has no similar specific purpose.

In what circumstances could the Ceding Company draw upon the Letter of Credit? Presumably in the same circumstances as it could encash a premium reserve, which must be when the Reinsurer fails to honour his obligation under the treaty. Then the Ceding Company may use the premium reserve in lieu. With a Letter of Credit this would require careful drafting to ensure that both the rights of the Ceding Company and Reinsurers were safeguarded. An obvious circumstance would be when a Reinsurer became insolvent and was unable to fund or pay future losses on business already ceded. Outstanding losses could be paid from outstanding loss advances but future losses on the business ceded would be reimbursed from the premium reserve.

Therefore a Letter of Credit used in lieu of a premium reserve could be drawn upon by the Ceding Company if the Reinsurer was unable to pay future losses, or did not do so, on the unearned premium portfolio of business or, alternatively, failed to repay the unearned premiums to the Reassured if the treaty were cancelled and the treaty terms entitled the Reassured to reassume the unexpired portfolio of business.

There are also practical difficulties. Some time limit would have to be set on the period of default before encashment and someone, other than the Reassured, would have to be appointed by both parties in advance to authorise encashment. Nevertheless, greater use of Letters of Credit and Bank Guarantees has such obvious advantages in periods of high interest rates and currency fluctjuations that greater use of them must surely come about.

Use of Letters of Credit (LOCs) in the U.S.A. is permitted by many state insurance authorities. These authorities require certain conditions which may vary state by state. In the main, to be acceptable, a LOC must:

(1) Be irrevocable for a period of time.

(2) Be renewable automatically if liability still exists after the LOC has expired unless notice is given by Reinsurers.

(3) Be unconditional and *not* itself tied down to particular losses or circumstances.

This means the LOC becomes just like a bank account upon which the Ceding Company can draw upon as it wishes. Obviously with a Ceding Company trusted by Reinsurers these LOCs may represent no risk. However, with an unscrupulous company or should a Ceding Company go into liquidation there could be a risk that such LOCs are drawn down for improper purposes.

I enclose at the back of this Chapter the conditions laid down by the New York Insurance Department (1983) under which it will give credit for Letters of Credit.

Outstanding Claims Advances (OCAs)

A letter of credit is a line of credit established by a Bank on Reinsurers behalf. The Bank will normally want collateral security but will not necessarily require that in the form of a full matching cash deposit. An outstanding claims advance is an advance of cash usually equal to the outstanding claim or loss amount made by the Reinsurer to a third party, a bank, a lawyer or a loss assessor under trust and the trustee is authorised to release the necessary amounts to the Ceding Company once the Ceding Company produces proof of loss settlements which have been agreed by the Reinsurer or for which the Reinsurer is liable under the treaty.

Where an OCA is used under a treaty for an aggregation of losses which will vary as some losses are settled and new ones are added, it is usual to review the aggregation of outstanding losses every quarter and to adjust the OCA amount accordingly. Such arrangements are known as revolving fund OCAs.

The use of Letters of Credit in place of OCA is a modern development which gives Reinsurers more flexibility in the use of their money but if the LOC is unconditional does pose greater risk to the Reinsurer than an OCA under control of a trustee.

Outstanding Loss Portfolios

Whether a treaty is accounted on a written basis or an earned basis, it is not possible to finalise any one year of account until all losses and liabilities on that year's business are settled and salvage and recoveries obtained. Even on a physical damage treaty, this can take years and on long tail classes it can take many years. This means that on a continuing treaty several years' accounts will be open at one time, with adjustments being made to all "open" years until final settlements are made. The profit commission, or the actual ceding commission with a sliding scale, may also have to be adjusted each time there is a variation in settlement. At best this is tedious; at worst it is a considerable expense to both parties.

It is common practice, therefore, for the liability for outstanding claims to be transferred from the old closing year to the new reinsuring year. The new Reinsurers receive a premium equal to the estimate of these outstanding losses and assume responsibility for their payment in the future. It must be noted that the consideration or premium paid from one year to the next for this outstanding loss portfolio is not necessarily the same as an outstanding loss reserve.

An outstanding loss reserve is an amount deposited by Reinsurers with their Reassured to meet the reserves carried in the Reassured's account for those losses or liabilities. A loss portfolio transfer is the amount of premium that a Reinsurer will need to discharge the liability on those losses. Let us take a few examples:

> With a fire treaty the Reassured will tend to reserve known out standing losses conservatively. Often, in times of low inflation of values, the actual settlements will be less than the loss reserves. This may be due to successful future litigation or recoveries or just conservative reserving.

Therefore, it is not infrequent for an outstanding loss portfolio on fire business to be transferred at a lesser figure than the reserves for such losses. Often a figure of 90% of the estimated outstanding loss reserves is used. However, a lower figure will only be justified if the Reassured's estimating procedures are both reliable and conservative and can be proven from past experience.

During the 1980s fire and physical damage business has become more and more long tail and it is highly unlikely that a portfolio transfer done at 90% of known loss reserves would be sufficient for the 1990s. My belief would be that 100% plus some estimate for IBNR or unfavourable loss development would be more realistic.

Quite different considerations apply to long tail business, where the advice of claims is delayed the known outstandings at the end of any year inevitably will only be a fraction of the eventual loss settlements. Normally, on a long tail treaty, for example, a quota share third party business, it would be most unwise to assume a loss portfolio at the figure of known outstanding losses. It is best not to transfer until such time as all outstandings are stabilised. This may take many years.

In addition, on long tail business the loss portfolio is a sum of money which will be used to settle losses as they mature.

In the meantime the money will earn interest at a compound rate. The value of a loss portfolio may be discounted by the value (estimated) of future earnings on it. Therefore, this negotiated reinsurance premium may not be the same as the loss reserve carried in the Reassured's books. It may be greater or less; often very much greater. The "reinsurance to close" of a Lloyd's Syndicate is a good example of this in action.

A Lloyd's Syndicate keeps its account open for three years and then "closes" that account and collects the loss or distributes the profit on that year's account to its Members. In order to close or wind up the account all outstanding liability must be reinsured by someone else. The premium paid for this reinsurance of the outstanding liability portfolio at the 36th month will not necessarily be the same as the Syndicate's reserves (audit or technical reserves). For example, on very short tail business, such as livestock, the reinsurance to close can be a lower figure than the audit or technical reserves. For a Syndicate with a very long tail account and a doubtful record, the premium paid or quoted for a reinsurance to close may be in excess of the technical or audit reserve, which would be required if that Syndicate did not reinsure but left the account open.

Certain words of warning are necessary over loss portfolios:

(1) Even with short tail business a transfer made at the close of a year can be inequitable and it may be better to close 12 months after the close of the treaty year.

(2) With long tail treaties loss portfolios can be very dangerous animals for oncoming Reinsurers. Any inadequacy in the amount transferred may build cumulatively from year to year until such time as the amount of portfolio transfer is quite inadequate for the potential liability. If this happens at a time when the treaty is terminated the last year's Reinsurers may be left with a horrific run-off of liability

on many past years for an inadequate consideration. Loss portfolio transfers on long tail business, therefore, should not be undertaken without very great analysis of the treaty pattern of settlement.

THIS WORD OF WARNING NEEDS UNDERLINING IN RED. TIME AND TIME AGAIN PEOPLE ARE ATTRACTED TO ASSUME RUN-OFF PORTFOLIOS ON LONG TAIL BUSINESS OR DO NOT REALIZE THAT THEY ARE TAKING THEM ON WITH DIRE RESULTS 10 YEARS LATER.

(3) On property treaties some special provision often should be made for special treatment of large claims, for example catastrophes such as hurricanes and earthquake, and for large claims subject to litigation or substantial potential recoveries. It is best that where a loss portfolio contains such claims, either the transfer is held pending settlement of those claims or loss reserve itself excludes these claims, provision for this being made in the treaty wording.

Having said this, the transfer of outstanding loss portfolios is regular treaty practice sometimes entered into too lightly.

APPENDIX TO CHAPTER VII

Extracts from NEW YORK INSURANCE Department's Letter of October 1983 regarding the conditions required for a Letter of Credit to be admissable.

(1) The letter of credit must be "clean". irrevocable and unconditional. By "clean" and unconditional, it is meant that the letter of credit stipulates that the beneficiary need only draw a sight draft under the letter of credit and present it to obtain funds and that no other document need be presented. The letter of credit must also indicate that it is not subject to any conditions or qualifications outside of the letter of credit. In addition, the letter of credit itself cannot contain references to any other agreements, documents of entities.

(2) The heading of the letter of credit may include a boxed section which contains the name of the applicant and other appropriate notations to provide a reference for such letter of credit. The boxed section must be clearly marked to indicate that such information is for internal identification purposes only and does not affect the terms of the letter of credit or the bank's obligations thereunder.

(3) The letter of credit must contain a statement to the effect that the obligation of the bank under the letter of credit is in no way contingent upon reimbursement with respect thereto.

(4) The term of the letter of credit must be for at least one year and must contain an "evergreen clause", which prevents the expiration of the letter of credit without due notice from the Insurer. In addition, the "evergreen clause" should allow for a period of no less than 30 days notice prior to expiry date for non-renewal.

(5) The letter of credit must state whether it is subject to and governed by the Laws of the State of New York or the Uniform Customs and Practice for Documentary Credits of the International Chamber of Commerce (Publication 290), and all drafts drawn thereunder must be presentable at a bank office in the United States.

(6) If the letter of credit is made subject to the Uniform Customs and Practice for Documentary Credits of the International Chamber of Commerce (Publication 290), then the letter of credit must Specifically address and make provision for an extension of time to draw against the letter of credit in the event that one or more of the occurrences specified in Article 11 of Publication 290 occur.

(7) The letter of credit must be issued or confirmed by a bank authorized to issue letters of credit and which is either a member of the Federal Reserve System or is a New York State chartered bank.

(8) The aggregate of all letters of credit issued or confirmed to any one licensed insurance company by one bank on behalf of any one entity must not exceed 5% of the bank's capital and surplus, as shown in its annual report as of the end of its preceding fiscal year, as filed with the New York State Banking Department or the appropriate Federal banking regulatory agency.

Exhibit A is a form of letter of credit that the Department finds acceptable.

(9) If the letter of credit is issued by a bank authorized to issue letters of credit, other than a bank described in condition No. 7 then the following additional requirements must be met:

(a) the letter of credit, in a form similar to Exhibit B, must be confirmed by a bank described in condition No. 7,

(b) the issuing bank must formally designate the confirming bank as its agent for the receipt and payment of the drafts,

(c) the confirmation must be in a form similar to Exhibit C,

(d) condition No. 8 above must be met by the confirming bank,

and

(e) the "evergreen clause" must provide for 60 days notice prior to expiry date for non-renewal.

(10) (a) When a letter of credit is obtained in conjunction with a reinsurance agreement, then such reinsurance agreement must contain provisions which:

(1) Require the Reinsurer to provide letters of credit to the Reinsured and specify what they are to cover.

(2) Stipulate that the Reinsurer and Reinsured agree that the letters of credit provided by the Reinsurer pursuant to the provisions of the reinsurance agreement may be drawn upon at any time, notwithstanding any other provisions in such agreement, and shall be utilized by the Reinsured or its successors in interest only for one or more of the following:

(i) to reimburse the Reinsured for the Reinsurer's share of premiums returned to the owners of policies Reinsured under the reinsurance agreement on account of cancellations of such policies,

(ii) to reimburse the Reinsured for the Reinsurer's share of surrenders and benefits or losses paid by the Reinsured under the terms and provisions of the policies Reinsured under the reinsurance agreement,

(iii) to find an account with the Reinsured in an amount at least equal to the deduction, for reinsurance ceded, from the Reinsured's liabilities for policies ceded under the agreement. Such amount shall include, but not be limited to, amounts for policy reserves, claims and losses incurred and unearned premium reserves, and

(iv) to pay any other amounts the Reinsured claims are due under the reinsurance agreement.

All of the foregoing should be applied without diminution because of insolvency on the part of the Reinsured or Reinsurer.

(b) Nothing contained in (a) above shall preclude the Reinsured and Reinsurer from providing for: (1) an interest payment, at a rate not in excess of the prime rate of interest, on the amounts held pursuant to (a) (2) (iii) above, and/or (ii) the return of any amounts drawn down on the letters of credit in excess of the actual amounts required for (a) (2) (i), (ii) and (iii) above, or in the case of (a) (2) (iv) above any amounts that are subsequently determined not to be due.

(c) When a letter of credit is obtained in conjunction with a reinsurance agreement covering risks other than life, where it is customary practice to provide a letter of credit for a specific purpose, then such reinsurance agreement may in lieu of (a) (2) above require that the parties enter into a "Trust Agreement" which may be incorporated into the reinsurance agreement or be a separate document. Such "Trust Agreement" shall conform in substance to Exhibit D.

(11) A letter of credit may not be used to reduce any liability for reinsurance ceded to an unauthorized Reinsurer in financial statements required to be filed with this Department unless an acceptable letter of credit with the filing Ceding Insurer as beneficiary has been issued on or before the "as of date" of the financial statement. Further, the reduction for the letter of credit may be up to the amount available under the letter of credit but no greater than the specific obligations under the reinsurance agreement which the letter of credit was intended to secure.

(12) The conditions stated herein, shall apply to letters of credit issued, confirmed, amended or renewed on or after October 1, 1983. However, Condition No. (10) (a) shall not apply to reinsurance agreements entered into prior to October 1, 1983, provided that the reinsurance agreement does not restrict the drawing down of the letter of credit in any way and no new business is ceded under the agreement.

Chapter VIII

CATASTROPHE — EXCESS OF LOSS REINSURANCE

Introduction — Period — Territory — Perils — Insuring clause — Coninsurance — Loss occurrence — Hours clauses — Ultimate net loss — Net retained lines — Premiums and rates — Premium income — Reinstatement — Excess of loss reinsurance extended expiration — Underwriting practices — Loss settlements — Rates of exchange

Introduction

It is doubtful if anyone can say with certainty who originally devised the first catastrophe protection. However, I think the modern development stems from the San Francisco earthquake of 1906. From that time U.S.A. companies sought, negotiated and placed such business through Brokers in Lloyd's. Some of the contracts, changed and amended of course, are still continuing today after 90 years.

However the development of excess of loss contracts (not properly referred to as treaties) protecting a whole account is a 20th Century development and mainly from the 1920s onwards. It contrasts with the more traditional resinsurance developed in the 19th Century of passing on liability on individual policies by treaties.

Quite different considerations can arise because protection of a whole account may divorce the reinsurance contract from the terms and conditions of the original policies, and before Reinsurers have any liability, some contingency must take place other than just a loss on an original policy. In the case of a catastrophe reinsurance this contingency, i.e.,"a catastrophe" must have occurred.

The protection of an insurance account by means of an excess of loss contract is now of world-wide significance and there is hardly an insurance Underwriter in the world who does not use or write such reinsurance. Like all important and successful operations the basic concept is simple. If an insurance company or Underwriter is unfortunate to suffer a very large loss then catastrophe Reinsurers will reimburse him for that proportion of his loss which exceeds an agreed figure (the deductible) up to an agreed limit. Simple though the concept is, many difficulties arise in practice. Through the years considerable thought has had to be given to defining more precisely the terms of contracts to eliminate these difficulties.

It is interesting to note that where disagreements have arisen between contracting parties in the past they have been settled normally by mutual agreement, with occasional resort to arbitration. Disputes or disagreements have very rarely been taken to the courts. This means that, unlike Marine insurance, there are very few legal or case interpretations of excess of loss contract reinsurance wordings. In some ways this is a disadvantage, though undoubtedly the trust between excess of loss Reinsurers and their Reassureds is still very real today and I doubt whether we shall ever build up a case history of court interpretations.

In 1996 this has changed and the Courts have now entered the field of interpreting excess of loss contract in some force. See Chapter XVI.

Chapter VIII contains a synopsis of a typical catastrophe contract and this chapter will consider various problems in detail. I have attached to the chapter a specimen excess of loss catastrophe wording which was drafted by myself and others after 1965. As a result of Hurricane Betsy, the winter weather losses of 1962/63 in the United Kingdom and other incidents, many of us in London, both in Lloyd's and other companies, felt that a revised and standard wording was desirable. This wording is now in general use in Lloyd's and the London market for reinsurance of direct underwriting companies. It is not generally used for U.S.A. business.

I will follow this wording article by article in my discussion. I will deal firstly with the principles behind the contract terms and then in Chapter IX will turn to problems of fixing the actual terms of the contract.

ARTICLE 1

Term of Agreement. This agreement shall apply to losses occurring during the period commencing the ______________ and ending the ______________ .

Normally catastrophe contracts are for a fixed non-cancellable period of 12 months. Sometimes the contract is a continuous one subject to annual cancellation by required notice, usually 90 days, to a fixed anniversary date. The idea of a continuous contract is to give continuity. In practice it often causes problems; renewal information may not always be available 3 months before the anniversary date. In addition, in the Northern hemisphere the typhoon and hurricane season is early autumn and it is often impossible to finalise renewal for the next annual period until the major period of typhoon and hurricane exposure is past. This often means that the 90 days notice has to be given either by one party or the other, or reduced from 90 days by mutual consent. I feel personally that the continuous contract gives rise to more problems than it solves.

Catastrophe contracts normally cover losses occurring on all policies issued by the Reassured regardless of when the original policies attached, i.e. a contract for 12 months from the 1st January 1999 will cover business written in 1998 and possibly 1997 and earlier years, as well as business written in 1999 itself.

Sometimes catastrophe contracts cover losses arising on business written during a year, i.e. during an annual "account". This is not unusual with Lloyd's Syndicates and Underwriting Agents writing for a group of companies. In these cases, where the Reassured changes every year, a catastrophic loss may well affect two or more years of account. The Syndicates, or Pool, may have to bear two or more retentions and their Reinsurers may have to bear possibly two or more loss payments from the same loss occurrence. Often such contracts contain a bridging clause which has the effect of combining all accounts together in one loss recovery with a common deductible and limit and allowing the loss recovery to be distributed pro rata between the individual accounts involved in proportion to the share of those accounts in the loss concerned.

ARTICLE 2

Territory. This agreement shall apply to losses occurring within __________________________.

This can be extremely important in relation to catastrophic perils such as tropical windstorms, earthquake and flood and, in some cases, riots, bush fires and conflagration exposures. A Reassured will obviously desire the widest territorial coverage but he may be advised to limit the territories to those in which he is actually operating. There is little point in his Reinsurers becoming worried and making a charge for earthquake exposures in Israel or Mexico if the Reassured does not operate in those territories and has no intention of so doing.

ARTICLES 3 & 4

Policies or perils covered. Often these are defined in broad terms such as — "All policies written in the property department" and specific exclusions would be added to Article 4.

ARTICLE 5

> *Insuring Clause. The Reinsurer hereby agrees to indemnify the Company for ___ % of that part of its ultimate net loss which exceeds _________ on account of each and every loss occurrence and the sum recoverable under this agreement shall be up to but not exceeding ___ % of ________ ultimate net loss on account of each and and every loss occurrence (subject to the provisions of Article 11).*
>
> *The balance of ___ % of the excess ultimate net loss together with the first ________ shall be retained net by the Company and not reinsured in any way. However, it is understood and agreed that the Company have an underlying reinsurance for ___ % of ________ each and every loss occurrence, recoveries under which shall be disregarded in computing the ultimate net loss hereunder.*

This clause sets out the coverage provided, the percentage of loss covered, the deductible and the policy limit for any one loss occurrence. It then stipulates the retention by the Reassured of its coinsurance and retention of the deductible with a proviso that specified underlying reinsurances are permitted.

In catastrophe covers the deductible is normally set in monetary terms at the commencement of the contract and reviewed each year. I will discuss the way in which deductibles are chosen and negotiated later on. Sometimes a deductible on a catastrophe excess of loss cover is adjustable automatically on sums insured or the Reassured's premium income, but this is unusual. In other cases a deductible can be indexed automatically, for example, to the cost of building index. This would mean an automatic variation in the deductible corresponding to building or repair costs.

Again, the policy limit is normally a fixed monetary sum but can be adjustable on sums insured, or premium income or indexed with the deductible. Both the deductible and limit are on account of each and every loss occurrence (which is defined in Article 6). Many Reassureds take out a catastrophe programme which often consists of a series of layers of cover adding up to the total limit of protection required. Normally the deductible of the second excess will be directly over the first excess. However, some programmes are placed with gaps between the finish of one "layer" and starting point of the overlying "layer".

Coinsurance

Most catastrophic covers protect only 90% of that part of the Reassured's loss in excess of the deductible, the balance of 10%, being warranted, maintained net by the Reassured. The reasons behind this requirement are twofold:

Firstly, the maintenance by the Reassured of an insurable interest in his business. Without a coinsurance a Reassured might be tempted to expand his business in hazardous areas or hazardous perils. A good example is provided by Florida in the United States. It is a State which is extremely flat and in the regular path of tropical hurricanes. Its climate is superb, if a trifle hot for my taste, and it has developed very quickly in the past generation. Therefore there has been a continuous demand for insurance protection.

Of course, the normal fire and extended coverage insurance, or various private house comprehensive forms, provide protection against wind damage, including hurricane, and with a considerable potential peril the rates charged are not insignificant. In addition, the fire results on private houses have been profitable.

In years when no hurricanes occurred a profit of around 30% or more was not unreasonable. When a hurricane did strike, then of course the loss ratio could climb into the hundreds. The answer is to rely on a catastrophe protection for the hurricane when it comes. If such protection is for 100% cover, and if the deductible remains at a fixed figure, then there is a great temptation to increase writings as the whole of any extra loss from those extra writings will fall upon the catastrophe Reinsurers whilst the extra profit in the non-hurricane years remains mainly with the Reassured.

The second reason for coinsurance is to make certain that the Reassured retains financial interest in loss settlements, the theory being that they will handle original loss settlements with more skill and relish if they have an involvement themselves.

To my mind coinsurance is sensible for these reasons and also because reinsurance is always, and always should be, a partnership and it is no bad thing if that partnership is expressed in this monetary way.

Coinsurance is perhaps an unfortunate word for the retention by the Reassured of part of his own catastrophe policy and I would prefer to use the word co-reinsurance. Co-reinsurance of more than 10% by the Reassured is unusual but is used, for example, where a Reassured wishes to increase his retention and prefers to keep the deductible of his reinsurance the same. Where a Reassured has several layers of catastrophe protection he may well reduce the percentage to Reinsurers on his first layer as a prelude to dropping that layer altogether.

We have referred to coinsurance or co-reinsurance but strictly speaking the policy itself is expressed as providing 90% cover for a premium and a rate. The Reassured retains the other 10% but does not retain part of the reinsurance premium. In some contracts, more particularly in Europe, the rate and premiums are quoted as 90% of a figure.

The retention is sometimes reduced, particularly on higher excess contracts, to 5% or 2½% and on occasions eliminated altogether. This is not unusual where the Reassured retains a gap between the finishing point of one layer and the deductible of the next layer. The gap is a form of co-reinsurance. It is now quite common on International Catastrophe XL layers (ex USA layers) to have no coinsurance at all.

Another safeguard to make sure that the Reassured's insurable interest is maintained is the requirement that the deductible is kept net and not reinsured in any way. Of course, where it is known that an underlying policy exists, and the contract has been negotiated with this knowledge, the underlying layers are stipulated in the wording. Loss recoveries from such underlying policies will not then breach the requirement that the amount of the deductible must be kept net by the Reassured before any recovery is made against this contract.

In many contracts Reinsurers often require a further stipulation that no higher layers of catastrophe protection are taken out by the Reassured without their consent. Normally this will appear on the slip and in the wording as a simple warranty. Where contracts are placed in layers this warranty is usually only included in the top layer. The thinking behind this warranty lies in the fact that a top layer catastrophe policy usually covers the maximum foreseeable loss that the Reassured can envisage on his account. The Reassured, after all, knows his own account best and if after the contract is placed he feels that he needs more protection, because his account has become more exposed or he has reassessed his liabilities, or local conditions have changed the vulnerability of his account, then the taking out of additional cover may definitely affect the Reinsurers of the previous highest layer.

ARTICLE 6

Definition of Loss Occurrence. The words "loss occurrence" shall mean all individual losses arising out of and directly occasioned by one catastrophe. However, the duration and extent of any "loss occurrence" so defined shall be limited to:

(a) 72 consecutive hours as regards a hurricane, a typhoon, windstorm, rainstorm, hailstorm and/or tornado.

(b) 72 consecutive hours as regards earthquake, seaquake, tidal wave and/or volcanic eruption.

(c) 72 consecutive hours and within the limits of one City, Town or Village as regards riots, civil commotions and malicious damage.

(d) 72 consecutive hours as regards any "loss occurrence" which includes individual loss or losses from any of the perils mentioned in (a), (b) and (c) above.

(e) 168 consecutive hours for any "loss occurrence" of whatsoever nature which does not include individual loss or losses from any of the perils mentioned in (a), (b) and (c) above

and no individual loss from whatever insured peril, which occurs outside these periods of areas, shall be included in that "loss occurrence".

The company may choose the date and time when any such period of consecutive hours commences and if any catastrophe is of greater duration than the above periods, the Company may divide that catastrophe into two or more "loss occurrences", provided no two periods overlap and provided no period commences earlier than the date and time of the happening of the first recorded individual loss to the Company in that catastrophe.

Loss Occurrence

I will now turn to one of the most difficult and contentious clauses in any catastrophe wording and discuss the definition of "loss occurrence".

My own views on this are prejudiced by the fact that Article 6 is very much my own baby as I was largely instrumental in drawing up this wording in the 1960s. The following remarks may be interesting if they give the reader some of the reasoning behind the wording. It will be interesting to see in the years ahead if arbitrators and the Courts interpret the words in the way in which they were intended.

In the early years of catastrophe policies the contract merely paid "excess of each and every loss". The word "loss" gave rise to trouble; did it mean an individual loss? Did it mean a general financial loss? Soon wordings along these lines were used: "excess of any one loss or series of losses arising out of one event (or one disaster)". Then the definition of "event" or "disaster" became difficult and time periods were used to arbitrarily limit the "event" or "disaster".

During the 1950s and the 1960s significant changes took place in the way insurance companies dealt with their catastrophe Reinsurers. Generally speaking, up until then, if difficulties arose over the interpretation of definitions they were argued over between the professional insurance managers or Underwriters. However, in the 1950s and 1960s Boards of Directors, often advised by lawyers, tended to take a greater interest in technical matters. Quite rightly; after all, that was what they were paid for.

The result was that when an insurance company or Underwriter sustained a serious loss, naturally the duty of the Board and advisers was to make certain that they recovered the largest amount legally possible from their Reinsurers. In particular, the definition of one loss and the hours clause began to be interpreted by Reassureds and their advisers in a way which Reinsurers generally felt was not the intention, and in a way which was possibly contrary to the original information given when the reinsurance contract was negotiated.

Here are a few examples of the problems:

In the Spring of 1948 there was a series of tornadoes which sprang out of a warm front of air from the South-East meeting a cold front lying across the North-West of the U.S.A. Tornadoes in Texas, Kansas and up into Illinois and Indiana did extensive damage, including hail and flash flooding. They then blew out over Canada and in their course blew down an electric transmission line at Rimouski in Canada which set fire to a wood-yard and the high winds caused a major conflagration.

Two interesting points were made evident; firstly, no-one claimed that the Rimouski loss was the same event as the tornado damage. Secondly, many reinsurance contracts contained 48-hours clauses with the words:

> "all losses arising from *one atmospheric disturbance* during a continuous period of 48 hours ..."

Were tornadoes 1,000 miles apart and separate in time, i.e. not continuous, individual atmospheric disturbances or was the cold/warm front a disturbance? Meteorologists who were consulted said that they did not recognise "an atmospheric disturbance". They recognised fronts and high and low pressure areas, and anyway the whole atmosphere was nearly always disturbed. The 1948 tornado losses and associated hail and flash floods were all settled as one event but not the fires in Canada. However, we Reinsurers were using words, i.e. "atmospheric disturbance" which were not capable of definition.

In Kansas City a few years later floods brought down power lines which ignited oil and petrol on the water. This caused fires which spread. All these losses were regarded as "one event". In the Worcester tornado in Massachusetts in 1949 a policy holder got out of bed at the height of the storm to go downstairs to make a cup of coffee. At the top of the stairs the electric lights failed; he fell down and was killed. The P.A. claim was not included in that company's catastrophe collection.

In Australia the problem of bush fires became important and, with the development of residences in the bush, insurance companies had considerable liabilities. Bush fires in an exceptionally dry summer could spring up independently in N.S.W. or Victoria, miles apart and separated by weeks or even months. Was the dry summer an event or a disaster? To help the original insurance companies some Reinsurers gave an aggregate bush fire clause which treated all bush fire losses arising during an entire year as one loss for the purposes of collecting under catastrophe covers.

In an exceptional period of cold lasting over a month one U.S.A. company claimed for all its automobile damages from frost, freeze and collisions due to ice as one loss. In the winter of 1962/63 the United Kingdom had an extremely cold season. The cold weather set in after

Christmas 1962 and lasted well into March (with breaks above freezing in some areas). Some U.K. insurance companies considered the losses of the whole winter as one event or one disaster. It was a "disastrous" winter; certainly in an historic context.

To revert to flood, which had always caused Reinsurers some worry, would heavy rainfall over a continent over a few wet months, giving rise to widespread flooding in many disconnected river valleys, be one disaster or many? A number of Reinsurers in the U.S.A. and elsewhere designed a flood definition which limited one event to:

"flood damage arising in any one river valley".

In the Californian floods of 1948 some Reassureds who had losses in many river valleys, all directly resulting from a violent rainstorm, could make no collection due to this clause. Other Reinsurers paid all flood losses as one event.

Hurricanes gave problems too. These are carefully monitored by meteorologists and are given code names. Some male chauvinist pig (at that time they had not actually been invented) gave them girls names (since amended to include boys). The first one recorded in a year being an "A" name, the second a "B" and so on. Anyway, some of these ladies would arrive in Florida on Monday, go out to sea again and arrive in New England or Louisiana on Thursday. They were clearly one hurricane but due to the 48-hours clause they became two reinsurance losses. Then, in 1965, came hurricane "Betsy" and some companies sustained losses which exhausted the limit of their catastrophe protection. One of them looked very carefully at its 48-hours clause. Here, one must bear in mind that all the damage from "Betsy" in Louisiana occurred within a continuous period of 48 hours.

As near as I can recall the wording read as follows:

> "As regards hurricane one disaster shall mean all losses or losses arising out of one atmospheric disturbance occurring during a continuous period of 48 hours. The Reassured may choose the date and time when any such period of 48 hours shall commence provided no two periods overlap".

They chose one period starting well before "Betsy" hit Louisiana and finishing half way through the damage period, then started a second period immediately and finishing well after "Betsy" had departed. This enabled them to claim two total losses from their Reinsurers. It was literally correct but never intended. I was not a party to the contract but I believe Reinsurers felt that they had no option but to pay up twice. 1 believe, too, that there may have been some reluctance to reinstate the policy and to give the company future reinsurance protection.

I must also add that the problem of riots, civil commotions and later acts of terrorism and malicious damage added to the confusion. Was a series of riots over a wide area, and hours or days apart, one event if they followed on, say, a shooting by the authorities of an agitator or a speech on the radio or television by a leader? What was an event in this context?

Such difficulties led a number of us in Lloyd's and the London company market to feel that a revision of this definition was needed and Article 6 in the wording attached and quoted above was the result, and I would comment as follows:

First of all, Article 5 reinsures the Reassured on the basis of one "loss occurrence", not one event or one disaster. The term 1oss occurrence is a hybrid term with no dictionary definition and it is not a term commonly used in the press or media, such as disaster or catastrophe. We use the term deliberately so that we could define it in reinsurance terms in the contract. We define it as "all individual losses arising out of and directly occasioned by one catastrophe". Here there is no restriction by peril or by proximate cause. A flood loss arising out of, and directly occasioned by, a hurricane is part of that loss occurrence, along with the wind losses. The term "arising out of and directly occasioned by" will no doubt be subject to interpretation and we hope will be capable of reasonable flexibility to cope with individual cases.

It is impossible to envisage all the forms future catastrophes will take. I can only recall one catastrophe where this wording has been tested — the Managuan earthquake of 1974. Here the earthquake shock did extensive damage within minutes. Fires broke out almost straight away and caused extensive damage as well. Fires continued for some time and in the general chaos, looting and other fires occurred. Even a week later, fires also occurred; some many miles from Managua itself. These were attributed to such things as reconnecting electricity and arson fires started in a period of civil disturbance. Reinsurers applied the dictum "arising out of and directly occasioned by". Obviously, the fires which broke out immediately after the quake formed part of the same loss occurrence. Fires 10 miles away a week later were not normally held as "directly occasioned by the earthquake". Of course, there were borderline cases but the wording, coupled with the "72-hours" clause contained in Article 6, seems to have worked well and prevented any real argument over the definition of one loss occurrence in the case of fire and earthquake losses.

The Managua earthquake as a catastrophe also provided several important and fascinating problems. The fire insurance policy form in use in Managua by the Managuan Companies in 1974 excluded fire following the earthquake. If an Insured wished he could pay an additional premium and obtain an extension covering earthquake shock and fire following earthquake. This followed the general custom of the British and European Companies.

In the USA after San Francisco in 1906 the US custom was different. Fire following quake was normally part of the Extended Coverage document along with coverage for windstorm, hail and other perils. As most people bought Fire and Extended Coverage together, the fire following quake risk was normally provided under the fire policy and the premium charged as part of the Extended Coverage premium. Earthquake shock, on the other hand, was treated separately and rated separately.

Some US Companies who had issued policies in Managua particularly to US Assureds and to the property of the then dictator of Nicaragua General Somosa had used the US Fire and Extended Coverage form.

After the earthquake happened, great pressure was brought to bear on all insurance companies to pay all losses as fire losses even though many of these properties were only actually burnt after they had been reduced to rubble by the Earthquake itself.

There was no way that the Nicaraguan companies could pay their Assureds unless their Reinsurers put them in funds either before or at the same time as payments were made by them to their policy holders. I was the leader of the treaty and excess of loss reinsurance of one of the Nicaraguan insurance companies involved and the world wide reinsurance market were all involved too. The Nicaraguan Insurance companies had been ordered by General Somosa to pay all losses as fire losses. Once this was known many heaps of rubble and standing structures not previously burnt were promptly set on fire. The Nicaraguan companies then approached their Reinsurers and said that they had to settle losses under Nicaraguan law as Fire losses and not as Fire following earthquake and Reinsurers were contractually bound to follow their loss settlements.

I remember Beau Wentworth the boss of one of the major US companies involved telephoning me and asking me to Chair a Meeting of Reinsurers in New York. At that meeting London and the major European Reinsurers such as the Munich and Swiss Re were present along with the major US Reinsurance and Insurance companies. It was clear that where the US form had been used by US companies insuring directly in Nicaragua then the fires following the quake were covered under F and EC policies and had to be paid as such. Clearly, though such F & EC policies did not cover earthquake shock as such.

These direct policies were not the main problem which was, that under the British form of coverage used by the Nicaraguan companies fire following quake was specifically excluded under the fire policy and was only covered provided the Assured had taken out earthquake shock and fire following endorsement.

The world wide Reinsurers under my chairmanship in New York agreed that they would not pay for fire following quake losses unless the original Assured had taken out and paid the premium for that cover. Those with fire policies which specifically excluded fire following quake should not expect payment unless they could show that their fire losses were due to other causes.

However, how could we as Reinsurers not follow the fortunes of, or follow the loss settlements of our Nicaraguan Reassureds if they were compelled by Nicaraguan courts to settle all such losses as Fire?

The Nicaraguans asked us to come to Nicaragua to discuss the matter. We refused to enter the Lions' Den but agreed to a joint meeting in Mexico City. The two delegations met, business was conducted in Spanish and really for a day and a half we got nowhere and it was obvious that unless the Nicaraguans paid up for all losses under fire policies, they would not only be bust but would end up in prison or worse. They could not pay unless their Reinsurers paid them first, so the ball was very firmly in the Reinsurers'court and we needed a plan which Somosa would have to accept.

By lunch time on the second day I went aside with a US Broker and one of the European Reinsurers and we sat down and wrote out what we were prepared to do, which was:

(a) we would arrange to put the Nicaraguan insurance companies in funds to pay all valid insurance claims provided our funding went specifically to pay our share of those losses i.e. we would not insist that they pay first.

(b) all policy holders who had taken out earthquake and fire following earthquake under either a separate policy or by endorsment to a fire policy would be paid in full.

(c) those policy holders who had fire insurance only and no earthquake nor fire following the quake coverage, whose property had collapsed due to the earthquake would not be paid.

(d) those policy holders who had fire insurance only and no earthquake nor fire following quake and whose property had burnt down on the day of the quake would receive 20% only of their loss.

On day 2 40%
3 60%
4 80%
5 and after 100%

provided that the building was still standing when it caught fire and provided the owner did not set light to it!

(e) Any special cases could be put forward on their own merits.

To implement the above plan we would set up an office in Managua manned by a loss assessing team run by Topliss and Harding to make funds available immediately for all loss payments which were due to be settled in accordance with the above.

We finally said that if the Nicaraguan companies insisted on paying 100% of all losses as fire losses, we would not pay whatever the verdict of a Nicaraguan court and they would have to sue us individually either in London, Zurich, Munich and New York or in the International Court at the Hague. That they should put our plan to their Government as a fair and honourable suggestion.

It was so put and the international reinsurance market backed us and the Managuan losses were so settled. Nobody was put in prison. Somosa got most of his claims paid but did not last long as he was deposed and shot by a Bazooka in Columbia. End of Story.

Back to the wording which goes on to say: "occasioned by one catastrophe", not one disaster or one event. We felt that the words "disaster", or "catastrophe" had little difference in meaning and we saw no point in using two words where one would do. "Disaster" could have been used instead of "catastrophe". We used the word "catastrophe" instead of "event" because we felt it was more specific. It implied a violent happening which in itself caused damage. The word "event" we felt might have applied to something which might have been the cause of a catastrophe rather than the catastrophe or disaster itself.

The next sentence reads …

"However the duration and extent of any loss occurrence so defined shall be limited to …"

Here we were careful not to define the duration and extent of the catastrophe itself. This was the prerogative of man or nature or the Almighty but we limited the definition to our own chosen words … "loss occurrence".

I feel that the hours clause which follows is self-explanatory. The indefinite article is used before hurricane and typhoon deliberately but not before windstorm, hailstorm and/or tornado as the former are capable of individual and precise definitions as individual entities. The words "… and no individual loss from whatever insured peril which occurs outside these periods or areas shall be included in that loss occurrence" imply that we cover individual loss, whatever the insured perils, arising out of and directly occasioned by the one catastrophe, provided the individual loss occurs within the periods or, in the case of riots, civil commotions and malicious damage, the areas.

This wording excludes individual losses occurring outside the periods. Here the interpretation intended would exclude the fire which started 4 days after the earthquake in Managua. It should not exclude an individual loss which started within a period chosen and where the monetary payment was made or assessed later.

The last paragraph gives the Reassured the right to choose the date and time when a period starts *only* when the catastrophe is longer than the hours period and no period must start before the first recorded individual loss to the Reassured. The Reassured cannot select two periods and divide a catastrophe into two loss occurrences artificially where that catastrophe is less than 72 or 168 hours in duration.

As I have stated, I feel personally that this definition clarifies the position for both contracting parties in a fair and clear way. Only time will tell whether future parties' arbitrators, and on occasion judges, take the same view. I would hope that this definition would be allowed to stand this test of time unaltered.

Writing in 1985 this is still true except that Lloyd's Underwriters have modified my wording by addition of Paragraph (d) which clarifies my original intention.

In addition an optional extension to the clause is offered to cope with the special problems of winter freeze losses which reads as follows:

Notwithstanding the above, as regards loss or losses from collapse caused by weight of snow and water damage from burst pipes and/or melting snow, the Company shall have the option to deem any one "loss occurrence" to be the aggregate of all such individual losses which occur during a period of 168 consecutive hours within one continent. No period may commence earlier than the date and time of the happening of the first recorded individual loss to the Company in that "loss occurrence" and the periods of two or more "loss occurrences" may not overlap. It is understood and agreed however, that if the Company exercises the option set out in this paragraph then the amount in excess of. which this agreement attaches shall be be increased for the "loss occurrence" or "loss occurrences" involved by the greater of £ or % of the Company's premium Income for the period from
to

1999 Hours Clauses Review

The hours clauses which date back to the 1960s have been very successful but there has been a demand to amend the clauses on occasion. As mentioned earlier the Freeze extension was agreed which included it in for a period of 168 hours and it could be reinstated. In the United Kingdom Insurance companies were concerned that if a windstorm arose at the same time as a high tide significant flooding could happen like in 1953. The problem was that because the peril of windstorm was involved, then the traditional hours clause of Article 6 limited the event to 72 hours even if the flooding took a week to subside. The Reinsured was entitled to take another period of 72 hours but would have to retain a further deductible. Two clauses were produced which addressed the problem.

Firstly: *LIRMA NP 65* of which the main details are:

The Reinsured is permitted to treat a loss involving 72 hours peril(s) with 168 hour peril(s) as a single loss occurrence provided that the individual insured losses included therein are limited to:

(a) *72 consecutive hours with regard to the losses which arise from the 72 hour perils.*

(b) *168 consecutive hours with regard to the losses which areise from the 168 hour perils.*

Secondly: *Lloyd's — LPO 98A* amended has the following loss occurence definitions:

(a) *72 consecutive hours as regards a hurricane, a typhoon, windstorm, rainstorm, hailstorm and/or tornado unless the "loss occurrence" includes arising from flood.*

(b) *72 consecutive hours as regards earthquake, seaquake, tidal wave and/or volcanic eruption.*

(c) *72 consecutive hours and within the limits of one city, town or village as regards riots, civil commotion and malicious damage.*

(d) *168 consecutive hours as regards flood or flood in combination with perils mentioned in (a) above.*

(e) *72 consecutive hours as regards any "loss occurrence" which includes individual loss or losses from any of the perils mentioned in (a), (b), (c) and (d) above.*

(f) *168 consecutive hours as regards any "loss occurrence" of whatsoever nature which does not include individual loss or losses from any of the perils mentioned in (a), (b), (c) and (d) above.*

And no individual loss from whatever insured peril, which occurs outside these periods or areas, shall be included in that "loss occurrence".

The company may choose the date and time when any such period of consecutive hours commences and as respects those "loss occurrences" referred to in (a), (b) and (c) above and if any catastrophe is of greater duration that 72 hours, the company may divide that catastrophe into two or more "loss occurrences", provided no two periods overlap and provided no period commences earlier than the date and time of the happening of the first recorded individual loss to the company in that catastrophe. As respects "loss occurrences" other than those referred to in (a), (b) and (c) above only one such period of 168 consecutive hours shall apply with respect to one catastrophe.

Please note that *LIRMA NP 65* requires the Reinsured to differentiate between windstorm losses and flood losses and this may be tricky for the Reinsured to do. The Amended *LPO 98A* doesn't have this problem but it does not allow a reinstatement in the same event for 168 hour perils other than freeze and 72 hour perils.

Following the shortage of Reinsurance capacity in the Mid 80s it was normal in the USA not to allow a reinstatement in the same event for windstorm. This was because a hurricane could take more than 72 hours to travel from Florida to New England and Reinsurers felt unable to take potentially two total losses from the same hurricane. Some companies purchased catastrophe cover for the difference between the 72 hours and 168 hours and they collected a total loss on hurricane Hugo in 1989.

In the floods which affected Czech republic and Poland in 1997 most of the catastrophe programmes allowed a reinstatement in the same event and some of the lower layers had two total losses as the floods continued for more than 10 days. Some programmes counted flood damage in any one river valley as one event and these were difficult to sort out as some of the rivers eventually met. There must be a good argument to not allow flood to reinstate for the same event otherwise a flood spreading all the way down the Danube could lead to multiple occurrences in many countries weeks apart. I have seen the opposite approach in Scandinavia where a one month hours clause has been used for flood. In that case the catastrophe programme becomes almost a stop loss for flood perils and one needs to make sure it really is the same event. Flood is one of the largest catastrophe perils but because in many countries only restricted insurance coverage is given (USA, Germany and Italy) therefore it is not given the concern it deserves. The increase of building in river plains and the modern less flood resistant construction, will lead to a few surprises in the future as always.

Riots are generally restricted to 72 hours any one city, town or village. This can mean that in a period of civil commotion a company could have a large number of separate “occurrences”, which can lead to the exhaustion of the reinstatements on lower layers. If however a ‘Nation-wide’ hours clause is used the riots losses will all be aggregated together and they could exhaust the programme, as happened in Venezuela in the 1980s. Most catastrophe programmes cover riot, civil commotion and malicious damage but civil war and political risk are excluded. As was shown in Indonesia in 1998 the gap between civil war and civil commotion is very small. Most of the losses that occurred were paid reluctantly by Reinsurers as they felt the motives were political, however much of the original coverage was ambiguous, since then the original coverage has been tightened so that hopefully these losses will not be covered in the future.

Bush fires, which are common in Australia where the eucalyptus burns very well in a dry windy summer, are now generally covered by a 168 hours nation-wide clause.

This and the other amendments illustrate the flexibility of the hours clause which can be tailor-made to any Reinsured’s requirement. It is such an important clause of a catastrophe contract that I feel it should appear on all cover notes and slips rather than hidden in the wording. There have been reinsurance disputes on the hours clauses but they have usually been settled by negotiation rather than in court and therefore few legal precedents have been created.

ARTICLE 7

Ultimate Net Loss. The term "ultimate net loss" shall mean the sum actually paid by the Company in respect of any loss occurrence including expenses litigation, if any, and all other loss expenses of the Company (excluding, however, office expenses and salaries of officials of the Company) but salvages and recoveries, including recoveries from all other reinsurances, other than underlying reinsurances provided for herein, shall be first from such loss to arrive at the amount of liability, if any, attaching hereunder.

All salvages, recoveries or payments recovered or received subsequent to any loss settlement hereunder shall be applied as if recovered or received prior to the aforesaid settlement, and all necessary adjustments shall be made by the parties hereto. Nothing in this clause shall be construed to mean that a recovery cannot be made hereunder until the Company's net loss has been ascertained.

A definition of ultimate net loss is one of the traditional clauses in excess of loss contracts. The wording varies somewhat, but not greatly, between contracts and the clause used in my wording is perhaps slightly more restrictive than some. It defines loss as the amount actually paid whereas some contracts might use the words — "... sums actually paid or for which the Reassured has admitted liability for payment."

It will be noted that litigation expenses are included as part of the total of the Reassured's ultimate net loss. This is the opposite of many excess of loss contracts covering third party or liability business which often contain a "costs clause" and which makes Reinsurers responsible for litigation expenses in proportion to their share in the actual loss.

All loss expenses are included in the ultimate net loss of the Reassured excluding the Reassured's own office expenses and salaries of officials. In some contracts an apportionment of the salaries and expenses of a Reassured's officials are included as part of the loss if they are diverted from normal duties and undertake adjustment duties outside their offices.

Often, when a catastrophe happens outside, adjusters are fully committed and a Reassured may well find it necessary, cheaper and more efficient to adjust claims using his own staff. Reinsurers would benefit from this and it is not unreasonable to allow such expenses and a proportion of salaries of a Reassured's employees to be included in the ultimate net loss.

The final sentence allows a Reassured to make a recovery before he knows his final net loss. He can then make additional claims until his final net loss is ascertained.

In 1990 further thought needs to be given to this problem. The definition of ultimate net loss given here dates back to the 1920s if not earlier. The operative words are "The sum actually paid by the Company". In other words, reading these words in conjunction with Article 5, the insuring clause, Reinsurers are **not liable** until the Reassured has actually paid.

The other alternative reading is that under an excess of loss contract the liability of Reinsurers follows the liability of the Reassured and the actual payment is a discharge of that liability i.e. it is a secondary stage. In the USA as a result of a Court case many years ago the State Regulatory authorities insist on the ultimate loss clause being extended to include an insolvency clause. This says that if the insolvency of a Reassured prevents him paying his direct loss in full he can still claim against his excess Reinsurers as if he had paid.

However, outside the USA such an insolvency clause has never been adopted. The world Reinsurance Markets have always paid excess claims to insolvent companies in good faith and without insisting on actual payment first. This has now been challenged in at least one arbitration.

The actual decision in any, future cases may well depend very much upon the precise phraseology used in the individual wording as a whole. It is an unsatisfactory situation and it would be wiser in my view to adopt the USA practice and include an insolvency clause in all non-USA excess of loss contracts. This would make it quite clear that a Reinsurer cannot refuse to pay valid claims merely because the insolvent Reassured is not lawfully permitted to make settlement to their original policy holders.

It is quite common for the ultimate net loss clause to be amended to allow the Reinsured to have the benefit of underlying reinsurances that do not benefit Reinsurers, i.e. risk excesses. Refer to the ultimate nett loss clause shown in Chapter XI liability. Reinsurers must make sure that the

Reinsured still has a sensible retention. Our preference is that there should be no difference in the inuring reinsurances and the clause should not be amended. Watch!

It is now common practice as a result of the House of Lords' decision to include the new G86 insolvency clause that makes it clear that Reinsurers cannot avoid payment due to insolvency of the Reinsured.

The House of Lords has now settled this matter. They have upheld the traditional honest practice that under English Law, payment cannot be refused on grounds of the Reassured's insolvency. Hooray!

Written in 1978

There are two changes which I would suggest for a modern wording.

Article 7 line 5 should have the word *"due"* added viz:

"salvages and recoveries including recoveries due from all other reinsurances".

The word *"due"* should make it clear that recoveries not actually collected because of, say, insolvency of Reinsurers, are still deductible. Alternatively, add the words *"whether collected or not"* after *"recoveries from all other reinsurances"* in line 5.

Article 7 line 3 *"loss expenses"* should read *"claims expenses".* Again to make it quite clear that expenses in defending claims which do not become losses are part of the ultimate net loss. The Market has assumed for as long as I can remember that this must be so as such costs inure to Reinsurers benefit in reducing his losses, but in today's legal framework one never knows whether sense will prevail. (See comments in Chapter XVI.)

INSOLVENCY CLAUSE 'G86'

Where an Insolvency Event occurs in relation to the Reinsured the following terms shall apply (and, in the even of any inconsistency between these terms and any other terms of this Agreement, these terms shall prevail):

1. *Notwithstanding any requirement in this Agreement that the Reinsured shall actually make payment in discharge of its liability to its policyholder before becoming entitled to payment from the Reinsurer:*

(a) the Reinsurer shall be liable to pay the Reinsured even though the Reinsured is unable actually to pay, or discharge its liability to, its policyholder; but

(b) nothing in this clause shall operate to accelerate the date for payment by the Reinsurer of any sum which may be payable to the Reinsured, which sum shall only become payable as and when the Reinsured would have discharged, by actual payment, its liability for its current net loss but for it being the subject of any Insolvency Event.

2. The existence, quantum, valuation and date for payment of any sum which the Reinsurer is liable to pay the Reinsured under this Agreement shall be those and only those for which the Reinsurer would be liable to the Reinsured if the liability of the Reinsured to its policyholders had been determined without reference to any term in any competition or scheme of arrangement or any similar such arrangement, entered into between the Reinsured and all or any part of its policyholders, unless and until the Reinsurer serves written notice to the contrary on the Reinsured in relation to any composition or scheme of arrangement.

3. The Reinsurer shall be entitled (but not obliged) to set-off, against any sum which it may be liable to pay the Reinsured, any sum for which the the Reinsured is liable to pay the Reinsurer.

An Insolvency Event shall occur if:

A. (i) (in relation to (1), (2) and (3) above) a winding up petition is presented in respect of the Reinsured or a provisional liquidator is appointed over it or if the Reinsured goes into administration, administrative receivership or receivership or if the Reinsured has a scheme of arrangement or voluntary arrangement proposed in relation to all or any part of its affairs; or

(ii) (in relation to (1) above) if the Reinsured goes into compulsory or voluntary liquidation;

or, in each case, if the Reinsured becomes subject to any other similar insolvency process (whether under the laws of England and Wales or elsewhere) and

B. the Reinsured is unable to pay its debts as and when they fall due within the meaning of section 123 of the Insolvency Act 1986 (or any statutory amendment or re-enactment of that section).

ARTICLE 8

Net Retained Lines. This agreement shall only protect that portion of any insurance or reinsurance which the Company, acting in accordance with its established practices, retains net for its own account. Reinsurer's liability hereunder shall not be increased due to an error or omission which results in an increase in the Company's normal net retention nor by the Company's failure to reinsure in accordance with its normal practice, nor by the inability of the Company to collect from any other Reinsurer any amounts which may have become due from them whether such inability arises from the insolvency of such other Reinsurer or otherwise.

Again, this is a traditional clause in excess of loss contracts. The exact wording can vary but the clause quoted is fairly typical. It sets out that the contract applies only to the amount of any insurance that the Reassured retains for his own account and that recoveries from other Reinsurers are deducted first. It also states that failure to reinsure in accordance with normal practices shall not prejudice Reinsurers' position, nor shall errors and omissions and failure to collect from other Reinsurers due to insolvency or other causes. The wording, which precludes collection due to failure to reinsure in accordance with normal practices, is not universally used, but it should be so.

In my opinion errors and omissions and failure to insure are not proper hazards to be reinsured under a catastrophe contract. These are properly covered under an error and omissions policy which should be rated and taken out separately from a catastrophe contract. Normal catastrophe contracts never have taken this hazard into account in their rating.

As to insolvency of other Reinsurers, this is not a matter which should concern catastrophe Reinsurers as they have no control over it and no method of assessing a proper premium therefore.

ARTICLE 9

Premium Clause. The Company shall pay a deposit of _______________ at the inception of this Agreement. As soon as possible after the expiry of this Agreement, the above deposit premium shall be adjusted to an amount equal to a rate of _______________ % applied to the Company's premium income as defined hereunder, subject, however, to a minimum premium of _______________ .The payment of any adjustment due between the parties being made at once.

It is a normal procedure to charge a deposit premium which is payable at inception of the contract. A catastrophe contract is an insurance taken out by an insurance company against it having an insured loss and is similar to a direct insurance policy. A direct Insured normally pays his premium in advance where the premium is known in advance. On such direct insurance policies, e.g. a stock reporting policy, where the premium is adjustable at the close of the policy, a provisional premium is paid at inception and subsequently adjusted.

A catastrophe contract is similarly adjusted at the close of the contract and a deposit premium paid at inception. Logically, the deposit premium should approximate to the estimated final premium. In practice it is often set lower than this and charged at around 80% of the estimated final premium.

Normally a deposit premium is payable at inception of the contract. However, some contracts allow a payment of deposit premiums by instalments, often half yearly, i.e. one half at inception and the second half after 6 months. Alternatively, payments can be made quarterly in advance. Where deposit premiums are so paid it would be normal to make them equal to the estimated final premium rather than a lower figure. In other words, if you pay at inception you expect a reduction; if paid in instalments you pay in full. Of course, the final payment on adjustment is the same.

In general, the single deposit payable at inception is preferable, even on the grounds of less paper work. It is normally used unless the premium is a sizeable one and the Reassured prefers to spread the payment to equalise his cash strain.

Some catastrophe contracts have used a different approach, charging a small deposit premium or even a nominal one, with the contract being adjustable quarterly at the close of each quarter when the Reassured's premium income for that quarter is known. This equates the payment of catastrophe premiums to a similar basis of accounting as a pro rata treaty with quarterly accounts. However, it means a considerable delay in catastrophe Reinsurers receiving any premium and catastrophe Reinsurers are still expected to make prompt payment for losses which may occur any time after the inception date of the contract. It also adds to the paper work.

My personal opinion is that such a method of quarterly adjustment is not suitable to a catastrophe contract. Under a pro rata treaty one is dealing with a regular flow of premiums and losses and a quarterly balance adjustment is sensible. With a catastrophe contract the position is different. A Reassured pays a premium for a contingency; the losses may never happen. If and when they do, they can be very large in relation to the premium. The whole theory of catastrophe reinsurance is the same as direct insurance. The premiums of the many pay the losses of the few and this is difficult to achieve if the many do not pay their premiums in advance.

Except where quarterly adjustments are made, catastrophe contracts are adjusted after expiry of the contract at an agreed rate percent of the Reassured's premium income for the period of the contract, the payment of the adjustment being made at once.

Minimum Premiums

Invariably, however, such adjustments stipulate a minimum premium and such a minimum premium is agreed as part of the original contract negotiations. Why is a minimum premium required? There are three basic reasons:

Firstly, the Reinsurer is giving an indemnity fixed in money terms, i.e. the amount of the cover purchased for each and every loss occurrence. This does not vary with the Reassured's premium income and the minimum premium reflects the minimum charge for the fixed amount of cover.

Secondly, the Reinsurers and the intermediaries, if any, all incur certain expenses and the minimum premium is a method of making a minimum charge to cover these expenses.

Thirdly, a catastrophe Reinsurer has to put a limit on his own acceptances. A book of catastrophe reinsurances has to be balanced with so much liability accepted in Germany, so much in California and so much in Japan. All catastrophe Reinsurers set themselves limits by liabilities accepted. Each of his clients takes up part of his allocation of liability and, therefore, the minimum premium is a booking fee for reserving this capacity and it is right that it should be paid even if, subsequently, the liability turns out to be very little. It should also be remembered that a catastrophe Reinsurer will himself reinsure or and pay a premium negotiated in advance for his own protection. The catastrophe Reinsurer, therefore, must have a certain minimum income to pay his own reinsurance costs.

The amount of the minimum premium on a catastrophe contract is negotiable, of course. Very often it is around 70% or 75% of the estimated final adjusted premium. Often contracts have a common minimum and deposit premium mutually agreed at a figure around 70% to 80% of the final estimated premium. Sometimes the deposit premium is the higher of the two.

Let us assume that a catastrophe contract for 90% of 500,000 × 150,000 has a rate of 2% on a premium income estimated at 2,000,000. The final estimated premium will be:

$$2\% \times 2{,}000{,}000 = 40{,}000$$

A Min. & Dep. Prem. 30,000
adjustable on expiry at 2% premium income, or

B Min. Prem. 25,000
Dep. Prem. 35,000
adjustable on expiry at 2% premium income, or

C Min. Prem. 25,000
Dep. Prem. 40,000 payable 10,000 quarterly in advance,
adjustable on expiry at 2% premium income, or

D Min. Prem. 30,000
Dep. Prem. 5,000
adjustable quarterly in arrears at 2% premium income.

D is the method which I regard as the least desirable.

ARTICLE 10

Definition of Premium Income. The term premium income hall mean the gross premium written by the Company on business protected hereunder during the period of this Agreement, less only return premiums and premiums paid for reinsurance recoveries under which inure to the benefit hereof.

We have talked about the normal method of rating a catastrophe contract, which is to apply a rate per cent to the Reassured's premium income for the period of the contract. We now have to decide what premium income we are talking about. Readers should by now mentally equate earned premium with business in force during the year. If a contract covers loss occurring on business written during the year (whenever the loss occurs), then the correct income is the written income. If a contract covers losses occurring during the year (i.e. on business in force during that year, whenever it was written) then at first glance the correct income is the earned income.

The first supposition is correct; the second requires a further look. We must do a little probing to see why the basis of written premium is normally used for rating catastrophe contracts covering losses occurring during the period of the contract, and why the basis of earned premium is not so used.

Assume that a contract for 90% of 500,000 × 150,000 is placed with a 3% rate on g.n.e.p.i. and covers losses occurring during 12 months — 1st January 1980. Let us assume a contract negotiated on the assumption that the account is not changing and the written P.I. for 1979 and 1980 is 2,000,000 and the earned premium income for each year is the same figure, then the contract would earn 60,000 whether on a written or earned basis. However, the 1980 written premium turns out to be 3,000,000 not 2,000,000 and the earned 2,500,000. Also, the increase of business written between 1979 and 1980 is not due to a change in the original rates, neither to an increase in the Reassured lines on individual risks, rather that the increase is due to additional business.

Which is more correct to apply? The 3% rate to the 1980 earned premium of 2,500,000 or to the 1980 written premium of 3,000,000?

It is a fair assumption that the greater the exposures a Reassured has at risk the greater will be his loss. As premium income is a reflection of the exposures the greater premium income, the greater the monetary loss suffered.

Thus, to revert to our example, let us assume that the Reassured's 1980 earned premium had remained at 2,000,000 and represented a liability at risk of 200,000,000. An insured damage from a windstorm of .15% of the property values insured would cause a loss of 300,000. On a catastrophe contract of 90% of 500,000 × 150,000 the recovery would be 90% of 150,000 against a premium of 60,000.

Let us now take the 1980 actual earned premium of 2,500,000 which means an *average liability* at risk during 1980 of 250,000,000. The same percentage damage of .15% would now cause a loss of 375,000 not 300,000. The recovery on the catastrophe contract of 90% of 500,000 × 150,000 would be 90% of 225,000. The premium is of course 3% of 2,500,000 or 75,000. The original estimates were:

	Prem. 60,000	100% loss	150,000	1:2.5
Actual results:	Prem. 75,000	100% loss	225,000	1:3

Had the 1980 contract been adjusted on the written premium the comparison would have been:

Original estimated	Prem. 60,000	100% loss	150,000	1:23
Actual	Prem. 90,000	100% loss	225,000	1:23

In this example (which is chosen carefully) the use of written premium preserves the *status quo*.

The point is that a catastrophe contract has a deductible fixed in monetary terms. If exposures increase then the loss to the catastrophe contract increases out of proportion to the original loss increase. The use of written premium instead of earned premium compensates in some measure for this. Therefore, the earned basis of premium income should only be used where the deductible of a catastrophe contract automatically increases with increase in income or liabilities.

There is one counter argument to this which the reader will have noticed — exactly the same argument can be used in relation to the limit of the contract. That remains fixed as well and, of course, provides a help to Reinsurers in that with a growing income the recovery does not increase. In spite of this, the rule of using written premium income on catastrophe excess of loss contracts is sound and logical. Please note the difference on stop loss contracts and underwriting or risk excess of loss where other arguments apply and an earned basis is correct.

Before leaving this argument we should mention the seasonal element. Tropical storms hit in the autumn; typhoons in Japan; hurricanes in the West Indies and the U.S.A. For a contract starting 1st January, where the major exposure occurs in the second half of the year, the written premium must be more equitable than the earned premium. Please note that in Australia the storms come in February/April; the renewal dates of Australian reinsurance contracts is not 1st January but 1st July, so, for a major part of both hemispheres, this philosophy works.

Lastly, we must deal with the situation where the written premium income falls. Here a catastrophe Reinsurer will receive less premium on a written basis that he would on an earned basis. This is also fair as the reader can do a few examples and see that the argument used above works equally well in reverse. Furthermore, if a Reinsurer is worried over this he should take care of the situation by increasing the minimum premium in the contract. Of course, where catastrophe protection is sought on a running off account, i.e. where there will be no written income but only an earned income, then the catastrophe premium should either be a flat monetary premium or adjustable on the earned income. There is no other way.

I hope we have now talked ourselves into using gross net written premium income as the basis of rate adjustment on catastrophe contracts. Gross means *before* deduction of original costs; agents commissions, brokerage, taxes, overheads and any other charges or costs. Net means after deduction of the cost of other reinsurances (i.e. premiums), recoveries under which inure to the benefit of the catastrophe contract, i.e. where the losses recovered from such reinsurance are deducted in computing the Reassured's ultimate net loss.

Please note:
The cost of the catastrophe contract itself and the cost of underlying or overlying catastrophe contracts are not deductible as they do not "inure to the benefit ..."

Reinstatement

It has become common practice for a catastrophe contract to pay two total losses and no more. In some ways, as the reinsurance is drawn up as a limit each and every loss occurrence, it seems stupid to talk about reinstating that limit. However, the insuring clause and the reinstatement clause are pretty unambiguous and again are traditional. The effect is that with "one reinstatement" a catastrophe contract really has unlimited reinstatements for partial losses but an overall limitation on the aggregate of losses collectable in a year to twice the occurrence limit. Once a loss occurrence has occurred the amount of loss is reinstated from the commencement of that "1oss occurrence" for a premium. It was common practice for reinstatements to be pro rata for time as well as for amount. This meant that if the loss happened on the last day of the contract year the Reinsurer would receive only 1/365 of the premium as a reinstatement. Sensibly reinstatements are usually now pro rata as to amount but 100% as to time. This saves also on complicated calculations.

When is such a reinstatement premium due? Most reinsurance contracts do not specify. There seem to be three possibilities:

(1) At the close of the contract, when the final premium is ascertainable.

(2) When the loss itself is paid, when it simply reduces the loss collection.

(3) Immediately reinstatement is made.

In my opinion, the third alternative must he correct and the payment is due at once. I would, however, accept the argument that payment should follow the payment of the original policy premium, i.e. that pro rata of the deposit premium should be due at once with pro rata of the adiustment on expiry. In the late 1990s, it was common practice to settle the reinstatement simulatneous with the payment of the loss. It is the easiest to administer.

I cannot see that a Reassured has any right to wait until a loss is settled until payment of the reinstatement premium is made, unless of course the amount of loss cannot be determined before then. In the example above, once the loss of 200,000 is known, then an A.P. of $\frac{2}{5} \times \frac{9}{12} \times 30{,}000$ (Min. & dep.) should be payable at once.

The whole question of the principle of reinstatement is a nice juicy subject. There are those who argue that reinstatement should be unlimited. Rather that a contract with a limit per occurrence should not then have an overall aggregate limitation. Everything has a price which can be agreed at inception.

The difficulty here is twofold. One, that any Reinsurer has to remain solvent himself. A catastrophe Reinsurer, writing a considerable book of catastrophe excess of loss reinsurance, will find it quite imprudent to make himself liable for unlimited recoveries at inception because he may have to assume that all of his exposed commitments may be total losses several times over.

The situation may be different after the first major disaster has occurred. A Reinsurer may have a much smaller loss than he envisaged on his portfolio and, having escaped lightly on the first disaster, may then be in a position to take on a commitment for the third or fourth loss. Reinsurers themselves buy protection and are reluctant to give unlimited reinstatement if they themselves can only obtain a limit on their own reinsurance of two total losses. Therefore, a Reassured is unlikely to find cover on a normal catastrophe policy for more than two total losses. However, it may be possible to find a Reinsurer who is prepared to quote at inception a policy to pay, say, the third or the third and fourth total losses, and Reassureds who desire this can normally buy the cover.

Alternatively, a Reassured can wait until his catastrophe cover has paid one total loss and then buy a second reinstatement or third loss cover. At that moment of time the second reinstatement has become a first reinstatement, due to the occurrence of the first loss. Therefore, the premium for the reinstatement will be considerably higher than if he had purchased a third loss at inception.

ARTICLE 12

> *Excess of Loss Reinsurance. This Agreement in no way applies to protect any liability of the Company other than that in respect of its direct underwriting, cessions under reinsurance treaties or pooling agreements, and acceptances of specific reinsurances. Liability in respect of Excess of Loss Reinsurances is excluded from the protection of this Agreement and cannot be taken into account in arriving at the amount of excess of which liability attaches hereto.*

This is another standard clause on all catastrophe contracts protecting a direct writing company's account. The reason behind the excess of loss reinsurance exclusion is quite simple. When a catastrophe contract protects direct underwriting and pro rata reinsurance, the reinsurance rate is charged upon a pro rata premium income. Where the Reassured's account contains excess of loss reinsurance, the original premium income will be considerably reduced without necessarily a reduction in liability. At best the inclusion of excess of loss reinsurance in the original business distorts the balance between exposure and rate. At worst it can leave the Reinsured with a very considerable increased exposure with less premium:

Assume Company "A" reinsured an 80% Q.S. treaty with Company "B" and Company "A" has a premium income of 200,000 and suffers a single catastrophe loss of 100,000. Company "B"s position is:

G.N.W.P.I.	160,000
His share of the loss:	80,000

Company "C" reinsures Company "B" for 90% of the excess of 50,000, each loss occurrence at a rate of 2% of Company "B"s g.n.w.p.i.

Company "C"s position is:

Premium $2\% \times 160{,}000 = 3{,}200$

Loss 90% of $30{,}000 \times 50{,}000$ or 27,000

Assume now that Company "B"s contract with Company "A" is itself an excess of loss contract for 100% of 80,000 x 20,000 at a rate of 10%. Company "B"s position is:

G.N.W.P.I. $10\% \times 200{,}000 = 20{,}000$

Loss 80,000

Company "C"'s position as Reinsurer of Company "B" now becomes:

Premium 2% of 20,000 = 400
Loss 80% of 30,000 × 50,000 = 27,000

The loss to Company "C", is identical but the premium he receives is only ⅛th.

Of course, examples can be chosen to show an opposite case but, in the vast majority of cases, an excess of loss on an excess of loss account is a much more dangerous and vulnerable proposition than an excess of loss on a pro rata account. Thus the excess of loss reinsurance clause.

ARTICLE 13

Extended Expiration Clause. If this Agreement should expire or be terminated while a loss occurrence covered hereunder is in progress it is understood and agreed that, subject to the other conditions of this Agreement, the Reinsurer hereon is responsible as if the entire loss or damage had occurred prior to the expiration of this Agreement, provided that no part of that loss occurrence is claimed against any renewal of this Agreement.

If a "loss occurrence" commences within the period of the contract and continues after the expiry date, then this clause makes the total "loss occurrence" collectible as if it all fell within the contract. It should be noted that with an hours clause limitation to a "loss occurrence", should a catastrophe start within one contract and continue into its renewal, and should that catastrophe be divided into two or more "loss occurrences", then separate "loss occurrences" from the same catastrophe can be collected in some circumstances. A nice little case could be made out for a contract expiring at midnight on 31st December and renewed at 00 on 1st January.

A catastrophe starts at midnight on 25th December and ends on 7th January. A Reassured could collect four "loss occurrences", two on each contract under the 72-hours clause:

(1) 26th, 27th and 28th December

(2) 29th, 30th and 31st December

(3) 1st, 2nd and 3rd January

(4) 4th, 5th and 6th January, It is a nice little situation which this wording could allow.

ARTICLE 14

Underwriting Policy. The Company undertakes not to introduce any change in its established acceptance and underwriting policy in respect of the classes of business to which this Agreement applies without prior approval of the Reinsurer and any reinsurance arrangements relating thereto shall be maintained or be deemed to be maintained unaltered for the purpose of this Agreement.

This clause is not always contained in a catastrophe contract in this form because of the difficulties which can arise in its application. What constitutes "a change in its established acceptance and underwriting policy"? Presumably it would be held to mean a significant alteration in policy but not, for example, a minor adjustment in reclassifying its acceptance limits.

However, most catastrophe contracts normally contain a warranty relating to a change of underwriting practices, or a material increase in a Reassured's line limits, or a reduction in reinsurance protection.

In my view the Reinsurer is entitled to know if his Reassured makes a material change in his underwriting which increase the exposure to the catastrophe contract significantly and is entitled to ask for renegotiation if he considers he is prejudiced. Thus a clause like this is vital.

ARTICLE 15

Notification of Claim. The Company undertakes to advise the Reinsurer as soon as possible of any circumstances likely to give rise to a claim hereunder together with an estimate of the Reinsurer's liability and thereafter keep the Reinsurer fully informed of any developments regarding the claim and the Reinsurer shall not be liable for any claim of which it has not been advised by the Company before the expiry of one year from the date upon which the Company received the first notice of any loss resulting in such a claim.

A Reinsurer is entitled to have prompt advice, not only of a claim against his contract but also of any circumstances likely to give rise to a claim. For example, if a natural disaster occurs it may be some time before a Reassured can estimate his eventual liability but he will know fairly quickly whether he is likely to be involved significantly or not. If he is likely to be involved he will notify his Reinsurers and keep them informed of developments as they arise.

ARTICLE 16

Loss Settlement. All loss settlements made by the Company, provided same are within the terms of the original policies and within the terms of this Agreement, shall be unconditionally binding upon the Reinsurer and amounts falling to the share of the Reinsurer shall be payable by them upon reasonable evidence of the amount paid being given by the Company.

The settlement of losses is left to the Reassured and his settlement is unconditionally binding upon his Reinsurers, provided such settlements are within the terms of the original policies and within the terms of the reinsurance agreement.

Here one must distinguish between a loss settlement and a claim settlement. Settlement of a loss implies that the Reassured has suffered a loss within the original policy terms. However, settlement of a claim may well be a settlement to dispose of a claim which is not a loss to the Reassured within the terms of the original policy. Where such claim settlements are made without admission of liability, they are not normally binding upon Reinsurers and would require their specific agreement before they can become part of the Reassured's ultimate net loss. Where a Reassured has such cases and wishes his reinsured to contribute to them, it would be wise for him to keep his Reinsurers advised and to ask whether they wish to co-operate in such claims settlements or agree with them. Normally catastrophe contracts do not contain claims co-operation clauses. The 10% coinsurance clause and the clause making a Reinsurer only liable for loss settlements within the original policy conditions render them unnecessary.

ARTICLES 17, 18, 20 and 21

Most catastrophe contracts will contain an arbitration clause, a books and records clause, an intermediary clause and a right to terminate in the event of war or insolvency. These clauses are common to other reinsurance contracts.

ARTICLE 19

Rates of Exchange. For the purpose of this Agreement currencies other than the currency in which this Agreement is written shall be converted into such currency at the rates of exchange used in the Company's books or where there is a specific remittance for a loss settlement at the rates of exchange used in making such remittance.

A normal procedure is for currency conversions to be made at rates of exchange used in the Reassured's books. In other words, the Reinsurers follow the settlements of the Reassured. However, the effect of varying rates of exchange upon a catastrophe contract can be difficult and complicated and at this point we should delve into some of them just a little.

Assume that a catastrophe contract is expressed in Sterling as follows:

90% of £ 100,000 × £50,000
M & D £8,000 adj. @ 2% g.n.w.p.i., the g.n.w.p.i. being estimated at £500,000.

When the contract is negotiated the D.Mk. rate of exchange is 6 Mks. = £1 Sterling and the Min. & Dep. premium is paid at inception.

Translating the Sterling policy into terms of D.Mks. at inception, i.e. using 6 D.Mks. = £1 we have:
90% of D.Mk. 600,000 × D.Mks. 300,000
M & Dep. D.Mks. 48,000 adj @ 2% g.n.w.p.
estimated g.n.w.p.i. D.Mks. 3,000,000.

Now assume the rate of exchange becomes 9 Mks. = £1

On the premium side a 2% rate on D.Mks. 3,000,000 on adjustment will produce D.Mks. 60,000 or £6,667 which is less than the minimum premium already paid.

If a loss should occur the D.Mk. deductible has increased 50% and a loss of D.Mks. 400,000 previously collectable is now below the deductible. Because of the exchange movement the Reassured has been penalised by paying more premium for a contract which is less exposed. However, the Reassured is not seriously affected by the change in the deductible and the limit because the loss in his own account is in Sterling and at the same rate of exchange as his contract recovery. He has, however, paid a penalty Min. & Dep. premium.

Now turn to the opposite movement where the rate of exchange changes from D.Mks. 6 = £1 to D.Mks. 4 = £1. A loss of D.Mks. 300,000 previously uncollectable is now worth £75,000 and a collection of 90% of £25,000 can be made. On the premium side adjustment will be at 2% on £750,000 or £15,000. The Reinsurer will obtain a higher Sterling premium for a contract which is now, however, considerably more exposed to loss.

The lesson to be learned from this is that wherever possible deductibles and limits should be expressed in terms of the currency of the country of origin of the business. If this is not done then the relationship of deductible and limits to exposure will change.

However, it may not be reasonable to expect a Reassured who accounts in £s to have a catastrophe contract in original currency, particularly where there are many of them. In such cases special rates of exchange clauses are sometimes built into contracts to deal with currency fluctuations greater than, say, 10% and automatically reconverting the Sterling limits of the deductible and limit of the policy. For example:

> In the case where the rate of exchange moved from 6 to 4 D.Mks. the deductible and limit would be changed from £100,000 × £50,000 to £150,000 × £75,000, thus preserving the original ratio of limit, deductible and premium.

The Reassured, accounting in Sterling, suffers a larger Sterling loss against which, of course, his total D.Mk. premium income has increased from £500,000 to £750,000.

A currency stability clause such as above is often used where a Reassured feels that the currency concerned, i.e. the currency in which the contract deductible and limits are expressed, is a weak one in relation to the currencies in which the original exposures have been assumed.

We have considered, at some length, some of the problems of excess of loss catastrophe contracts and most of the clauses in such contracts. In the next chapter we will discuss the information needed and the way in which the terms of such contracts are decided.

(RJK (B) LLOYD'S — AUGUST 1969)

PHYSICAL DAMAGE EXCESS LOSS WORDING

Reinsurance Agreement No. ████ *made between*

called the Company) and *(hereinafter*

(hereinafter called the Reinsurer).

ARTICLE 1 *Term of Agreement. This agreement shall apply to losses occurring during the period commencing the* __________ __________________ *and ending the* ____________________.

ARTICLE 2 *Territory. This agreement shall apply to losses occurring within ______________________.*

ARTICLE 3 *Classes of Policies or Perils Covered. This agreement shall apply to all policies and binders of insurance and reinsurance written by the Company covering the following:*

ARTICLE 4 *Exclusions. This agreement does not cover any liability assumed by the Company on the following:*
War and Civil War Exclusion Clause (as attached)
Nuclear Exclusion Clause (as attached)

ARTICLE 5 *Insuring Clause. The Reinsurer hereby agrees to indemnify the Company for ____% of that part of its ultimate net loss which exceeds ________________ on account of each and every loss occurrence and the sum recoverable under this agreement shall be up to but not exceeding ____% of ________________ultimate net loss on account of each and every loss occurrence (subject to the provisions of Article 11).*

The balance of ____% of the excess ultimate net loss together with the first ________________ shall be retained net by the Company and not reinsured in any way. However, it is understood and agreed that the Company have an underlying reinsurance for ____% of ________________ each and every loss occurrence, recoveries under which shall be disregarded in computing the ultimate net loss hereunder.

ARTICLE 6 *Definition of Loss Occurrence. The words "loss occurrence" shall mean all individual losses arising out of and directly occasioned by one catastrophe. However, the duration and extent of any "loss ocurrence" so defined shall be limited to:*

(a) 72 consecutive hours as regards a hurricane, a typhoon, windstorm, rainstorm, hailstorm and/or tornado

(b) 72 consecutive hours as regards earthquake, seaquake, tidal wave and/or volcanic eruption

(c) 72 consecutive hours and within the limits of one City, Town or Village as regards riots, civil commotions and malicious damage

(d) 72 consecutive hours as regards any "loss

occurrence" which includes individual loss or losses from any of the perils mentioned in (a), (b) and (c) above

(*e*) *168 consecutive hours for any "loss occurrence" of whatsoever nature which does not include individual loss or losses from any of the perils mentioned in (a), (b) and (c) above.*

and no individual loss from whatever insured peril, which occurs outside these periods or areas, shall be included in that "loss occurrence".

The Company may choose the date and time when any such period of consecutive hours commences and if any catastrophe is of greater duration than the above periods, the Company may divide that catastrophe into two or more "loss occurrences", provided no two periods overlap and provided no period commences earlier than the date and time of the happening of the first recorded individual loss to the Company in that catastrophe.

Notwithstanding the above, as regards loss or losses from collapse caused by weight of snow and water damage from burst pipes and/or melting snow, the Company shall have the option to deem any one "loss occurrence" to be the aggregate of all such individual losses which occur during a period of 168 consecutive hours within one continent. No period may commence earlier than the date and time of the happening of the first recorded individual loss to the Company in that "loss occurrence" and the periods of two or more "loss occurrences" may not overlap. It is understood and agreed however, that if the Company exercises the option set out in this paragraph then the amount in excess of which this agreement attaches shall be increased for the "loss occurrence" or "loss occurrences" involved by the greater of £ or % of the Company's premium income for the period from to

ARTICLE 7 *Ultimate Net Loss. The term "ultimate net loss" shall mean the sum actually paid by the Company in respect of any "loss occurrence" including expenses of litigation, if any, and all other claims expenses of the Company (excluding, however, office expenses and salaries of officials of the Company) but salvages and recoveries, including recoveries due from all other reinsurances,* *other than underlying reinsurances provided for herein, shall be first deducted from such loss to arrive at the amount of liability, if any, attaching hereunder.*

All salvages, recoveries or payments recovered or received subsequent to any loss settlement hereunder shall be applied as if recovered or received prior to the aforesaid settlement, and all necessary adjustments shall be made by the parties hereto. Nothing in this clause,shall be construed to mean that a recovery cannot be made hereunder until the Company's net loss has been ascertained.

ARTICLE 8 *Net Retained Lines. This agreement shall only protect that portion of any insurance or reinsurance which the Company, acting in accordance with its established practices, retains net for its own account. Reinsurer's liability hereunder shall not be increased due to an error or omission which results in an increase in the Company's normal net retention nor by the Company's failure to reinsure in accordance with its normal practice, nor by the inability of the Company to collect from any other Reinsurer any amounts which may have become due from them whether such inability arises from the insolvency of such other Reinsurer or otherwise.*

ARTICLE 9 *Premium Clause. The Company shall pay a deposit premium of ____________________ at the inception of this Agreement. As soon as possible after the expiry of this Agreement, the above deposit premium shall be adjusted to an amount equal to a rate of ____ % applied to the Company's premium income as defined hereunder, subject, however, to a minimum premium of ____________________ . The payment of any adjustment due between the parties being made at once.*

ARTICLE 10 *Definition of Premium Income. The term premium income shall mean the gross premium written by the Company on business protected hereunder during the period of this Agreement, less only return premiums and premiums paid for re-insurances recoveries under which inure to the benefit hereof.*

ARTICLE 11 *Reinstatement. In the event of any portion of the indemnity given hereunder being exhausted, the amount exhausted shall be automatically reinstated from the time of commencement of any loss occurrence to the expiry of this agreement and an additional premium, calculated at*

100% of the premium hereunder, for the period from the date of such reinstatement to the expiry of this Agreement shall be paid by the Company upon the amount of such loss, but nevertheless the Reinsurer's liability shall never be more than the limit of liability as stated in Article 5 in respect of any one loss occurrence nor more than twice that amount in all during the term of this Agreement, representing one reinstatement only of the above limit of liability.

ARTICLE 12 *Excess of Loss Reinsurance. This Agreement in no way applies to protect any liability of the Company other than that in respect of its direct underwriting, cessions under reinsurance treaties or pooling agreements, and acceptances of specific reinsurances. Liability in respect of Excess of Loss Reinsurances is excluded from the protection of this Agreement and cannot be taken into account in arriving at the amount of excess of which liability attaches hereto.*

ARTICLE 13 *Extended Expiration Clause. If this Agreement should expire or be terminated while a loss occurrence covered hereunder is in progress it is understood and agreed that, subject to the other conditions of this Agreement, the Reinsurer hereon is responsible as if the entire loss or damage had occurred prior to the expiration of this Agreement, provided that no part of that loss occurrence is claimed against any renewal of this Agreement.*

ARTICLE 14 *Underwriting Policy. The Company undertakes not to introduce any change in its established acceptance and underwriting policy in respect of the classes of business to which this Agreement applies without prior approval of the Reinsurer and any reinsurance arrangements relating thereto shall be maintained or be deemed to be maintained unaltered for the purpose of this Agreement.*

ARTICLE 15 *Notification of Claim. The Company undertakes to advise the Reinsurer as soon as possible of any circumstances likely to give rise to a claim hereunder together with an estimate of the Reinsurer's liability and thereafter keep the Reinsurer fully informed of any developments regarding the claim and the Reinsurer shall not be liable for any claim of which it has not been advised by the Company before the expiry of one year from the date upon which the Company received the first notice of any loss resulting in such a claim.*

ARTICLE 16 *Loss Settlement. All loss settlements made by the Company, provided same are within the terms of the original policies and within the terms of this Agreement, shall be unconditionally binding upon the Reinsurer and amounts falling to the share of the Reinsurer shall be payable by them upon reasonable evidence of the amount paid being given by the Company.*

ARTICLE 17 *Inspection. The Reinsurer may at any time during normal office hours inspect and take copies of such of the Company's records and documents which relate to business covered under this Agreement. It is agreed that the Reinsurer's right of inspection shall continue as long as either party has a claim against the other arising out of this Agreement.*

ARTICLE 18 *Arbitration.*

(1) All disputes arising out of the above Agreement or concerning its interpretations or validity whether arising before or after its termination shall be referred to a Court of Arbitration which shall consist of two Arbitrators who shall be active or retired officials of Companies or Underwriters carrying on a similar type of insurance or reinsurance business to that covered hereunder; one to be appointed by each party, and an Umpire who shall be appointed by the Arbitrators immediately after they themselves shall have been appointed and in the event of the Arbitrators being unable to reach agreement on the reference the Umpire shall forthwith enter on the reference in lieu of the Arbitrators.

(2) If either of the appointed Arbitrators for any reason whatsoever fails to act for the party by whom he was appointed shall by writing appoint an Arbitrator in his place and if either party fails to appoint an Arbitrator within one month after being requested by the other party in writing to do so, or in the event of the Arbitrators failing to agree as to the appointment of the Umpire within one month after their own appointment such Arbitrator or Umpire as the case may be shall be appointed in writing by the Secretary General for the time being of the Court of Arbitration of the International Chamber of Commerce at the written request of either party.

(3) *The Arbitrators or Umpire as the case may be shall determine any reference in accordance with current reinsurance market practice pertaining during the period of this Agreement and in making their award shall at the same time decide as to the payment of the cost of the arbitration.*

(4) *The Court of Arbitration shall take place in the country in which the head office of the defendant party is situated and the law applicable to both the aforesaid Agreement and this arbitration agreement shall be the law of that country.*

(5) *This arbitration agreement shall be construed as a separate and independent contract between the parties hereto and arbitration hereunder shall be a condition precedent to the commencement of any action at law.*

ARTICLE 19 *Rates of Exchange. For the purpose of this Agreement currencies other than the currency in which this Agreement is written shall be converted into such currency at the rates of exchange used in the Company's books or where there is a specific remittance for a loss settlement at the rates of exchange used in making such remittance.*

ARTICLE 20 *Intermediaries. Messrs. ________________________ are recognised as the intermediary negotiating this Agreement, through whom all communications relating thereto shall be transmitted to both parties.*

ARTICLE 21 *Termination.*

(1) *Either party shall have the right to terminate this Agreement immediately by giving the other party notice:*

(a) *If the performance of the whole or any part of this Agreement be prohibited or rendered impossible de jure or de facto in particular and without prejudice to the generality of the preceding words in consequence of any law or regulation which is or shall be in force in any country or territory or if any law or regulation shall prevent directly or indirectly the remittance of any or all or any part of the balance of payments due to or from either party.*

(b) If the other party has become insolvent or unable to pay its debts or has lost the whole or any part of its paid up capital.

(c) If there is any material change in the ownership or control of the other party.

(d) If the country or territory in which the other party resides or has its head office or is incorporated shall be involved in armed hostilities with any other country whether war be declared or not or is partly or wholly occupied by another power.

(e) If the other party shall have failed to comply with any of the terms and conditions of this Agreement.

(2) All notices of termination served in accordance with any of the provisions of this Article shall be addressed to the party concerned at its head office or at any other address previously designated by that party.

(3) In the event of this Agreement being terminated at any date other than that stated in Article 1 then the premium due to the Reinsurer shall be calculated upon the premium income of the company up to date of termination or pro rata temporis of the annual minimum premium, whichever is the greater. The rights and obligations of both parties to this Agreement shall remain in full force until the effective date of termination.

Chapter IX

CATASTROPHE — EXCESS OF LOSS CONTRACTS *(continued)*

Fixing deductibles — Fixing limits — Fixing the price — Aggregate deductibles on catastrophe contracts — Multi-year contracts — Financial markets response

In the last chapter we dealt with the wording and problems related to catastrophe contracts. In this chapter I shall deal with the various considerations relating to the terms of such contracts and some of the underwriting detail. I must emphasise that my views will colour this chapter and there will be plenty of opportunity to tear me to pieces if you so desire. Bear in mind that I am dealing with catastrophe contracts for direct writing companies.

Fixing the Deductible

A Reassured wishing to purchase catastrophe cover will normally select the deductible he considers most suitable for his needs. In asking for quotations he will probably seek a number of alternatives, again in a range that will suit his needs. The final decision as to which he chooses will often be a compromise between the deductible he wants and the price he can afford or wishes to pay.

In general terms catastrophe deductibles should relate to a Reassured's resources (i.e. his surplus), his premium income and his maximum net line on a single risk and his profitability. Firstly, the deductible will normally be set at a figure in excess of the maximum net retention on a single risk. Secondly, it will be set at a figure which prevents a single disaster affecting the results of his account too adversely, or prevents an underwriting loss which would need funding from a Reassured's assets, or profits if any, on other parts of his trading.

A small company, writing only fire department business, has a net written premium income of 1,000,000. It has a pro rata treaty to limit its maximum net line to 10,000 or 1% of its premium income. It is adequately reserved and has a surplus of 500,000 reasonable investment income and its normal underwriting profit is around 5%.

The sort of thought process goes like this ... "On an ordinary fire I lose 1% of my premium income. A fluctuation of 5% would lose me my profit, which is not too serious. Therefore a deductible of 50,000 looks sensible. However, 1 will have to bear 10% coinsurance and I could have two disasters in a year so I will ask for quotations in excess of 40,000, as alternatives — 50,000 and 75,000. Even. 100,000 might be worth considering. It would take away my year's profit plus most of my investment income. A 100,000 deductible is really too high for comfort, particularly with 10% coinsurance excess of 100,000 and a possible second loss. I might have to take a chance if it saves me considerable premium".

The correct procedure for a Reassured to take is to work out for himself the deductible that makes him feel reasonably secure in relation to his assets, surplus and profitability, both on underwriting and investment, and then to modify his requirements as necessary to cope with the price. The contrary of say, "I can afford 'x' for catastrophe protection, what can I buy?" is, I am sure, a snare and a delusion.

A larger company may do its calculation firstly department by department, relating the deductible in the first place to the specific department's net lines on a risk, its department's underwriting profit in normal non-catastrophic years, that department's premium income and most important point the point at which the department's Underwriters feel secure and happy; they will need to have a feeling of balance on their account. It must be emphasised that one main purpose of reinsurance is specifically to give Underwriters reassurance to allow them to underwrite without too much worry and to sleep at night and not to impair their normal functions as loving spouses. Secondly, the deductible will be related to the company's overall profitability, surplus and assets.

In fixing deductibles for catastrophe protection, the tendency can be to fix it high when, things are good. With a good profit plus a good surplus and a strong investment income, a company can obviously afford a high deductible. When times are hard, a lower deductible is desirable because there is less money to play with. This, although logical, can be unsound. When things are good, it is the time to pay out a big premium. After all, it is tax deductible! When times are rough a company can least afford a big premium. It may, therefore, make sense to buy more reinsurance at a lower deductible in good times.

It may be that the catastrophe contract may suffer no losses and the higher premium may merely increase Reinsurer's affluence, but given a good Reinsurer, who gives continuity, the accumulated premiums will act as a bank or sinking fund which can be drawn upon when. times are hard, either to pay losses or to improve the protection.

Fixing the Limit of the Policy

Here again, this is the Reassured's prerogative and the amount of cover purchased will be dictated by a combination of need and price. The same argument applies as above. When things are going well, this is often the time to buy maximum cover. Firstly, the premium can be afforded more easily when a Reassured's account is profitable, and with a good Reinsurer the premium is not really "lost". Secondly, when things are going well, one often finds that more cover is available from the reinsurance market and, in good times, the price may be more reasonable.

There is another advantage in this philosophy; Reinsurers are mostly human and mostly loyal to their clients. When times turn difficult and a reinsurance market contracts, it may be very difficult and costly to buy new cover in such a market. However, if the cover is in existence and is being renewed, Reinsurers will normally give it priority over new business. In difficult times Reinsurers' capacity will be kept for old friends.

Therefore, a wise adage is to buy extra cover when you can afford it in good times and not wait until the hard times. Do not forget that when you are making profits a reinsurance premium is tax deductible. However, if it has to be paid out of assets, because you have no profits, it is not tax deductible.

After that little piece of Brokers' propaganda let us turn to deciding the cover required by a Reassured. Firstly. there is almost invariably a tendency on the part of direct writing companies to underestimate their potential exposure to catastrophic losses. Direct Underwriters are often optimists in relation to their own underwriting; perhaps they have to be to continue their hazardous trade. Financial directors also have a nasty tendency to regard catastrophe premiums as money down the drain. Funnily enough, one often finds that where a board of directors of a company are consulted, the non-executive directors take a more realistic view than the Underwriters themselves.

Let us assume that a Reassured is offered a new catastrophe layer of cover of 1,000,000 at a premium of 30,000. The Underwriter will argue that he cannot possibly need it and anyway he cannot afford 30,000. A Banker on the board will say, "If you can get a line of credit for 3% (with 2 losses — 1½%) don't be a fool, take it". A farmer on the board will say, "I'd feel safer lad if you took it".

Now to the nitty gritty. The only way to try and calculate the catastrophe cover you need as a direct writing company is to work out your liabilities and then work out the worst that can happen to them. Do not work on premium income. Think of all the worst possibilities — a major earthquake with fires and floods following; a major hurricane or windstorm; a major explosion spreading through an industrial complex through sympathetic explosions; fires in a high wind or the explosion of a heavier than air vapour that has filled low ground throughout a complex before exploding; a riot blazing up in a city; a 747 bouncing and exploding; forest fires — then consider your sums insured in the widest possible area that can be affected and estimate the maximum percentage damage that could be suffered in that area from the eventuality.

2000 Note

There are now many computer modelling companies which sell their services to help insurance companies analyse their exposure from various catastrophic events. They take into account such things as return periods of certain events, the class of insurance business written, the age and type of construction of the property and the exact location of the property etc. These are very useful tools for the insurance companies and also Reinsurers. However, it is always difficult to predict the actual event. For example, in 1998 Canada had a large icestorm, whereas most people were concerned in that territory of an earthquake or windstorm. Furthermore, in 1998 many insurance companies in Indonesia suffered catastrophic claims from riot losses partly caused by the political instability in the region. In some cases these riot losses affected all layers of the catastrophe programme. These layers were only rated by many Reinsurers for earthquake and windstorm with little or no consideration given for riot. That will now change.

Let us take earthquake as an example. It is probably the most difficult of all to estimate because of its widespread area of devastation and the possibility of fire in addition to the shock. Assume there is an island in an earthquake prone area, with a known fault line running through it. You, as a company, have a fire department premium income of 200,000 and each policy includes earthquake and fire following, and 80,000 of that premium income is close to that fault line and very little of your business is from truly earthquake resistant construction. Of course, if you know your actual liabilities, use them. If you do not log your liabilities you will be able to estimate your average rate, which, for this exercise, we will take as .50%. This gives a liability of 16,000,000 close to the fault line and 24,000,000 of liability further away.

Assume that a major shock along the fault could do 40% damage close to the fault and 10% away from the fault, we have a maximum probable loss of:

40% of 16,000,000 =	6,400,000
plus 10% of 24,000,000 =	2,400,000
	8,800,000

Then think of fire following that quake and, if construction is poor and properties are congested, or have inflammable scrub between them, or there are gas pipelines and other horrors, the extra exposure could be large. For the sake of argument let us assume an extra 10% destruction on the island or:

10% of 40,000,000 or 4,000,000

totalling in all 12,800,000. This is the sort of protection you will need if and when the disaster comes. Compare this with the original premium income of 200,000. We are envisaging a loss of sixty times your premium income.

These figures are not wildly unrealistic and could be matched by actual experience in major disasters and take no account of the next door island or the resulting tidal wave or the breaking of a dam.

Another useful check is to take your percentage share of the insurance business in an area — a state or a country. Let us assume you have 3% of the private houses in a particular state. Let us say that in a major hurricane the authorities and you yourself feel that that state could suffer insured hurricane damage of 2,000,000,000, of which 60% will be on houses. Your potential is:

3% x 60% x 2,000,000,000
or 36,000,000 loss in that State

and do not forget the state next door as well. The process must be repeated for each catastrophic peril in each area.

This sort of exercise may turn out a frightening result but it is better to be frightened than ruined. If it does throw up a frightening potential liability, such an exercise can often make a direct writing company sit down and think through its original underwriting policy with regard to catastrophic exposures. It may need to revise its original rating or institute tougher limits to its aggregate liabilities by areas or to effect quota share reinsurance as well as buying catastrophe protection.

Here I have used a very simple example. In practice, of course, many companies will use more sophisticated figures but even a fairly simple calculation, such as we have made, can at least put the exposure into the right area of magnitude. In dealing with portfolios which include properties other than buildings, one must add to the building totals damage to vehicles, loss of profits, goods in transit, valuables, personal accident losses and never forget that the really large disaster may cross state or country boundaries with ease.

Lastly, always add a factor to take care of any increase in your business and the effect of inflation on your existing liabilities. The probable maximum loss, plus a contingent factor of anything between 10% and 50%, is the cover you want. If it is not obtainable, or if the price is too great, then, as I say, it may mean re-underwriting your account or protecting it by other methods of reinsurance, or both. The easiest and quickest way of doing this is often by a quota share treaty, either on your whole account or of the particular area and classes most exposed.

If price is the essential criterion in purchasing a catastrophe cover it may be better to take a higher deductible and buy more cover. The lack of cover when the ultimate happens may ruin you; the higher deductible is unlikely to do so.

One last word on price and quality. In purchasing catastrophe protection you are buying ultimate "sleep at night" cover. It is no good paying money for such protection if your Reinsurers have slunk off as darkness falls. Like the best prostitutes, you want them in bed with you when dawn arrives, not disappearing with your wallet in the early hours!

The quality of Reinsurers and their financial stability on catastrophe reinsurance is of paramount importance to you, and the higher the layer of protection the more important is the quality of Reinsurers because that is the layer which will have to pay when all the market is stuffed with losses on your lower layers and the lower layers of all other Reassureds. In the words of Kipling's "If" … "If you can keep your head when all about you" … So, vet the security of your Reinsurers on your top layer protection, at least as closely as on your lower layers. It is your money they are taking so make sure they will still be there when you need them.

Fixing the Price

The Reassured chooses his limit and deductible subject to the price he can afford to pay. It is the Reinsurer's prerogative to fix the price at which he is willing to take the risk. No two reinsuring Underwriters will necessarily agree on that price and in a free market the Reassured has to decide which quotation he feels he should accept. It will not necessarily be the cheapest. Very often security and continuity are more important to a Reassured than the cheapest price.

Secondly, at times the cheapest Underwriter may only be able to accept a limited share of the proposition and it may be impossible for the Reassured or his Broker to complete the placing at that price. It is legally possible, of course, and sometimes feasible, to place a layer of catastrophe reinsurance at several different prices. It has been done but it is not to be recommended except in exceptional circumstances and as a temporary measure, unless the consent of all Reinsurers on the policy has been obtained. A Reinsurer will feel aggrieved and very unkindly towards a Reassured who pays him "x" for a share of a policy and 150% of "x" to other Reinsurers for the same share of the same policy.

Now, to turn to practical methods used in rating catastrophe business, the whole procedure boils down to an assessment of future probabilities. It is necessary to know or estimate a Reassured's exposure and the susceptability of those exposures in each area likely to sustain a catastrophic loss and then to calculate the odds of catastrophes of varying severity happening and to apply those odds to the exposures.

To take a relatively simple case of tropical windstorm in Australia firstly, from the study of past meteorological evidence, one first of all calculates the area which a major storm is likely to affect. Let us assume, and it is not an invalid assumption, that most tropical storms hitting the East Coast of Australia are moving NE to South West. As the coast line runs approximately NNW to SSE, storms normally strike the coast approximately at right angles. therefore, each storm will normally strike a limited coastal area. How limited? Well, the diameter of a tropical typhoon or hurricane can be several hundred miles across, but the really destructive winds are around the eye or centre of the storm and rarely exceed a diameter of more than 200 miles, and 100 miles diameter is often enough.

Next, we need a map of the main areas of population or exposures and we could make an assumption that areas with a 200 mile gap between them are unlikely to be both badly hit by the same storm. On Northern and Western coasts the storm moves N to S or NW to SE, so a similar pattern emerges. Then we calculate the possible frequency in each area of major storms and assess the likely percentage damage that a major storm should cause to property and this may mean differentiating between different types of property. Beach front holiday homes will be much more susceptible than well built industrial properties. Wind resistive or tied down roofs will be less susceptible, and so on.

We then apply our odds to the actual sums insured at risk on a particular Reassured's account. Say Darwin is one isolated area with one major storm likely every 30 years, and say damage to private houses is likely to be 40%, and to industrial risks 10%, then we can apply these factors to a Reassured's liabilities.

Assume private house liability of A.$ 2,000,000 — this would give a loss of 40% or	A.$800,000
Assume industrial liability of A.$ 3,000,000 this would add a loss of 10% or	A.$300,000
Total anticipated loss	A.$1,100,000

Such a loss has a frequency of 1:30
Therefore a policy for:
90% of A.$ 1,000,000 × A.$ 100,000
should carry a "risk" premium of A.$ 30,000 which has to be loaded for expenses, error and profit.
A premium of around A.$ 50,000 might be sustainable.

In practice, of course, not every storm will be of the same magnitude and smaller ones may occur more frequently than every 30 years and, in all probability, the premium would have to be increased to, say, A.$ 70,000 to take care of smaller and more frequent storms and for other perils, such as conflagration or riots. The individual company's own experience on past catastrophes will also be a relevant factor and market competition, or lack of it, will also determine the eventual price.

There are so many varying factors by which Underwriters may be influenced but I consider that the method of exposed liabilities and the probability of loss on any account is both a good basic method in determining a premium and also a valuable method of checking the validity of a premium arrived at by other methods.

Following this example, how do we rate the next layer of:

A.$ 1,000,000 x A.$ 1,100,000?

In theory it is above the loss area. However, we have the possibility of a real whopper storm every 100 years or so and the possibility of our calculations being wrong. In addition, we have to consider the cost of writing such a policy. The following, therefore, is a minimum premium situation:

A Reinsurer has to say:

(1) What do I need to cover my expenses; plus
(2) the cost of reserving this capacity;
(3) the chance of the whopper loss;
(4) the fluctuation or inaccuracy of my assumption that large losses will not expose this layer, i.e. the 30 year storm?

The result is the premiums needed which, doing my mental thinking, might be made up as follows:
(1) A.$1,000
(2) A.$3,000
(3) A.$2,000 or one in five hundred years
(4) A.$5,000
Total : A.$11,000
Add a profit and call it A.$12,500
Then compute our two layers:
90% of 1,000,000 x 100,000 at 70,000
90% of 1,000,000 x 1,100,000 at 12,500

The premium for the two layers appears to have the right feel.
Add them together..
90% of A.$ 2,000,000. x A.$ 100,000. Premium A.$82,500.

Then we would have to consider the actual experience. If no storm has occurred for 15 years, and this company has been in existence for 10 years and has never suffered a loss over A.$100,000, then no doubt it will consider itself overcharged if it pays this type of premium. If, on the other hand, it suffered a A.$1,100,000 loss a year ago, it may be extremely lucky to find a Reinsurer to take its reassurance at this price. It requires a brave Insurer, who is very sure of his betting or mathematical odds, to take on a proposition such as — 90% of A.$1,000,000 x A.$100,000, for a premium of A.$70,000 for 1980 if he, or someone else, has just paid a total loss of A.$1,000,000 in 1979.

Of course, the Reinsurer who is sure of his odds and is brave enough to underwrite after a loss rather than before a loss, may well make more money than his rival who does not get his odds right and reduces the premium he charges for a loss-free experience and catches the next loss. The art of catastrophe underwriting has often lain in taking a calculated risk after a high loss has been sustained and, conversely, refraining from taking business after a loss-free period when market pressures, due to optimism, have brought rates down below an economic level. The practice of assessing liabilities and the frequency of catastrophes can at least stop the prudent Underwriter from committing this folly.

However, one must always remember that because a catastrophe occurred in 1979, the odds of it occurring in 1980 can be unaltered. Sometimes the odds can shorten; a major riot in one city can tend to spark off similar riots elsewhere. A major earthquake may have released pressures and thus reduce the probability of future earthquakes in the same fault, or it could increase pressures in other faults or further along the same fault.

To sum up:

(a) *from a Reassured's standpoint* — catastrophe protection purchased from stable markets you know and trust is the best form of investment for the future, particularly if the tax man pays a substantial part of the cost. Never underestimate the potential loss to your account, work out your maximum potential exposure on the liabilities you have. If price is a criterion consider a higher retention or deductible rather than a smaller cover,

(b) *from a Reinsurer's standpoint* — calculate the premiums you charge on your estimates of potential exposures and loss frequencies. Do not be misled by a few years loss free experience unsupported by changes in the risk or by other people's price. Log your exposures and potential losses by areas to obtain a balanced book. Keep your own liabilities at a level which you can afford to pay in each area and overall.

Comments 2000

When purchasing a catastrophe programme the main question to ask is how much cover do I need. The answer will depend not only on the exposures the company has, the financial strength of the company but also the philosophy of the company (and/or the Reinsurance buyer). Company A may wish to purchase the bare minimum of coverage at the cheapest possible price and not to be too bothered by security. Company B however may wish to purchase sufficient catastrophe coverage to be confident that any foreseen disaster will be retained within their catastrophe programme. They would also be extremely concerned about security but not so concerned about price. Hence the price of these two programmes could vary considerably. The larger the size of the catastrophe programme purchased the higher would be the price, as a higher price would be needed to eke out the capacity to complete the programme.

The price charged for each catastrophe layer should be based on the probability of events happening which may affect the relevant layer with a loading for expenses and profit. The pricing will also be distorted by the fact that each layer has a reinstatement premium due in the event of a loss and often lower layers which will give a discount taking this potential extra premium into account. Thus the price will reduce as you go further up the programme due to the reduced probability of the loss affecting the higher layers. The change of these prices is best illustrated graphically. Let us take a fictitious UK catastrophe programme, the structure and prices are shown below:

layer	limit £'000'	deductible £'000'	premium £'000'	R.O.L. %	deductible % income
1	£3,000	£2,000	£612	20.4%	2.0%
2	£5,000	£5,000	£660	13.2%	5.0%
3	£10,000	£10,000	£910	9.1%	10.0%
4	£20,000	£20,000	£1,120	5.6%	20.0%
5	£30,000	£40,000	£990	3.3%	40.0%

The estimated premium income is £100m, which is made up of 80% private dwellings and 20% commercial lines. The loss record is:

event	Incurred claim
87J. Oct 1987 Windstorm	£17,400,000
90A. Jan 1990 Windstorm	£22,504,000
90G Feb 1990 Windstorm	£ 3,370,000
95K Dec 1995 Freeze	£ 2,200,000
97A Jan 1997 Windstorm	£ 3,550,000

What we can do with this programme is to produce a graph by plotting the mid-points of the rate on lines for each layer (which are really percentage probabilities) against a measure of exposure. The best measurement of exposure is the total sums insured for the company in the area of exposure. This figure is often not readily available but the premium income is, which is the next best thing. If the original insurance rates have remained fairly constant then the size of premium income is directly porportional to the sums insured. In 1990 most UK companies lost approximately 37.5% of their premium income from the large windstorm Daria or 90A which occurred on the 25th and 26th of January. This percentage increased for companies with a large private home account and reduced for those with an industrial account. The companies also lost approximately 0.08% of their total sums insured throughout the UK but the total sums insured were not available prior to 90A.

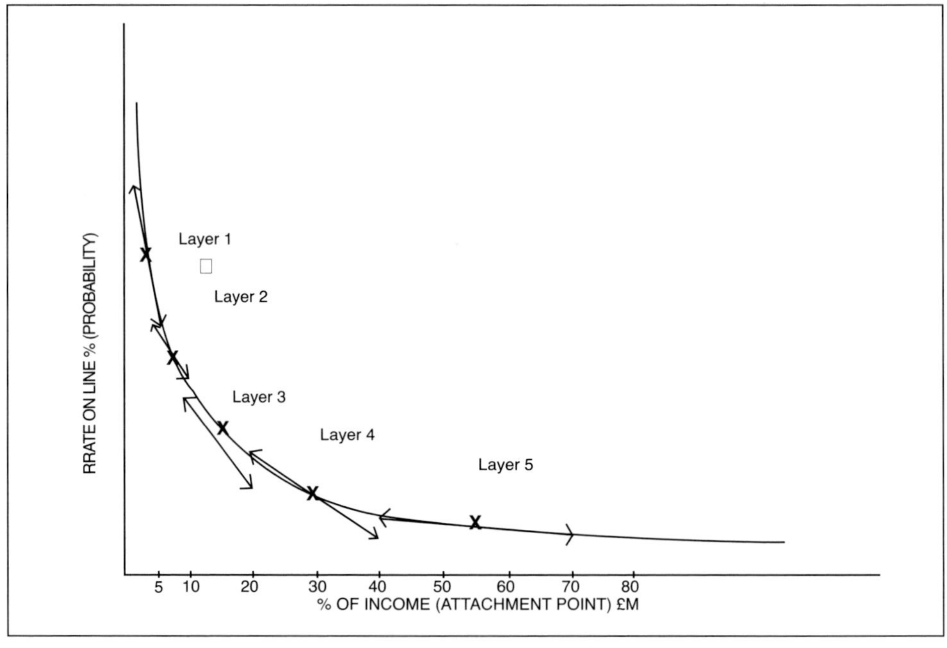

The graph obtained produces a curve with each layer touching the graph at its midpoint. This 'Rate on line' graph will vary slightly for each company. It is probable that some layers do not fit readily to the line of the graph. Why could this be? A new layer may have been purchased after the loss and as it is not in deficit therefore it will be cheaper than the other layers. Conversely another layer may have a large financial deficit so that this layer is paying an above average price. We could plot other UK company's catastrophe programmes on the same graph and we could obtain a comparison between them. This graph would show which programmes appear cheaper. We could use the graph to give a guide of what rate or rate on line to charge for a new layer. These curves can be readily entered in a computer and a rating programme developed.

The market tends to get cheaper following a period of low loss activity and the whole graph although retaining its shape shifts to produce lower rates at the same attachment point. The shape of the curves will vary however dependent on the type of exposure being covered. For example if we were protecting a company in the Midwest USA where the main exposure is an earthquake in the New Madrid fault, then we would produce a very flat graph above a certain level. Such an event is very severe but rare and therefore if the event happened it would exhaust more or all of the layers, hence the price differential is small. At the low level the company may however be affected by localised tornadoes. Compare the two graphs opposite.

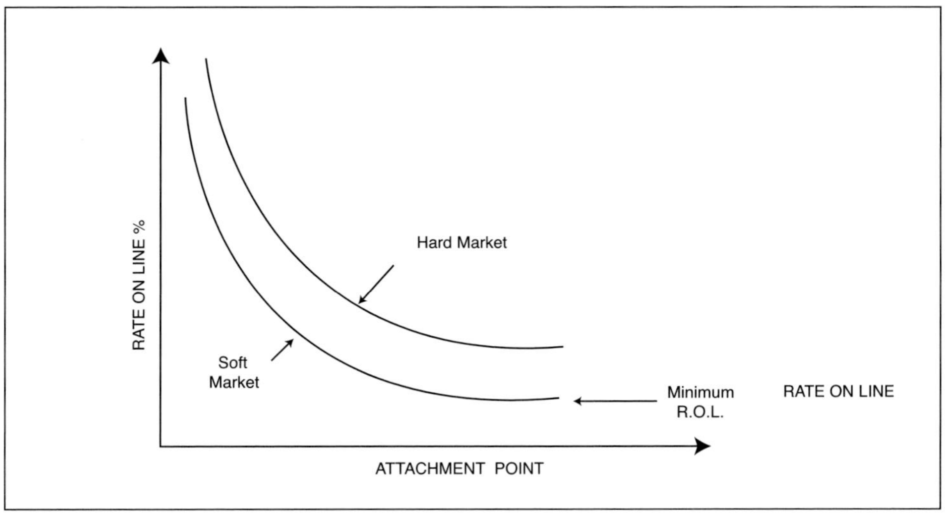

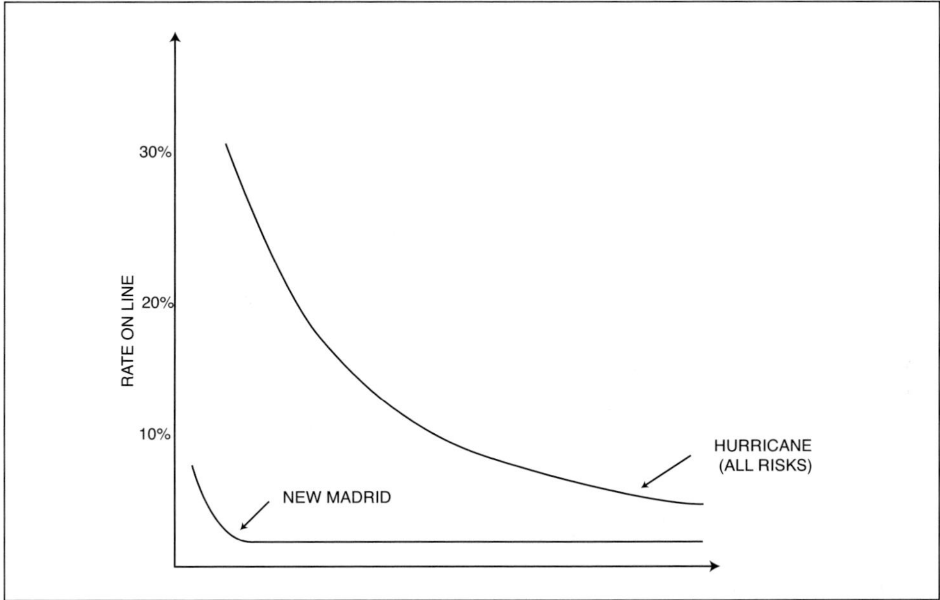

These days, catastrophe models have been developed which can simulate the likely events, and they can be run against the insurance company's own portfolio. These models run many different storm paths for hurricanes or tornadoes and can come up with the suggested prices on each layer of a programme. Hence these models are becoming essential rating tools for catastrophe Underwriters and reinsurance buyers alike.

Use of Aggregate Deductibles on Excess Catastrophe Contracts

In an ideal world the catastrophe contract that a Reassured would like to buy might be as follows.

> Unlimited cover excess of 1,000,000 for the first catastrophe and then excess of 200,000 for the second and subsequent catastrophes.

This means that the Reassured can say … "I can stand 1,000,000 on one catastrophe but if more than one happens then 200,000 is enough on the second and all subsequent ones".

These types of contracts can be placed but Reinsurers look at them with bloodshot eyes. So we turn it round and place the cover as follows:

> Excess of 200,000 each and every loss, with an aggregate deductible on such losses of 800,000.

Reinsurers can then rate the cover excess of 200,000 and give whatever is an appropriate reduction for the fact that they will not pay for the first 800,000 loss to the cover. One loss of 1,000,000 would involve no collections. Two losses of 500,000 i.e. 300,000 x/s 200,000, would involve no collection. Three losses of 500,000, i.e. 300,000 excess of 200,000 three times, would involve a collection of 100,000 x/s 800,000 in the aggregate.

Intelligent use of aggregate deductibles, particularly on low layers of catastrophe programmes, can be very useful. Taking our example a stage further, say we envisage a Reassured who wants protection up to 10,000,000 in respect of any one disaster, we might suggest a programme in 3 layers:

> Top layer 5,000,000 x/s 5,000,000
> 2nd layer 3,000,000 x/s 2,000,000
> 1st layer 1,000,000 x/s 1,000,000

If he worries about the size of the 1,000,000 deductibles on second and subsequent loss, we might suggest, as an alternative to the first layer, that he has a layer of:

> 1,500,000 x/s 500,000 e.e.l. with an aggregate deductible of 500,000.

It will cost him more premium but, after a first loss of 1,000,000 or more, he will collect subsequent losses excess of 500,000 from the ground up, and two losses of 900,000 will give him a recovery of 300,000 from Reinsurers. The rating of such contracts needs care but they are a very useful method of protection.

Multi-Year Catastrophe Excess of Loss Contracts

There has been a demand for catastrophe reinsurance contracts, which last from 3-5 years or in some cases longer.

Why have they developed?

There has been a demand by Reinsurance Managers to stabilise the price of their catastrophe reinsurance cost over a longer period. It has been difficult for Reinsurance Managers to justify to their Financial Officers why the cost of their reinsurance has trebled from one year to another due to predictable catastrophe losses that they have suffered. Whereas the price changes in the insurance market tend not to be as dramatic, they may only have rate increases of say, 10-20% following poor experience. The cost of catastrophe reinsurance following a series of good years however, falls well below the price needed for Reinsurers to make a profit, and some major correction following a major loss is often needed. Some pros and cons for multi-year catastrophe contracts are as follows.

For the Reassured

Pros

1. Predictable pricing over the next few years.

2. No need to spend time renegotiating the contract each year.

3. There may well be a profit commission if the results are profitable for Reinsurers.

4. Will save money if there is a major loss in the first two years, i.e. before the contract is renegotiated.

5. Do not have to worry if contracts are fully placed by the inception of the contract each year.

6. Long term relationship with Reinsurer.

Cons

1. Do not have the in-depth annual review of one's reinsurance needs with Brokers.

2. The price may be more expensive than purchasing on an annual basis when the market is softening.

3. The annual contract can be tailor made more accurately to the portfolio for that year.

For the Reinsurer

Pros

1. Long-term relationship with Reassured guaranteed.

2. No annual negotiation of contract terms necessary.

3. Price cannot fall unless there is a cancellation clause.

Cons

1. No ability to increase the price following major losses in the first two years.

2. Portfolio may change significantly and no amendments or terms. Must have a review clause in order to change these.

3. If you have written the contract at way below the burning cost, you are going to have to wait three years or more to get off!

The Financial Markets Response to Traditional Catastrophe Programmes

The financial or capital markets have always been keen to break into the reinsurance market and have developed many products, which are competing with property catastrophe reinsurance. I quote from an excellent publication *Alternative Risk Financing* published by Jim Bannister Developments Limited and I thank them for letting us publish it.

1. Catastrophe Bonds

The last few years have seen the beginnings of a stronger link between the insurance and capital markets. Essentially by the development of bonds and other vehicles where the returns and, in some cases, the capital is directly related to insurance results of a particular company or more generally to the insurance market sector's results.

Over the last few years a new and innovative type of risk financing has developed and is now making a significant contribution to new catastrophe capacity.

In essence, the catastrophe (or Act of God) bonds are issued by an Insurer or other body. They provide for normal redemption at the end of a pre-determined period, but in the event of a catastrophe that falls within defined limits (e.g. geographic area, type of loss and size of insured loss) the holders of the bonds contribute. This contribution may be the forfeiture of all/part of interest and/or late payment of debt or interest.

Catastrophe bonds, like reinsurance catastrophe options, are not insurance or reinsurance. There is no requirement for insurable interest and they do not provide indemnity against loss. A user has to calculate his own exposure and allow for any difference between that exposure and recovery under options or funding through bonds.

The early bonds were privately placed with limited public knowledge of their existence or terms. In 1996 the attempt to include a US$1.5 billion layer of earthquake risk bonds, within the California Earthquake Authority scheme, attracted much publicity (this layer was ultimately written as conventional reinsurance). Then in 1997 there have been a number of successful issues of catastrophe bonds which have attracted very wide support and the terms have therefore become public.

2. AIG Bonds

The first bond to be widely noted was issued by a dedicated offshore vehicle to support reinsurance of AIG. The total of US$25 million was divided among five separate areas: U.S., Caribbean, Europe, Australia and Japan. It paid an enhanced interest, but the capital was at risk if a loss exceeded a defined level.

3. USAA Bond (United Services Automobile Association)

The bond that attracted most was that issued to cover some of the reinsurance risk of USAA. Some US$477 million was raised in one-year bonds providing US$400 million as the pure bond with US$77 million in zero-interest securities to provide repayment of principal to some bondholders.

The operation is managed by an offshore Reinsurer, Residential Reinsurance Co, in Grand Cayman which reinsures USAA. The US$400 million reinsurance of USAA's exposure to a single hurricane protects 80% of US$500 million excess of US$1 billion and covers 20 Eastern states. USAA retains the other 20% of this US$500 million layer.

There are two separate categories of bond:

1. Class A1 of approximately US$87 million whose interest is protected by the US$77 million zero coupon securities. The risk to bondholders is of payment delayed for up to ten years, when the zero coupon securities mature.

2. Class A2 of US$313 million where the principal is at risk.

The US$400 million made up of US$87 million class A1 and US$313 million class A2 will be in trust and invested in commercial paper.

The differing risk status is reflected in differential rates of interest with A1 receiving the London inter-bank rate LIBOR plus 2.73% and A2 receiving LIBOR plus 5.76%. Both groups lose interest in the event of a loss, but A2 lose principal as well.

Comment

These Bonds are fixed interest investments, which either lose the interest or delay the interest or in some cases lose the capital if a specified catastrophe happens. They are extremely costly to set up, some of them involving opening up offshore companies and also the lawyers, accountants and financial market fees are high. The way the catastrophe element is priced in the initial offerings was in my view high but I am sure this element of the pricing and the fees will fall as the markets become accustomed to them. One advantage is that the price will not vary as much as the catastrophe market and I doubt if it will get as competitive but it opens up a new market and new ideas and in the event of a major catastrophe the extra capacity will be useful. Will it be around after a major disaster? I would have thought so as the investors that have gone into it had their eyes open, but we'll see!

4. Contingent Equity

1996 saw the development of a new hybrid instrument, the Catastrophe Equity Put (CatEPut), which gives the buyer an option to secure additional equity capital at pre-determined interest rates following a defined catastrophe event.

The first transaction for a specialist U.S. property casualty Insurer in Illinois, RLI Corp, was devised by AON Capital Markets and placed with Centre Re. It provides for:

- An option for US$50 million of cumulative convertible preferred shares with payment of an option premium (which was said to cost about 20 to 25% of comparable catastrophe reinsurance). The option can be exercised if a California earthquake exhausts RLI traditional catastrophe reinsurance.

This contract triggers if a major California earthquake exhausts the whole of RLI's catastrophe programme this being the only significant catastrophe exposure they have. The reasoning behind this deal is that it is easier to raise capital before the earthquake than after and the original earthquake rates will become attractive also afterwards.

5. Catastrophe Futures

These were developed by the Chicago Board of Trade futures exchange (CBOT).

Insurance and Reinsurance companies could purchase a futures contract related to catastrophe losses in different USA zones for up to a year ahead. If the market suffered significant losses, which triggered the conditions, of the contract they could recover and it would only cost them the price of the futures option. They could be cheaper than the traditional catastrophe market but because the option is based on market data the Insurer could suffer a large loss and still collect nothing from the option as the market loss was small. Another problem was that they were not very liquid, either plenty of sellers and few buyers or vice versa. For more details see the publication Alternative Risk Financing.

The above either cost a lot of money to set up, are complicated to understand or have a large miss factor that may not be attractive to Insurers. They will get cheaper as the methods and advantages are understood. My own personal point of view is that a traditional catastrophe reinsurance is very simple and flexible. It can compete quite effectively against these products as it can be tailor made with additional features such as profit commission or free reinstatements amended as required. It can also be much cheaper but certainly catastrophe pricing can be volatile.

Chapter X

PROPERTY RISK EXCESSES

Introduction — Term — Policies issued basis (risks attaching) — Ratio of limit and deductible (balance) — Variable limits — Reinstatement and occurrence limits — Risk definition — Advantages and disadvantages of risk excesses — Underwriting factors — Rating methods — Burning cost — Flat rated — First loss scales — Cession contracts — Other options and uses

Introduction

In the last chapter we discussed the classic type of excess of loss reinsurance, that is the protection of a Reassured against a catastrophic loss on his net retention. The application of the excess of loss contract, to give protection to a Reassured within his exposure on an individual risk, seems to have developed somewhat later.

Right away we must distinguish between such a risk excess on, for example, a fire account and an excess of loss on a liability or third party account. The use of the excess of loss method to protect an account against unusually large awards, on individual policies, on third party or similar business, is dealt with in the next chapter. Here, we are concerned with the use of an excess of loss contract to protect an Assured's known retention on first party business. Such a method will be used as an alternative, or a supplement, to the pro rata method, e.g. a quota share or a surplus treaty.

One of the first pioneers who used this excess of loss method was

policies attaching before the inception date of the contract. However, it does cover losses which occur on policies issued or attaching during the contract period whenever those losses occur.

Normally, a risk excess on a policies issue or policies attaching basis would stipulate that the maximum period of an original policy is 12 months plus odd time not exceeding 18 months in all, or is so deemed for the purpose of the contract. Where such a stipulation is not made, then of course the risk excess Reinsurer will continue on risk until the natural expiry dates of the original policies. This could be for a number of years for some types of business, such as builders' or construction risks. We will discuss the effect of these two bases on the contract premium a little later.

Comment

It is rare these days to have 3–5 year risk excesses, they are usually annual but often on a risks attaching basis.

ARTICLES 2, 3 and 4

Territory, classes and exclusions

These set out the territory to be covered, the classes of risk or perils and the exclusions. All these are self-explanatory.

ARTICLE 5

> *Insuring Clause. The Reinsurer hereby agrees to indemnify the Company for 90% of that part of its ultimate net loss which exceeds $20,000 on account of each and every loss each and every risk and the sum recoverable under this agreement shall be up to but not exceeding 90% of $160,000 ultimate net loss on account of each and every loss each and every risk. (Subject to the provisions of Article 11.)*
>
> *The balance of 10% of the excess ultimate loss together with the first $20,000 shall be retained net by the Company and not reinsured in any way.*

The wording follows very closely that used under a catastrophe contract except, of course, the deductible and limit are "on account of each and every loss on each and every risk" and not "on account of each and every loss occurrence". However, you will notice that the contract does contain a limit in respect of each loss occurrence, which is set out in Article 11. You will also notice that a definition of loss occurrence will be required

(Article 6b), a definition of ultimate net loss (Article 7) and a definition of "each and every risk" (Article 6a).

Co-reinsurance

You will see that we have retained the 90% cover feature common to most catastrophe contracts and that the limit of liability at 90% of $160,000 any one risk is 90% of 8 times the deductible of $20,000.

With regard to the first of these two features, the co-reinsurance requirment of 10% and the ratio of cover to deductible, in this case 8:1, the function of co-reinsurance is similar to that described in catastrophe contracts, that is to preserve the partnership between the two parties. However, in the late 1990s, this co-insurance is rarely seen as a risk as much of the 'partnership' seems to have disappeared. The Reassured is looking for the lowest price with no extra retention. Firstly to dampen down any tendency the Reinsured may have to increase his gross exposures on any one risk because he knows he is protected for 100% in excess of a fixed monetary amount. For example, in the past a Reassured has accepted a maximum line of $60,000 on brick built private houses. He requires a contract for $160,000 x $20,000 each loss each risk, because he will write up to $180,000 on a reinforced concrete office building. If his contract is for 100% of $160,000 x $20,000 each loss each risk, he might be tempted to increase his normal $60,000 acceptance on private houses because he bears no part of any loss in excess of $20,000 on those risks.

Secondly, the use of co-insurance is to preserve the basis of partnership as regards loss settlement. As with catastrophe resinsurance, the use of co-reinsurance has a practical advantage in theat Reinsurers can agree to follow the loss settlements of the Reassured without the necessity to agree loss settlements. (See Article 16.)

However, whilst the use of 90% cover or 10% co-reinsurance is normal on catastrophe covers, it is rare on most risk covers and is frequently omitted, particularly when the ratio of the limit per risk to the deductible per risk is low. Let us pursue this a stage further ...

Variable Limits and Deductibles

Our Reassured is going to accept up to $180,000 on reinforced concrete offices — a Class "A" risk — and $60,000 on a brick built private house — a Class "C" risk. It might be reasonable to assume that he would keep net on the office, say $60,000 each and every loss each and every risk and $20,000 on Class "C". In that case we could re-phrase our risk excess to:

Class "A"— $120,000 each and every loss each and every risk x $60,000 each and every loss each and every risk.
Class "C"— $40,000 each and every loss each and every risk x $20,000 each and every loss each and every risk.

Here we are using a variable risk excess where the limit and deductible bear a fixed relation to each other of 2:1 but the monetary limits vary by class of risk. We might just add a couple more classes and rephrase our contract as follows:

		Acceptance limits
		$
Class "A"	$120,000 x $60,000	180,000
Class "B"	$80,000 x $40,000	120,000
Class "C"	$40,000 x £20,000	60,000
Class "D"	$20,000 x $10,000	30,000

Now, in this example, provided the Reassured's acceptance limits are as stated, i.e. the amount of the deductible plus the contract limit, then one of the necessities for co-reinsurance disappears. We have substituted a variable risk excess of 2 lines x 1 line for a fixed limit of 8 lines x/s 1 line.

Therefore, it has become a practice on property risk excesss to dispense with co-reinsurance where the ratio of contract limit per risk is not more than, say, five times the deductible and thus where the Reassured acceptance limit is not more than six times the deductible.

The insurance clause contains a limitation in accordance with Article 11 and it would be logical to discuss this here.

ARTICLE 11

Occurrence Limit. In the event of any portion of the indemnity given hereunder being exhausted, the amount exhausted shall be automatically reinstated from the time of commencement of any loss to the expiry of this Agreement but nevertheless the Reinsurer's liability shall never be more than the limit of liability as stated in Article 5 in respect of any one loss on any one risk, nor more than twice that amount in respect of any one loss occurrence regardless of the number of risks involved.

The occurrence limitation normally limits the policy to pay on one loss occurrence three times the loss limit on any one risk. Now, this limitation per occurrence is of very great importance and needs explanation.

In theory, a risk excess could be rated on its exposures, i.e. a Reinsurer will be told of all the exposures excess of $20,000 and will rate his contract on those exposures. In practice that would mean keeping bordereaux and accounts similar to a first surplus treaty and a very complicated calculation of premium. This can be done and such ceding excess of loss treaties are sometimes placed and these are discussed later.

In practice one great advantage of the risk excess basis of re-insurance is its simplicity. This means that most contracts are either rated at a flat rate percent on the Reassured's gross premium income or they have variable rates, according to the contract experience. Very often such rating will not take into account the possibility of the accumulation of liability from a major catastrophic peril. In any case, the premium developed under a risk excess will be very much less than that which would be payable under a pro rata treaty for the same limits and retention.

The case I have used — a cover of $160,000 x $20,000 each loss each risk — on past records, with no catastrophe losses, might carry a premium rate, of say, 15% of the Reassured's gross premium income. A first surplus treaty for up to 8 lines surplus to $20,000 a risk might well receive 60% of the same Reassured's premium income. On the surplus basis the treaty Reinsurer is being ceded automatically with his share of all catastrophe risk premiums charged to the direct policy holder. On the risk excess basis the Reinsurer is almost certainly not being so paid unless he makes a special charge for it.

Therefore, in practice, an occurrence limit is often used in a risk excess to relieve the Reinsurer of a potential liability for which he has received little or no payment. How serious is this potential liability, and who covers it? The second half of this question is easy to answer. The potential liability in excess of the occurrence limit remains with the Reassured and, of course, could drastically increase his net retained loss if such a disaster happened. A Reassured needs to be aware of this and he should either take out a special policy to protect himself or pay more money for his own net catastrophe cover and purchase additional catastrophe protection.

On the other hand, it may pay a Reassured to negotiate with his excess risk Insurers to delete the occurrence limit for an extra rate or premium. The serious nature of this potential liability needs careful thought. Some catastrophic perils, such as windstorm, normally affect a wide area and cause partial losses, e.g. roof damage, T.V. aerials, to a large number of risks. Riot, flood or water damage often have a similar effect.

Where a Reassured has a first surplus or contributing treaty he will recover such losses on a contributory basis. Where a Reassured has a risk excess the vast majority of these partial losses will fall within the first loss net retention of the Reassured. Therefore, in general terms, with these types of catastrophes, few collections may be made against the risk excess Reinsurers. The major part of the loss falls against the net account of the Reassured and his general catasptrophe Reinsurers.

On other catastrophes, where the damage to individual risks is of a total loss nature, a very different pattern emerges. For example, a conflagration causing total destruction of a number of risks. An earthquake often causes similar total destructive damage. Other examples are bush fires or tornadoes. Where this happens to a Reassured with a first surplus treaty, again, reinsurance recoveries are on a pro rata basis and both the Reassured and his Reinsurers suffer in proportion to their liability.

On a risk excess without an occurrence limit the effect of such catastrophes can be very severe on the risk excess Reinsurers and out of all proportion to the premium they have received. On the other hand, on a risk excess with an occurrence limit the collection from such excess risk Reinsurers will be strictly limited and the loss thrown back to the Reassured's net account can be huge.

A very fine example occurred in the Darwin storm in December 1974. This violent tropical storm caused a great deal of total losses to a large number of properties. Local companies, who reinsured on a risk excess basis, collected very large sums on those excesses as they did not contain any occurrence limits. Where risk excesses contained such occurrence limits, then the loss fell on companies' net accounts and catastrophe Reinsurers. Thus, the distribution of this disaster amongst Reinsurers varied considerably.

ARTICLE 6

> *(a) Definition of one risk. The Company shall be the sole judge of what constitutes one risk but shall act in accordance with its normal underwriting practices as recorded in its underwriting records.*

The definition of one risk is another difficult task. In simpler times a single building within four walls, separated by a fire break from other properties, was one risk. Not a large warehouse with a party wall through the room may be two risks. A factory spread over acres may be regarded as several risks. This definition of one risk gives rise to many problems on surplus treaties and some of these problems are discussed in that chapter.

On risk excesses, the onus of deciding what is “one risk” is almost invariably left to the good sense and direction of the Reassured, who, of course, will mark his own records when the business is accepted. Such records will be available to Reinsurers should a loss occur.

The definition of one risk often leads to disputes as to what is actually one risk. It is quite often entirely at the discretion of the Reinsured (look at the wording). Therefore, it is imperative that the Reinsurer understands what the Reinsured calls one risk and how the markets operate in the country being covered. The original risk definition of one risk being, “any one building or location” is no longer always used.

In the USA for example, policies are often written on an occurrence basis for one insured. Therefore, if there is an earthquake, which affects many locations, the insured and the reinsured will probably refer to the Insured as one risk, although different locations are affected. Therefore Reinsurers have to be on their guard.

ARTICLE 6b

“Loss occurrence” definition

This clause is only necessary where the risk excess contains a loss occurrence limit and should be identical to the definition used in the Reassured’s own catastrophe protection. This clause is commented upon in full in the chapter on catastrophe reinsurance.

ARTICLES 7 and 8

Ultimate net loss and net retained lines clauses

These require no comment here as they are covered in detail in Chapter VIII on catastrophe reinsurance.

ARTICLE 9

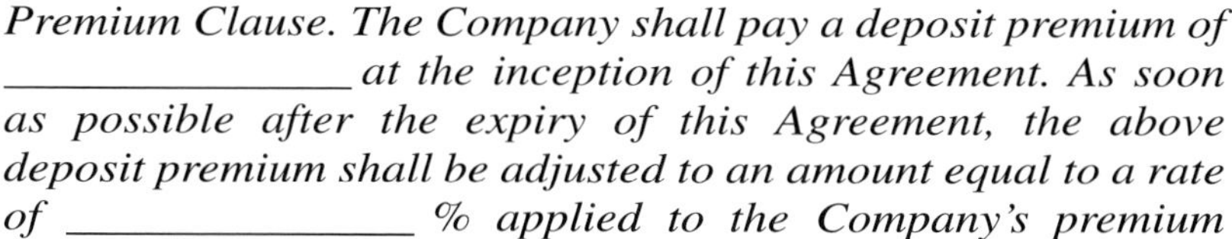

Premium Clause. The Company shall pay a deposit premium of ________________ at the inception of this Agreement. As soon as possible after the expiry of this Agreement, the above deposit premium shall be adjusted to an amount equal to a rate of ________________ % applied to the Company’s premium

approximations and it would not be unusual or unsound to vary the rates somewhat by allowing a small profit commission and setting the rates a little on the high side. For example, instead of 10%, 25% and 40%, we might charge 12%, 30% and 45% with a 25% P.C.

ARTICLE 13

> *Extended Expiration Clause. In the event of non renewal or replacement of this Agreement by the two parties, the Company shall have the option to require Reinsurers to extend this contract by twelve months in respect of losses occurring during this extension period in respect of risks in force at the original termination date of this contract.*
>
> *The Company shall exercise its option by giving notice at least 30 days prior to the original termination date of this contract. The premium for such an extension shall be 135%, the rate stated in Article 10 applied to the premium earned during the extension period on such business. The Company shall pay a deposit premium for this extension calculated at 62½% of the total deposits paid during the previous four quarters, such deposit being paid on the date the extension takes effect.*

This is a clause which applies only to contracts on a loss occurring basis and provides some continuity should a Reassured be unable to renew his risk excess cover. This clause is not commonly used as most Reinsurers dislike it and in practice it is very rare indeed for a Reassured not to be able to obtain coverage albeit at an enhanced rate. However, it is perhaps useful for a Reassured who is embarking on the risk excess method for the first time and is nervous about continuity.

The wording in Article 13 is often varied and sometimes the rate applicable to the run-off is the correct rate itself, but in Article 13 I have used a figure of 135% of the contract rate. The reason for this is that this extension is at the option of the Reassured and he should pay a surcharge if he exercises that option. Also, if the option is exercised, it is likely to be so because of a bad experience.

It is unlikely in the 1990s that the run off coverage would be rated as high as it is in this instance and very often the run-off terms are set at terms to be agreed. This means that if the reinsured opts to run-off the contract, the terms will have to be agreed between the two parties. It would be normal to set the run-off terms at the same adjustable rate on an estimate of the unearned premium for the following 12 months. However, if the experience had been good, more favourable terms may be obtainable and if they are poor, the reverse. It is relatively uncommon for Ceding Companies to opt for run-off as once companies have opted for a risk excess programme, they tend to retain them, unless either the companies close down or pull out of the class of business.

ARTICLE 14

> *Underwriting Policy. The Company undertakes not to introduce any change of in its established acceptance and underwriting policy in respect of the classes of business to which this Agreement applies without prior approval of the Reinsurer and any reinsurance arrangements relating thereto shall be maintained or be deemed to be maintained unaltered for the purpose of this Agreement. In particular, the Company undertakes not to take out any high excess cover on any one risk and all amounts in excess of $180,000 any one risk shall be Reassured on a pro rata basis or so deemed.*

This warranty regarding no higher excess is very important and relates, of course, to the Reassured's underwriting policy. The warranty states that the Reassured will not take out any higher risk excess protection over $180,000 (when the limits and deductibles are variable, as in my classes "A", "B", "C" and "D" previously mentioned, the $180,000 would be reduced for class "B", "C" and "D") and any reinsurance in excess of these figures will be reinsured on a contributing basis, or so deemed.

I think the reader will be aware by this time of the need for this warranty to prevent this risk excess reinsurance becoming a first loss policy itself and thus being unfairly exposed on partial losses.

This underwriting policy clause is relatively uncommon these days, however, it would be normal practice for the Ceding Company to advise the Reinsurer of any major changes to underwriting so that the appropriate changes can be made to the contract by endorsement

ARTICLES 10 and 15 to 21

Miscellaneous clauses

The rest of the Articles in this wording are very similar to those contained in an excess of loss catastrophe contract and have been commented upon in that chapter.

Practicalities of Underwriting

Having discussed the contract wording of a simple flat rated risk excess. We will now consider some of the advantages and disadvantages of risk excesses against proportional treaties. These advantages and disadvantages vary whether one is a Ceding Company or a Reinsurer. We will deal with the Ceding Company first.

Advantages and disadvantages of risk excesses versus Proportional treaties

Ceding Company

Proportional Treaty Advantages

1. Large premium volume — useful for surplus relief or for new companies who have little capital or experience in underwriting.

2. Help stabilise the results of an insurance company as not only does it follow the fortune as far as original rates are concerned but also provides good catastrophe protection. There are generally no occurrence limits under proportional treaties.

3. This is very much a partnership with a Reinsurer and therefore the Reinsurer can give help and advise on the business written.

4. If the results are successful then normally an overrider is obtainable. This can either be an actual overrider worked out, as a percentage of the premium income or it is the difference between the commissions obtained and the actual costs of running the business. This overrider will effectively reduce the overall costs of the company.

5. Generally proportional treaties will give good cash flow for the Ceding Company as the premium is usually paid out quarterly in arrears and cash losses can be made if in between the accounts any exceptional losses occur to the treaty.

6. Generally good continuity with Reinsurers.

Proportional Treaty Disadvantages

1. A large premium volume is paid away to Reinsurers — this may not be acceptable to an insurance company who wants to retain more of their premium income.

2. The administration of a proportional treaty is generally very complicated, needing not only a computer to help prepare the accounts but also to insure the correct cessions to the various treaties. Also, quarterly accounts have to be prepared until the expiration of all risks under the treaty and for a proportional contractor's all risks treaty, this can go on for many years.

Risk Excess Advantages

1. A small premium volume of income is ceded away.

2. Easy administration relative to a proportional treaty.

3. Very flexible — limits can be changed readily — new layers can be either bought above or below the existing programme.

4. More markets will look at risk excess business, rather than proportional business and therefore Ceding Companies can probably obtain a large variety and possibly better terms.

Risk Excess Disadvantages

1. Less continuity although this is helped by a run-off clause.

2. Generally risk excess business is on a losses occurring during basis, whereas a proportional treaty is usually on a risks attaching basis. Therefore in the event of run-off limited coverage may be available to the Ceding Company and the terms may have to be negotiated.

3. Little catastrophe cover is given; generally the occurrence limit is three times the risk limit. Therefore the Ceding Company will have to buy more catastrophe cover.

4. Generally poor cash flow as the premium is paid up at the beginning of the year and losses can only be collected when they become paid.

5. Difficult to revert to pro rata treaties once companies have switched to risk excess. This is because you would have to set up a computer programme to run the pro rata treaty and re-educate people on how to use the proportional treaty. However it is rare that people want to switch back from risk excess to pro rata treaties.

THE REINSURER

Proportional Treaty Advantages

1. A large volume of premium income — fairly stable results.

2. A partnership with the Ceding Company — will probably receive other business as well.

Proportional Treaty Disadvantages

1. Costly to administer.

2. Reinsurance margins generally low.

3. Cash flow poor with accounts generally coming in slow and cash losses being made against the treaties.

4. Can be subject to large catastrophe losses.

5. Unable to get payback following poor loss experience.

Risk Excess Advantages

1. Generally good cash flow with the premium up front and losses only payable when they become paid by the Ceding Company.

2. Able to adjust very rapidly to either poor or good results by changing the rates and conditions at renewal.

3. Very flexible contract can be based on a burning cost basis, a flat rated basis or with aggregate deductibles etc. These will be dealt with later on in the chapter.

4. Generally these contracts are on a 12 months losses occurring during basis and therefore little run-off cover is given and if it is, it can be charged for as appropriate.

Risk Excess Disadvantages

1. The results of these treaties can be extremely volatile, either because the rates charged are too low or else due to a succession of losses, either due to economic conditions or else catastrophic events.

2. Little or no continuity from Ceding Companies.

3. These treaties can be extremely unbalanced, i.e. the contract limit can be in some cases either 10 times or 100 times greater than the limit given; but this is rare on the proportional treaty.

Word of Warning

Risk excesses are not for the unsophisticated and it should not be recommended for small companies, either requiring many lines of reinsurance or else without the experience. I would refer people to the little parable in Chapter 17 (XVII) — "Philosophy Programmes and People". It is much better to start off with a quota share and first surplus treaty and then as experience grows to consider switching over to a risk excess programme.

A risk excess must have a balance of premium income to the maximum risk exposure to enable it to endure, otherwise it will not last and continuity will be lost. Again, a Reassured using a risk excess must be sophisticated enough to realise that the rating, particularly on a flat rated basis, presupposes a continuity of direct underwriting. Any Reassured who is foolish enough to increase his acceptance limits materially, will soon lose his risk excess with dire consequences to himself.

However, given a proven account, with a good balance of premium to losses, and a Reassured and Reinsurer who are both sophisticated and trust one another, then the risk excess to replace part of, or the whole of, a treaty can reduce considerably the volume of outwards reinsurance. It will not necessarily reduce the profit ceded. However, it will undoubtedly cut down very considerably on the administration costs of both the Reinsured and Reinsurers, and thus lead to considerable economies. No sizeable company can afford to ignore these advantages these days, unless, of course they cannot shed or re-employ the staff made redundant.

Factors in Underwriting

1. General

If we are happy that the Ceding Company is sophisticated enough, then we can think about the various types of risk excess treaty available. There are three main types of risk excess 1) Burning Cost, 2) Flat Rated and 3) Coded or Cession Contracts. The burning cost contracts usually have a deposit rate, the final rate being determined by the loss experience subject to the maximum and a minimum rate. The flat rated contracts have a fixed rate, which will be reviewed at renewal with the rate adjusted for the following year on exposure changes and the loss experience. This is the most common type of risk excess. The coded or cession contracts usually have a deposit premium with the final premium decided by the number and size of the risks exposing that contract.

These types of risk excess fit quite well with the three ways of rating risk excesses:

A. On the basis of risk exposures;
B. On the basis of past experience;
C. By the seat of your pants.

All three have their advantages, but method (C) does require asbestos trousers which, in this day and age, may cause a products liability claim, and for that reason and others, is not recommended except as a very useful check on results derived from (A) or (B). The exposure rated method equates well with the coded rating basis, Rating by past experience to the burning cost basis and seat of the pants to the flat rated basis; all are analysed below. Let's start with the burning cost method.

Risk Excesses on a Burning Cost Basis

Burning Costs and Loss Costs

The Burning Cost Method of Rating

Description

One of the many factors taken into account in rating any excess of loss or stop loss contract is the past experience which a contract has suffered or would have suffered if the contract had been in force. For example, a direct writing company writes fire business on farms and wishes protection for:

40,000 x 10,000 a.o. loss any one farm.
The fire loss experience for the past 5 years in excess of 10,000 has been:

1976 1 paid loss of 20,000 from the ground
1977 Nil
1978 1 paid loss of 40,000 from the ground
1979 Nil
1980 1 outstanding loss of 50,000 from the ground

The cost of these fires, or "burning cost", excess of 10,000 each loss, has been:

1976	10,000
1978	30,000
1980	40,000
Total	80,000

For the five year period the average annual burning cost has been

$$\frac{80,000}{5} \text{ or } 16,000$$

Now this gives us a valid figure but it is not a great help for future rating unless we know the exposures over those 5 years. Perhaps the account in 1976 was only one third of the size that it was in 1980. We need to calculate the burning cost on some basis that reflects the changing exposure. We could use the number of farm sites written where values exceed 10,000 but one thatched farm might be more hazardous than 5 tiled-roof ones.

The Reassured's premium income from farms should give a better yardstick by which to judge the loss experience, and as we are discussing losses which have occurred during each year, whenever the original policy incepted, then the Reassured's earned premium income will be more accurate a gauge than his written income.

Our experience, then, can be put down as follows:

Year	*Gross net earned premium*	*Loss — included loss expenses excess of 10,000 any one loss*	*Annual burning cost*
1976	100,000	10,000	10%
1977	100,000		Nil
1978	150,000	30,000	20%
1979	200,000		Nil
1980	250,000	40,000 o/s	16%
Totals	800,000	80,000	

Now, the burning cost for each year is shown in the right-hand column but the burning cost for the five-year period, expressed as a percentage of the five-year income is arrived at by dividing the five years' losses by the five years' premium income; i.e.

$$\frac{80,000}{800,000} \times 100\% = 10\%$$

The average of the five individual years' burning cost, is

$\frac{46\%}{5}$ or 9.20%

The burning cost normally, and more correctly, used is the former and not the latter figure.

Therefore, we can say that the five-year burning cost percentage is 10% of the g.n.e.p.i. This burning cost could be a very useful guide as to future experience. Its usefulness or accuracy will depend very much on whether this farm business has remained the same.

For example: Have the original rates remained unchanged?
Have the Reassured lines and exposures changed?

and so on.

The B.C. will also only be of help if the experience has been "normal". For example, if there has not been a spate of bush fires or some pyromaniac setting fire to hayricks. It will also only be a reliable guide if there are sufficient losses of all sizes to give validity to the experience. The burning cost we have used of three losses in five years is not a very valid one. The losses are too few to constitute a reliable sample.

Given an account which has remained constant, and experience which is valid, then it is possible and reasonable to use the burning cost method as the main or exclusive method of rating. The rate for our farm account for 1981 might be a pure factor of the previous five years' burning cost of 10%. What factor? This depends very greatly on the validity of the past experience for the future contract.

Take a fixed deductible of 10,000 and an inflation of 10% per annum. A 10,000 loss in 1976 will cost 16,000 odd in 1981. As previously mentioned, many other factors may change. Therefore the loading factor to convert a burning cost rate into a proper premium rate must take all these factors into account. It must also take into account the "catastrophic" exposure. On our farm account a very dry period producing a catastrophic period, our pyromaniac or an agricultural depression might produce an abnormal catastrophic experience. No Reinsurer can take on a reinsurance without costs — his own and any brokerage or tax. Hopefully, a profit is envisaged? We used to expect profits in the 1950s, 1960s and early 1970s and Underwriters used to buy their houses with it; now they are lucky to get a double gin!

The loadings often are: 66.6% or $\frac{100}{60}$

50% or $\frac{100}{66\frac{2}{3}\text{rd}}$

42.857% or $\frac{100}{70}$

33% or $\frac{100}{75}$

25% or $\frac{100}{80}$

The loading used on a burning cost formula based on past experience must be very considerable to deal with inflation of values unless, of course, the deductible of the contract itself increases with inflation and in proportion to it. Before going any further we will consider a typical burning cost premium clause.

> "The Reassured shall pay to the Reinsurers within 60 days of the close of each calendar quarter a provisional premium calculated at 'x'% of the Reassured gross net earned premium for that quarter. At the close of each calendar year the provisional premium paid for that year shall be adjusted by applying the rate calculated according to the formula below to the Reassured's gross net earned premium for that year. This final rate for any year shall be calculated as follows:
>
> By multiplying the burning cost of this contract during the five years immediately prior to the year in question by a factor of $\frac{100}{70}$ subject to a minimum rate of 'x'% and a maximum rate of 'y'%.
>
> The burning cost shall be calculated by dividing the losses incrred on the basis of this contract by the Reassured's gross net earned premium for the same period and expressing the result as a percentage.
>
> Losses incurred on the basis of this contract shall mean the actual losses sustained by this contract or which would have been sustained by this contract had it been in force. Losses shall include loss expenses as included hereunder and shall include both settled and outstanding losses.
>
> Where a calculation includes outstanding losses such a calculation shall be provisional and shall be adjusted annually until such time as all such losses are settled and a final calculation is possible."

The clause itself is self-explanatory but there is a provision for a minimum and maximum rate. This is necessary both because there could be outstanding losses which may not materialise, or late advised losses may occur. If these changes were very violent they might upset the validity of past experience as a rating basis for the future.

Take our farm example: the 1981 rate would be $\frac{100}{70}$ x 10% or 14%, but say the 1980 o/s loss never materialises, the burning cost reduces to 5% and the rate to 7%, which could be dangerously low in view of the known exposures and the limit of 40,000 per loss. To guard against this, a minimum rate of, say 10% would make sense. The reason in our example is easy to see; that is, if the 1980 loss disappears, it leaves only two losses and neither greater than 20,000 excess of the deductible to rate a contract with an exposure of 40,000 excess of 10,000.

Similarly, if a spate of late losses occurred, or our pyromaniac struck at Christmas 1980, the 14% rate might escalate to, say, 30% plus, which again could destroy the validity of past experience, so a maximum rate of around 20% or 22% could be valid.

To sum up, the use of a "burning cost" calculation as a help or guide to fixing a flat rate for a contract is sensible and widespread. The use of a "burning cost" as the sole and automatic method of determining the rate for any contract, within a minimum and maximum, should only be used where the past experience used in the calculation is valid for the future. This pre-supposes:

(1) That the rates and terms of the original business are constant.

(2) The type of business is reasonably stable.

(3) The exposures or policy limits are stable.

(4) There are sufficient numbers of losses in the past experience to produce a valid sample.

(5) There is at least one loss equal to the coverage granted under the policy.

(6) That no undue exposures exist (e.g. a large catastrophic exposure) which have not produced losses during the burning cost period.

(7) Above all, that inflation is not going to play havoc with the experience.

The first six points are known facts on which the Reassured and Reinsurer can agree and for which allowances can be made. Item (7) (inflation) is the real killer.

Contracts using a 5-year back period burning cost were popular both on property and mixed property and liability excess Reinsurers during the 1920s, 1930s, 1940s and even the 1950s. When, in the Western world, the post war economic recovery generated a rate of inflation of over 5% per annum, this type of contract, without an indexed deductible, became virtually impossible to underwrite. Various expedients were tried. Firstly, instead of using the 5 back years, 4 back years plus the current year were used.

e.g. the rate for 1959 was $\frac{100}{70}$ x burning cost for 1959, 1958, 1957, 1956, 1955.

This quickened the formula and thus damped down the effect of inflation. Then even quicker formulae were used, e.g. current plus back 2 years. An example of the relevant clauses from the wording of such a contract commencing in 1967 is set out below:

> Example of a quick acting burning cost contract wording. (Only the articles dealing with the term and cancellation and calculation of premium are quoted. In other respects the contract would be similar to any excess of loss risk excess.)

Term and Cancellation

This contract applies only to loss occurring during the period from 12.01 a.m. 1st January 1967 to midnight 31st December 1971, but may be terminated at 31st December 1969 or 31st December 1970 by either party giving 90 days cancellation notice.

PREMIUM FORMULA

1. *The Reassured shall pay to the Reinsurers a deposit premium of "X" on 1st January, 1st April, 1st July, and 1st October of each year that this C ontract is in force. At the end of each year the premium due Reinsurers will be calculated in accordance with the following formula and the deposit premium shall be adjusted accordingly.*
2. *The rate of premium due to Reinsurers shall be calculated as provided hereunder and shall be payable on the gross net*

earned premium income of the Reassured on all business covered hereunder. Gross net earned premium income shall mean the earned portion of the gross written premiums less return premiums and less also the earned portion of premiums paid for reinsurances, recoveries under which would inure to Reinsurers' benefit.

3. *The rate payable to Reinsurers for each contract year shall be computed as follows:*

   Add to the Reassured's gross net earned premium income on business covered by this Contract for the current contract year, the gross net earned premium income for the two preceding years. Divide the total amount of said premiums into losses which occurred during the same period which would have been covered by this Contract and multiply the resulting percentage by 100/70ths. All losses hereunder shall be included in the year of occurrence and the rate will be readjusted annually until such time as all losses are finally settled.

4. ***MAXIMUM AND MINIMUM RATES FOR ALL YEARS***

   Notwithstanding the rates which derive from the calculations above provided:

   (a) The maximum rate shall never be more than 200%

   (b) The minimum rate whall never be less than 50% of the rate for the first year as finally adjusted.

5. *The first year's rate and all subsequent years' rates are based on the Reassured's losses recoverable under this Contract, irrespective or whether claim is made against the Reinsurers or not.*

Burning Cost Contracts

Contracts such as this, where the rate is determined automatically by a burning cost formula, are known as burning cost contracts. Normally they are written for periods exceeding one year; often for five years with an option after three years, or for a firm 3-year term, or sometimes on a continuous basis with annual cancellation after a two year or three year non-cancellable period.

The theory of such continuity is that the Reassured's own experience determines his future reinsurance costs. Both parties understand that if such experience is good then the Reassured is entitled to continuity to enjoy the consequent reduced cost of reinsurance. If, on the other hand, the experience is bad, then the Reassured will automatically pay a higher reinsurance cost to his Reinsurers, who are entitled to continuity to enjoy that. In theory, should such a contract continue for ever, then it would be a guaranteed profit for Reinsurers with past losses always being repaid with a loading in future rates. In practice, the finite term of the policy and the maximum rate of the contract prevent this.

In an inflationary period, where losses excess of a fixed deductible inevitably increase, then Reinsurers may forever cause their tail until cancellation happens and reimbursement is then cut off. Therefore, the use of burning cost contracts becomes very difficult in an inflationary period unless some method is used to adjust the deductible and the limit of the contract itself to inflation.

This has been done, and is being done, by the use of deductible and limits which are indexed in some way to inflation. This is fully explained in Chapter XI under "Indexation". Where such indexing is a reflection of inflation, then a burning cost contract, with a reasonable loadings of $\frac{100}{75}$th or $\frac{100}{70}$th is a logical mathematical exercise. The past experience used in the future rate calculation is based on an indexed deductible and limit and not on a fixed monetary deductible or limit.

Let us assume that we wish to start a burning cost contract effective 1st January 1981, with a limit and deductible of 40,000 x/s 10,000 each and every loss. The 10,000 deductible will apply to losses which are settled in January 1981 and losses settled thereafter will be indexed. In computing the past burning cost we need to index the limit and deductible backwards for losses which occurred during 1976 to 1980 inclusive. Assume that 10,000 indexed backwards was 9,000 on 1/1/80, 8,000 on 1/1/79, 7,000 on 1/1/78 and 6,000 on 1/1/77, then a loss which occurred in 1976, and which is settled, say, on 1st January 1978 must go in our burning cost calculation in the 1976 experience *but on the basis of a deductible of 7,000 not 10,000.*

Similarly with a limit of 28,000 not 40,000. Assuming this can be done, it does provide stable basis for a burning cost calculation. It should be noted that although losses are included in the year in which they occur the limit and deductible applicable to that loss is that which would have been in force at the date *the loss was settled*, i.e. an "as if" basis which corresponds with the future basis of the contract.

The use of actual premium income figures for the past years burning cost calculation is correct and logical as these actual premium incomes reflect actual values and do not need indexation. Where indexation is used it is often extremely difficult to find an index which reflects the effect of inflation on losses accurately. With a fire or property business an index related to building cost per area, say, per square metre, can be an extremely accurate guide where one is dealing with fire and allied perils insurance on building. Many direct insurances in Europe are indexed in this way automatically and a burning cost reinsurance could also be so indexed and would parallel the direct indexation.

With third party or liability or motor excess, however, an index based either on wages or material inflation can be a very poor guide to the inflation of liability claims. The inflation of liability claims owes much more to the views of juries or judges, changing social values, consumerism, medical improvement, and so on. Social inflation is very difficult to index. In fact the only valid index is one based on court awards themselves. Failing this type of index, then the use of a past burning cost as the sole and automatic method of rating, even with indexation, is often neither logical nor sensible.

Loss Cost Rating

The terms loss cost and burning cost ought to be synonymous. In fact they have come to be applied to two different things. A loss cost refers to the cost of losses during the period the contract is in force. As we have already seen, a burning cost refers to the past cost of losses on the basis of the contract. If a contract for 1st January 1980 has losses during 1980 of 20,000 then its loss cost is 20,000. If the Reassured's premium for that year is 100,000 then the loss cost is 20% of the premium income.

The use of a loss cost method of rating for an excess of loss contract is to rate that contract on its own experience subject to fixed minimum and maximum rates. It is used where the use of a burning cost is not thought logical or where a flat rate cannot be arrived at or agreed by the parties concerned. Often an untried class of business is not easy to rate until the business has built up an experience of its own or its exposures can be assessed accurately. In these sort of circumstances the Reassured and the Reinsurers may not be able to agree on an acceptable rate and a self-rating formula or loss cost rate, with a minimum and a maximum, may be an acceptable decision. A typical 12 months' contract could be rated as follows:

> Min. & Dep. premium adjustable on expiry at $\frac{100}{80}$ th of the losses hereunder, subject to a minimum premium calculated at 7½% of the earned premium income and a maximum rate of 20%.

Unlike a burning cost, where the contract experience may be quite different from the past rating experience, a loss cost is a guaranteed profit to Reinsurers, provided the losses do not exceed the maximum rate. The amount of this profit varies with the quantum of loss and in the example above is greatest when the losses are nil and second largest when losses equal 16% and the contract rate is 20%, and least when the losses equal 4% and the rate 5%. Bearing in mind Reinsurers' expenses, the margin of profit can be very marginal to run the risk of paying losses in excess of 20%. In fact, this loss cost contract is really a stop loss contract imposed on the original excess loss contract where the stop loss deductible is 16% and the premium for the stop loss being variable between 1% and 5%.

This loss cost method of rating can be a snare and a delusion to Reinsurers unless the risk of losses exceeding 16% is remote. In my opinion, the use of this method of self-rating can rarely be justified. It is far better to effect an excess of loss reinsurance at a flat rate with some form of profit commission or return of premium if there is no claim. However, a flat rate is not always possible and loss cost contracts often appeal to Reassureds who may feel that they are likely to pay the minimum rate most years.

This method of rating, used for an annual contract only, really makes sense where it is anticipated that there will be a number of losses during the annual period and that these losses will generate a rate normally between the minimum and the maximum.

The type of contract of a catastrophic nature, which has infrequent losses, say, every decade, is not suitable for this type of rating as it will run at the minimum rate when the Reassured can afford to pay the most and the maximum rate when the catastrophe happens and the Reassured can afford to pay least.

Most loss-cost contracts are rated on a 12-month basis. However, contracts can be based on a three-year or even five-year basis. In the 1970's and 1980's these contracts were quite common, however, more and more contracts are now on an annual basis. For a full explanation of the workings of a three-year loss cost contract, one should refer to the third edition of Reinsurance in Practice – Chapter 13, entitled 'Global Excesses'. This section depends very much on the present or past experience of the contract in order to come up with a rate. The next section relies more on the exposures falling to the particular risk excess layer.

Flat Rated Risk Excess Contracts

The flat rated contracts we compared with the seat of the pants method because the other methods generally are self-adjusting either by exposures or by loss cost whereas if the price is much too low on a flat rated contract it will take a while for the Reinsurer to get their money back. Therefore the two main rating criteria are the two E's, Exposure and Experience. By far the most important consideration is Exposure.

Exposure

The most important information we need in order to see the exposure is a risk profile. A risk profile is a table showing by band size 1.) The number of risks written 2.) The premium for those risks and 3.) The total insured values for each band. Sometimes these risk profiles are by class of business as well, this will enable a more accurate quotation to be done; a sample risk profile is shown below:

Bands	Risk no	Premium	Sums Insured
0-24,999	259	17,483	3,885,000
25,000-49,999	659	108,076	18,452,000
50,000-74,999	1,105	255,255	67,405,000
75,000-124999	821	241374	69,785,000
125,000-149,999	401	137,844	56,500,000
150,000-249,999	50	22,550	9,400,000
250,000-499,000	11	8,470	3,850,000
500,000-999,999	3	4,185	1,875,000
Total	**3,309**	**795,236**	**231,077,000**

Risk profiles produced are often not as detailed as this. Common problems are that they are produced on a gross basis before both facultative reinsurance and proportional treaty cessions which is of no great help. Sometimes the risk profile is on a PML basis with no details of the sums insured involved. Sometimes 'risks' are policies covering many separate locations. Therefore it is important to understand the basis of the profile before doing much analysis and especially quoting.

Let's suppose that this risk profile was produced by a company that largely writes a household account but also writes a few commercial risks, mainly offices and shops. The profile is on a gross basis and the company wants to replace their surplus treaty with a risk excess programme. Their current retention is 250,000 with a three-line surplus which gives the company gross capacity per risk of 1,000,000. The company has a premium income shown on the profile of 795,236 and the annual premium estimate is showing a minor increase to 800,000.

The Broker has requested quotations of the following:

(1) 125,000 xs 125,000
(2) 250,000 xs 250,000
(3) 500,000 xs 500,000.

How do we measure the exposure and work out a rate for each layer? We could work out the number of risks exposed to each layer and also the premium income for these risks exposed to each layer. See below:

Band	Risk no	%	Premium	%
under 125,000	2,844	85.9%	622,188	78.2%
125,000-249,000	451	13.6%	160,394	20.2%
250,000-499,999	11	0.3%	8,470	1.1%
500,000-999,000	3	0.1%	4,185	0.5%
Total	**3,309**	**100.0%**	**795,237**	**100.0%**

If the number of risks was used as a rating method too little premium would be charged for the risk excess layers above 125,000. In the above example 86% would be kept for 125,000 and below and only 14% of premium for 125,000 and above and of that only 0.4% of premium above 250,000. This is because a large percentage of the risk numbers fall below the 125,000 deductible.

If it was done by the exposed premium too much premium would be given to the risk excess layers as no credit is given for the value of the deductible and the cost of servicing the policyholder (i.e. paying agents commission, producing the policy, handling claims etc.). In this case 20.2% for the 125,000 to 250,000 band and only 1.6% for the top two bands. How do we come up with a fairer method?

Much work has been done studying the loss distribution on property business relative to the percentage of sums insured. In other words, how many losses out of say 100 fires result in damage, say above 10% of sums insured or 50% of sums insured etc. With these loss distribution patterns, first loss scales have been developed. On page 258 is an example of four first loss scales.

Excess point as % of value	Premium for Retention of Insurance Co. Scale A good	Scale B fair	Scale C poor	Scale D high risk
0%	0.0%	0.0%	0.0%	0.0%
0.5%	20.0%	15.0%	9.0%	7.0%
1%	31.0%	23.5%	12.0%	9.5%
2%	37.0%	29.0%	19.0%	11.5%
3%	41.0%	32.5%	23.0%	14.0%
4%	45.5%	36.0%	25.5%	16.3%
5%	49.0%	38.3%	28.0%	18.3%
6%	52.0%	40.5%	30.0%	20.0%
7%	54.4%	42.5%	32.0%	21.7%
8%	56.2%	44.3%	34.0%	23.3%
9%	58.0%	45.8%	35.8%	24.9%
10%	59.5%	47.4%	37.4%	26.3%
12%	62.2%	50.0%	40.3%	29.0%
14%	64.6%	52.7%	42.8%	31.6%
16%	66.7%	54.9%	45.0%	34.0%
18%	68.7%	56.9%	47.0%	36.0%
20%	70.4%	59.0%	49.2%	38.2%
22%	72.0%	61.0%	51.3%	40.4%
24%	73.5%	63.0%	53.4%	42.4%
26%	75.0%	65.0%	55.2%	44.3%
28%	76.3%	66.8%	57.0%	46.2%
30%	77.5%	68.4%	59.0%	48.2%
32%	78.6%	70.0%	60.8%	50.0%
34%	79.6%	71.4%	62.3%	52.0%
36%	80.6%	72.6%	63.7%	54.0%
38%	81.5%	74.0%	65.0%	56.0%
40%	82.5%	75.0%	66.5%	57.8%
45%	84.5%	77.8%	69.9%	62.0%
50%	86.6%	80.4%	73.0%	65.9%
55%	88.6%	82.7%	76.0%	69.8%
60%	90.6%	85.2%	79.0%	73.7%
65%	92.5%	88.0%	82.0%	77.4%
70%	94.0%	90.6%	85.0%	81.3%
75%	95.3%	92.5%	88.0%	85.5%
80%	96.5%	94.4%	91.0%	89.3%
85%	97.7%	96.4%	93.9%	93.0%
90%	98.6%	98.0%	96.5%	96.0%
95%	99.4%	99.1%	98.6%	98.3%
100%	100.0%	100.0%	100.0%	100.0%

These scales are best seen on a graph and they produce the so called banana-shaped curves.

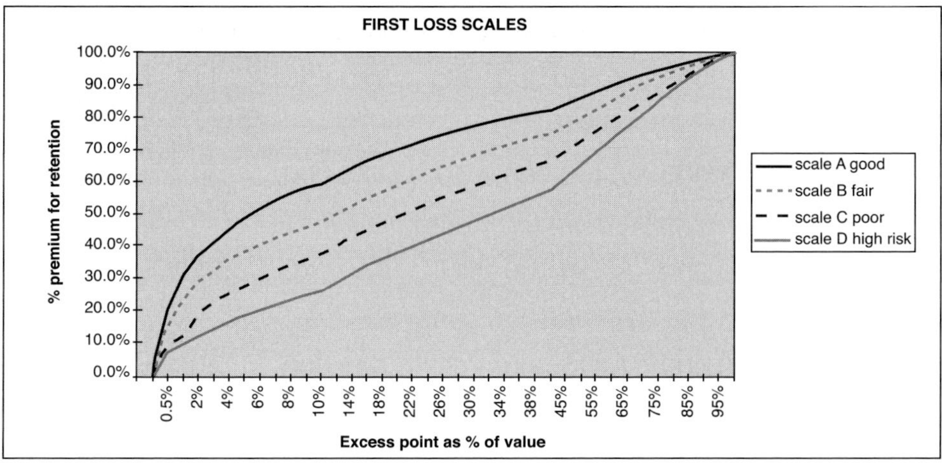

The first loss scales vary for different types of construction. For the more hazardous types of building, a higher percentage of premium is needed for the excess Reinsurers as it is more likely to have a major fire or explosion etc. How do these scales work?

Let us go back to the risk profile shown earlier. There are three risks in the band between 500,000 and 1,000,000. We know that the total sums insured for these three risks are 1,875,000 combined. That is an average of 625,000 each risk, we will assume that we have three risks of exactly 625,000. We will assume that these risks are offices or shops. We will therefore use the scale B, as we do not know if they are of good construction. We are trying to work out how much premium should be charged for the 500,000 excess of 500,000 layer.The deductible or excess point is at 500,000 which is at 500,000/625,000 or at 80% of the values at risk. If we look at the scale B we require 5.6% of the premium for each of those 3 risks or 234 in all. It would not be economic to charge so little a premium for so much capacity and therefore we may possibly charge the Reinsured near the whole of his exposed premium. This would be 0.52% or 4,185, which only produces a rate on line of 4,185/500,000 or 0.84%, which is barely economical.

If we apply the same methodology for the first layer 125,000 xs 125,000 we get the following premiums required.

	Values	No	Ave.Values	125,000 %ages
25,000 xs 125,000	56,500,000	401	140,898	11% xs 89% is 2.3% of 137,844 or 3,170
125,000 xs 125,000	9,400,000	50	188,000	34% xs 66% is 11.8% of 22,500 or 2,661
250,000 xs 250,000	3,850,000	11	350,000	35.7% xs 35.7% is 18% of 8,470 or 1,525
500,000 xs 500,000	1,875,000	3	625,000	20% xs 20% 16% of 4,185 670
			Total	8,026

For the 3 layers we get following premiums by using the same methodology.

Band	Premium	Rate	Rate on Line
125,000 xs 125,000	8,026	1.009%	6.42%
250,000 xs 250,000	2,119	0.266%	0.85%
500,000 xs 500,000	234	0.029%	0.05%

These rates and rate on lines are effectively for unlimited reinstatements and are technical prices but not commercial prices. As indicated before the rate on line of 0.05% is equivalent to a return period of once every 2000 years. This rate is too low as there is no way a Reinsurer can recover his costs let alone a loss at this rate on line. Therefore we would offer a premium of say 2,500 or 0.5% rate on line for two reinstatements free with an occurrence limit of 1,000,000 or twice the risk limit. In order to keep the rate on line of the second layer to be more differentiated from the third we might offer a premium of 3,000 or a rate on line of 1.2% and with 2 free reinstatements and an occurrence limit of 500,000. The first layer we could put up the technical price quoted but also with limited reinstatements and an occurrence limit.

There is some flexibility to adjust the pricing level by giving different occurrence limits, number of reinstatements and by using different first loss scales. One may also adjust the excess prices if the original rates are high or low.

Experience

One should always look at the experience of the contract as well as the exposure. Any pricing is probably a combination of the two. If the experience is worse than the technical price then you have to ask yourself why? Is it due to bad luck? Poor underwriting? A particular class of risk that they have now excluded? etc. If the experience is much better than the technical price then you may be able to give a discount but you should check past exposures to make sure there has not been a radical recent change in underwriting philosophy resulting in a large exposure increase, and have they been lucky?

One should refer to the Burning Cost section earlier in the chapter before analysing the loss experience. Rating any form of excess of loss reinsurance by reference to past experience can only be viable if past conditions can be guaranteed to continue in the future. As we are in an inflationary age past losses need to be inflated to adjust them for current building costs. In a time of high inflation these adjustments can be significant.

Let us assume that we are rating one layer of $250,000 xs $250,000.The loss record is as follows:

Year	Claim Amount	Loss Details
1985	155,000	Jones Industries – Fire
1986	175,000	Calliper & Son – Arson
1987	225,000	Benson – Flood
1989	325,000	De Vroom – Explosion
1992	124,000	Jones Industries – Theft.
1994	340,000	Gomes – Fire
1996	450,000	Eat all Supermarket – Fire
1997	245,000	Benson Warehouse – Fire
1998	450,000	Crunch Foods – Fire

All Claims above $100,000 shown.

The Contract is for 12 months at 1st January 1999.

Let us suppose the Inflation Rates for building costs were in this Territory 1985-1990 – 20%, 1991-1995 – 10%, 1996 onwards 5%. We will assume all the losses all occur at the middle of the year. The adjusted claims experience and loss record to our layer is:

Year	Act Loss	Loss to Layer	Infl Loss	Infl Loss to Layer
1985	155,000	nil	852,880	250,000
1986	175,000	nil	811,850	250,000
1987	225,000	nil	869,839	250,000
1989	325,000	75,000	872,524	250,000
1992	124,000	nil	210,165	nil
1994	340,000	90,000	476,247	226,247
1996	450,000	200,000	520,931	250,000
1997	245,000	nil	270,113	20,113
1998	450,000	200,000	472,500	222,500

If we then work out the annual average loss cost both for the inflated loss and non-inflated loss. We get the following results.

Period	Annl Act Loss	Annl Infl Loss
Last 5 years	98,000	143,772
Last 10 years	56,500	96,886
Last 14 years	40,357	122,776

Therefore if you do not apply inflation the loss record appears to get better over the longer period. The annual inflated loss cost is always greater than the actual loss but for the 14 year period. The inflated loss record is almost three times higher than the unadjusted loss. Which are the most meaningful loss periods the 5, 10 or 14 years? They are all useful, however the last 5 years is more likely to reflect current underwriting practices. But the longer period is more likely to pick up the exceptionally large loss so it is more important on a catastrophe layer or where there are rarely losses. Please note that the loss record does not show losses below $100,000 and with the high inflation rate in the 1980s some of the losses below $100,000 would probably encroach into our layer after inflation is applied. We would also need to add in our own costs on top of this factor before we quote a price. On layers with no losses at all, even on an inflated basis, make use of the exposure prices as experience is of no help? One useful way to check-up on inflation and also growth of the account is to ask for the historical premium incomes by year. If you can find out the historical line sizes, that can help as it can indicate any major changes.

As we said earlier it is best to use both an exposure and an experience rating method for risk excesses and use your own judgement to decide which method should carry more emphasis.

Risk Excess — Cession Contracts

If a Ceding Company elects to purchase a risk excess programme, then they may opt to go for a loss cost contract on the first layer where the experience is extremely volatile.

Then they may elect to buy several layers of flat rated risk excesses. For the top layer they may elect to buy a flat rated contract. However, because the Ceding Company is unsure how many very large risks they may be writing, they may elect to buy it on a cession basis. Rather than pay a minimum and deposit premium and then adjust it on a percentage of the earned or written premium during the year, they may elect to adjust on the number of risks ceded to the layer of risk excess. This is a bit like a surplus treaty but with a lower percentage of the premium being paid away

Therefore, say a company has a net retention of $10 million on a risk, they may elect to buy the top layer of $5 million excess of $5 million on a cession basis. The Reinsurer would charge the Ceding Company a percentage of the premium for any risks exposed to the 5 million over 5 million layer. The layer would be split into say, five bands of 1 million each. By using the first loss scales referred to earlier, we can calculate what percentage of premium we would require for each band. We have used scale B in the first loss scales with a loading for our costs.

Band	Percent Exposed	% Premium Needed
5m to 6m	17 xs 83	7%
6m to 7m	30 xs 70	12%
7m to 8m	37.5 xs 62.5	15%
8m to 9m	44 xs 56	18%
9m to 10m	50 xs 50	22%

The advantage of this type of treaty for the Ceding Company is that the reinsureds only pay premium when they expose the risk excess layer. Therefore, if they do not expose it much it is very cheap, but if they do expose it a lot then it is probably more expensive than buying a flat rated risk excess programme. It is common practice on these types of treaties to give unlimited reinstatements because you are getting the applicable premium for each cession made. However, these treaties are not universally popular with Reinsurers as these contracts are often very unbalanced, there are risks attaching and they require more administration and premium comes in slowly. Very often these contracts have an event limit of one or two times the risk limit and sometimes a limited number of reinstatements to avoid any huge deficit.

Reinsurers need to be very careful that the business ceded to an excess of loss cession contract is standard business and should not have a loaded rate for each cession made. For example, for a petrochemical account one would expect to get a higher percentage of a ceded premium than for an office block. Please refer to the first loss scales given earlier.

Other Options

Reinstatements

The number of reinstatements given on a risk excess layer varies on a contract by contract basis. It is quite common on most USA insurance company risk excesses for unlimited reinstatements to be given but with a three times occurrence (event) limit. If the reinstatements are limited then for the Reinsurer the maximum down side of this particular risk layer is limited and this will lead to a reduction in the premium charged. It is quite common on contracts rated on a loss cost basis to have no limitation on the number of reinstatements. This is because if the experience is adverse then the rating will be adjusted up to the maximum rate. It is common though to still include an occurrence limit under these contracts.

Aggregate Deductibles

In order to keep the price of a risk excess layer down for the Ceding Company, one can include an aggregate deductible. This means that the Ceding Company retains this aggregate deductible before they can recover from the risk excess programme. Reinsurers should be aware that because an aggregate deductible is usually applied when there has been a lot of loss frequency, it may be better to raise the deductible to avoid the frequency rather than apply an aggregate deductible. However, the application of aggregate deductibles can mean that in many years this particular layer would probably have no losses and the cost of administration both for the ceding companies and the Reinsurer is reduced.

Profit Commissions and No Claims Bonuses

If the rating of these risk excess programmes is not clear cut, i.e. because the Ceding Company has had no experience or because they are going in to write a new class of business, then it may be sensible to charge a little bit more money up front, and then give a profit commission or a no claims bonus if the experience is good.

Risks Attaching Versus Losses Occurring During

When a risk excess programme is replacing a series of proportional treaties, then the reinsurances usually change from a risk-attaching basis (i.e. the proportional treaties) to a losses occurring during basis (the risk excess programme). This will mean that the exposure to the risk programme will build up as individual cessions and will expire under the proportional treaties.

One important thing for the Reinsured to remember is that the movement from pro-rata reinsurance to risk excess generally means that the Reinsured will have to buy substantially more catastrophe excess of loss protection. Pro-rata treaties are often undervalued as a form of catastrophe protection especially where a proportional treaty can be purchased in a high catastrophe exposed territory or zone.

In most cases therefore the new risk excess programme would be on a losses occurring during basis and would only pick up losses from risks written new or renewed that year and occurred that year. Risk excess programmes can also be placed on a risks attaching basis which would be more in line with a proportional treaty and would likewise give run-off protection. However, they are not so popular with Reinsurers; the main reason is that on a risks attaching treaty it takes many years to know if the risk excess has run profitably or not. So therefore it is more difficult for the Reinsurers to adjust the rating to cope with the actual experience of the treaty. An additional problem is that if a Ceding Company is writing a portfolio of contractors all risks business, some of these policies may last up to 10 years, and therefore it may be many years before they are reported. It is standard practice on risks attaching contracts to put a limitation of 12 months or 12 months plus odd time with a maximum period of 18 months for the original policies, so that the tail of the losses being reported is reduced.

When Reinsurers are protecting a surplus treaty and it usually makes sense to protect this on a risks attaching basis because then it follows the fortunes with the surplus treaty Reinsurer, although these can also be placed on a losses occurring during basis. One word of warning to Reinsurers writing surplus treaty reinsurances is that they are usually bought on an opportunistic basis and therefore there is often very little continuity on such contracts and they are not usually renewed when you charge the right price.

Application of Risk Excess to Other Lines of Business

The underwriting and rating of motor and third party liability risk excesses are dealt with in Chapter XI.

Using the three main methods of risk excess, i.e. the loss cost, the flat rated or the cession based risk excess; these can be applied to all classes of business. They could be applied to a portfolio of burglary business, a personal accident account, a contingency account and even a political risk account. Care must be taken by both Ceding Companies and Reinsurers to define firstly what is an individual risk and also sometimes more importantly, what is the date of loss. It is clear on a portfolio of fire business when the date of loss occurs. However, on a political risk treaty, does the date of loss occur when the Government in a particular country collapses, or does it occur when the waiting period of the contract frustration policy has passed, or does it occur when the Insured lets you know of potential loss?

Chapter XI

MOTOR AND THIRD PARTY

Introduction — Reinsuring clause — Disputes — Costs inclusive — Indexation — Claims co-operation — ECO — Claims made basis — Excess cession — Professional indemnity — Underwriting considerations — Thoughts in 1984 and in 2000 — Reinsurance claims made

Introduction

The excess of loss method of reinsuring these types of business is the main method, unless of course there are particular reasons for placing a quota share or excess aggregate reinsurance.

The surplus method is impossible to operate where unlimited liability is given on, say a European third party motor policy. It is possible, in theory, to use the surplus method where policies are for fixed amounts but it is rarely used. The quota share method is often used where the Reassured desires to reduce his volume on, say, motor business, either overall or in any class, e.g. heavy goods vehicles, or in any particular country or territory.

However, the major method of protection of liability and motor business is by the excess of loss method and it is one of the most difficult types of reinsurance to underwrite and control. The reader should review this chapter, the chapter on law and the asbestos appendix before proceeding, as much can and has gone wrong. In general it contains many of the clauses incorporated in a catastrophe wording described and commented upon in an earlier chapter. I will, therefore, confine my comments to the points where it differs from such contracts. This chapter has been substantially altered since the third edition by the editor. The editor has used a modern United Kingdom motor and household liability as an example.

ARTICLE 1

Reinsuring Clause

> *This Agreement shall indemnify the Reassured for that part of their Ultimate Nett loss which exceeds say £100,000 except as provided in the London Market Severe Inflation Clause Article10, (referred to herein as "the retention") each and every accident.*
>
> *The liability of Reinsurers shall never exceed £ 100,000 Ultimate Nett loss, except as provided in the London Market Severe Inflation Clause Article10, (referred to herein as "the limit of liability") each and every accident.*

It will be noticed that there is no coinsurance unlike some catastrophe programmes. The severe inflation clause will increase the retention on those losses, which take a long time to settle we will talk about indexation later.

ARTICLE 2

> *It is understood and agreed that loss or losses, if any, paid by the Reassured in currency or currencies other than Sterling shall be converted into Sterling at the rates of exchange as used and contained in the books of the Reassured.*

Typical currency conversion clause.

ARTICLE 3

Period

This agreement is in respect of losses occurring during the period commencing with the 1st January 2000 and ending with the 31st December 2000 both days' inclusive local standard time at the location of the loss.

On motor business the excess of loss contract is the major underwriting protection, performing the same functions as the surplus treaty or risk excess on the property side. The contract covers losses occurring during the contract period and this is normal.

ARTICLE 4

Territorial scope standard not shown here.

ARTICLE 5

> *For the purpose of this agreement the term "each and every accident" shall be understood to mean each and every accident and/or occurrence and/or series of accidents and/or occurrences arising out of one event.*

We have discussed the definition of one loss on catastrophe contracts at some length. Under motor and liability contracts a great variety of definitions are in use today and a few samples are shown below:

> "The term loss occurrence shall mean a loss or series of losses arising out of one event."

or

> "The term loss occurrence shall mean a loss or series of losses arising out of one accident."

or

> "The term loss occurrence shall mean one or more occurrences, disasters and/or casualties arising out of one event."

or

> "The term loss occurrence shall mean one or more losses arising out of and occasioned by one occurrence."

Generally speaking, the variety of definitions is confusing and there is little definitive case law which covers all these various distinctions. Even in marine insurance, which goes back some way and which often uses a similar type of wording, e.g. "all losses arising out of one event", the definitive interpretation by Courts of what is an "event" does not exist in all countries and arbitration decisions have been variable, from treating the sinking of one vessel to be an event to regarding one storm or another period of bad weather over a large area, as an event.

On the liability side the problem is rather more as to how far back

this wording is written there are few disputes on what is one occurrence or event. This is because motor and household accidents normally happen at a clearly defined time and place. Generic losses such as Savings and Loans, Asbestos, Pollution, Pension mis-selling which affect a large number of policies cannot be contained within a short time period and therefore should not be events. These situations cause substantial financial losses to Insurers and Reinsurers alike and there must be ways of providing protection for these situations. I will cover this later in this chapter under "thoughts in 2000".

ARTICLE 6

The term "ultimate net loss" shall mean the sum actually paid by the Reassured in settlement of losses or liability after making deductions of all recoveries, all salvages and all claims upon other Reinsurances, whether collected or not, and shall include all costs and adjustment expenses arising from the settlement of claims other than the salaries of employees and the office expenses of the Reassured.

All salvages recoveries or payments recovered or received subsequent to a loss settlement under this agreement shall be applied as if recovered or received prior to the aforesaid settlement and all necessary adjustments shall be made by the parties hereto. Provided always that nothing in this clause shall be construed to mean that losses under this agreement are not recoverable until the Reassured's ultimate net loss has been ascertained.

Except as is otherwise provided for herein it is understood and agreed that recoveries under all underlying excess of loss reinsurances are for the sole benefit of the Reassured and shall not be taken into account in computing the ultimate net loss or losses in excess of which this agreement attaches nor in any way prejudice the Reassured's right of recovery hereunder.

It is understood and agreed that the amount of the Reinsurers' liability shall not be increased by reason of the inability of the Reassured to collect from any other Reinsurers any amounts which may have become due from them, whether such liability arises from the insolvency of such other Reinsurers or otherwise.

Ultimate Net Loss and Costs

The words "ultimate net loss" shall be understood to mean the amount actually paid in cash in settlement of the liability of the Reassured after making recoveries from other reinsurances. Please note that the recent House of Lords decision does not allow the Reinsurer to avoid payment to Reassured due to the Reassured's insolvency where they could not actually pay the loss.

This ultimate net loss clause is **costs inclusive**.All costs incurred by the Reassured to adjust the claim including court costs and lawyers fees are covered. These costs can be substantial and in some cases greater than the claim payment. It used to be normal that the costs were split between the Reassured and the Reinsurer in proportion that the retained loss was to the Reinsured loss (**costs in addition**). Please note that the costs inclusive contract has the advantage that Reinsurers can pay no more than their share of the limit, but they could pick up a claim where the claim payment is in the retention and only the costs breach the excess point. Please refer to the professional indemnity section later where "costs in addition" is used widely. On a costs in addition policy please note that in a successful defence of a claim no indemnity could be paid and the whole of the costs would be borne by the retention. In some of these cases the main beneficiaries to a successful defence are the excess of loss Reinsurers and they are sometimes asked to contribute to the legal costs.

ARTICLE 7

Premium Clause – Contract specific not shown here.

ARTICLE 8

In the event of loss or losses occurring under this agreement, it is hereby agreed to reinstate this Agreement to its full amount from the time of the occurrence of such loss or losses to expiry of this agreement without payment of additional premium. Nevertheless the Reinsures shall never be liable for more than £100,000 in respect of each and every accident.

It is understood and agreed that the aforementioned limit of liability shall be subject to the terms of the London Market Severe Inflation Clause Article 10.

On this contract unlimited free reinstatements are given. This is a very dangerous thing to do unless one is very comfortable about the number of likely losses and the likely tail. There were many such contracts written in the period from the 1950s to the 1980s, that have a growing, number of claims still hitting them.

On this contact it protects UK motor and household liability where the tail is probably 5 to 8 years and the number of claims fairly predictable. This is not the case on USA general liability (casualty). Even so please make sure the deductible is not too low and there is an index applied to the excess (deductible) so that in a few years time you do not scoop every small loss up. Only one limit is given per accident, which protects the Reinsurer in an "event " situation.

ARTICLE 9

Nuclear and civil war exclusions not shown here.

ARTICLE 10

INDEX CLAUSES

Before we look at these I quote from the earlier editions:

Indexation

Before considering this in detail let us look at the effect of inflation on excess of loss Reinsurers where deductibles are fixed in monetary terms. Assume a deductible of 50,000 for a contract for 12 months 1st January 1976. Assume that 2 identical claims happen on 2nd January 1976. The first is settled in 1976, the second, which would have cost the same if settled in 1976, is delayed and not settled until 1977:

Loss "A" costs 60,000
Loss "B" costs 66,000 (due to 10% inflation) i.e. a 10% increase.
The excess Reinsurer pays:
10,000 x 50,000 for "A" and
16,000 x 50,000 for "B" – an increase of 60%

The effect of this on excess Reinsurers will vary with the length of settlement and the rate of inflation. In all cases, with a fixed deductible, the excess Reinsurer's experience will show a much higher percentage increase than the increase in the original claim. Often such an increase approximates to the square of the original increase, i.e. original increase – 5%, excess Reinsurer's increase – 25%, but, where the original increase is over 10% this rough formula may produce too high a figure.

Therefore, in order that the original balance between the Reassured and Reinsurers is kept, our 50,000 deductible should increase as inflation increases. Thus, in our simple example:

> Loss "A" – Reinsurer pays 10,000 x/s 50,000
> Loss "B" – Reinsurer pays 11,000 x/s 55,000
> Note that both parties have a 10% increase in the loss, i.e. they share in the increase proportionately.

Therefore, the introduction of an indexed deductible can have a dramatic effect on Reinsurers' eventual loss payments and will have the effect of making both parties share in the cost of inflation proportionately.

To achieve the above a deductible fixed at 50,000 on the lst January 1976 should be indexed automatically from that date *until the date the loss is settled.* In practice, a monthly index can be used, i.e. all losses settled in January 1976 have a deductible of 50,000 but with a 1% monthly increase in inflation. Losses settled in February will have a deductible of 50,500 and in March 1976 51,005.

> Note that the increase is cumulative from 1st January 1976 to the date of the *settlement* of the loss, not the date of *occurrence* of the loss.

In some cases the use of a monthly indexation may be postponed for 12 months, in which case all claims settled in 1976 would have a deductible of 50,000 and one settled in March 1977 would have a deductible of 51,005. (Here the base is 50,000 at lst January 1977 and I have assumed a 1% monthly increase in 1977.)

Alternatively, a less rapid formula can be used on an annual basis, i.e. all claims settled in 1976 will have a deductible of 50,000. All claims settled in 1977 will be on the basis of a deductible increased to the index at 1st January 1977. Assume an annual increase of 12% (rather less than 1% monthly) then all claims settled in 1977 would be on a deductible of 56,000.

It will be seen that the index used is vital and should relate to the actual increase in the claims themselves. For example, an excess W.C.A. or E.L. excess for workers in the steel industry might have its index based on wages and salaries in the steel industry. In practice the index used will not relate so directly to the effect of inflation on the claims concerned.

A general or motor liability excess could be indexed on a general wages index, or upon a cost of living index, or upon the cost of new motor cars or the cost of repairs. However, an index must be found which can be recognised by both parties, i.e. one which is produced by an outside body and which is published and has general acceptance. This limits the possibilities. In practice one is forced into an index based either on the cost of living or on wages or values.

It could be argued that an index based on the price of medical treatment would be more appropriate for a W.C.A. or E.L. excess and some indices are so based on the published cost of hospital beds. However, whilst such indices have a validity, and any index is better than none, the fact remains that liability awards have a life of their own. In many countries they are subject to what I have always called social inflation. This is the inflation caused by changing social (and social political) pressures. In the U.S.A. this is particularly dynamic as awards are often made by juries and accentuated by the method of paying lawyers with a fee related to results or awards given.

Awards have been increased in other areas too, due to a variety of social factors which have no relation to either wages or the cost of living e.g.:

(1) Increased monetary awards for pain and suffering.

(2) Change of status of widows.

(3) Medical advances involving the high cost of new treatment and drugs.

(4) Impairment of future earnings or marriage prospects.

(5) Life expectancy increasing.

In the last generation a whole new concept of consumerism, plus social aspirations and conscience, has meant that the cost of liability awards has escalated far faster than either the cost of living or wages. The only index which would keep abreast of this would be one based on the average level of such awards themselves. There is a very strong case, for example, for the index used on English motor excess to be based on a selection of actual awards on motor liability in the English Courts.

Assume that in any year the top two awards in that year could be abnormal. Assume, too, that our excess contract is dealing with claims exceeding £50,000, then our index could be based on the change from one year to the next in the aggregate amount of the third, fourth, fifth, sixth and seventh highest awards made in any year. This would always index our £50,000 deductible to the increase in large awards.

Alternatively, the use of an arbitrary pre-fixed indexation has a great deal to recommend it. If current Court verdicts indicate a rate of increase of around 20% per annurn (not an unusually large increase) then a contract might have a deductible increasing automatically at 1½% per month, and each year such an arbitrary indexation could be altered by the parties.

My first use of indexed deductibles was made in the immediate postwar period in Europe. No doubt these were used before the second World War but I can find no record of them. Unfortunately, competition for liability and motor excess in the early 1950s became so fierce that we were unable to maintain indexed deductibles. During the 1960s and 1970s they came back into vogue in Europe but not in the U.S.A. or Canada.

It is my personal view that some form of indexation of deductibles and limits on liability and similar classes is essential if award inflation is to be checked. However, if I were a Reassured I would do my level best to obtain an un-indexed contract, even if the price was a lot higher. Where liability business is concerned it has almost always been worthwhile to purchase a fixed excess deductible at the lowest possible deductible and forget the price, provided the Reinsurer is sound and will be solvent in 10 or 20 years time.

In the U.S.A. and Canada there has always been a somewhat different attitude to indexation. Europe has unlimited liability on motor or automobile liability; in the U.S.A. policies are limited. Again, in the U.S.A. deductibles can be set at a fixed figure which relates to the fixed maximum liabilities under the original policies. For example, if a U.S.A. company can warrant that it will limit its maximum acceptance to $250,000 any one person, $500,000 any one accident and $100,000 any one accident for property damage, then a Reinsurer having an excess of U.S. $500,000, with a costs clause in his policy, will only be involved in a combined loss of $600,000 maximum, or an accident involving 2 policies. Even if the deductible were $250,000 he will not be involved for a single person claim.

Of course, in practice, such a warranty may be difficult to insert and recent tendencies to award extra damages in excess of the policy limits against the original Insurers may make such a warranty ineffective. The reason indexation of liability deductibles has never caught on across the Atlantic is basically the policy limitation and availability of non-indexed reinsurance. There is also another reason, and that is that the large professional Reinsurers in the U.S.A. tend to keep a much closer claims control than on this side of the Atlantic. The result of non-indexation does mean that U.S.A. liability excess reinsurance has the longest and most wicked tail.

Robert would have been appalled that now it is common practice to use the 35% Severe inflation clause rather than a full index clause which he was describing above where the deductible is increased to account for annual inflation. This is a very weak index clause as it only comes into affect after the wages have increased above 35% and only then does the index apply. In these days when normal inflation is only 2.5% and say wage inflation is say 5% then it will take six years before the index starts to apply. This in no way accounts for award inflation, which is in excess of 10% annually.

A. *Reinsurer(s) shall be adjusted by reference to an index, as hereinafter. In the event of any Bodily injury loss hereunder the retention of the Reassured and the limit of liability of the Reinsurer(s) shall be adjusted by reference to an index, as hereinafter defined, for the period embracing 1st January 2000 in the manner hereinafter set out. The index for the period embracing the above mentioned date shall be called the base index. There shall be no adjustment to the retention of the Reassured until the increase in the base index exceeds 35% (thirty five percent)*

B. *In respect of any loss settlement(s) made under this agreement the Reassured shall submit a list of payments comprising such loss settlement(s) showing the amount(s) paid and the date(s) of payment. All payments made by the Reassured in respect of Bodily Injury claims and legal costs shall be aggregated and the index used shall be that for the period embracing the date of payment as defined below.*

The amount of each payment shall be adjusted by means of the following formula:

Amount of Payment X (Base Index X 1.35 = *Adjusted Payment Value*

Index for the period embracing date of claims payment.

All payments and adjusted payment values shall be separately totalled and the retention of the Reassured and the limit of liability of the Reinsurer(s) shall be multiplied by the fraction:

Total of payments

Total of Adjusted Payment Values.

If, however the index for the period embracing the period is less than the base index the retention of the Reassured and the limit of liability of the Reinsurer(s) shall remain as stated in this agreement.

The index used within the United Kingdom is "Average earnings of all employees for the whole economy"

The clause goes on to define what other indices are used outside the UK and how the date of payment is defined

Comment

The two reasons this clause has come in is probably due to the soft state of the market and secondly to the fact that the index clause will only have to be calculated on those claims which are unsettled after say six years. This saves a lot of work.

Where deductibles are indexed it is logical and sound that reinsurance limits are indexed in the same way. In fairness to the Reassured, if he accepts indexation of the deductible, he should receive an indexed limit. Of course the Reinsurer will have an increasing limit which could in time vastly increase his loss. However, excess reinsurances are often placed in layers and some Reinsurers have been willing to have fixed deductibles at a high enough level. There can be a huge difference to the affect of the index on various layers, if the index is not matching the award inflation, then the lower layers will receive an increasing number of claims that might carry on for ten years with an increase in the monetary loss per claim. The high layers however may have a deductible high enough to avoid anything but the exceptional claims and with the extra claims management these claims might keep out of the top layers. However if landmark decisions in the Courts or new legislation lead to an unprecedented increase in the size of the major claims even the high layers are vulnerable. UK Reinsurers in the 1960s who wrote unlimited policies excess of £100,000 and in the 1970s excess of £500,000 and got caned. The same happened to Reinsurers of Spanish and Portuguese motor Insurers who following their entry to the European Community paid catch up, with the motor awards to match other countries already in the EEC.

Flat Deductible Increases

It is common on some USA Professional Indemnity contracts in the working area to have a fixed limit with a flat monetary deductible increasing by say $25,000 each year. This is done for administration simplicity and has the affect of keeping a frequency of claims out of the layer. At the end of the first year if the claim has not been paid it simply has an extra $25,000 deductible. I would welcome this method to be used on some low motor layers.

ARTICLE 11

Claims notification and co-operation

In the event of the Reassured receiving notification of a possible claim or claims arising out of one accident where the quantum, regardless of any questions of liability is estimated to exceed 75% of the retention hereunder the Reassured shall report such claim or claims to the Reinsurers as soon as possible.

The Reassured shall furnish the Reinsurers with all available information respecting such claim or claims. In addition, the following categories of claims shall be reported to the Reinsurers as soon as possible:

a) fatal injuries to third parties where such third party or parties leave a spouse or issue or other dependent(s).

b) bodily injuries as specified below:
- *brain injuries resulting in impairment of physical functions,*
- *spinal injuries resulting in partial or total paralysis of upper or lower extremities,*
- *amputations or loss of use of upper or lower extremities,*
- *All other injuries likely to result in a disability rating of 50% or more.*

c) bodily injuries resulting in payment of an annuity.

d) bodily injury claims made in USA and Canada

The Reassured shall keep the Reinsurers advised of all significant developments relating to above claims.

Whenever a claim or claims arising out of one loss appears likely to exceed the retention hereunder the course to be adopted in connection with the defence or settlement of such claim or claims shall be determined between the Reassured and the leading Reinsurer participating in this agreement.

Claim co-operation and claims consultation between the two parties is vital. This clause sets out clearly what is required by the Reassured for claims notification and it enables the Reinsurer to assess to some degree what the claims might cost. All typical problem claims are highlighted and these reports can be easily put onto spreadsheets or e-mailed to the Reinsurers as required. A good Reinsurer may often take over either the handling of a difficult individual claims or the handling of a large number of claims. This type of help or service is offered to many clients by some large Reinsurers and by some professional Reinsurance Brokers.

Annuities are very common in continental Europe; a third party is often awarded a fixed annuity for say, permanent disablement rather than a lump sum payment to produce a future income. Where this is done the law often requires the setting aside, or payment to a fund in trust, of the capital sum. This annuity reserve is normally treated as an outstanding claims reserve and deposited by Reinsurers with the Reassured, often with interest being paid to the Reinsurer. The reserve may need adjustment and of course, may be released when the annuity ceases, for example on death. When a fixed annuity is purchased for the injured party, that is discharge of liability, then the purchase price becomes a full settlement and not a reserve.

OTHER ARTICLES

The other articles in this wording were not specific to liability wordings. Other clauses that might appear in other wordings that need mention.

Acts in Force clause

Another aspect of long tail already touched upon is the retrospective changes in law, particularly in relation to benefits and coverage under workmen's compensation and employers' liability. Reinsurers should be entitled to limit their coverage on an excess W.C.A. reinsurance " to the Acts and benefits in force at inception of their reinsurance policy". If the Act or the benefits change, then appropriate amendments can be made to the reinsurance. If the Act changes retrospectively, e.g. benefit increases for claims which have already occurred, then Reinsurers will not be liable for those increases. Without such a clause Reinsurers may well find themselves covering retrospective increases in past claims already settled and such increases may go back 10, 20 or 30 years.

Extra Contractual Obligations clause

> *This agreement shall exclude all cover in respect of Extra Contractual Obligations howsoever arising, such Extra Contractual Obligations being defined as any award made by a Court of competent jurisdiction against an Insurer or Reinsurer, which is not within the coverage granted by any insurance and/or reinsurance contract made between the parties in dispute.*
>
> *Notwithstanding the foregoing this Agreement shall extend to cover any liability arising from a "Claims Related Extra Contractual Obligations":*
>
> *a) awarded against the Reassured*
>
> *or*
>
> *b) Incurred by the Reassured where they have paid their share of a "Claims Related Extra Contractual Obligation" awarded against one or more of their Co-Insurers.*

The clause goes on to define some points carefully and then defines a claims ECO as:

> *a) The failure of the Insurer or Reinsurer to agree or pay a claim within the policy limits or to provide a defence against such claims as required by law;*
>
> *b) Bad faith or negligence in rejecting an offer of settlement;*
>
> *or*
>
> *c) Negligence or breach of duty in the preparation of the defence or the conduct of a trial or the preparation or prosecution of any appeal and/or any subsequent action resulting therefrom.*

I have left out the remainder of the clause for conciseness.

The reason for this clause is entirely due to large punitive awards being made in the USA courts. These could be made against an Insured, Insurer or Reinsurer. These awards have been in some cases far in excess of the policy limits issued hence the name used of "Extra Contractual Obligations" or ECO for short. It is not the intent to exclude bad-faith or negligence of the Insurer or Reinsurer in handling the claim so this is added back in. These ECO awards make the Insurer think twice before rejecting some claims and it makes the handling of suspicious or potentially fraudulent claims very difficult.

Occupational disease definition

The provisions of this article shall override any other article contained herein which may conflict.

1. *Insofar as liability in incurred by the Reassured under an Employers Liability Policy and/or Workers Compensation Policy in respect of the legal liability for Occupational Disease or Physical Impairment which does not arise from a sudden and identifiable accident or event this agreement shall provide cover only on the following basis:*

2. *Where the Occupational Disease or Physical Impairment results from exposure to a hazard of the employment of the claimant, any one claim in respect of one employee of an original Insured arising out of this exposure shall be considered individually as one event for the purpose of recovery hereunder.*

The clause continues to explain later how or if coverage is given on an exposure or any other basis and how the date of loss is determined.

This clause is from the same UK Motor and household liability as seen earlier. It is dealing with the difficult problem that arose from the Asbestos problem in the USA and elsewhere. This clause prevents the aggregation of all these occupational disease claims as one event. One individual is one event and it is unlikely they will reach the deductible hereon. One needs to be careful if this clause is included at a low level in a high risk class of employers liability i.e. manufacturing, as there could be many individual claims that exceed the deductible. Please note we cover claims from sudden and accidental events (say an explosion at work) on a normal basis. There are many different types of these clauses available.

Seepage and Pollution

It has been common practice to exclude all seepage and pollution claims since the enormity of the potential pollution situation became recognised. However there is usually a write-back for sudden and accidental events such as tank ruptures and oil spills. Even so very often only "letter of intents" are produced which may not give an absolute exclusion.

Claims-Made Basis

Indexation is one method by which Reinsurers have tried to cope with the "tail" and with the effect of inflation and social inflation with some success. A second method is the replacement of a loss-occurring (occurrence) contract with a Claims-made contract.

Claims-made contracts are very common on professional indemnity direct insurance where claims have to made against the Insured during the policy period regardless of when the claim occurred. This means that the tail of such business is considerably shorter than with a losses occurring policies. Losses that actually occur many years ago thus fall into the year that they are first advised. To avoid a new Reinsurer picking up known situations that have occurred many years ago usually "a retro date of inception" is agreed with the claims-made Reinsurers. This date limits how far back the Reassured can go to include losses that have occurred but have not been reported yet.

Claims-made policies usually start when no Insurer or Reinsurer is prepared to continue to participate on an occurrence basis. This is invariably because the claims are being reported so late and in such a great number there is no way can the Insurer or Reinsurer assess the ultimate quantum of these losses and thus the premium to be charged. In a situation like this the retro date of inception will be the start of the new claims-made policy. In the first year most of the claims reported will arise from losses that occurred prior to both the start of the policy and the retro date and thus will be excluded. In the second year of the claims made policy the retro date will remain at the inception of the prior year policy and thus a larger number of the reported claims will be covered by the claims-made policy, the remainder still fall back to the old occurrence form. At the end of about six years on Professional Indemnity business most claims that are reported will have occurred in the prior six years, and the policy is said to be "mature". This cannot be said of industrial general liability business where the claims are reported up to 50 years later as asbestos has proved.

Thus on claims made policies at the end of the policy period it is known exactly the number of claims made and an Insurer or Reinsurer can make a reasonable estimate of what the ultimate cost of these claims will be. On some excess claims made policies the date of claims made can be the date the claim is reported to the primary or first layer and therefore there can still be a delay before the claims are reported to them. Beware of this. On Professional indemnity policies it is common to include retirees or claims against those who died in service as occurrence policies at the date of retirement or death. This will increase the tail slightly. On fidelity and surety polices it is normal to use the words "losses discovered" rather than "claims made". The date of loss will be the date of discovery of the fraud or financial collapse rather than the date reported.

The major problem for "claims made" policies is that no coverage exists after the expiry of the policy, for the run-off of claims that have occurred but not been reported yet. It is therefore normal to agree prior to the inception of the policy the cost of say three or five years run-off. This can be at many times the cost of one years claims made premium. It therefore is not sensible for an Insurer who writes business on an occurrence basis to buy a claims made policy unless the run-off coverage is purchased both for any business covered by the new claims-made policy and also earlier purchased occurrence reinsurances. This discussion leads very neatly into a paper written by Ray Hunter on Professional Indemnity with an emphasis on medical malpractice. However I will include here Robert's explanation of excess cession treaties which fits very well with Ray Hunter's paper which follows.

Excess Cession Treaties

We have discussed some methods of rating facultative liability excess reinsurances and in Chapter III we referred to excess cession treaties which use some of these methods of rating. To illustrate this method I will use professional indemnity or malpractice business as an example.

Assume that an Insurer wishes to underwrite medical malpractice and wishes to retain a deductible of U.S. $1,000,000 on each and every policy, and to be able to accept policies up to a limit of $3,000,000 with automatic reinsurance protection.

The rating of a layer of reinsurance of $2,000,000 x/s $1,000,000 may be extremely difficult on an experience basis. It will be a contract exposed on individual policies and should be rated on the exposures falling to it. A very sensible method of achieving this is to take out an excess cession treaty whereby the Reassured is obliged to cede all insurances excess of $1,000,000 and Reinsurers are obligated to accept. Each cesssion is noted by bordereaux and individually rated at a percentage of the total policy premium or at the manual increase premium, that is the premium charged by the original direct writer for increasing the original policy from, say, $1,000,000 to $3,000,000. The M.I.T. (Manual Increase Table) premiums are set out or referred to in the treaty. Each cession is thus rated individually by the M.I.T.

Alternatively, a premium is calculated as a percentage of the premium for the primary million, these percentages will vary by size and type of risk and will be set out in a table in the treaty, for example, a table for a treaty with a deductible of $1,000,000 might have:

	Premiums as % of premium for the primary $1,000,000	
Class of Risk	*Reinsurers limit up to $1,000,000 x/s $1,000,000*	*Reinsurers limit up to $2,000,000 x/s $1,000,000*
(1) Nurse	5%	10%
	10%	15%
	10%	20%
	20%	30%
	25%	40%
(10) Brain Surgeon	30%	50%

Such a rating method can, of course, be applied in bulk to all risks within a class on, say, monthly or quarterly bordereaux or by use of a cession record and quarterly or monthly accounts.

Professional Indemnity

This section was written by Ray Hunter an experienced actuary and Professional Indemnity Underwriter from the London Company Market and Lloyd's. May I thank Ray for this contribution which is included with the minimum of amendments and it will give the reader an understanding of the class with an emphasis on medical malpractice.

Professional indemnity insurance represents a significant proportion of liability reinsurance business. Coverage is purchased by members of the recognised professions such as Lawyers, Doctors, Accountants, Architects, Actuaries etc., and by many other individuals and entities which provide professional services such as Management and Computer Software Consultants, Public Officials, Directors and Officers, Brokers, Bankers, School Guards, Hospitals etc.

Professional indemnity is of interest to Reinsurers because it is a class of business that can produce substantial individual losses. Major insolvencies and other financial disasters often lead to lawsuits being brought against Directors and Officers, Auditing Accountants and other professional advisors. In the medical profession, a successful outcome can never be guaranteed. At some time we all face serious illness and death, but it is becoming increasingly common for disappointed patients, or their families, to look for ways to recover damages from medical professionals. Multi-million dollar medical malpractice awards have, for some years, been common in the USA but they are now also becoming common in other countries.

Professional Indemnity is prone not only to individual loss severity; from time to time generic loss situations occur which have the potential to cause major loss frequency problems, sometimes involving billions of dollars. (Examples that come to mind are the US savings and loan crisis in the 1980's and the recent pensions mis-selling problems in the UK.) For this reason, it is normal for professional indemnity policies to carry an aggregate limit in addition to a per event limit.

The susceptibility of professional indemnity business to occasional severe losses has, from time to time, led to the withdrawal of commercial insurance capacity. This, in turn, has led to the establishment of a multitude of specialist mutual Insurers and insurance pooling arrangements, which are managed by the professional societies. These mutual insurance schemes have often been established with very little initial capital, which has meant that they have been significant buyers of reinsurance and therefore a major source of reinsurance business.

A professional indemnity mutual Insurer, owned and managed by members of the Insured profession, has the advantage that the managers have a detailed knowledge of the risk and probably also a detailed knowledge of a large proportion of the membership. From the reinsurance Underwriter's point of view, this is an attractive feature, which should lead to a superior level of expertise in the original underwriting. A prudent reinsurance Underwriter will, however, recognise that there could be a lack of understanding of insurance principles and a lack of the financial expertise necessary to manage an insurance company. He would therefore be well advised to confirm that there are suitable insurance professionals employed within the mutual's organisation, and that appropriate actuarial advice is sought when establishing rate tables and reserves. It is common practice for P.I. mutuals to make their actuarial reports available to Reinsurers, and these reports can be of great assistance to the reinsurance Underwriter when he is considering the structure and rating of the reinsurance programme.

The reinsurance of the professional indemnity account of a commercial insurance company presents different problems. Commercial insurance companies should have plenty of insurance expertise. However, the reinsurance Underwriter will wait to ensure that the company has a sufficiently detailed understanding of the risks associated with the particular professions that it is insuring. He may be concerned that the commercial Insurer could suffer anti-selection when competing with non-profit mutuals, managed by the professional associations, (though, of course, the commercial Insurer will not suffer the political pressures to accept Insureds that are members of a particular association). Commercial Insurers rarely share their actuarial information with Reinsurers, which is a distinct disadvantage from the reinsurance Underwriter's point of view.

Professional Indemnity is now written predominantly on claims made policy forms, however, some occurrence form still persists notably within medical malpractice business and occasionally within public officials errors and omissions. The use of a claims made original policy form is a great advantage to Reinsurers because it should give a significant insight into both the nature and potential quantum of claims, which have been experienced by the Reinsured account. However, the Reinsurer would be well advised to commission an independent review of loss reserves because cedants' own reserves can often be misleading. Professional Indemnity claims frequently take several years to settle and the quantum can be difficult to estimate. More significantly, the cedants may adjust the estimate to reflect their thoughts on the probability of their insured being found liable, (for example, $2 million damages times 0.5 probability of liability gives a reserve of $1 million on the original business. For a Reinsurer excess of $1 million, the same logic would lead to an FGU reserve of $1.5 million; i.e. $1 million exposure to the layer times 0.5 plus the retention). Furthermore, cedants often will not put up reserves on claims where there is a coverage dispute and some cedants are reluctant to establish high case estimates for fear that they may be discovered by the claimants during litigation.

Medical malpractice is written almost exclusively on a "costs in addition" basis and medical malpractice reinsurances normally give pro rata costs in addition to the reinsured limit. However, reinsurances with a "costs inclusive" limit are not uncommon. Please note that as discussed earlier in the chapter "costs in addition," means that the Reinsurer can pay more that his limit due to the costs. On the other hand costs on claims that have no indemnity payments all the costs will all be borne by the Reassured.

For other professional indemnity classes, both the original policies and the reinsurances are usually on a costs inclusive basis. Reinsurance Underwriters should beware of costs in addition coverage on professional indemnity classes where there could be major discovery of documents during claims litigation (i.e. anything financial). The writer can only too clearly remember a claim on a U.S. savings and loan, directors officers policy, where the attorneys had to hire a warehouse to store five million documents, taken in discovery, while they worked through them. In such a case the costs could became a large proportion of the total amount paid.

In order to protect professional reputations, it is common for policies to require the Insurer to obtain settlement authority from the policyholder before the payment is made, so it is not always possible to make a commercial settlement to save costs.

The structure of reinsurance programmes, which protect professional indemnity accounts, can vary widely. Indeed, for many commercial insurance companies, the professional indemnity account is protected within the general casualty reinsurance programme, and there are no specific principles to consider.

However, for specialists, mutual Insurers, some reinsurance structural features are common, and the following hypothetical example will help illustrate some of the common features and basic principles of programme design.

A U.S. physician mutual insurance company operates in a state where minimum insurance coverage of $1 million per event, $3 million annual aggregate, is required before physicians can be licensed to practice in hospitals which are located within that state. The mutual therefore offers a standard $1m/3m, claims made, medical malpractice policy ($1m/3m denotes $1 million per event limited to a maximum annual aggregate of $3 million). Some Doctors, recognising that they would be potentially exposed to verdicts excess of $1 million, wish to buy more than the minimum requirement. This would occur with Physicians involved with obstetrics and gynaecology or in wealthy neighbourhoods. As a consequence the company offers alternative limits of $2m/4m and $5m/7m. Standard, manual increase factors are used calculating the premium for the chosen higher limits from that which would have been charged for the normal $1m/3m limit. 60% of the company's policyholders buy the standard $1m/$3m limit, 30% buy $2m/$5m and the remaining 10% buy the maximum offered limit of $5m/$7m.

The mutual's reinsurance programme consists of four layers. There are two excess cession layers, which cede the exposure excess of the standard $1m/$3m limit. This effectively reduces all the policies to the standard limit exposure and they are then protected by a working risk excess and a contingency layer. The manual increase factors used for the difference between the $1m/$3m standard limits and the larger limits of $2m/$5m and $5m/$7m enable the premiums for the two excess cession layers to be calculated accurately. Some deductions are made for commissions to the mutual to cover their own costs for claims handling and policy production etc. The contingency layer would protect the mutual against two or more Physicians involved in the same case or an extra contractual loss (ECO).

The reinsurance limit for the first excess cession is expressed as the difference between \$2m/\$4m and \$1m/3m. It would be tempting, but wrong, to express the limit as \$1m/1m excess of \$1m/3m because \$4 million of aggregate could be used up by two \$2 million losses and a reinsurance limit of \$1m/1m would only allow one loss to be recovered. By expressing the limit as the difference between \$2m/4m and \$1m/3m both losses could be recovered excess of \$1 million.

Similarly, the second excess cession limit is expressed as the difference between \$5m/7m and \$2m/4m.

For both excess cession layers, the Reinsurers receive the normal increase premium less an allowance for the mutual Insurer's management expenses. Only policies, which have ceded premium to the excess cessions, will be eligible for recovery from those reinsurances.

The excess cession reinsurances are on a risks attaching basis. When a Physician dies or retires, his final policy has attached to it an extended reporting endorsement which allows that final policy to respond within the limit, to all future claims made in respect of incidents which occurred while he was a policyholder. Policyholders who move to another Insurer also have the option to buy such an endorsement. Excess cession reinsurances follow the fortunes on extended reporting and these endorsements can greatly increase the potential loss reporting tail.

For the primary working risk excesses the reinsurance limit for our hypothetical programme is expressed as:

Section A: The difference between \$2 million each and every loss, each and every policy and \$250,000 indexed at \$25,000 per annum each and every loss each and every policy.

Section B: The difference between \$4 million each and every loss event and \$500,000 indexed at \$25,000 per annum, each and every loss event. Section A insures to the benefit of Section B.

This reinsurance is on a claims made during basis with the condition that the claims made date on the first policy to report determines the reinsurance loss date for all other involvement in the same event. The reinsurance carries a run-off option in the event of non-renewal so that the mutual can be sure of being able to buy protection for unexpired policies and extended reporting endorsements, which were issued prior to non-renewal.

Section A gives protection up to \$2 million per policy, whereas the maximum original exposure per loss is only $1 million net of the excess cession reinsurances. The additional cover is to give further protection for excess of policy limits verdicts and potential bad faith litigation brought against the mutual. In this case the loss adjustment expenses are pro rata in addition. If the reinsurance was cost inclusive then that would be another reason for the higher limit for Section A.

Section B gives clash protection for involvement of more than two insureds and additional protection for the non-contractual exposures (ECO) described above.

Both reinsurance deductibles are indexed to protect the Reinsurer from inflationary increase in loss frequency on what would likely be a heavily working layer. The index is a flat $25,000 per annum for administrative simplicity.

The primary working risk excess is rated on a loss cost, burning cost or swing plan basis. The initial rate is 20% of gross net earned premium income adjusted 24 months after inception and annually thereafter at:

4% GNEPI plus 110% of incurred losses subject to a maximum of 30% GNEPI.

This type of adjustment is called "minimum plus". It is often used when reinsuring professional indemnity because it gives a clearer picture of the Reinsurer's profit margin. It also allows the swing to start from a very low percentage which is attractive to cedants who feel that they can influence their loss experience with superior underwriting selection and claims management.

The risk excess illustrated here is on a claims made during basis. Similar risks are often written on a risks attaching basis with the premium based on gross net written premium income rather than earned income. Risks attaching has the advantage that it avoids what could be a rather onerous run-off obligation in the event of non-renewal, however, the administration of risks attaching could be messy where there are a large number of events involving multiple Insureds. An interlocking clause would be required.

The final layer reinsurance layer for our hypothetical mutual is a $9 million excess $1m excess of policy limits protection on a "verdicts during" basis. All other reinsurances inure to the benefit of this protection. This reinsurance has one paid reinstatement whereas all the other layers have unlimited reinstatements. Professional indemnity Insurers often have to take claims to a verdict in court and, on rare occasions, where they previously had the opportunity to settle within the policy limit, they could be held responsible for substantial awards, which are in excess of the policy. This type of rare contingency can only be rated using Underwriters' subjective judgement. Prudent reinsurance Underwriters will only write this type of cover on a verdicts during basis because the existence of the protection could change a cedant's attitude towards taking claims to trial.

The hypothetical reinsurance programme described above is typical of what one might see in a normal reinsurance market. But obviously, reinsurance markets are cyclical. In a harder market one might see maximum recoverable limits added to the risk excess and excess cessions. In a softer market one might see significant profit commission added to the excess cession treaties and pressure applied to reduce the swing plan percentages on the risk excess, even to the point where the maximum rate is below the equivalent manual premium for the reinsured layer (which can be derived from the rating actuarial report), a dangerous situation for the Reinsurer. Also, in a soft market other coverage may be added to the risk excess, such as per policy or even whole account aggregate protections.

The final area which we need to consider under the heading of professional indemnity is the interpretation of a Reinsured event. The 1980's US savings and loan crisis and the 1990's Lloyd's agents' errors and omissions problems have led to several reinsurance disputes being brought to UK courts, which have sought to clarify what is an Insured event for professional indemnity business. They have produced only greater confusion. There have been a number of verdicts within the UK Commercial Court (e.g. *1996 American Centennial Insurance Company v INSCO Ltd* and *Axa Re v Field*), which have found that the original acts of negligence of the professionals were the events which led to the insurance claims and they could not be aggregated for event purposes with losses which resulted from other professionals' negligent acts. *Axa Re v Field* was appealed up to the House of Lords and the House of Lords found that a reinsurance event could differ from the original cause, which triggered the loss under the original policy. *Axa Re v Field* was then sent back to the Commercial Court for reconsideration but is believed to have been settled before a revised verdict was given.

We must hope that the UK Courts produce more clarity of thinking regarding the interpretation of event for professional indemnity purposes. In professional indemnity the event is the outcome which results from the original acts of negligence (e.g. the death of a patient, the insolvency of a company or the collapse of a building). If the original negligent acts were the events, and then it would be virtually impossible to have a clash loss within professional indemnity business, in which case it would be absurd for Reinsurers to continue to sell clash coverage to their cedants.

Written by Ray Hunter-1999

Liability General Underwriting Considerations

Robert wrote this passage in 1981

A Reassured has two objects in mind when buying excess long-tail reinsurance. Firstly, he desires to protect himself against the large loss which may be known quickly — for example, an explosion — and which can be settled quickly. Secondly, he desires to protect himself from the effect of inflation of awards so that his premium fund can be invested in the knowledge that it will not be eroded by this inflation of claims. In addition, claims can be limited to the amount of his known retention.

Therefore, a buyer of excess long-tail reinurance should, wherever possible, purchase non-indexed or low-indexed cover on a loss-occurring basis, thereby relieving himself of the effect of future inflation.

Basically, Reinsurers fall into three schools:

Firstly, there are those who believe that they can write excess reinsurance with a sufficiently high deductible to escape most individual awards however much they may be inflated on final settlement. Of course, where direct policies have a fixed monetary limit, this can be achieved. The writing of such high excess liability business is done at a judgement rate with little or no experience. To be successful the Reinsurer must reassess the height of his deductible each year and increase it for his renewals and new business. The premium charged will be based on:

(a) the costs of the Reinsurer;

(b) the catastrophic risk involving two or more policies;

(c) the chance of a very large settlement on a single policy.

As claims will be infrequent, the Reinsurer's premiums will be invested to produce a maximum return. Often it will be many years before such an account can be said to be "profitable".

The art is to build a fund as quickly as you can and keep it, not disperse it. The eventual success or failure of such an operation will depend not only on investment but also on timing. In "hard" markets the premiums for high excess contracts may be considerable; in "soft" markets — negligible. If the book can be built in former times and shed or trimmed in latter times, then the premium fund may be kept ahead of claims.

The second school of Reinsurers reinsure within the known loss area. Here the assessment of loss frequency above the deductible is of as great concern as the size of losses. Such Reinsurers must keep in close touch with their Reassureds' claims departments and with original settlements and estimates of outstandings to be successful. If deductibles are not indexed then they will need annual revision. Rates must be based on realistic progression of past experience into the future. This progression will, of course, be much easier to achieve if contract deductibles are indexed realistically, as future inflation of past awards will be taken care of automatically by future deductible increases. Again, with a claims made basis, the task is easier as the tail is much shorter.

In addition, Reinsurers may rate their excess contracts on the number of policies exposed to their layer or, better still, to the premium from such policies, and I would like to turn to one method of achieving this in a moment. Investment is vital and if loss reserves are put up, proper interest or investment gain must not be sacrificed. Either Letters of Credit should be used or a proper investment return paid by the Reassured.

The third school is best illustrated by a quotation from one of the most successful liability excess writers of the 1970s given to me personally for this book.

Question: "Tell me, how do you write excess long tail business? Do you mix deductibles?"

Answer: "I don't worry about indexing; leave that to the experts. I want a juicy premium; if the client won't pay it let him try elsewhere for a year or so. He'll come back when they've had enough.

Then tuck your premiums away, investing every penny, After 3 years look at your reserves and make sure that they are 150% of premiums you wrote 3 years earlier. Tuck those away to produce lovely investment gain. Another 3 years — tuck some more away. You lose on your underwriting every year but that is tax recoverable and the fund gets juicier and juicier."

Any Reinsurer writing long tail reinsurance should keep the

progression of his experience by year of account or at least 10 years, preferably for 20 years. Such progression will be done probably contract by contract, class by class, country by country and even by classification of deductibles, e.g. low, medium and high deductibles. I would refer the reader to the progression triangle in dealing with long-tail quota share treaties. The use of such progression triangles, or pyramids, for excess liability reinsurance results is strongly recommended. Finally, any successful Underwriter of non-indexed loss occurring business (he must have a least a 25-year record) has my profound respect.

Thoughts in 1984

Since writing this chapter in the late 1970s a good deal has happened in the whole field of third party and casualty excess reinsurance. Notably, the effect of asbestosis, the escalation of professional indemnity awards, the looming menace of pollution and environmental impairment and the constant move by society, Courts and Politicians to expect an "injured" party to receive compensation often, retroactively geared to cost of living or medical services, without having to prove negligence of any third party.

Often the insurance industry has been simply forced to pay regardless as to whether it was liable under the terms of the original insurance contract when that was taken out. In many cases primary carriers have turned to Reinsurers to protect them often on a basis which was never envisaged within the original reinsurance contracts and for which a reinsurance premium was never paid.

The reserving of claims has become almost impossible on any adequate basis and many Insurers are at present grappling with their long-tail run-offs from the '50s, '60s and the early '70s. No one has a clear idea how the tail of the late '70s and early '80s will turn out.

In Chapter XIV I refer to some methods of reinsurance which have been increasingly used by long-tail Underwriters to at least alleviate or solve their problems. The problem can only be solved by reinsuring ones run-off in full (i.e. with unlimited cover) for a finite premium with someone else. This is a solution only provided that someone else does not dispute the reinsurance and is and will remain solvent for the period of the run-off; today 50 years would be a reasonable period.

Many have taken advantage of the soft reinsurance market since 1970 to so reinsure their run-offs. They only remain viable entities today because they did so and found someone else to shoulder the burden of their run-off.

Reinsurers of run offs on the other hand are in some instances facing tremendous accumulation of liability losses due to the relatively recent explosion of latent disease and pollution claims from the USA.

The problem has been contained, at least by the more astute, by using the historical high rates of interest available particularly when the interest is tax free, e.g. in tax-free havens or special tax-free investments or because of the Company's own tax position. The success in underwriting this type of business is essentially geared to the investment of this fund either by yourself or using someone else via the reinsurance route. There is no point in writing this business unless one is organized in this field.

No Underwriter can expect to make a technical profit in this business and the professionals do not expect to do so. An eventual loss ratio of 150% to 200% may be perfectly acceptable. The difficulty is that you must start out to acheive a technical profit otherwise your eventual settlements will be several hundreds percent and will swamp the investment gain.

The whole problem is really a social and political one. If the insurance industy is to continue to provide a welfare cushion for aggrieved persons, for impaired life and for many other aspects of an industrial society, then it has to prevent itself going bankrupt in the process and it can only do this at a cost in premiums or restricting coverage in a way which policy holders cannot economically accept.

The effect of huge medical malpractice premiums in the USA has already impaired the service that a Doctor is willing to provide to his patients and undoubtedly other professions are being similarly effected.

I have already discussed a "claims made basis" as one which will shorten the Insurers and Reinsurers tail. But will this be socially acceptable or will the Courts in the USA, for example, find some way in the future of finding this illegal?

Our industry has got to convince society, i.e. the Politicians, the Judges and Lawyers, the lobbies and above all, the public, that we Insurers and Reinsurers are being asked to carry a burden which is not supportable and the alternative of governments taking over this social burden is no real solution as they only pass it on to future taxpayers in the same way that many of us today are passing it on to our future policy holders, presuming we are still in business to have any!

We are in effect being asked to provide indexed pensions to injured or aggrieved people. No Life Company can afford to provide such pensions to the fit. In the UK life and pension funds enjoy tax-free status for their policy holders funds. We should all at least try and convince our governments that our policy holders funds should enjoy the same status, i.e. be tax-free investments whilst they remain in a trust for our policy holders being taxed only when they move to shareholders funds. At least then tax-free havens would not have it all their own way.

Without such a change in the attitudes from the courts and society, how can we as Reinsurers honestly continue to shoulder the burden for the direct writers?

Firstly we must not relieve them of their burden entirely. We must use such devices as coreinsurance, aggregate limitation of coverage, indexation of deductibles, variable rates, to make sure that primary carriers suffer with us if things go wrong. Of these, it is my view that indexation of the deductible from the start of the policy until the settlement of the claim is the most effective and least likely to be upset by Courts. It is also the fairest to be insured as this index will preserve the parity between the parties as inflation takes place. We must not put up loss reserves without agreeing quantum and having an adequate return for providing this service. We must charge a proper premium which means a premium which is several times the "mathematical" or "risk" premium calculated at the time of writing.

We must ourselves have a highly efficient investment operation tied in to our underwriting. We must take advantage of any reinsurances which will enhance this. We must be efficient in our IBNR reserving and we have got to convince our fiscal authorities not to tax these reserves. We must never assume that we have made a "profit" until the "run-off" is either complete or we are sure that we can evaluate it. On the long-tail business that means at least 10 years and on the very long-tail probably 20 years and in 1990 25 years and more!

The accumulation of exposures from industrial disease and pollution has become a huge risk and the basis of reinsurance must be carefully defined with an aggregate limit per annum and carefully rated.

For myself, since I became an active Reinsurer in the late 1940s, I have always believed that this long-tail reinsurance is not for me. A little may be necessary for commercial reasons and occasionally one may be tempted by a short-term shortage of market but my advice remains, keep short and keep your powder dry.

Thoughts in 2000

The liability Reinsurance market can sometimes adapt well to provide new reinsurance products when a crisis arises in the market.

When the USA medical malpractice market was in disarray in the mid-1980s following an increase in the severity and frequency of claims as well as the continuing problem of late reporting; the whole insurance and ongoing Reinsurance market switched almost universally to the claims made form. This allowed Reinsurers and Insurers to assess much quicker whether they were making or losing money. At the same time the original rates were increased and some legal reforms were made which restricted the size of some awards. The changes made, allowed Reinsurers to make a profit again and therefore they could continue to provide coverage. At the same time Insurers who had good results would in time achieve a reduction in their reinsurance rates. Any Insurer who still produced poor results would have further rate increases and there would be a reluctance for Reinsurers to provide coverage anymore, maybe putting the Insurers out of business. Therefore a healthy market economy was produced where there were willing buyers and sellers.

At the same time there was also a crisis on USA general liability business for Fortune 1000 companies. Some Reinsurance coverage was provided by new companies often writing this business on a claims made form situated offshore where they would get tax and investment benefits.

As a contrast however following the disastrous foray of certain infamous Underwriters into providing unlimited run-off contracts from the mid-1970s until the early 1980s no easy replacement of capacity was found. This was because no market was produced, as there were then plenty of buyers but no sellers. This situation led however to the development or ART (Alternative Risk Transfer) products dealt with in Chapter XIV. The new products produced i.e. ART and Claims made have provided partial solutions and have enabled some continuity of coverage with the reinsurance market.

Why have these solutions worked?

(1) The length of the tail has been reduced.

This has been achieved by switching from the occurrence form to the claims made form. It has made the management of the claims easier for the Reinsurer as at the end of the first year no new claims will be reported although of course the ultimate cost of the known claims may take six or more years to develop. The switch of an entire account can only be achieved if there is a consensus in the market; it is not possible if good reinsurance security is still offering the occurrence at say only two times the price of the claims made policy.

A similar solution was achieved by the introduction of the index clause, which led to a gradual improvement of the old underwriting years.

(2) The contracts were experience rated.

This was normally, but not always, written into the contracts but it was an essential part. As Ray Hunter showed earlier in the chapter the working layer malpractice contracts had minimum and maximum rates which were usually applied to three- year contracts. The minimum rates encouraged the Insurer to produce a good experience and the maximum rates protected the Reinsurer if everything continued to go badly. On the higher layers there were no experience rate adjustments but there was an understanding between the parties that if Reinsurers were making good profits after say 3 or 4 years, when the results of the first two years are predictable, then there would be an improvement in terms. The whole mechanism led to the development of a close relationship between the parties and encouraged continuity.

(3) Contracts were capped

The unlimited run-off contracts were particularly problematic as there was no maximum limit that could be paid and the losses kept rising.

The ART contracts that developed all had a maximum limits and in order to develop the relationship aspect they generally also had profit commissions. On the clash layers on the malpractice programmes it was normal to have one or two reinstatements only.

Continuity and Close relationships

The development of a close relationship between the Insurer and Reinsurer is essential on liability reinsurance. There is often a long time between when the contract incepts the losses are paid. If this tail gets too long it is almost impossible to retain the continuity. The Underwriters who wrote the risks have probably retired or died and Reinsurers may well be out of business due to the losses sustained. The only way to keep these relationships going is to keep the tail short and have a regular review of the results of the business written for all underwriting years. It helps to have an annual renewal so that terms can be changed where necessary to reflect past profits and losses.

On this class one of the major problems has been, "what is the definition of one event or one occurrence"? This will continue in the future due to large amounts of money involved in these disputes. Many of the disputes are between parties who no longer have a close relationship. Examples are where the liquidators of a reinsurance company are suing their Reinsurers or where one company has purchased another. There is a tendency for the financial controllers to take over the handling of the disputes due to the large amounts involved and they may be prepared to test any grey areas in a wording in the courts rather than agree a compromise settlement due to the amounts at risk. Therefore, I was pleased with the development of the reinsurance claims made contracts by R. K. Carvill in the late 1980s which went some way to address the problems of what is one loss and it also has kept the tail of the reinsurances as short as possible to help with continuity problems.

Reinsurance Claims Made

Key points

1. The contracts are for 12 months where all claims have been discovered within the twelve months and an extra 60-day reporting period. This allows the Reassured 60 days only to report any claims advised right at the end of the year.

2. The contracts are claims made but the original business can be either claims made or occurrence business. There is an exclusion for all losses where part of the loss occurred before the inception of the contract. This excludes known events written on an occurrence form e.g. asbestos, Agent Orange etc. but it does not exclude claims from claims made only contracts where the claims have not been made yet.

3. The contracts generally have one reinstatement at 100% additional premium. This means the downside is limited.

4. There is a sixty month extended discovery period which allows the Reassured in event of non-renewal of the contract to buy for an additional premium the ability to present any additional claims that

were discovered during the twelve months period to be reported to Reinsurers.

5. The event definition is as broad as possible but the decision of what is one event is made by an exclusive arbitration panel of market practitioners. The aim of the panel is to resolve what is one event as soon as possible and to be binding on both parties. In order to help the panel and the contracting parties to know what is one event before the loss, a series of examples of what is one event are described in the renewal package. As illustrated in the *Axa v Field* Court case the definition of what is one event can differ between the original policies and the reinsurance contract. Examples of loss events defined as such by the reinsurance panel were.

   The E&O claims arising from the underwriting of Outhwaite in Lloyd's in the early 1980s resulted in claims made in the early 1990s. These were treated as one loss .The claims from the Gooda Walker agencies which affected three syndicates in the early 1990s were also treated as one loss event. The losses from the Savings and Loan crisis in the USA in the early 1980s was not treated as one event but all claims whether D&O, Fidelity, Lawyers and Accountants E&O were treated as one event as long as the claims came from the collapse of the same financial institution. Some of these definitions are at loggerheads with some Court cases but the good thing is that it offers some Reassureds who are affected by these losses, some coverage which is not available elsewhere.

6. There are specific exclusions for asbestos, tobacco, dioxin, silicon, electromagnetic fields, Year 2000 change, seepage and pollution other than specific events etc.

7. A recent development in line with ART and to encourage continuity is a contingent or profit commission.

8. The contracts are renewed annually and because of the reporting conditions, losses are known about quickly. Therefore in the days of concern about security the security is effectively upgraded as required each renewal season.

9. This product has been recently adapted to cover products liability on an aggregate basis. The coverage is only where the products losses have shown an exceptional increase in the last 12 months and they have the exclusions as in 6 above.

Chapter XII

STOP LOSS REINSURANCE

Introduction — Insuring clause — Earned or written income basis — Other reinsurances — Advance loss payments — Outstanding losses — Incurred loss basis — Past statistics and underwriting practices — Uses — Types of business — Fixing the deductible — Fixing the limit — Fixing the premium and rate — Quota share stop loss conversions — Variable rates — Loss settlements — Stop loss on surplus treaties — Stop loss on excess of loss

Introduction

We now turn to the second main type of non-proportional reinsurance; excess aggregate or stop loss reinsurance or excess loss ratio reinsurance, all of which are different names for the same animal. Correctly, the term excess of loss ratio is restricted to a certain type of stop loss or excess aggregate.

We have dealt at some length with excess of loss reinsurance and many of the clauses and conditions common in excess of loss are used in a stop loss reinsurance contract. I will only discuss in detail those articles which differ.

The stop loss reinsurance indemnifies the Reassured against sustaining an aggregation of losses during a period of time. Normally the losses would be those occurring during the term or period of the contract as they are finally settled. However, where settlement is unduly prolonged, the contract may make provision for outstanding losses to be commuted or settled on a basis laid down in the contract. A typical example of this in the case of a reinsurance of long-tail business. The term of the contract is normally an annual one as this coincides with the accounting period of most Underwriters. However, there are exceptions; notably in dealing with seasonal risks, such as hail damage on crops.

ARTICLE 5

> *Insuring Clause. If the total of the Company's ultimate net loss, in respect of all losses occurring during the term of this agreement, exceeds a deductible equal to _____% of its gross net earned premium income (as finally determined) or _________ whichever amount is the greater, then Reinsurers agree to reimburse the Company for 90% of that part of its aggregate ultimate net loss which exceeds the said deductible up to but not exceeding 90% of a further _____% of its gross net earned income or 90% of whichever _________ the lesser.*
>
> *The balance of 10% of the excess ultimate net loss together with the first _________ shall be retained net by the Company and not reinsured in any way. However, it is understood and agreed that the Company have an underlying reinsurance for 90% of _________ excess of _________ in the aggregate, recoveries under which shall be disregarded in computing the ultimate net loss hereunder.*
>
> *If the Company's final gross net earned premium income is not known at the time any claim is made under this agreement, an estimate of the Company's gross net earned premium income for the full term of this agreement shall be used in determining the deductible hereunder, subject to adjustment when the gross net earned premium income is determined.*

The insuring clause of the contract will set out the deductible of the contract, that is the point at which Reinsurers' liability in respect of the aggregate loss attaches. It will also contain the limit of Reinsurers' liability for losses exceeding the deductible.

The limit and deductible can be set as straight monetary figures, but, to make sense, the limit and deductible should change with variations in the Reassured's original exposures. For example, a stop loss might be based on a Reassured's total original sums insured. More normally, as in the Article above, the limits and deductible are expressed as a percentage of the Reassured's gross net premium income on the business protected.

In most cases this is sensible, for this premium income will reflect the type of exposures and the volume of such exposures. Of course, when the original premiums are variable according to original results, such as with an assessment mutual, a deductible and limit based on the average net sums insured at risk during the contract period is more sensible.

Where deductible and limits are based on premium income, such a contract is often referred to as an excess loss ratio reinsurance. Normally, a minimum deductible is set in money terms and, similarly, the contract will often contain a maximum liability set in money terms as well. Most stop loss contracts will contain a coinsurance by the Reassured in excess of the deductible and the contract will be expressed ... "to pay 90% of that part of its aggregate ultimate net loss which exceeds the deductible".

ARTICLE 8

> *Premium Clause. The Company shall pay a deposit of _________ at the inception of this Agreement. As soon as possible after the expiry of this Agreement, the above deposit premium shall be adjusted to an amount equal to a rate of ______% applied to the Company's gross net earned premium income as defined hereunder, subject, however, to a minimum premium of _________. The payment of any adjustment due between the parfies being made at once.*

The premium of a stop loss contract can be a flat monetary one but, as with the limit and deductible, the premium is normally based on the original exposures and calculated on premium income or average sums insured. Normally, as in excess of loss reinsurance, a minimum premium is set in monetary terms and a deposit premium paid in advance, such a deposit being adjusted after expiry of the contract.

Here, I suggest that the reader peruses the wording at the end of this chapter — particularly Articles 5, 8, 9 and 11.

So far, I feel that everything is straightforward. The concept of a stop loss or excess aggregate reinsurance is easily understandable and deceptively simple. However, such contracts are technically the most difficult of all reinsurances to underwrite successfully so,we will probe a little deeper.

It is my opinion that no other type of reinsurance requires such care in making certain that all the words used in the contract are fully understood and defined. Draft and read the wording with great care. No other type of reinsurance requires such care in setting out clearly the information and statistics upon which the contract is negotiated.

Earned or Written Premium Basis

With this warning behind us let us proceed. Where a contract covers losses occurring during its term, it is vital that the calculation of the deductible and limit are based upon the *earned* premium income during the same period. A simple example will illustrate this point.

During 1978 a Reassured has written a net premium income of £100,000. He desires a stop loss to protect all his losses occurring during 1979 in excess of 80% of his premium income in 1979. Assume that in 1979 his net written premium income is only £10,000. If the deductible is 80% of the written premium income it will be set a £8,000. Losses during 1979 will occur, however, on the run-off of that business written in 1978. On a 1978 written volume of £100,000, and a favourable loss ratio on that volume of as low as 40%, these losses are likely to be around £20,000 (a 40% settlement on the premiun earned in 1979 on the 1978 writings). The result to the 1979 stop loss Reinsurer will be both disastrous and ludicrous. Of course, where one is dealing with a seasonal business, and the stop loss covers the whole of a season's business, the written and earned premiums are the same and the problem does not arise. The golden rule is — **losses occurring: earned premiums**.

The contrary is true where the stop loss covers business attaching during the contract term and not losses occurring during the contract term. Here the measure of exposure is not the premium earned during the contract term but the premium written on the business attaching during the contract term. Therefore, the second rule is — **business attaching: written premiums**.

It must be realised that the results of writing a stop loss on a business attaching basis will not be known until all such business has expired and all claims arising on that business are settled or can be accurately reserved. On property business this will be many years. If the account contains longer tail business it will be decades.

Deduction of Other Reinsurances

We turn now to another aspect of losses and premium income. A stop loss contract is designed normally to give protection to a Reassured's net account, i.e. it pays the aggregation of his ultimate net losses after deduction of all other reinsurances, after deduction of recoveries from facultative reinsurances, treaty reinsurances and excess of loss reinsurances. The premium income is also net of premiums paid for such reinsurances. These reinsurances "inure to the benefit" of the stop loss Reinsurer because recoveries from them reduce the losses covered by the stop loss contract.

Now, just pause a moment. The premium paid for the stop loss reinsurance itself does not inure to its benefit and therefore must not be deducted in calculating the net premium income. Neither should the premium paid for an underlying or higher stop loss because they do not inure to the benefit of the stop loss Reinsurers.

We have discussed the basis of earned premiums — losses occurring. In deducting the cost of premiums for reinsurances which inure to the benefit of the stop loss contract, care must be taken to deduct the earned portion only of premiums paid for such reinsurances, because that earned part is the part which inures to the benefit.

For example, a Reassured has a stop loss covering losses occurring during 1979 on his fire business. The premium is based on the net premium earned in 1979 after deduction of premiums paid for reinsurance which inure to the benefit of the stop loss contract. In September 1979 the Reassured deems it right to take out a new excess of loss contract for 12 months to protect him and his stop loss Reinsurers for losses occurring during the period 12 months at Ist October 1979. Only 3 months, or one quarter of that excess of loss reinsurance, inures to the benefit of the 1979 stop loss Reinsurer, and only 25% of the excess loss premium should be deducted in computing the Reassured's net earned premium for the calendar year 1979.

Do I hear mutterings? If so, they are unjustified because with an excess loss ratio contract, where the deductible is based on premium income, any inaccuracies or inequities in that premium income not only affect the premium paid to the stop loss reinsurance, but also the deductible. They affect the point at which the Reinsurer will start paying his losses to the Reassured and thus the very basis of the contract itself.

It is of vital importance on an aggregate excess contract to make sure that all reinsurance recoveries due whether collected or not are deducted so that the stop loss Reinsurer does not pay for the insolvency or failure to pay by such Reinsurers. This may not be true if a stop loss protecting a run-off.

Advance Payments of Losses

Losses will be defined clearly in the contract as net after recoveries from all other reinsurances and normally will include loss settlement expenses. Most stop loss contracts will be based on losses as finally settled, i.e. the loss ratio will not be determined finally until all the Reassured's losses for that year are settled. This may take a long time, even on fire or simple business. Very often a stop loss contract will allow for provisional settlements before the final result is known, based on estimates of losses, and in some cases estimates of premium income as well. For example, a European insurance company has taken out a stop loss in respect of its season's hail writings on crops. Normally the season will commence in April or May and continue until the late crops, such as vines, are harvested in the autumn. Its hail premiums for the season are paid early in the season.

Let us assume that disastrous losses occur in July on cereal crops and the company knows full well that the season's operation is bound to be bad and will produce losses to its stop loss Reinsurers. In fact, the experience may be so bad that the company may be unable to pay the losses out of its own resources. This is not uncommon where crop hail insurance is undertaken by a farmers' mutual or a farmers' co-operative.

Therefore, it is essential for the Reassured to call upon its stop loss Reinsurers for an advance payment. The Reassured would estimate its total seasonal premium income and its total paid losses and be entitled to collect on that basis from its Reinsurers. In addition, there will be losses on which it has admitted liability for payment but has not actually made payment to its Insured. A stop loss Reinsurer would help the Reassured either by funding a part of these outstandings or allowing the Reassured to draw upon money quickly as he needs to settle.

A similar situation may arise on an annual stop loss contract on a normal continuous business. For example, a stop loss on an Underwriter's personal accident account, covering losses occurring during the period of 12 months from the 1st January to pay 90% of losses in excess of 100% of the gross earned premium income. During the early months of the year the account suffers a very bad experience and the situation at the end of June looks like this:

A	Earned premiums to 30th June	500,000
B	Estimated earned premiums for year	1,000,000
C	Losses paid to 30th June	900,000
D	Losses where liability is admitted but not yet paid	200,000
E	Known outstandings at 30th June	300,000

F	Estimated losses for second 6 months assuming a normal loss ratio of 50%	250,000
G	Estimated loss for second 6 months assuming a continuation of first 6 months' experience	1,500,000

Firstly, the eventual outcome of the year's activities will be pretty dismal and quite obviously the stop loss Reinsurer is bound to have a claim, and if the estimate of the annual earned premium is correct at 1,000,000, with paid and admitted losses of 1,100,000, a provisional payment on account of 90% of 100,000 is really the least that can be expected. However, unless the stop loss contract specifically provides for earlier payment, a Reinsurer might be entitled to refuse such a payment until the earned income is known.

Secondly, the Reassured may wish, or may have to ask, for a large provisional settlement. There are various methods by which this can be achieved. One could base it on the results of the six months trading, i.e.

Earned Premium Income to 30th June	500,000
Losses paid and admitted at 30th June C+D	1,100,000
Provisional settlement	600,000

or estimate the conservative 12 months' position

Estimated earned Premium Income	1,000,000
Estimated final losses	1,650,000
C + D + E + F	
Provisional settlement	650,000

Both of these would produce a result exceptionally beneficial to the Reassured. Normally I would not expect a settlement to be made on six months' figures, neither would I expect a basis of settlement based on outstanding losses. A more reasonable suggestion would be a provisional settlement to be adjusted monthly or quarterly until the year was closed using:

Estimated annual premium of	1,000,000
Paid and admitted to pay losses	1,100,000
Plus: assumed losses for last 6 months on a minimum basis of, say, 50% of estimated earned premiums	250,000
Provisional settlement — 90% of	350,000

In any contract it is best for the basis of a provisional settlement to be stipulated as this can avoid a lot of argument and possible ill will after the event. Without such stipulation in the contract the Reassured has no real right to any advance, although it would be difficult in equity to refuse to pay on the basis of actual paid or admitted losses against the final estimated premium income. In my example this would produce an advance of 90% of $100,000.

Loss Settlements: Outstanding Losses

I revert to the more normal situation of an annual stop loss, where adjustment of the contract premium and settlement of any claim is postponed until the results of the annual period are known after the close of the year. When the contract is based upon earned premiums and losses occurring, the earned premiums will be known shortly after the close of the year, say, within 60 days. At that time the deductible and the premium for the contract can be finalised accurately. However, there may be claims which are still outstanding.

The collection of losses, if any, from the stop loss Reinsurers will be based on paid or admitted to pay losses only and will not include outstanding losses unless the contract provides otherwise. However, it is usual to make a provisional settlement on the whole annual period using known outstanding as well. Adjustments are then made periodically until all settlements are finalised.

It is often desirable to finalise settlement of the stop loss contract on the basis of estimates where a stop loss contract covers classes of business with a long tail, i.e., where the claims will be outstanding for years. Sometimes a contract may give the Reinsurer only the right to commute outstanding losses, say three years after the close of the annual period. In other cases the commutation may be automatic.

A stop loss reinsurance of a Lloyd's Underwriter's whole account normally will be commuted when the Lloyd's Underwriter himself "closes" his account. This usually takes place three years after the commencement of the account. This process of "closing" a Lloyd's account means that all outstanding liabilities, including known outstandings and incurred but not reported losses, are commuted or assessed and a premium is paid to a Reinsurer who takes on the liability to settle all future claims on the account in return for the premium. The amount of this "reinsurance to close" is often the technical reserve, which is part of the Lloyd's audit, and most stop loss reinsurances of a Lloyd's Syndicate would make final settlement on the basis of the "reinsurance to close" at the end of this three year period.

It should however be noted that an Underwriter of a syndicate may often not be able to close his account after the end of three years and may simply not do so. In that event any stop loss Reinsurer may have no commutation clause and will be on risk for the full run-off.

So if commutation is desired, the contract must so specify and specify also the basis of that commutation.

Incurred Loss Basis

A stop loss reinsurance can be based upon earned premiums and incurred losses rather than loss occurring as finally settled. By this time the reader is familiar with the transfer of liability for outstanding claims under treaties by way of loss portfolios. A stop loss reinsurance may be based on incurred losses in the same manner. The calculation of losses will be based on the usual formula of:

Losses paid during the year
Plus losses outstanding at the close of the year
Less losses outstanding at the start of the year

Of course, such a basis means that a final adjustment of the stop loss reinsurance can be made once these figures and the earned premiums are known, which would usually be shortly after the close of the annual period. Therefore, it provides an obvious way of finalising such contracts quickly and is following the same practice of using incoming and outgoing loss reserves as is used under pro rata treaties.

HOWEVER, THE METHOD IS FRAUGHT WITH DANGER WHEN APPLIED TO STOP LOSS CONTRACTS and it should be used only for very special cases where the estimating of loss reserves is not under the Reassured's control or where a very close understanding exists between the two contracting parties.

Under a pro rata treaty any variation in loss reserves will level out over a period of years. For example, if in Year 1 of a treaty the outstanding loss reserve turns out to be over estimated, that overpayment by Year 1 treaty Reinsurers will be paid back to them in subsequent treaty years when the losses are settled.

This is often not the case under a stop loss reinsurance and is best illustrated by an example:

therefore the success of the operation.

Fourthly, there is the question of funding. We have considered at length ways in which advances for losses may be negotiated under stop loss contracts. However, the fundamental difficulty remains. Under pro rata reinsurance of a risk, if that risk burns down, the share of that loss can be collected from a pro rata Reinsurer. Under an excess of loss contract, if a loss happens, the Reinsurer's share is collectable quickly. Under a stop loss programme, collection may have to wait until the overall results of the year are known. Even if arrangements are made for advance stop loss payments a considerable element of funding remains with the Reassured. In adverse times the strain on his finances or his cash flow can be detrimental.

It is my firmly held belief that stop loss programmes used to cover a whole account on a long term basis, often turn out to be disadvantageous to the Reassured and Reinsurers alike, and that such contracts, to replace the more normal methods of pro rata and/or excess of loss reinsurance, are very dangerous animals which can only be undertaken successfully by highly trained people with phlegmatic temperaments and considerable cash resources.

6. Protection of a "run-off" account.

We have discussed the use of a Quota Share contract to reinsure the run off of an account. The excess aggregate method can be used equally effectively.

Assume a company having written a property account in Canada ceases to write such business at 1/1/90. He has a portfolio of inforce business with an unearned premium of C$ 1,000,000. Rather than placing a Quota he buys a stop loss for, say, $200,000 in the aggregate excess of $1,000,000 in the aggregate. In other words, he protects his run-off for a 200% loss ratio in excess of 100% loss ratio.

The above example is simple but where the run-off accounts comprise long-tail business a very difficult and very detailed underwriting study is necessary and very full disclosure must be made by the potential Reassured if the contract is to be viable. Such aggregate protections on run-off accounts, including long tail business, are best left to very brave, very sophisticated and very wealthy Reinsurers and even then, such protections should always contain a limit of liability.

However such excess aggregate contracts have become a feature of the Lloyd's and other markets in the 1980s and 1990s and are dealt with in my chapter on financial reinsurances.

Types of Business

I will list here some of the major types of business where stop loss reinsurance is frequently, or can be sensibly, used.

Hail and other perils on growing and standing crops.
Fire and storm on growing and standing timber.
Protection of property account against weather losses.
Protection of private house and other simple "comprehensive" accounts.
Protection of life companies or life accounts against adverse mortality experience.
Protection of personal accident accounts.
Protection of hospitalization and medical insurance accounts.
Protection for assessment mutuals or protection of their Assureds against such assessments. (Such mutuals normally are small with accounts limited to agricultural or simple rural business.)
Protection of a potential hazardous part of an underwriting account, for example, war, confiscation, riots.
Protection of new or experimental accounts until established.
Protection of a whole account on a short term basis.
Use of excess aggregate method superimposed on an excess of loss contract.
Run-off accounts.

The reader will be able to add a considerable number to this list from his own experience.

We should now discuss the various processes which are undergone by the contracting parties and their advisers when a stop-loss reinsurance is negotiated and I will follow the format of the wording at the end of this chapter.

Article 1 to 4 dealing with the term or period of the contract, the territory, the classes of business covered and exclusions need no further comment. We can, therefore, concentrate on Article 5 and discuss the fixing of the deductible and the limit of the contract.

Fixing the Deductible

The Reassured normally will select the deductible and limit which he considers suitable for his purposes. For example, a stop loss reinsurance could be taken on as a special class of business where the Reassured only wants to protect himself against a major adverse experience on that particular piece of his business. In such a case a deductible of at least 200% gross earned premium income is quite common. More normally, however, the Reassured will wish to protect himself against adverse losses at a lower level.

A company writing hail on crops may have an expense ratio of 32% and will want stop loss protection at a level of around 75% loss ratio, i.e. limiting its loss to 7%, plus the stop loss premium. If it can obtain cover at a lower deductible, it may wish to purchase it. On the other hand, if the hail company has good reserves and capital, it may consider a higher deductible excess of 80%, 90% or even 100%. The deductible will be determined very much by the Reassured's ability to stand a loss and, of course, by the price of the various. alternative deductibles.

The crucial question, which the Reinsurer must always consider, is one of making the Reassured keep a reasonable insurable interest for his net account. In other words, a stop loss Reinsurer is very foolish if he issues a contract which guarantees the Reassured against having an annual loss or guarantees that he only suffers a loss which he can shrug off as insignificant.

With an expense ratio of 32% the crucial loss ratio is 68%, but of course the Reassured will have to pay the cost of the stop loss reinsurance, so the break-even point is where the deductible plus the premium equals 68%, i.e. a stop loss contract x 60% cost 8%, x 50% cost 18% meet this criteria. Of course, where the deductible is over 68% the criteria is met. Normally the Reassured should lose money and if it is reasonable to lose, say, 10% of his premium income, one may be talking of a stop loss x 70% rate 8%.

The Reassured also maintain an interest by co-reinsurance. Like most excess of loss reinsurance contracts, the co-reinsurance in a stop loss contract is normally 10%. Where the stop loss deductible is very high in relation to expected fluctuations, then the co-reinsurance may be reduced and in some cases eliminated (unwisely, in my opinion). There are, however, occasions when greater co-reinsurance is sensible.

To revert to our example above, where the critical loss ratio was 68%, a stop loss cover for 90% of unlimited cover x 60% loss ratio for a rate of 90% of 5% would guarantee the Reassured a profit until his loss ratio reached 95%, which would be an unwise contract. However, if the coinsurance is increased to 25% and the contract becomes:

75% of unlimited cover x 60% L.R. Cost 75% of 5%

then the Reassured will break even at 75% and lose 25% of anything over 75%. Such a contract may well make insurable sense.

In these examples I have assumed that the limit of the stop loss is infinite. In practice the above calculation will have to be modified to take account of the possible cost of an unlimited cover excess of the limit of the stop loss cover. We will revert to this a little later when we consider fixing the rate for a stop loss cover and do a little gentle mathematics.

Of course, when the stop loss deductible is fixed upon net premium income, then the critical point is 100% N.P.I. With a Lloyd's Syndicate N.P.I. is normally the basis but a Syndicate's N.P.I. is usually calculated net of brokerage and commission but not net of the Syndicate's own internal expenses. If these are, say, 4% then the critical point becomes 96%. A contract to pay 100% of losses x 90% L.R. to a Lloyd's Syndicate, at a cost of 4%, will leave the Syndicate with no insurable interest. Not a very sensible contract.

Where the stop loss deductible is based upon average total sums insured one uses one's nut and sticks to the rule — "Make sure that the stop loss deductible plus the cost of the stop loss cover means that the Reassured loses money".

We have already discussed the function of a minimum monetary amount for the deductible of a stop loss. This is necessary because if the premium income is small, then the chances of abnormal loss ratios increase and the stop loss reinsurance with a deductible fixed on premium income is more vulnerable to loss if that income is small. Therefore a minimum deductible, say at around 50% of the estimated deductible, is a rough and ready guide. There will be many cases where 50% is too low and 100% of the estimated P.I. may be more logical. Normally a figure around 70% is often used. The bigger the base (i.e. the premium income) in relation to possible fluctuations, e.g. largest exposure on a risk or area, then the lower the minimum deductible can be set.

A good way of assessing this is to say, "On this account would it make any difference to the rate and terms of the contract if the income was half or 50% of the estimated income?" If the answer is no then there can be no logical reason against a minimum deductible of 50% of the estimated deductible.

Fixing the Policy Limit

Here the Reassured should calculate the maximum foreseeable loss he can envisage. If he is a cautious Underwriter then add 50%; if he is an Actuary then add 100%, this being a rough guide to expected fluctuations. The Reassured should then buy protection up to this figure if he can afford it. Of course, he may not be able to do so, in which case he may have to soldier on with a Volkswagen instead of a Mercedes.

In making calculations of this maximum foreseeable loss it is probably wise to think in terms of the original sums insured and the maximum percentage loss that they could sustain. This works quite well in dealing with crop insurance and similar portfolios where the original rates are sizeable, e.g. for original rates of ½% to 10% or more. It works less well in dealing with, say, personal accident business where one is dealing with rates in the realm of one per mille or less. For example, take a stop loss reinsurance in respect of sugar cane in a single country against windstorm; if the original rates are 4% and one can estimate the maximum foreseeable loss at 30% of total values at risk, then the amount of stop loss protection should be:

30% + (50% for error of 30%) = 45% x T.S.I.
or 45% of 2500% L.R.
which equals a L.R. of 1125%.

A contract or layers of contracts for 90% of 1000% in excess of 100% L.R. might make sense if it can be afforded. If it cannot be afforded then one must question whether the original rates charged (in this case 4%) are sufficient for the high potential loss exposure.

A Reassured is generally best advised to buy the cover he needs and to save on his reinsurance costs by increasing his deductible rather than reducing the cover. An increase in the deductible normally will not ruin him but inadequate cover, when the crunch comes, can well do so.

With an account such as a personal accident account, or an abnormal mortality stop loss to a life company, the amount of cover is best assessed by calculating the possible fluctuations in the account. This can be done by assuming an unfavourable mortality involving the largest sum insured in the original portfolio and a percentage of the larger policies at risk, and adding to this a fluctuation of normal losses on the rest of the portfolio. Of course, past experience must also be a guide to possible future disastrous experience.

Fixing the Premium

Let us now turn to the main action in buying or writing a stop loss cover, that is the price and how we arrive at it.

ARTICLE 8

> *Premium Clause. The Company shall pay a deposit premium of ____________ at the inception of this Agreement. As soon as possible after the expiry of this Agreement, the above deposit premium shall be adjusted to an amount equal to a rate of _____ % applied to the Company's gross net earned premium income as defined hereunder, subject, however, to a minimum premium of ____________ . The payment of any adjustment due between the parties being made at once.*

Firstly, deposit premiums normally are dealt with in a similar way to an excess of loss contract and fixed at between 70% and 100% of the estimated final earned premium. The minimum premium under a stop loss contract can be treated rather more flexibly than under an excess of loss contract for the following reason: unlike a catastrophe cover the limit of a stop loss cover is expressed in relation to premium income (of course, with a maximum monetary amount). If the premium income turns out to be half, then the limit will be halved. Of course, the deductible will also be halved. The fixing of a minimum deductible has been discussed previously. Provided this is done to protect Reinsurers against abnormal fluctuations on a reduced income, then theoretically a stop loss cover does not need a minimum premium except to cover Reinsurers' costs.

Certainly, on stop loss covers, where the limit of liability is not a fixed amount, a minimum premium of 50% of the estimated final premium is justifiable.

Fixing the Rate

In theory, arriving at a rate is simple. One has to estimate the probabilities of future losses to the stop loss contract; add an error factor; add for Reinsurers profit and expenses and your answer is there. Take a contract for 100% L.R. x 90% L.R. If we break down the proposition in layers and then calculate the probabilities of a total loss to that layer ...

	Probabilities of total loss	*Rate*
10% × 80%	1:4	2.5%
20% × 90%	1:10	2.0%
20% × 110%	1:30	.66%
50% × 130%	1:50	1.00%
	Total rate:	6.16%

load by $\frac{100}{70}$; round it off and "Bob's your uncle" and the rate is 8.8% or with 90% cover around 8%.

So, how can we give some credence to estimating these future probabilities? Basically there are three methods and all should be used. Firstly, the past results of the account one is reinsuring. Secondly, the past statistics of other similar accounts or other relevant statistics. Thirdly, the inherent dangers of fluctuations in the account and the likelihood of them occurring.

Let us assume that a Reinsured has ten years' experience in the business and that these past statistics are valid on the basis of future underwriting practises, then these can be used to provide some of our probabilities for us. The contract we are trying to rate is for 90% of 100% × 80% L.R. and the past 10 years' results are as follows:

	A P.I.	B Losses	C Monetary Loss × 80%	D L.R.	E Points of L.R. × 80%
	100,000	70,000	—	70%	—
	110,000	121,000	33,000	110%	30%
	120,000	72,000	—	60%	—
	120,000	60,000	—	50%	—
	140,000	126,000	14,000	90%	10%
	150,000	75,000	—	50%	—
	180,000	90,000	—	50%	—
	200,000	180,000	20,000	90%	10%
	230,000	126,500	—	50%	—
	250,000	175,000	—	70%	—
Total	1,500,000		67,000		50%

Taking column "E" we can say that the annual burning cost over 10 years for our contract is 5%, or taking the actual monetary B.C. divided by premium income, column "C" divided by column "A" will give us a burning cost of $\frac{67}{15} \times 100$ or 4.47%. Both are correct but 15 which is more valid? We are dealing with a steady growth in income and a fairly steady account, and the B.C. based on Column "E", i.e. actual points of loss ratio, is likely to be the better guide. The statistics contain several L.R. of between 70% and 80%, which gives stability to these figures. Therefore we would be justified in saying that a B.C. of 5% looks sensible, but of course it is the B.C. for a cover 30% × 80% not 100% excess of 80%.

We then have to rate 70% × 100% L.R. Here we have no experience and perforce we have to look at other people's statistics on the same class or make a judgement rate based on probabilities. To help us in this let us use our probability method using the known burning costs to help us:

Layer	*B.C.*	*Probability*	*Rate*
10% × 80%	3%	1:3⅓	3%
20% × 90%	2%	1:10	2%
20% × 110%	Nil	say 1:20	1%
50% × 130%	Nil	say 1:100	.5%
			6.5%

The loss trend falls away sharply over 90% and the above assumptions look reasonable. Again, using a $\frac{100}{70}$ths loading our overall rate for our cover will be 90% of 9.3, i.e. 8.4%.

The effect of raising our deductible from 80% to 90% will produce a rate of 90% of $\frac{100}{70}$ths of 3.5% or 4.5%, leaving a rate of 3.9% for 90% of 90% × 80%. The next stage is to stand back and say, "Do these rates look right? Are they sensible? Can the Reassured afford them? Can the Reinsurer take a chance on the future being more stable with a bigger income? Is the loading of $\frac{100}{70}$ths too great, particularly in the layer 10% × 80% where with 3 total losses in 10 years the fluctuations must be more limited? On the other hand, our suggested rate of $\frac{100}{70}$ths × 1½% for 70% × 110% may look decidedly thin. Is the account well balanced? Is the type of business such that a L.R. in excess of, say, 120% is virtually impossible? What is the character and experience of the Reassured? What continuity are we likely to have?"

Quota Share/Stop Loss Conversions

Another very useful method is to convert a stop loss into a quota share treaty and to see if the resultant quota share would be a treaty you would write or cede. This is a mathematical exercise which should be done for all stop losses where the deductible is around 80% or less. Taking our example of 90% of 100% × 80%; at a rate of 90% of 9%, and assuming that unlimited cover excess of 180% is worth 1%, then 100% unlimited cover excess of 80% is rated at 10%. This hypothetical cover will lose money to the Reinsurer at a loss ratio of 90%; so will a quota share of the account paying 10% ceding commission. Arithmetically the contracts are the same except that the stop loss can never receive more than 10% of the original premium however low the original loss ratio. Therefore, we must put in the quota share contract a 100% profit commission of any profit over 10% so that its profit in any year is also limited. The two contracts then produce the same arithmetical result.

Would a quota share of this account, paying 10% ceding commission, with such a limit of profit in any year to 10% make underwriting sense? Compare it with the terms of a possible quota share treaty on the account concerned. Let us say the original costs on our example are 25% and that a quota share with 25% ceding commission and no P.C. is on offer; the results for such a quota share would have been as follows:

A P.I.	B Losses	C Commission	Monetary Loss or Gain	L.R.	C.C.	L.R. Result
100,000	70,000	25,000	+ 5,000	70%	25%	+ 5%
110,000	121,000	26,000	–38,000	110%	25%	–35%
120,000	72,000	30,000	+18,000	60%	25%	+15%
120,000	60,000	30,000	+30,000	50%	25%	+25%
140,000	126,000	35,000	–21,000	90%	25%	–15%
150,000	75,000	37,500	+37,500	50%	25%	+25%
180,000	90,000	45,000	+45,000	50%	25%	+25%
200,000	180,000	50,000	–30,000	90%	25%	–15%
230,000	126,000	57,500	+57,500	50%	25%	+25%
250,000	175,000	62,500	+12,500	70%	25%	+ 5%
		Profit	116,000		Result	+60%

Actual Q.S. Profit 116,000 Average annual profit 6%

Would you write a quota share paying 25% ceding commission? Surely it is not an unreasonable treaty. If so, what about 10% ceding commission with a 100% profit commission over 10% profit? Again, it looks a good contract to write. Do a few conversions yourself.

Let us convert a quota share paying 40% ceding commission with a profit commission of 100% with 10% expenses into a stop loss. Firstly, where do quota share Reinsurers start to lose money? Answer: at a 60%

loss ratio. Therefore, the stop loss deductible plus stop loss premium must equal 60% and the stop loss premium must equal the maximum profit of 10% under the quota share treaty i.e. a stop loss unlimited x/s 50% loss ratio for a 10% rate. Make the quota share profit commission 50% and not 100%. Answer: stop loss unlimited x/s 50% loss ratio for a 10% rate plus an additional rate equal to 0.5% for each 1%. The original loss ratio falls below 50%. Check it!

L.R. 10%	Q.S. Profit 10% + 50% of 40% = 30% Stop loss premium 10% + 50% of 40% = 30%
L.R. 100%	Q.S. loss 40% Stop loss deficit 40%

Variable Premium Rates

This leads us naturally on to another method of rating a stop loss contract. This is the idea of a basic rate plus a participation in the good years. Revert again to our example and this time we will merely set down the past 10 years' loss ratios and results each year in loss ratios for two contracts, both for 100% × 80% loss ratio, the first "A" at a flat rate of 9% and the second "B" at a flat rate of 6% with an extra rate of 0.5% for each point the loss ratio is less than 70%:

Loss Ratios	*"A"*		*"B"*	
70%	+ 9%		+ 6%	
110%		–21%		–24%
60%	+ 9%		+11%	
50%	+ 9%		+16%	
90%		– 1%		– 4%
50%	+ 9%		+16%	
50%	+ 9%		+16%	
90%		– 1%		– 4%
50%	+ 9%		+16%	
70%	+ 9%		+ 6%	
Result	+63%	–23%	+87%	–32%
Gain	40%		55%	

To the Reassured a contract of 90% of 100% × 80% at a cost of 8.1% may be less attractive than a contract at a basic cost of 5.4% with an extra rate of 0.45% — for each 1% their loss ratio is below 70%.

In concluding this short discussion on some of the factors and methods which can be used by all parties in assessing stop loss rates I must emphasise that Underwriters, both Reinsurers and Reassured, are individuals and many of them may use methods which I have not mentioned. Some would maintain that the only place a rate is obtainable is from the seat of his pants; others, that one must use a full actuarial approach in assessing probabilities. In my opinion underwriting is both an art and a science (simple mathematics). Rating the probabilities on a stop loss contract cannot be done entirely actuarily — there are too many imponderables; and pure art inspired from the seat of the pants, or from higher places, can be disastrous. It is the blend of art and mathematics, checked by commonsense and founded on experience which will create a successful rating approach.

Loss Settlements

I have spent some time stressing the vital importance in a stop loss contract of warranties about line limits, underwriting policies, continuance of other reinsurance and similar points. I have also stressed the vital importance of making sure that the information of past statistics and past practices are clearly set out as part of the original or renewal placing of the contract. If a loss is advised the Reinsurers will be very foolish if they do not check to make certain that warranties in the wording have not been breached and they should certainly review the placing or renewal information afresh after the loss. Should doubts arise, these can either be resolved by question and answer between the parties or, if not, recourse may have to be made to Article 14 and the Reassured's records examined. Should this be necessary such an examination may well be a very difficult and technical one and, in my view, needs an expert versed in stop loss procedures to carry it out successfully.

In general, adjusting loss settlement under stop loss contracts requires very considerable loss adjusting and loss settlement skills.

Stop Loss on Treaties

Often a Reassured will cede a quota share and protect its net retention and its quota share Reinsurers with a stop loss treaty. There is no problem as the stop loss protects 100% of the account and the quota share Reinsurers pay their share of the premium and receive their share of any stop loss recoveries. This is a straight joint account stop loss in favour of a Reassured and his quota share Reinsurers.

The use of a stop loss to protect a surplus treaty is more unusual but can be a very useful device. If the treaty is subject to possible wide fluctuations of loss ratio, then a stop loss protection will even out these fluctuations giving the treaty more "balance". Also, a stop loss will even out profit commission to a Reassured. The underwriting of such stop losses follows the lines we discussed above. Of course, with a surplus treaty, large risk exposures may make the account more liable to violent fluctuations than a net account. An interesting use of a stop loss on a treaty account is where a Reassured desires to retain part of its own treaty or even the whole of it. Protecting such a treaty by a stop loss is a very useful way of limiting the Reassured's liability on its "take back".

Stop Losses on Risk Excesses

At the end of Chapter IX we discussed the grafting of aggregate deductibles onto catastrophe contracts. Here, I would like to carry this one stage further and discuss the introduction of aggregate deductibles on risk excess covers; a combination of stop loss superimposed on a risk excess. As an example let us assume a risk excess for a period of 12 months for 40,000 x/s 10,000 each and every loss, each and every risk. The Reassured's net premium income is 1,000,000 and contract rate is 20%, producing a premium per annum of 200,000 to the risk excess contract. The Reassured may wish to cut down on this 20% premium and one simple way to do so would be to insert an aggregate deductible of, say, 12% of the premium income into the risk excess contract. The risk excess contract would then read ...

To pay 40,000 x/s 10,000 e.e. loss, e.e. risk, but no liability shall fall on Reinsurers unless and until the losses on such a contract occurring in the contract period exceed an aggregate amount equal to 12% of the reassured g.n.e.p.i. for that period.

In our example the Reassured would only collect if losses on the basis of 40,000 x/s 10,000 exceeded 120,000 in the aggregate for that year. If set at 8%, the premium with the deductible would equal the original premium of 20%. The Reassured would then reap a bonus if any year's losses were less than 12% as the "profit" he cedes away is limited to 8%. Therefore, technically the premium should be set a little higher, say 9%. This becomes a stop loss to the risk excess of unlimited cover excess of 12% g.n.e.p.i. for a 9% premium.

Such use of a superimposed stop loss on an underwriting excess can be a very useful way of cutting down a Reassured's premium without cutting down on his recoveries. However, we must dwell a little on one grave danger. Assume our 20% rate is developed by a loss cost or formula of $\frac{100}{70}$ths, i.e. the rate is $\frac{100}{70}$ths of losses equal to 14%. If the contract is converted to a loss cost with an aggregate deductible of 12%, and the rate is still formulated by use of a $\frac{100}{70}$ths loss cost formula, the rate for the aggregate will be $\frac{100}{70}$ths × 2% (14% loss less deductible of 12%) or 2.86%.

Now, whereas the original excess loss cover had a premium of 20% against losses of 14%, a margin of 6%, the use of an aggregate deductible plus the same loading reduces this margin to .86%. Where rates are based on past burning costs a similar pattern emerges, e.g.:

	Premium Income	*Losses 40,000 x/s 10,000*	*Losses with a 7% deductible*
Year 1	1,000,000	140,000	70,000
Year 2	1,000,000	90,000	20,000
Year 3	1,000,000	70,000	Nil
	3,000,000	300,000	90,000

3 years burning cost 40,000 x/s 10,000 — 10%
3 years burning cost with aggregate — 3%

If a contract was entered into for year 4, with, say, a loading of $\frac{100}{66\frac{2}{3}\%}$ 'the rates developed would be:

40,000 x/s 10,000 — 15%
40,000 x/s 10,000 — 4½%
with a 7% aggregate

If the contract's first proposition, i.e. 40,000 x/s 10,000 at 15%, is correct, then the second contract is a snare and a delusion to Reinsurers as it will lose money at 11½% not 15% and can never make more than 4½% profit however good the experience. The use of rate loadings where stop losses or aggregates are superimposed on excess losses needs very careful vetting.

To my mind excess aggregate reinsurance has always been associated with hail reinsurance and I thought it appropriate, therefore, to close this chapter with the story of the placing of one of the first hail stop loss reinsurances in the London market.

"The Crop Hail Reinsurance market at Lloyd's, which in these latter days has developed a formidable premium income from worldwide sources, has, perhaps surprisingly, only attained its present importance during the last 45-50 years.

Prior to the very early thirties, there was little significant reinsurance market, if any at all, at Lloyd's and 'Hail' was a dirty word; a controversial class of business which no enlightened and experienced Underwriter would contemplate. This general prejudice arose from the pre 1914-18 war era, when the renowned Cuthbert Heath entered into certain crop hail reinsurance commitments in Italy with disastrous results; perhaps one of his few failures during an epic underwriting career.

The Lloyd's market shied away from this class of business for almost a quarter of a century in consequence. Who would dare to know better than 'the master?' It was around 1932-1933 when an eminent Banker (who possessed a Lloyd's brokering subsidiary) was authorised by an old established German Mutual Hail Insurance Company to approach the Lloyd's market with an aggregate excess loss proposal, instigated by a disastrous year which they had just suffered. Being a Mutual Company, they possessed limited resources which had been severely strained by the catastrophic season and it was prudent to hedge against an early repetition.

A prominent leading Lloyd's Underwriter was approached and was tempted to decline the proposal out of hand but, hesitating, thought it might be useful and intellectual exercise to try out his young and resourceful deputy with a proposition which was novel and untried by his contemporaries. In fact, Excess Aggregate Reinsurance on any class was rarely placed and there was little recognised market in the days when the conventional pro rata treaty held sway in reinsurance practice.

The deputy was, therefore, instructed to "have a go" and report back to his master. Meanwhile, there had arrived in London a high powered delegation from Germany and the deputy was invited to attend in the Banker's London Board Room for consultation. Much overawed, he was confronted by two dignified German gentlemen, with goatee beards, wearing cravats and long morning coats who, standing very erect, almost literally clicked their heels and slightly bowed from the waist in salutation! Indeed, old world courtesy belonging to a byegone age!

The proceedings commenced and right across the Board Room table was spread a detailed column of statistics in Reichmarks stretching back to Napoleonic times; indeed to 1814. The recent disastrous year stood out like a sore thumb in this welter of statistics. By question and answer, the aspiring Underwriter acquired an understanding of the original business and what was entailed, having previously no knowledge or understanding of this class of business and very little experience of Excess Aggregate Reinsurance. He departed from the meeting with no Brokers' slip but merely a bulky portfolio of papers and statistics under his arm.

After careful consideration, he duly submitted to his chief an improvised slip and a summarised memorandum indicating a quotation of 4% of the gross premium income for indemnity excess of 90% aggregate settlement in the season on the gross premium income. He stressed that the indemnity should be for 90% only, with the Reassured being Coinsurers for 10%, so that they would have a self-pecuniary interest in their loss settlements after the 90% settlement mark was reached! (A prophetic stipulation for the future development of excess aggregate reinsurance!) These were embryonic days in the Excess Loss Reinsurance business.

15% brokerage, being the customary excess loss reinsurance allowance, was inserted in the improvised slip. The suggested quotation, in detail, was now placed before the Underwriter of the Syndicate who, like his deputy, had little knowledge or experience of the class. Partly influenced by a pioneering instinct and partly, perhaps, to encourage the aspiring deputy, the Underwriter authorised the quotation but, picking up his quill pen, he struck out the 15% brokerage and substituted 10% with the remark, in effect ... "Why allow them the usual 15% when you have done the exploratory work, most of the negotiation and will personally have to draft the contract, extempore, word for word?"

The junior who now felt considerably taller, conveyed the quotation and a firm order was immediately forthcoming. On placing the formal slip before his master for a lead line he was enquired, "How much?" The deputy, in a quavering voice, said, in effect, "They will not get home, sir, with less than a £10,000 lead!" In those days, on a dubious and hazardous class of untried business, that was an exceedingly large and bold commitment. However, down the line went; the slip was completed in the Lloyd's market and the Broker returned to his office rejoicing!

Thus, recommenced the Crop Hail Reinsurance market at Lloyd's (and now, of course, the London market generally) and thus 10% brokerage on Hail Excess Aggregate Reinsurance has prevailed and become sacrosanct during the ensuing 45-50 years."

These words conclude a chapter which I hope throws some light on to a type of reinsurance which has an enormous potential development but which, of all the types of reinsurance, requires the greatest expertise and care if success is to be achieved.

(RJK LLOYD'S)

PHYSICAL DAMAGE EXCESS AGGREGATE WORDING

Reinsurance Agreement No. made between ________ ________________ (hereinafter called the Company) and ____________________________(hereinafter called the Reinsurer)

ARTICLE 1 *Term ofAgreement. This agreement shall apply to losses occurring during the period commencing the _________ _____________and ending the ___________________.*

ARTICLE 2 *Territory. This agreement shall apply to losses occurring within ____________________*

ARTICLE 3 *Classes of Policies or Perils Covered. This agreement shall apply to all policies and binders of insurance and reinsurance written by the Company covering the following:*

ARTICLE 4 *Exclusions. This agreement does not cover any liability assumed by the Company on the following:*
War and Civil War Exclusion Clause (as attached)
Nuclear Exclusion Clause (as attached)

ARTICLE 5 *Insuring Clause. If the total of the Company's ultimate net loss, in respect of all losses occurring during the term of this agreement, exceeds a deductible equal to _____% of its gross net earned premium income (as finally determined) or _________________________ whichever amount is the greater, then Reinsurers agree to reimburse the Company for 90% of that part of its aggregate ultimate net loss which exceeds the said deductible up to but not exceeding 90% of a further _______ % of its gross net earned premium income or 90% of _________ _________whichever the lesser.*

The balance of 10% of the excess ultimate net loss together with the first ________________ shall be retained net by the Company and not reinsured in any way. However, it is understood and agreed that the Company have an underlying reinsurance for ______ % of ______________________________ excess of in the aggregate, recoveries under which shall be disregarded in computing the ultimate net loss hereunder.

the Reinsurer's right of inspection shall continue as long as either party has a claim against the other arising out of this Agreement.

ARTICLE 15 *Arbitration*

(1) All disputes arising out of the above Agreement or concerning its interpretations or validity whether arising before or after its termination shall be referred to a Court of Arbitration which shall consist of two Arbitrators who shall be active or retired officials of Companies or Underwriters carrying on a similar type of insurance or reinsurance business to that covered hereunder; one to be appointed by each party, and an Umpire who shall be appointed by the Arbitrators immediately after they themselves shall have been appointed and in the event of the Arbitrators being unable to reach agreement on the reference the Umpire shall forthwith enter on the reference in lieu of the Arbitrators.

(2) If either of the appointed Arbitrators for any reason whatsoever fails to act the party by whom he was appointed shall by writing appoint an Arbitrator in his place and if either party fails to appoint an Arbitrator within one month after being requested by the other party in writing to do so, or in the event of the Arbitrators failing to agree as to the appointment of the Umpire within one month after their own appointment such Arbitrator or Umpire as the case may be shall be appointed in writing by the Secretary General for the time being of the Court of Arbitration of the International Chamber of Commerce at the written request of either party.

(3) The Arbitrators or Umpire as the case may be shall determine any reference in accordance with current reinsurance market practice pertaining during the period of this Agreement and in making their award shall at the same time decide as to the payment of the cost of the arbitration.

(4) The Court of Arbitration shall take place in the country in which the head office of the defendant party is situated and the law applicable to both the aforesaid Agreement and this arbitration agreement shall be the law of that country.

(5) This arbitration agreement shall be construed as a separate and independent contract between the parties hereto and arbitration hereunder shall be a condition precedent to the commencement of any action at law.

ARTICLE 16 *Intermediaries. Messrs ______________________ are recognised as the intermediary negotiating this Agreement, through whom all communications relating thereto shall be transmitted to both parties.*

Chapter XIII

RETROCESSION

Introduction — What is Retrocession — Gearing effect and the spiral — Facultative accounts — Risk on risk — Catastrophe XL — Reinsuring a retro account — Tonners — Market loss warranties

Introduction

When the original book was written, little was written on Retrocession business, largely because Robert wrote little and generally avoided Retrocession business.

Different people have different opinions of what is Retrocession and what is Spiral. I will attempt in this chapter to try and explain these various terms and to give an idea of some of the pitfalls and opportunities of writing this business.

Retrocession was defined in the old edition as Contributing Reinsurance of Reinsurance and a term, Retrosurance was defined as Reinsurance of Reinsurance. The term Retrosurance never has been in common usage and it is rarely used these days.

Insurance is the "insurance of a risk" by an insurance company. Reinsurance is "insurance of some or all of that liability" by another insurance company or reinsurance company. I am taking Retrocession to mean the "insurance of some of that reinsurance liability" by another insurance company or reinsurance company. I will give you two examples of Retrocession.

Example I

The ABC Insurance Company writes a homeowners portfolio in Florida. They then purchase a catastrophe programme with Reinsurers in Lloyd's, in the USA domestic market and in Europe. One of the companies in Europe then purchases a catastrophe programme protecting their portfolio of catastrophe excess of loss business including ABC's contract, and other risk excess and proportional treaties. This is a Retrocession Treaty.

Example 2

The General Insurance Company of Asia, writes a commercial portfolio in their own country in Asia. They then purchase a surplus treaty which is written 50% by the State owned reinsurance company and 50% is placed in local markets in Asia. The State reinsurance company then purchases an excess of loss protection for their proportional cessions from the various companies in the country. This is also a Retrocession Treaty but such a treaty is generally not excluded from a Reinsurers catastrophe programme as no excess of loss reinsurance business is included. If, however, one of the local markets in Asia who also wrote some catastrophe excess of loss, bought a catastrophe cover, that would also be a Retrocession contract and that would be excluded from most Reinsurers own catastrophe programmes as it protects excess of loss reinsurance.

General Comments

When underwriting any Retrocessional business one needs to be extra cautious. This is because you are not reinsuring Insurance companies where the type and volume of the portfolio is unlikely to change dramatically from one year to another. Reinsurers can change their portfolio very quickly depending on the opportunities that arise and on the back of some cheap reinsurance that you may give them. Therefore, past results are only a limited guide to what a Reinsurer will do. You are reinsuring professionals who are trying to make a profit themselves on the reinsurance they write and some of this will be by careful risk selection and some by careful reinsurance purchase.

Having said that, Reinsurers do need reinsurance protection against an adverse catastrophe loss in one country where they have a significant market share or say, where they suffer a major fire loss on one particularly important cedant.

The advantages on reinsuring reinsurance companies is that only the major losses affect the Retrocession programmes. This is because only medium losses will affect the Reinsurances of the Insurance companies and only major losses will go through the retentions of the Reinsurance companies. Anyhow, this is what you hope will happen!

This business will generally be higher priced than other reinsurance business but in the event of a major market loss it will probably be more likely to be a total loss; therefore, there is less of a miss factor.

The Gearing Effect and the Spiral

If you refer back to Example 1, some Reinsurers will only reinsure direct catastrophe business, they will not write any Retrocessional contracts which include catastrophe business. Other Reinsurers will be attracted to the higher rates obtainable on the Retrocessional business that includes catastrophe business and also the fact that there will be fewer attritional losses. Therefore in years where there are fewer major market losses their loss ratio will be very low.

In the early and middle '80s, with the exception of Hurricane Alicia which hit Texas in 1983, there were no major market catastrophe losses. Markets around the world were attracted to write reinsurance contracts of Underwriters who wrote a portfolio of Retrocessional business. They in turn purchased a reinsurance programme including all of this business. The Reinsurers of these layers then sought reinsurance on their portfolio and they reinsured these with some of the Reinsurers who they in turn reinsured. An incestuous Spiral was created. When a loss was large enough to enter the Spiral, it would go round and round until all the so-called reinsurance was exhausted.

This is what happened. There was a series of major catastrophe losses starting with 87J which was a windstorm in 1987 which affected the United Kingdom, France and Norway. Then came Piper Alpha a major oil rig explosion in the North Sea in 1988. Then Hurricane Hugo affected the Caribbean and the USA in 1989, and finally 90A (Daria) blew through Northern Europe in January 1990. By the time that Hurricane Andrew hit Florida in August 1992, the Spirals in Continental Europe, in the London market, Lloyd's and the USA market had all been killed off and many companies and Lloyd's Syndicates perished. Since then the Spiral market disappeared, but people may well be tempted back into this, attracted by the excellent results in the good years. One clause that came in in 1991 to prevent the spiral was the LMX exclusion clause that excluded all retrocession and LMX business written and this has remained in force since.

In our book *Reinsurance Underwriting* published by LLP we studied three underwriting examples offered to us at the time of the Spiral market in 1989. Firstly, a USA insurance company writing direct insurance business; secondly, a Lloyd's syndicate writing only reinsurance business and no Retrocession and thirdly, a company underwriting all business including Spiral business. The table below illustrates the gearing or *leverage effect*:

	Premium	*Hurricane Alicia*	*Alicia % EPI*
A — Insurance Company	$1,000m	$25m	2.5%
B — Lloyd's Syndicate	$ 20m	$ 3.6m	18%
C — Spiral Company	$ 30m	$24m	80%

Therefore the insurance company A lost only 2.5% of its premium, the syndicate 18% of its premium and the company writing Spiral business 80% of its premium from the same event. What happens in the Spiral is that the rates on line on a Spiral programme tend to get lower the higher up in level one goes. However, if losses like Alicia enter the Spiral you are best to be on the lower layers at, say, 30% rate on line than on the top layers at 2% rate on line because they will both go! Looking at it another way. If you have a total loss at 30% rate on line it produces a loss ratio of 333% but at 2% rate on line it produces a 5000% loss ratio. Which would you prefer?

Reinsurance of Facultative Accounts

If a Reinsurer writes a portfolio of facultative reinsurance and protects this with a catastrophe excess of loss programme or a risk excess programme, I would not deem, this to be a Retrocessional programme. Care needs to be taken to understand the make-up of the portfolio. One could expect, as a Reinsurer, the following information.

For a Risk Programme

(1) The line guide. This should show the maximum line on primary policies, on an excess policy and on a whole programme and whether that line is a PML or Total Sums Insured etc.

(2) The territorial scope of business.

(3) A risk profile on a combined basis and broken down in the major categories.

(4) Historical premium income — so one can see the growth or stability of the account.

(5) The breakdown or the make up of the portfolio i.e. % petrochemical, % industrial, % office's and any differential line guide between them.

(6) Information or CVs about the Underwriters.

(7) Historical paid and incurred losses for the last five years excess of 50% of the deductible.

For a catastrophe programme additionally one would require the aggregate exposures per zone or country as appropriate.

The catastrophe programme and risk programmes should be analysed and rated as per the applicable chapters herein. Special points to bear in mind are:

(1) Often facultative Underwriters write excess of loss layers of portfolios i.e. Mortgage Bank portfolios, all locations of an Insured, windstorm pools, the property owned by the Government of a Caribbean island etc. These are to all intents and purposes catastrophe layers in themselves with some risk exposure thrown in. Therefore be careful of what is called one risk and whether the Reinsured is writing these classes of business.

(2) Some facultative Underwriters specialize in primary layers and therefore they are very exposed to catastrophe losses and will expect a frequency of risk losses.

(3) Some facultative Underwriters buy a lot of inuring facultative reinsurance which will significantly benefit their own Reinsurers.

(4) Facultative Underwriters used to write "transmission" and "distribution" lines and they called them, "single risks". However, they are a series of power or telephone lines spread over a wide area and are extremely catastrophe prone. In Hurricane Andrew, Florida Power and Light suffered considerable damage to their power lines and the cost to repair these lines was covered under the facultative policy. The various layers were extensively written worldwide and large losses affected many facultative risk and catastrophe programmes due to this one so-called risk. Because of this the following exclusion was added to many reinsurance policies. Make sure you have one on the policies you write.

Transmission and Distribution Line Exclusion

There are several of these all slightly different.

All transmission and distribution lines, including wire, cables, poles, pylons, standards, towers and any equipment of any type which may be attendant to such installations, including sub-stations of any description. This exclusion includes but is not limited to transmission or distribution of electrical power, telephone or telegraph signals, and all communication signals whether audio or visual.

This exclusion applies to both above and below ground equipment which are more than one mile radius from an insured structure.

This exclusion applies both to physical loss or damage to the equipment and all business interruption, consequential loss, and/or other contingent losses related to transmission and distribution lines.

Reinsurance of Proportional Portfolios

Where a reinsurance account consists of pro rata treaties they can be treated similarly to direct writing accounts. Care should be taken to ascertain the nature of quota share treaties as they may well be taken out specifically to cover part of an account with special hazards.

By its very nature a surplus treaty portfolio will contain large risks. The individual risk exposures often will be much larger than a direct written account. In addition, a number of individual treaties may well have the same large risks ceded to them. Therefore a large risk accumulation may build up. These accumulations may not be known to the Reassured but their possibility must be considered in rating the excess contract.

On the other hand, surplus treaties normally do not have cessions ceded to them on the smaller valued risks, e.g. private houses or small risks of poor construction. Catastrophic perils often affect these small risks to a greater extent than the larger industrial or commercial risks. A good example of this is storm damage to television aerials.

Therefore, in practice a surplus treaty account may be less prone to some catastrophic perils e.g. storm, damage, than a net account. This may not be true of earthquake or flood, where large losses can be caused to large risks, e.g. oil refineries or port and dock exposures.

Underwriting Information Required

The information required would be similar to that on the facultative accounts with the Underwriting CVs and the breakdown of the class of business written not being required.

As said earlier, the bulk of the exposures are probably Surplus treaties and therefore for earthquake and flood in particular, one would require aggregate liabilities and these may not always be available. Therefore you may have to rely on the premium income by territory and assess the likely catastrophe exposures. They can be shocking!

Insurance companies in wind-prone areas often place quota shares of simple portfolios to reinsure out of the bulk of their catastrophe exposures. Be aware of this.

Some territories operate with a significant coinsurance market. That means that the same risks are shared by many local insurance companies. Therefore if a Reinsurer writes many of these treaties, especially if they are the local national Reinsurer, then there will be a large clash potential from a single risk. Therefore this needs to be priced for.

Risk on Risk Protection

Generally speaking most reinsurance companies protect themselves from a single risk clash loss. This could be from a facultative account, a proportional treaty, a risk excess or even from a catastrophe layer which did not have a two risk warranty! Therefore it is good to know in this instance what the inuring programmes are in force. In other words, do they have a risk excess protecting their facultative and proportional accounts combined in place? If so, how much benefit would it give us?

The overall information we would require would be:

(1) Historical premium incomes by class of business i.e. facultative, binders and lineslips, pro rata treaties, risk excess of loss.

(2) The line guides by class of business as above in 1.

(3) The historical loss record showing the breakdown of the source of loss as in (1) above.

(4) Risk profiles of the risk excess, the pro rata treaty and the facultative accounts separately.

(5) The territorial breakdown of the account.

(6) Details of all the inuring programmes.

Most reinsurance companies would not buy a specific catastrophe programmes on their risk excess portfolio but would either purchase a combined layer with the facultative and proportional accounts, or as a general programme including their catastrophe reinsurance account as well. I will deal with these in a later section in this chapter.

Underwriting

These type of contracts and retrocessional catastrophe contracts are very difficult to underwrite. There is a bit of art, a bit of science, a bit of understanding human nature and a whole lot of common sense, and no right answer!

One has to weigh up the track record of the Reinsurer, will that continue? Are there changes of personnel? Are they growing? Are their line sizes going up? What is your experience with the company? Can you trust them? What are the exclusions? What is the price? What losses have they had? Do they accumulate with what you may have elsewhere? Are they writing only high up layers or low down layers or a mixture? Are they doing crazy things? When you have studied the information and the loss record, then you can make a judgement as to whether the price is right for the exposure you are taking on. These risks will probably be retained net to your company with no reinsurance so you need to keep a careful record of risk accumulations and catastrophe accumulations.If you are writing high up layers only then the catastrophe exposure is more remote. Good luck!

Retrocessional Catastrophe Excess of Loss

The Wording The wording would not be much different to a standard catastrophe excess of loss wording as shown in Chapter VIII, with the following possible differences.

1.

ARTICLE 1 (a)

This Agreement excludes:

(i) Workers' Compensation and/or Employers' Liability losses arising from the following perils:

Fire, Lightning, Explosion, Structural Collapse, Windstorm, Hail, Flood, Seismic Activity, Volcanic Eruption, Collision, Riots, Strikes, Civil Commotion, Malicious Damage.

(ii) Any Physical Damage and/or Consequential loss coverage contingent thereon effected by an Insured on behalf of another party.

This article excludes all casualty or third party losses but with the writeback of all losses if they occur due to a normal physical damage perils. Please note that following a major earthquake in California there would be a number of people injured and killed and there would probably be workers' compensation claims. This is what would be written back.

2.

ARTICLE 1 (b)

Liability arising out of Excess of Loss Reinsurances and/or Retrocessions thereof. However, this exclusion shall not apply to:

(1) Facultative Reinsurances on individual risks.

(2) Excess of Loss Reinsurances protecting direct, "captive" or facultative, or pro rata treaty accounts.

This is the key exclusion to exclude retrocessional business. Each clause is different depending on what the write backs are. In this case the following are protected. The facultative, risk excess, Proportional and Catastrophe excess accounts.

Please note that Risk Excess and Catastrophe Retrocession is excluded (i.e. contracts like this) but not Catastrophe Reinsurance.

(3) The Exclusions 1 (c) for Aviation business, I (d) war and Civil war and I (e) Nuclear Energy Risks are Standard Market Practice and are not shown here.

3.

ARTICLE 2

This Agreement applies only to that portion of any Insurance or Reinsurance which the Reassured retain nett for their own account (except as provided in Article 8) and in calculating the amount of any loss hereunder and also in computing the amount or amounts in excess of which this Agreement attaches, only loss or losses in respect of that portion of any Insurance or Reinsurance which the Reassured retain nett for their own account (except as provided in Article 8) shall be included.

The amount of liability hereunder in respect of any loss or losses shall not be increased by reason of the inability of the Reassured to collect from any other Reinsurers, whether specific or general, any amounts which may have become due from them whether such inability arises from the insolvency of such other Reinsurers, or otherwise.

ARTICLE 8

Notwithstanding anything contained herein to the contrary, it is agreed that recoveries under underlying reinsurances are for the sole benefit of the Reassured and shall not be taken into account in computing the ultimate nett loss or losses in excess of which this Agreement attaches, nor in any way prejudice the Reassured's right of recovery hereunder.

This clause shows that we are only protecting the Reassured for their net account not their quota share Reinsurers or surplus Reinsurers. However, Article 8 allows them to buy underlying specific covers which do not inure to our benefit, only to their benefit. We need to understand what they are buying so we can see whether the Reassured is retaining anything. You probably will not get a polite answer in some cases when you ask this question.

4.

This contract will not include an Hours clause which is different from a normal Catastrophe contract. The reason is that the Reassured is reinsuring many companies Worldwide all who in turn have Hours clauses, which may cover losses that start and end on different days, for example, in Hurricane Georges in 1998.

Hurricane Georges caused damage in St Kitts, then a few days later it hit Puerto Rico and later still the Dominican Republic and Florida. Then after a further few days it hit land in Mississippi. The damage occurred in a period well over a week but as far as the Reassured is concerned it is still one event. Therefore one has to be clear what is one event as the Hours clause cannot help you. This is usually decided by market agreement. Sometimes freeze losses are split into separate events, sometimes they are deemed to be one event, it depends on the length of the period of the damage and the key damage periods.

5.

It is not normal for the Reassured to have a coinsurance but in a hard market when reinsurance capacity is difficult, then this feature is sometimes forced on the Reassured. It is a good discipline.

6.

ARTICLE 13

This Agreement shall exclude all cover in respect of Extra Contractual Obligations howsoever arising, such Extra Contractual Obligations being defined as any award made by a Court of competent jurisdiction against an Insurer or Reinsurer, which award is not within the coverage granted by any insurance and/or reinsurance contract made between the parties in dispute.

Notwithstanding the foregoing this Agreement shall extend to cover any loss arising from a "Claims Related Extra Contractual Obligation"

(a) awarded against the Reassured or

(b) incurred by the Reassured where he has paid his share of a "Claims Related Extra Contractual Obligation" awarded against one or more of his Co-Insurers

It is warranted that any recovery under this Agreement in respect of "Claims Related Extra Contractual Obligation" shall only be for that part of any award which corresponds to the Reassured's share of the insurance and/or reinsurance policy and/or contract giving rise to the award and all proportional protection effected by the Reassured shall provide or shall be deemed to provide pro-rata coverage for such obligations.

This Agreement shall also extend to cover all loss from Extra Contractual Obligations howsoever arising where the loss is incurred by the Reassured as a result of his participation in any insurance or reinsurance which provides cover for such loss, it being understood and agreed that such loss results from a contractual liability incurred by the Reassured.

A "Claims Related Extra Contractual Obligation" shall be defined as the amount awarded against an Insurer or Reinsurer found liable by a court of competent jurisdiction to pay damages to an Insured or Reinsured in respect of the conduct of a claim made under an insurance and/or reinsurance policy and/or contract, where such liability has arisen because of:

(a) The failure of the Insurer or Reinsurer to agree or pay a claim within the policy limits or to provide a defence against such claims as required by law or

(b) bad faith or negligence in rejecting an offer of settlement or

(c) negligence or breach of duty in the preparation of the defence or the conduct of a trial or the preparation or prosecution of any appeal and/or subrogation and/or any subsequent action resulting therefrom.

There shall be no liability under this Agreement in respect of:

(a) any assumption of liability by way of participation in any mutual scheme designed specifically to cover Extra Contractual Obligation; or

(b) any Extra Contractual Obligation arising from the fraud of a director, officer or employee of the Reassured acting individually or collectively or in collusion with an individual or corporation or with any other organisation or party involved in the presentation defence or settlement of any claim.

Any loss arising under this Agreement in respect of "Claims Related Extra Contractual Obligations" shall be deemed to be a loss arising from the same event as that giving rise to the claim which the Extra Contractual Obligation is related; but recovery hereunder is subject to the Insurance and/or Reinsurance policy and/or contract which gives rise to the Extra Contractual Obligation falling within the scope of this Agreement.

This is a complicated clause. The main point of the clause was because Reinsurers did not want to give cover to *ex gratia* settlements where no coverage was given under the original policies. It was common practice for some USA Courts to give huge ECO awards with no regard for the original POLICY LIMITS or even the extent of the damage. This clause was to avoid these being passed to Reinsurers. There could be a situation where a compromise is made with the original Reinsured which is done for commercial reasons and yet the Reinsurer on this contract is paying for the generous gesture. However, one needs to protect the Reassured who is asked to pay an ECO loss by the Courts through the mishandling of a claims situation and this clause adds back some of the exposure.

Every wording is a little different and also the clauses change due to problems encountered in the market. One must keep abreast of these changes. For example, everyone in 1999 was developing their own Y2K Millenium, exclusion clauses. It was a non-event with very little disruption.

Information Required

The information required under retrocessional catastrophe contracts was revolutionized by the work done by Mike Kelly in the late 1980s and early 1990s in the London Market. Prior to that time the.information was requested as per the Charles Skey Questionnaire (see Charles Skey's article on Asbestosis in the Appendix) which was drafted in time for the Monte Carlo Rendezvous each year. The main information requested now is as follows:

(1) Historical breakdown of Premium Income by underwriting year between the various classes i.e. USA Cat XL, Canadian Cat XL, International Cat XL, USA and Canadian Risk XL, International Risk XL, USA and Canadian Pro Rata Treaties, International Pro Rata Treaties, USA Direct and Facultative, International Direct and Facultative.

This allowed the Reinsurer to get a good idea of the development of the Premium Income by class of business.

(2) Catastrophe aggregates were requested by Zone in the USA and by Country in the Rest of the World.

(3) Perhaps the greatest innovation was the production of Rate on Line Profiles by Territory for catastrophe Insurers. The rate on line is the premium divided by the limit on a catastrophe contract as a percentage. Therefore for a contract with a rate on line of 10% one would expect a total loss every 10 years. For a rate on line of 2% one would expect a total loss every 50 years.

This allowed the Reinsurers to assess how exposed they were on business the Reassured was taking on.

Rate on Line Profile Example		
ROL	*Liability*	*No. of Contracts*
40-50%	£ 250,000	3
25-40%	£ 435,000	5
15-25%	£ 485,000	2
10-15%	£1,150,000	6
5-10%	£2,500,000	11
2-5%	£1,650,000	7
0-2%	—	0

(4) There was also a request to produce Premium Income and Aggregate Liabilities for Retrocessional Risk XL and Retrocessional Cat XL. It was the intention to exclude these from coverage hereunder but if there was a request to include them their exposures could be clearly understood.

(5) There was a whole series of other searching questions which enabled Reinsurers to assess and also gave the Reinsurers some confidence or not about the Reinsured

Underwriting

The underwriting of this class up until the late 1980s had often been a question of write it all in and try and buy it out at a cheaper rate than you received it in. Some Underwriters managed to do it but they may have been unable to collect off insolvent Reinsurers. The information now requested enabled Reinsurers to assess each risk more accurately and with the high prices paid for this coverage enable them to write a net book without reinsurance. Restrictions put in at this time were the Two Risk Warranty, Retrocessional exclusion clauses, Marine exclusion clauses and Liability exclusion clauses.

Reinsurers could build a book of this business with the information provided, and could almost assess how a 5Bn Market loss in say the Northeast USA would affect the Reinsured. Reinsurers could write Retrocessional Contracts in different territories and on different classes and obtain a balance.

The most important piece of information was who were you reinsuring? Some people you could trust, some you could not, some would pay you back, some would not, some knew what they were doing, some did not. Some wrote all the lower layers and arbitraged, some wrote only higher layers and took a substantial coinsurance and had an excellent loss record. This class of business has made good profits since

1992 with the exception of 1998 and now 1999. It is bound to go wrong sooner or later but even during this period some people have lost money. Make sure you are not one of these!

Reinsuring a Retrocessional Account

If Reinsurers do offer capacity on this class of business then it makes sense for them, to protect themselves against major events.

Some Reinsurers because of their expertise and their good record will be able to place a quota share and maybe obtain an overrider and a profit commission. Some will be able to broaden the scope of their own retrocessional covers and include their non spiral writings. Some may be able to place a specific programme to cover their retrocessional business only. Another way is to purchase a Market Loss Warranty or Loss Franchise. Before I talk about these let us go back to the old days and talk about the bad word tonners and I quote from the original edition.

Tonners

In a non-marine reinsurance book "tonners" should have no place but it would be wrong not to make some reference to them. A long time ago, the London marine market underwrote most of the large marine vessels in the world and most Syndicates and companies in that market wrote most fleets with consistent lines per size or category of vessel. An Underwriter would be concerned if an abnormal number of large vessels were total losses during any year. Rather than effecting excess aggregate reinsurance on his net losses for such vessels he took out a "tonner" policy which paid a stipulated amount per casualty of vessels above a certain tonnage *whatever the actual losses of the Reassured on those vessels.*

Assume that the normal number of casualties of vessels over, say, 30,000 tons was four in a year. A tonner policy might be taken out to pay the Reassured £10,000 for each casualty in excess of six per annum up to a further six. If the premium was £10,000, then if casualties were six or under there would be no claim; if seven, the claim would equal the premium; if eight, the claim would be £20,000 against £10,000 premium, and so on up to twelve. The great advantage of the tonner is its simplicity. It is not a policy of indemnity. Even though several types of insurance or assurance, e.g. life, P.A., valued U & 0, are not policies of indemnity, at least the sum insured given bears some close relation to the Assured's potential loss.

"Tonners" originally fell into this same category. Now, however, even in marine markets, the Underwriter's loss on large vessels may bear no relation to the tonner recoveries he receives.

The extension of the "tonner" principle into aviation markets, for wide-bodied jets, or into non-marine markets for code-named hurricanes, or for fire losses exceeding a fixed amount, and the buying of tonners with fancy limits and deductibles has meant that "tonner" underwriting has really become bookmaking and the basic principle of indemnity which should underlie all insurance and reinsurance contracts has flown out of the box or the office window. The only winners in the long run are the Brokers. It was high time that this spurious method of reinsurance by laying of bets was laid to bed and I am delighted that Lloyd's have banned them!

The one main problem, with the "tonners" was there was not necessarily an insurable interest in the "tonner" contract.

For example in 1974 following cyclone Tracy in Australia, a Reinsurer could buy a "tonner" policy in case the Hurricane Tracy loss exceeded AS250M as indeed was the case and the Reinsurer may not have written any Australian policies at all and therefore they could have made a gambler's profit with no insurable interest.

However, what they did do was provide a mechanism to protect a Reinsured against losses they might suffer. Therefore, if 5 wide-bodied jets did go down, there is no doubt an aviation account would be very unprofitable unless in the unlikely event the Underwriter wrote none of the risks. The Market Loss warranties had their losses set by independant bodies and developed in the 1990s.

Market Loss Warranty

Territorial Scope – USA only

ARTICLE 6

This Agreement shall respond for a limit of up to $10,000,000 or equivalent in other currencies in each and every "qualifying event" (as defined in Article 7) excess of $100,000 (being the Reassured's retention) or equivalent in other currencies in respect of each and every qualifying event.

However, under no circumstances shall the Reinsurer be liable for more than $10,000,000 or equivalent in other *currencies for any number of qualifying events occurring during the period of this Agreement.*

ARTICLE 7

(i) A "qualifying event" for the purposes of this Agreement shall be a loss which is equal to or greater than the relevant "industry loss" set out below, which occurs during the term of this Agreement, is reported by Property Claims Services (hereinafter referred to as PCS) within the relevant reporting period set out below and for which the Reassured incurs losses on business protected hereon in excess of the Reassured's retention.

(ii) The relevant industry loss as set out in (i) above shall be any loss equal to or exceeding US$ 5,000,000,000 as so reported and defined by PCS.

(iii) The relevant "reporting period" for any loss falling within the scope of the qualifying event definition set out in (i) above shall be thirty-six months from the commencement date of that particular loss. This commencement date shall be the date as is so determined for that loss by PCS.

(iv) In the event that the publication PCS is discontinued or that PCS materially changes its methodology in a manner which makes it unsuitable for the purpose intended, the parties to this Agreement shall mutually agree on a comparable alternative source for the benefit of (ii) above. Failing mutual agreement on a comparable alternative source, a source will be determined by arbitration in accordance with the provisions of Article herein.

The Market Loss warranty would pay in this instance if the market loss in the USA from a catastrophic loss was over $5,000m, for the market as determined by PCS. The Property Claims Services (PCS) are a body which reports and measures USA Catastrophe losses. They publish their results regularly and update the major losses periodically after a major event.

There is no restriction under the Market Loss warranty contract as to what accounts are protected. There is a deductible on this contract that applies of $100,000. This loss warranty could be used to pay for reinstatement premiums due under other reinsurance contracts,

Retrocessional writings that incur losses, losses that come out of the top of existing programmes and retentions. Therefore it is a very flexible cover.

The problem is that if in this instance the market loss as deemed by PCS was only $4,950m, then not a single dollar is recoverable hereon. Therefore they are dangerous to rely on completely as you may have suffered a large loss but can recover nothing.

They are however a useful type of reinsurance for people who write retrocessional business and have no other form of protection.

It is important if one is an Underwriter of these types of risks to insure that the Reassured has suffered a financial loss and can prove it and is not gambling like the old days of the "tonners"!

The Market Loss warranties can be used for USA losses, International losses, (there the body used to determine the loss is SIGMA), Aviation losses, Satellite losses, Aggregate Catastrophe losses, Fire losses etc.

There are markets who specialize in writing these contracts and specialize in buying against them. Whether one thinks they are right or wrong they are here to stay.

Chapter XIV

CAPTIVES, FINANCIAL REINSURANCE AND THE DEVELOPMENT OF ART IN REINSURANCE

Some morality and philosophy on Honourable Trading *or* When is a "reinsurance" not a reinsurance?

[Note: The development of ART and Financial Reinsurance has been one of the major developments of recent years. In compiling this Chapter, I have quoted from "Alternative Risk Financing" by Jim Bannister – see the Bibliography. I have also used sections written from earlier editions of "Reinsurance in Practice" as Robert Kiln was a pioneer of Captive Reinsurance. This Chapter does not intend to cover all aspects of financial reinsurance but to give the reader a taster. As the world's capital markets and the reinsurance markets become closer, many other products and concepts have developed and will continue to develop.]

Competitors of traditional insurance and reinsurance — Captives — Islands in the sun — Catastrophe reserves — Bankers — Rollers — Time and distance — Development of Art

Self-insurance

The main competitor is self-insurance. This is a conscious decision not to insure probably because of the cost both in time and money is less than the financial and other benefits. The money normally paid to the Insurer or Reinsurer is kept in house and if the experience is favourable then the self-insurer will retain the profit, which would have gone to the traditional Insurer. The rationale being that the Insured knows its risks well and therefore will benefit from the good experience and refinancing the cash flows with the company to improve the IRR (Internal Rate of Return). However I am sure that there are many Reinsurance managers who took an increased retention or dropped a programme only then to be hit by a frequency of unexpected losses. Join the club!

Mutuals

Sometimes self-insurance is forced upon Insurers and Reinsurers alike when the price and terms of renewal become prohibitive . However one option they sometimes take is to form their own Mutual Insurance company. I quote from Alternative Risk Financing Examples of early mutuals are as follows:

(1) The marine mutuals formed by ship owners, such as owners of colliers and fishing vessels, bringing together most, if not all, of the fleets in a particular port.

(2) The fire mutuals formed in Scandinavian and other European countries to insure property in a town or region.

(3) The Factory Mutual system companies, originally formed by New England mill owners, who could not get fire insurance. They introduced loss control in the shape of automatic fire extinguishing systems and became market leaders in fire sprinkler technology with the conception of the Highly Protected Risk (HPR) where strong loss control allows lower rates.

(4) Trade mutuals formed by companies in a particular industry who found difficulty in securing insurance cover at a reasonable price or at all. By banding together and taking steps to control risk by exchanging knowledge they were able to mutually insure each other.

Some of these mutual companies like the New England Mill Mutuals (Factory Mutuals), State Farm and others in the USA and Zenkyoren in Japan have become very large and successful Insurers. There has however, been a tendency for mutuals in recent years to demutualise where they become stock companies and the policyholders receive some shares. The main reason given is that the stock companies have greater access to the capital markets to borrow funds for expansion etc. but on the flip side the stock market will require greater profits.

Captives

In a similar manner to the mutuals, an industrial or commercial company might decide to form its own insurance company because its own experience is superior to the average and rather than the Insurer keeping the profit the company will. This company because it retains its own insurance business is called a Captive Insurance Company. The first captive is thought to have been the Phoenix formed in 1782, although there may have been a Tuscan cloth merchant who did it earlier.

The development of captives was also helped by high post-war taxation, which caused many of these captives to be formed offshore or in low taxation areas. These tax havens allow the captives to pay lower corporation tax and to invest funds in a more liberal environment. Many tax authorities took the view that these captives were not truly independent of the parent and therefore all profits were taxed together with the parent, thus negating the tax benefit. Additionally the tax authorities would not allow any premiums charged by a captive to be tax deductible unless the premiums charged were reasonable. This was to avoid large funds being paid away to avoid tax. However despite these restrictions captives have been very successful. In 1998 there were over 3800 captives worldwide with an estimated premium of over $19billion.

Risk Retention Groups

In 1986, at a time of a shortage of liability insurance capacity in the USA, the US government passed an act called "The Federal Liability Risk Retention 1986". It allowed the formation of two types of new insurance vehicles.

(1) Risk Retention Groups (RRG) for collective insurance i.e. underwriting of risk.

(2) Risk Purchasing Groups (RPG) for collective insurance buying.

These groups had to be in a similar business or have similar liabilities. The risk retention group is thus an insurance company and is very similar to a captive but for an industry rather than a single industrial or commercial company. RRGs have been formed for scaffolders and for bars and taverns etc.

The RRGs still have to file annual financial statements in all the states they operate in like insurance companies and they have to pay corporation tax and insurance taxes. They avoid however much of the onerous insurance regulation. In 1996 there were 97 RRGs with premium of about $500million.

Reinsurance of Captive Companies

A great deal has been written, and no doubt will continue to be written, about captive insurance companies. This book is not the place to discuss the merits and demerits of such companies.

A captive insurance company must be defined as an insurance company owned by an industrial, commercial or financial organisation which writes, wholly or predominantly, the parent company's insurance. This means that a captive insurance company will have a very limited spread of business, often confined to a portfolio of risks in one particular industry.

As the captive insurance company set-up is often in tax free havens it will want to retain for itself the maximum premium income. If the captive is to be successful it is an essential prerequisite that the parent company's losses are kept to the minimum. This means an unusual concentration by the parent company and the captive company on loss prevention and engineering, to minimise the losses to the captive. In the main, the losses which can be minimised or eliminated will be smaller and medium sized claims. A good maintenance engineering and loss prevention programme may make the large disastrous loss less likely but no programme can prevent the major disastrous loss.

The captive portfolio then leads to an excess risk type of reinsurance with some form of facultative reinsurance to reduce peak values. By using the excess approach, with a deductible to absorb the "everyday" loss, the captive may achieve the best of both worlds. Firstly, it will pay away a smaller part of its income for its protection than if it effected contributing reinsurance and, secondly, it will benefit if, by loss prevention, the losses within the deductible are kept to a minimum.

Whether the captive's excess programme is on an actual risk basis or on an occurrence basis, with sizeable risk exposures, it is not important; what is important is that the excess Reinsurer will be exposed very substantially on single risks. The handling and rating of such reinsurance will follow basically that of a risk excess described in Chapter X and the third party excesses as described in Chapter XI.

However, before going into the more technical matters, any Reinsurer of a captive company will wish to establish certain basic facts:

(1) That the captive insurance company is adequately financed in relation to the size of business it will be writing. In other words, that it has sufficient paid-up capital and surplus or reserves to meet its likely vicissitudes of underwriting. In the event it is not comfortable, the reinsurer should seek parental guarantee/LOC or other structure to ensure the captive's financial obligations can be met.

(2) That it has experienced and adequate insurance management and underwriting.

(3) That it will be permitted by the parent company full underwriting control of the business it will take on.

(4) That its rating and policy forms will conform to accepted usage, e.g. that it will not cut rates on the business it accepts.

(5) That it will have experienced and efficient inspection and loss prevention programmes.

(6) That the captive company has a proper claims staff who will settle claims on a strictly legal basis and that they will be permitted to do so by the parent company.

Even with these assurances, however, as the captive company is itself under the control of the parent company, obviously a conflict of interest could arise. By this I mean that pressures may be placed on the captive company to make favourable loss settlements to its parent company and to quote competitive terms. Of course, if this happens, the life of the captive company will be a short one. In practice, most parent companies setting up captive companies tend to act in the opposite fashion and are prepared to modify loss collections and can even pay enhanced premiums! The onus is on the parent company to prove that the transfer pricing, or premium is reflective of the exposure.

A Reinsurer of a captive company should make quite certain, firstly, that he is aware and approves of the terms, conditions and rates charged by the captive company and that these are not changed without Reinsurer's consent, and, secondly, that the Reinsurer controls the settlements of either all losses or at least all large losses. In other words, a Reinsurer of a captive company must act very much as if he were a direct Insurer of the parent company's business. Naturally, in the course of time, a sufficient rapport will grow up between the captive company and its Reinsurers which will make it less necessary for the Reinsurer to act in this way.

However, the captive reinsurance should contain either a schedule of the original insurance which the captive company will write or a very full description of the properties and liabilities to be insured with perils, interest and monetary limits. Similarly, in the initial stages of a reinsurance relationship, the question of claims settlement is best dealt with by a claims clause which requires the captive insurance company not only to advise Reinsurers of any claim made, and to supply details, but to agree not to make any settlement without Reinsurers' prior agreement. Such a clause will make Reinsurers responsible for all claims handling once the Reinsurers are liable, or likely to be liable, for a claim. Once trust is established, such a claims clause can be eliminated and claims settlement left to the captive Insurer.

The captive insurance company provides two basic services to its parent company:

(1) That of a more efficient risk carrier for normal insurance cover than the parent company can obtain in the traditional insurance market. This efficiency can only be brought about by the captive operation improving the experience of the parent company's business and thus diverting the profit derived from this improved experience from the insurance industry to the captive, and thus to its parent company.

(2) Providing coverage for types of insurance not available or not readily available in the normal insurance market place.

A Reinsurer of a captive company will be well advised to distinguish between these two types of service. If it is the first, then the quality of engineering and loss prevention will be the key to a successful partnership. If it is the latter, then the Reinsurer should be fully aware of the coverage provided and ascertain very carefully whether he is to protect a type of business which may really be uninsurable. If so, then the reinsurance contract may have to be so designed so as to leave with the captive Insurer the greater part of the "uninsurable" risk. For example, a captive insurance programme covering loss by a parent company from strikes by its own employees is virtually a non-insurable risk in normal insurance markets. However, if written by a captive insurance company then reinsurance markets may be available to reinsure such a programme with a high monetary deductible, or deductible set excess of a sizeable number of weeks stoppage.

Captives and Off-shore Islands

We have discussed above the concept of reinsurance which requires a transfer of risk or risk shifting.

Can a reinsurance of a parent to a subsidiary or vice versa be regarded as a proper reinsurance? Has any risk been shifted? This whole subject is, of course, fundamental to the whole captive insurance movement.

Insofar as reinsurance is concerned, we can best consider it by taking an example of a large direct insurance company owning a reinsurance subsidiary 100%.

Today, provided the two companies operate independently and at arms length, and the reinsurance company's operation is a general wide-based reinsurance operation and not limited to, or under direction of, the parent, then risk transfer has taken place.

When the parent agrees, as a condition of the subsidiary accepting its business, that it will in some way hold the Reinsurer harmless from the bad results of such business or agree to inject fresh capital if things go wrong, then clearly no risk may have been shifted.

This whole subject is under constant review in the U.S. Courts and I can only suggest that readers keep abreast of the latest cases. I am sure the principles which decide these cases should be:

(A) are the transactions arms length?

(B) has there been a genuine shift of risk without any strings?

(C) does the subsidiary conduct its business without management or underwriting control from the parent?

I wonder, too, whether the highly-taxed societies such as the U.S.A. and E.E.C. are going forever to permit the trading of reinsurance to those areas of the world which pay no tax. However desirable freedom is to the reinsurance industry, it seems wrong for us to expect this freedom not to be curtailed and for some excise or other tax or limitation to be made for the proper and genuine protection of the home industry or at least that part of it that pays proper taxes.

In addition, so many of these tax-free islands have little or no regulatory rules.

The time is surely coming when the established reinsurance industry in Europe and the U.S.A. will itself welcome E.E.C. or U.S.A. moves in this direction.

Creating "Catastrophe" Reserves

Reinsurance is a cyclical business and these cycles last more than one year. In addition, major catastrophes happen infrequently.

An annual accounting period for a reinsurance operation is too short unless the back cycles and the incidence of catastrophes can be spread over the good years. Many Reinsurers do this in various ways. Unfortunately, the creation of reserves *per se* for losses which have not happened and may never happen are not tax deductible in most countries.

The situation has changed significantly in the UK and the rest of the EEC since the 3rd edition of this book was written. Insurance companies and reinsurance companies but not yet Lloyd's syndicates are now able to create their own catastrophe or equalisation reserves. The EEC directive allowing equalisation reserves was published in 1987 however the UK only approved the recommendations in 1996. This was speeded up probably because of the large European storms in 1990 and for the desire to make it more of a level playing field in Europe for Insurers and Reinsurers alike. For many years countries such as Germany and Switzerland had these reserves now the whole EEC does as well. Each country will have its own system of equalisation reserves but effectively one can put away premium as reserves in the good years and collect needed funds in the bad years.

In the UK on Non-life business the method is as follows. The categories of business are divided into five main classes (A-E) .The company can pay into the equalisation reserves up to maximum fixed percentages of net premium income varying from only 3%for categories A and B (Property & Consequential Insurance) and 75% for category D (Nuclear business) for each annual period. Non-proportional reinsurance is category E which allows payments of 11% of premium. The company can transfer out all funds in excess of a claims ratio trigger of 72.5% up to the value of the funds held. To prevent companies salting money away to avoid taxes there is a maximum aggregate limit of 20% of premium for categories A&B (Property & Consequential Insurance) and 60% for category D (Nuclear business). Non-proportional reinsurance (E) has a maximum limit of 75%. These reserves have the effect of reducing the need for reinsurance, as spreading the loss over many underwriting years is one of the main reasons for reinsurance and this is effectively done by catastrophe reserves. It is really a spread loss cover once outlawed in the UK, (see the financial section later). The development of catastrophe Reinsurers in Bermuda has been helped by the ability of them to put funds away for the bad years and the ability to build-up loss reserves tax-free. I envisage more Reinsurers moving to these tax havens or having holding companies based there. The main reason is that in a competitive market it gives them significant financial advantages.

Of course, the Reinsurer located in a tax-free area has no such inhibitions but, of course, as his profits may not attract tax either, he is tempted not to create extra reserves.

The Insurer or Reinsurer faced with the problem of spreading risk, normally attempts to solve it by the reinsurance route because reinsurance premiums paid away are tax deductible and generally are an allowable deduction for the calculation of technical reserves and solvency margins.

The difficulty here is to draw the line between what is reinsurance and what is a banking or loan transaction dressed up in a reinsurance cloak.

Nature of Reinsurance

Before discussing some of these ideas, we ought, therefore, to give greater thought as to the true nature of reinsurance. If we do not and we label transactions "reinsurances" which clearly are not, then we only have ourselves to blame if regulatory or fiscal authorities challenge us.

Similarly, if we deduct "premiums" for reinsurance ceded, sums which are not the true consideration for the liability ceded but are really loans for investment, then again we should not complain if regulatory and fiscal authorities say we are cheating and use "the dagger to rend our cloak!"

I assume that no one would dispute that reinsurance is an extension of insurance and that one cannot introduce into reinsurance concepts and principles that do not exist in insurance.

Insurance Concepts

Insurance is not in British Law defined except for marine insurance under the Marine Insurance Acts. However the Common Law cases all seem to arrive at the same conclusions which also make a great deal of common sense.

(1) There is a consideration paid for protection.

(2) Protection is for something that is adverse to that person.

(3) Protection is for something that is fortuitous or at least unpredictable in it effect or its timing.

(4) There must be an insurable interest (not necessarily a policy of indemnity). Protection implies that if the adverse happens you can collect more than your own money back on that insurance policy. In other words, there is a genuine and real transfer or shift of risk.

N.B. (a) you cannot insure against good things, i.e. to spread one's profits or gains.

(b) you cannot insure against something that is known to have happened unless its effect is unpredictable.

(c) you cannot insure against a certainty or something that is inevitable unless its timing and effect is unpredictable.

(d) you cannot insure where you have little or no insurable interest, otherwise it becomes a wager or a bet.

(e) there must be a transfer of risk from the Insured to the Insurer.

I would like the reader to consider a further concept. You will have noticed that my criteria about an insurance are all phased from the viewpoint of the Insured, not the Insurer.

It is not necessary to assume that the Insurer or Reinsurer necessarily stands to lose over a number of insurance policies. The concept of a mutual Insurer is perfectly valid.

Now another concept.

A limited company reports to its stockholders annually, its accounts are annual, its dividends are paid out annually and its share price will vary according to its annual prospects and its dividends.

It can be detrimental to shareholders for a company to pass its dividend. It is recognised that an insurance can be valid if it provides protection to each annual period *even if over a period of years the company pays its own losses*. In fact each annual period can be regarded as a separate Reassured. And this is even more valid for Lloyd's syndicates which can change every year.

Viewed as a continuing entity the company or syndicate might be regarded as receiving no protection as it is using its own money to fund losses. Nevertheless, spreading of losses over annual periods can be a valid reinsurance operation.

Now let us return to look at reinsurances. We have two types of reinsurance — see Chapter 1 Page 1 (*et seq*): contributing and non-contributing (or proportional and non-proportional).

Proportional Reinsurance

In contributing or proportional reinsuance the Reassured hands on or cedes all or part of his original insurance liabilities. As these liabilities are insurance ones, they embody the concepts of insurance we have been discussing. If they did not, they would not be insurances. There is no need to re-look at the contract whether facultative or treaty to see if it is a valid reinsurance, provided the basis of a common venture exists and the liability has truly been ceded.

In other words, that a net premium has been paid proportionate to the liability ceded away and no collateral or side agreement exists where the Reassured agrees or arranges for the Reassured to be relieved of the consequences of the reinsurance.

If the concept of sharing in a joint venture for good or evil does not exist then the deal is not a contributing resinsurance even though it may be so designated. I give a few examples where this principle had been breached and which clearly are not "reinsurances".

(1) Company A takes out a Q.S. Reinsurance with a Reinsurer B. Company A then arranges for Company C to provide B with an unlimited stop loss protection excess of 98% Loss ratio for a cost of 2%. Company A then takes a retrocession from C of 100% of that stop loss protection.

(2) Company X takes out a first surplus treaty with a Reinsurer Y with a sliding scale of commission. Minimum commission 5% at L.R. 90%. Commission rising 1% for each 1% decrease in loss ratio to maximum commission of 90% at loss ratio of 5%.

In both cases the "joint venture" has been broken. In example (1), in addition, no reinsurance exists as all liability has by arrangement come back 100% to A. In example (2) the contract is in effect a stop loss × 90% L.R. for a premium of 5% as explained in Chapter XIII and should be so accounted.

Non-proportional

If we now turn to non-proportional reinsurance and consider our criteria:

a. consideration

b. protection against something adverse to the Reassured.

c. protection for fortuitous losses.

d. insurable interest.

e. protection, i.e. "risk transfer" or in U.S.A. English "risk shifting".

(a) the consideration should be reasonable for the risk transferred.

(b) reinsurance must be for something that is adverse in its effect to the Reassured. "Reinsurance" where the effect is solely to store away excess profits to build up a fund which can be taken back as and when wanted may not be a reinsurance. "Reinsurance" where the intention is to spread profits is not reinsurance. However, a reinsurance where proper protection is bought against adverse loss or losses where a premium is paid from good years may well have a secondary effect of levelling experience and this is one of the proper uses of reinsurance. The test must be whether in substance the contract is one where genuine protection is bought against adverse losses or whether in substance it is a device to make reserves out of profits which can then be regained at will.

(c) the adverse loss must be fortuitous. Here fortuitous must mean a circumstance which has not happened and which cannot be accurately foreseen and must be extended to include something which is inevitable but where the timing is fortuitous, e.g. death of a person, or where the loss has happened and its effect upon the Reassured is not known. For example, it would be perfectly proper for a reinsurance company with massive potential exposures to purchase additional protection, after a disaster has happened, as its eventual loss from that disaster may not be certainable for many months.

What is not reinsurance is to reinsure when a loss is inevitable; for example, a company's loss ratio is consistently between 60% and 70%. Te effect a stop loss reinsurance for, say, 20%, L.R. excess of 30% is a certain loss and is not a reinsurance.

(d) normally, most reinsurances maintain the principle of indemnity. The Reassured is indemnified for the financial loss he suffers. However, there seems no reason why this must always be so. There are many insurances which are not policies of indemnity. Provided there is reasonable insurable interest or reasonable reinsurable interest such reinsurance should be valid. Where the insurable interest becomes very slight or non-existent then the reinsurance rapidly becomes a wager. An example of this was the old "tonner" policy — on which I have commented. These "tonner" policies are no longer permitted at Lloyd's.

Perhaps we can summarize things as follows:

(1) A contributing reinsurance can cease to become a valid reinsurance contract when the two contracting parties, by an agreement in the contract or by a separate reinsurance contract or by an arrangement between them, arrange for the ceding Reassured to assume back the liability ceded or assumes back the consequences of the liability ceded or a substantial part thereof.

(2) A non-contributing reinsurance can cease to be a valid reinsurance when the indemnity or the maximum possible recovery does not materially exceed the premium paid plus interest earned by the Reinsurer on that premium. But this will not apply where the contract covers a number of annual accounts and each account receives protection materially in excess of the premium it pays plus interest thereon.

Bankers

The classical "banking contract" usually either takes the form of an excess of loss reinsurance or a stop loss reinsurance. We need not detain ourselves here with the exact type of contract. They are fully dealt with in earlier chapters.

The guts of a banker is the premium clause. Essentially the banker is designed to store away a premium, i.e. "to bank it" and to retrieve it either for future losses or, if these do not occure, to receive it back, or part of it back in one form or another.

A banking contract can be a perfectly valid reinsurance contract.

Assume a 5-year non-cancellable losses occurring contract for 2,000,000 x/s 1,000,000 e.e. loss with one reinstatement each year (i.e. a

4,000,000 limit for each annual period) with an annual premium of 1,000,000. The contract contains a 50% PC on the 5 years' results.

This is a form of banking contract which, in my view, is perfectly valid and on which the annual premium is 1,000,000 (with a possible 500,000 returnable).

Insert a clause which limits the overall aggregate loss over the 5-year period to 5 m or 5 m plus interest earned, then the contract may still be a valid reinsurance because protection has been purchased by each annual period and these annual periods may be separate assureds.

Rollers or Roll-up Policies

The terms bankers and roll-overs are used fairly indiscriminatingly for a number of contracts. In writing a chapter like this, I am going to use the terms in what I consider to be their correct way.

A banker is essentially a contract where premium is banked and repossessed. A roller is a contract where the premium less losses, i.e. the profit on one year's contract, is rolled forward and added to the indemnity provided for the ensuing year.

Let us assume B the Reinsurer protects A the Reassured by a 12-month contract (for 1984) being a stop loss of 10% × 90% net Loss ratio for a premium of 3%. If the contract is clean, B agrees to issue a 12-month contract (for 1985) for 10% + 3%, i.e. 13% × 90%. (I assume, for simplicity, that the premium income stays constant.)

If that is clean then a 1986 contract for 13% + 3%, i.e. 16% × 90% and so on *ad infinitum*.

Now such a contract is reasonable and valid.

In fact, it often happens in the long-standing catastrophe market that Reassured with a long, clean record will expect and often receive either an annual increase in cover or a reduction in rate. Such a roll-over only puts a market practice in a formal way.

Let us now alter the scenario. Our roller above started with a contract for 10% × 90% at a premium of 3% with A's past loss ratios around 80%. The starting contract was a valid reinsurance. Now let us say that the indemnity for Year 1 was not 10% × 90% but 3.5% × 85% loss ratio for the 1984 year for a premium of 3% payable at inception with a proviso that no claim was payable until 6 months after the close of that year, i.e. June 1985 (which is when the result would be ascertainable anyway).

The 1985 policy, if the 1984 policy is clean, becomes 3.5% + 3.5% = 7% × 85%.

If 1984 and 1985 are clean the 1986 policy becomes 10.5% × 85% and so on *ad infinitum*.

This was how many rollers started in the late 1960s and early 1970s and, of course, the reader will quickly see that the first-year policy was not a valid reinsurance contract because no protection was bought, i.e. no risk transfer or risk shifting existed but that all subsequent years could be valid reinsurances.

Portfolio Reinsurances

We have discussed in earlier chapters the reinsurance of a portfolio of "in force" business. Where an underwriting operation is closing down or is sold, the entire outstanding portfolio of business is commonly reinsured for a premium sufficient to pay for all eventual liabilities leaving a margin for profit and allowing for investment and interest gain on the premium paid.

In modern times, the long tail nature of many insurance accounts and many reinsurance accounts means that an Insurer or Reinsurer should make very considerable reserves for I.B.N.R. and the unknown effect of the future on that I.B.N.R. progression. It may be very difficult to relate the prudent reserving to any actual past experience. Fiscal authorties are loath to allow such reserves as tax deductible. There is therefore an incentive for an Insurer, and more so for a Reinsurer, to find someone else who will take or reinsure the run-off for a premium which is tax deductible.

In addition, once such a reinsurance has been done with a Reinsurer whose security is unquestioned, then the Reassured can close his books. For a Lloyd's syndicate this is essential so that any year of account of a syndicate can be "closed" and names paid out. For a company, it may also be very beneficial to be able to close an account, particularly for taxation purposes.

Essentially, the Reassured pays over a sum of money to be relieved of the future movements (claims, return premiums) on that business and the future cost of claims handling and administration. The sum of money will have considerable investment gain until the liabilities have to be met.

If the Reinsurer fails to pay for any reason, then the Reassured still remains liable to his policy holders. This can only be removed if an actual transfer of liability is made from one Insurer to the other and this usually requires the consent of each policy holder or the Assumed Consent.

The advantages of these run-off reinsurances to a Reinsurer are twofold:

(1) The chance that he, through greater expertise or a greater claims-settling organisation, can settle the outstanding claims cheaply.

(2) The financial benefits of holding a substantial sum of money.

It is this second advantage that attracts reinsurance companies in tax-free areas such as Bermuda to this type of reinsurance. The great danger in assuming such business is that no one knows the length of the tail, and tails have a nasty habit of wagging for a very long time and wagging very vigorously.

Many portfolio reinsurances made in the 1950s, 1960s and 1970s have proved very costly to Reinsurers and many done in the 1980s have proven even more disastrous.

The advantages to the Reassured are, of course, the ability to sleep at night and close the books as well as the possible enhancement of his profit for the year in which the portfolio is reinsured.

The disadvantages to the Reassured are that he loses the use of his fund of money and, unless the security is above suspicion, he may be left with the liability and lose his fund of money too! This latter problem may be mitigated by a letter of credit or a bank guarantee which protects the Reassured against the solvency risk of the Reinsurer. However, such bank guarantees must be forever and irrevocable to be of much use.

The uses of run-off reinsurances by a Reassured are:

(1) For tax treatment

(2) For closing an account

(3) For selling a company

(4) To take advantage of someone else's greater investment expertise or tax advantages

(5) To take advantage of a Reinsurer's currency advantages

(6) To get rid of something you would rather be shot of at the price offered

(7) To enhance your profit and loss account by substituting a smaller reinsurance premium than your reserve.

The Reinsurer, having made his investment calculations according to the likely settlement patter on the run-off, must investigate fully the outstanding claimed estimates, the I.B.N.R. factors, the composition of the portfolio, the incidence of inflation and future currency movements. In fact, a lot will depend on the trustworthiness and Reinsurer's assessment of the whole claims accounting and reserving techniques of the Reassured.

Reinsurance to Close at Lloyd's RITC

Lloyd's Underwriters "Names" are Insurers with individual liability which is limited only by their means. That liability continues for as long as any insurance liability exists on the policies they have underwritten (say, today for 100 years). A Name is not permitted to effect a transfer of liability. In order to finalize his affairs, or his estates affairs, resort was and is made to a Reinsurance to Close (RITC). To be effective this RITC must have the effect of relieving the Name of all future movements on his commitments. Those movements are not limited to liability for losses, but include such items as: compromises on claims, expenses both loss and claims expenses, failure to collect from other Reinsurers due to insolvency or war or delay.

The wording of these run-off contracts has often used a more normal reinsurances one and often they have not clearly expressed the underlying purpose of both parties, which is clearly to give the Name complete release from all aspects of running-off his account, including such eventualities as failure to collect from his other Reinsurers due to insolvency, all claims expenses, all ex-gratia payments, punitive damages, etc., etc.

We have assumed in the previous paragraphs that the Reinsurer of a run-off will take over the future handling and settlement of claims and other movements and that he may be able to handle those more efficiently and cheaply than the Reassured. In 1996, we saw this in operation when Equitas took over the run-off of all Lloyd's Syndicates. Two of the arguments in favour were:

(1) Equitas as a continuing entity could make better use of the funds for investment.

(2) Equitas would be more efficient in handling and settling the run-off liabilities.

In the past at Lloyd's, the more normal transfer of liability the Reinsurance to Close (RITC) was done between the closing syndicate, the Reassured and another syndicate which was "open". "Open" simply means a syndicate which had not closed itself by a RITC.

Where the RITC was taken on by a successor syndicate under the same managing agent, the handling of the run-off was done by the successor syndicate using the same staff.

Where, however, the RITC was taken over by a different syndicate or a reinsurance company, then the claims handling on the run-off was often left with the "syndicate". In fact, what this meant was that the Reassured delegated the run-off settlement back to the managing agent of the successor syndicate. In other words, the successor syndicate became the Reassured's agent in this respect. In the event of their being no successor syndicate, then the assuming Reinsurer has to do this himself or find a run-off specialist to do it at a considerable cost.

Before leaving the subject of RITC, it must be emphasized that the original Names have only effected a reinsurance and they remain liable to the original policy holders. If in the future their Reinsurers do not respond (Equitas or whoever) then they, the Names, are still liable.

Stop Loss Reinsurances on Run-offs

A Reassured may well be able to achieve his objectives by not reinsuring his run-off in full but by protecting it by a stop loss reinsurance.

Assume that the Reassured has a run-off on which the known o/s losses are estimated to be 20,000,000 and the minimum I.B.N.R. is an additional 5,000,000 and his tax authorities will permit the figure of 25,000,000 as a proper reserve. The Reassured, to be prudent, wishes to carry an additional 10,000,000 of I.B.N.R. which would be unallowable for tax deduction.

The Reassured estimates that his 25 million will increase to say 30 million by the time the claims are settled. He then buys a reinsurance for 10,000,000 excess of 25,000,000 for a premium of 2 million. Provided this 2 million is tax deductible and provided his Reinsurer is secure, then he has solved his problems.

He has cover for 25 million (his own money) and 10 million of reinsurance for a reserve of 35,000,000. The Reinsurer has a potential loss of 10 million against a premium of 2 million, however, as the Reassured conservative estimate of the eventual outcome is 30 million. The "expected" loss to the Reinsurer is only 5 m × 25 m. Also, it will be many, many years, hopefully, before the Reassured's settled losses reach 30 m and thus involve Reinsurers. By that time the 2 m premium, having been well invested, may well be worth 5 m or more.

This is an over-simplified example but it illustrates the attraction of this type of reinsurance to both parties and the importance of investment of premiums to the Reinsurer. In fact, the terms of the contract will be determined by investment opportunities available to Reinsurers.

A portfolio transfer reinsurance or a stop loss thereon can be a valuable and valid method of reinsurance with a real transfer of risk for a consideration. The transfer of risk is in two parts, firstly the eventual settlement may be greatly in excess of the premium sum paid and interest earned upon it. The pattern of settlement may be quicker so that interest anticipated may not be earned. If, however, the settlement is limited in amount to the premium and interest thereon, then the first part of any risk may be eliminated. If a structural settlement is agreed, then the time risk can also be eliminated too. Then the deal may become not a resinsurance at all but a transfer of assets and liabilities from one party to another.

Such run-off reinsurances have become of great importance as the tail of insurance business lengthens and tax authorities do not permit I.B.N.R. reserves to increase to meet this lengthening tail. There is, however, a very grave danger and that is the security risk involved. These portfolio reinsurances can amount to massive sums and, of course, have equally massive liabilities which will be due for payment in the years ahead.

If these reinsurances have miscalculated the liabilities or miscalculated the investment returns and become insolvent or totally lacked liquidity, then those companies and Underwriters who are relying on them to pay the public may themselves become insolvent.

It is not just a misjudgement of the liabilities or investments but a misjudgement of timing, e.g. a quicker settlement of claims than anticipated which may cause a loss.

Regulating authorities in both U.S. and Europe may have taken this subject very seriously if the failure of Reinsurers of "run-offs" threatens the security of direct Insurers.

Time and Distance Policies

These are policies usually an excess aggregate or stop loss reinsurance where the indemnity provided is limited to the premium paid plus interest accrued on that premium. This is achieved by a date (time) in the policy usually some years ahead (distance) before which a collection cannot be made. Alternatively, a series of distances may be set with an increasing indemnity the greater the distance, a structured settlement.

Another alternative is to permit the Reassured to make a collection before the set distance but only with a penalty. In addition, some Time and Distance policies give the Reassured the right to have his premium plus interest earned back at the final date, loss or no loss. Clearly, this type of Time and Distance and some of those without this right of refund, are not reinsurances. The difficulty is to draw the line.

I suggest that the best way is to deal with this in disallowing part of the credit for Time and Distance policies in reserving (see Chapter XV).

I have set out a typical Time and Distance policy with a structured settlement at the close of this Chapter. I believe that this is a genuine reinsurance but needs to be discounted as in Chapter XV.

1999 Conclusion

The use of all the types of "financial" reinsurances discussed in this chapter have become valuable tools, if not essential tools, to allow the industry to take on business with a "tail". No doubt they will develop. The industry must, however, expect that, unless such policies are genuine reinsurances, they will be challenged either by tax or regulatory authorities. To give two examples:

(1) Portfolio reinsurances are a way of selling your reserves or part of them at a discounted price. A company sells its portfolio for which the reserve is, say, $100,000,000 to another company for a discounted price of $60,000,000. This has the effect, of course, of improving the Ceding Company's trading account by $40,000,000. The assuming Reinsurer received $60,000,000 and creates a reserve of $60,000, 000 which is quite illogical as he ought to be creating a reserve of $100,000,000. One can postulate two companies, each

writing identical accounts, reinsuring each other and each releasing £40,000,000. Poor policy holders — and what will the regulatory authority say!?

(2) Time and Distance. Where the indemnity is structured to the original premium plus the interest earned and, if no loss occurs on the policy, the premium plus interest is returnable in full to the Reassured, and if we are honest with ourselves we must admit that such a contract is not a genuine reinsurance and must raise the eyebrows of fiscal authorities.

Thoughts in 1990

As predicted above, the financial type of reinsurance has developed during the 1980s. The main problem which is also touched on in Chapter XV has been the very heavy discounting of insurance and reinsurance reserves, and the consequent enhancement of profits. My belief is that serious under reserving now exists and that this will surface in the 1990s and 2000s.

To put this in a very simple way. An insurance operation is reserved at US$ 50,000,000. Instead of carrying a reserve of this amount a "Time and Distance" policy for $25,000,000 × $25,000,000 is purchased for a $10,000,000 premium and the reserve reduced to $35,000,000 i.e. the first $25,000,000 plus the $10,000,000 premium. $15,000,000 extra profit is then produced and in many cases has been distributed to Names in Lloyd's or to Shareholders.

Thoughts in 2000

The main reason I feel for the development of the financial reinsurance market was that the traditional market was slow at realising "the time value of money". The financial reinsurance market very quickly allowed the buyer to receive a profit commission back, if the contract ran profitably as well as receiving a share of the interest. The financial reinsurance market was happy to do this providing they made their required profit margin on the premiums including investment income less the claims (often called the balance).

One concept the financial reinsurance market found difficult to live with, was unlimited liability. I quote from *Alternative Risk Financing* by Jim Bannister.

Steven Gluckstern and Michael Palm the founders of Centre Re came to the conclusion that: *"History shows that the insurance industry is not adequately compensated for taking unlimited risk."*

A fundamental concept of finite programmes is an ultimate limit on the liability of the risk taker in a given transaction. Beyond this limitation, there are no real constraints as to the exposures that can be covered or the duration of the commitments. There are, though, common features that appear in many finite programmes:

- a multi-year contractual commitment
- multi-risk or aggregate nature of coverage
- alignment of interest with the client, usually through profit sharing mechanisms which may explicitly recognise investment income on the profits paid
- aggregate limit of liability
- programmes usually written 100% net by a single carrier

None of the above features is unique on a stand-alone basis. It is the blending of these and other features into a single, innovative, tailor-made-for-the-client structure that has made the finite approach so successful.

In 1998, Swiss Re estimates that worldwide premiums paid by primary Insurers to 'finite providers' is about US$6 to 7 billion annually or about 5% of worldwide non-life reinsurance.

The tax havens which developed as the home for captives thus, developed as financial reinsurance centres due to the tax and regulatory advantages. The early time and distance policies were written there and in the 1980s the spread loss concept was developed. This spread loss concept allowed a loss to be spread over many years providing there was a provision for any negative contract balance to be paid back during the term of the cover. This pay back provision allowed all sorts of exposures to be covered including investment losses, which could not be insured in the traditional markets. The chief financial officer of an industrial company or an insurance company can now look at all his financial exposures i.e. natural disasters, stock market collapse, subsidence, negative cash flow, mortgage guarantees etc. and work out how they wish to manage these risks. He or she could form a captive, self-insure, purchase traditional insurance or reinsurance or use some financial spreading mechanism. The choice is large now thanks largely to the development of ART (Alternative Risk Transfer). The common features of the ART market are now being felt in the traditional reinsurance markets with multi-year contracts, profit commissions, no claims bonuses appearing on risk excesses and catastrophe programmes. There is a tendency to provide much more what the buyer wants than stick with traditional products.

AGGREGATE EXCESS OF LOSS REINSURANCE AGREEMENT

between

....

(Hereinafter called the 'Reassured'
of the one part

and

....

(Hereinafter called the 'Reinsurers')
of the other part

This Agreement shall protect the Reassured in respect of all liability howsoever and wheresoever arising which the Reassured may incur on their 1968-1978 inclusive Underwriting Years of Account of their so-called 'United States Dollar' Account and which is settled on or after 1st January, 1985 subject, however, to the following terms and conditions:

ARTICLE 1

This Agreement is only to pay in excess of an ultimate nett loss to the Reassured of U.S.$10,000,000 in the aggregate with a limit of liability to the Reinsurers hereunder of a further U.S.$10,000,000 in the aggregate.

Notwithstanding the foregoing, the limit of indemnity hereunder shall not exceed those amounts that are set out below or so deemed:

Settlement Period *At end of*	*Reinsurer's Maximum Ultimate Nett Loss payable hereon*
1st to 10th Calendar Year	U.S.$ 4,000,000
11th Calendar Year	U.S.$ 5,000,000
12th Calendar Year	U.S.$ 6,000,000
13th Calendar Year	U.S.$ 7,000,000
14th Calendar Year	U.S.$ 8,000,000
15th Calendar Year	U.S.$ 9,000,000
16th Calendar Year and all subsequent years	U.S.$10,000,000

ARTICLE 2

The term 'ultimate net loss' shall be understood to mean the sums actually paid movements by the Reassured (other than the salaries of employees and office expenses of the Reassured) after making deductions for monies acutally received by the Reassured.

Notwithstanding anything contained hereon to the contrary it is understood and agreed that recoveries under any underlying 'Run-off' reinsurances are for the sole benefit of the Reassured and shall not be taken into account in computing the ultimate net loss in excess of which this Agreement attaches nor in any way affect the amount recoverable hereunder.

ARTICLE 3

This Agreement is to take effect as from the 1st January, 1985 and shall be always open as from this date. It is expressly understood that this Agreement is non-cancellable by either party.

ARTICLE 4

As consideration for the protection afforded by this Agreement the Reassured shall pay to the Reinsurers a premium of U.S.$1,000,000 in full, payable by special settlement on the 1st April, 1985.

ARTICLE 5

In all things falling within the scope of this Agreement the Reinsurers shall share to the extent of their interest the fortunes of the Reassured.

ARTICLE 6

The Reassured shall exercise due diligence in dealing with all matters relating to this Agreement it being understood that all settlements made by the Reassured whether by way of compromise ex-gratia or otherwise shall in every respect be unconditionally binding upon the Reinsurers.

ARTICLE 7

As soon as practicable after the 31st December of each year the Reassured shall submit a statement in United States Dollars of their payments.

ARTICLE 8

As from inception or at any time thereafter, if so required by the Reassured, the Reinsurers agree to provide the Reassured with a Letter of Credit for an amount of not less than the incurred ultimate nett loss hereon less any collections hereon, whichever is the greater. In the event that the Reassured exercises this option then the Reinsurers shall arrange that such Letter of Credit be issued for a three year period and then renewed for further three year periods as at each annual anniversary thereafter. It is agreed however, that the costs of such Letter of Credit shall be borne by the Reassured.

Notwithstanding the foregoing it shall be specifically understood and agreed, however, that the Letter of Credit provided by the Reinsurers hereon shall never exceed U.S.$10,000,000 less the amount of the Reassured's ultimate nett loss recovered from the Reinsurers hereon. Should any Letter or Credit not be provided or not renewed then the Reinsurers shall if requested by the Reassured deposit in cash with the Reassured as a loss reserve an amount equal to amounts stated above in lieu of the Letter of Credit.

ARTICLE 9

It is hereby declared and agreed that any inadvertent delays, omissions or errors made in connection with this Agreement shall not be held to relieve either of the parties hereto from any liability which would attach to them hereunder if such delay, omission or error had not been made provided rectification be made as soon as possible after discovery.

Chapter XV

INSURANCE REGULATIONS, SOLVENCY OF REINSURERS AND LOSS RESERVES

PART 1
Solvency controls on direct writing companies — Technical reserves — Solvency margins — Supervision of reinsurance operations — Controls to protect local Insurers

PART 2
Evaluating Reinsurers' solvency — People — Past record — Assets — Technical reserves — Unearned premium reserves for a reinsurance account — A suggested evaluation of outstanding liabilities, including I.B.N.R., on a reinsurance account — A suggested evaluation of a Reinsurer's solvency margin

PART 1

Regulation of the insurance industry affects Reinsurers in three main areas:

(1) The solvency controls exercised over the direct writing companies for the protection of policy holders.

(2) Solvency controls of Reinsurers.

(3) Controls exercised for the protection of the local or national insurance industry.

Protection of the Policy Holder

Policy holders and members of the public rely on insurance policies should they suffer injury or loss. Thus, a car owner has come to expect that the Insurer to whom he has paid a premium will be solvent and in existence to pay his loss if his car is stolen. It could be argued that if he selects a "fly-by-night" company, which provides him with cover at a cheap premium, he has only himself to blame if he cannot collect his claim.

This argument is one with which I have considerable sympathy. Unfortunately, it strikes at the very root of the thinking of much of our society today, which assumes that the "ordinary" person must be protected from the result of his folly by "society", i.e. by the rest of us. Of course, if that car owner runs into someone and injures them, then it will not be the car owner who cannot collect but the injured third party. Therefore, it has to be accepted that members of the public do expect their Governments to regulate and control their insurance companies.

The main regulatory controls applied are:

(1) The approval of the establishment of an Insurance company to insure specified classes of insurance. Details needed would include the names of the people involved and their experience, a detailed business plan, sufficient management expertise and financial backing.

(2) The approval of any major changes in the life of the company, (i.e. appointment of directors, underwriting of a new class of insurance, an increase in capital, approval of a merger or take-over etc.).

(3) The regular reporting of financial figures either annually for long established companies or quarterly or even monthly dependent on the jurisdiction and their concerns. These reports will include premium and claims details by class of business. These would be for recent underwriting years as well as any loss development from older years.

(4) The production of an annual set of accounts that would be audited by an approved auditor.

(5) A valuation of all investments held, together with details of the paid up capital and any additional free reserves (or deficiencies) of the company. These will probably be required quarterly but certainly annually and audited.

(6) The right to inspect the records of the company at any time and in the case of problems, to suspend or wind-up the insurance company at any time.

The production of the financial figures allows the regulators to evaluate the following and thus apply the necessary financial controls.

(a) technical reserves.

(b) solvency margins.

(c) valuation of assets.

(a) Technical reserves

Technical reserves or audit reserves are to make certain that an Insurer has sufficient funds to discharge his future liabilities on the business he has already written and these consist of two parts — unearned premium reserves and o/s liability reserves, including reserves for incurred but not reported liabilities, i.e. I.B.N.R.

The unearned premium reserve and the reserve for the known outstanding liabilities are factual and, provided good records are kept, should present no problems. I.B.N.R. reserves. However, are a major problem. Whether reserves are calculated net or gross of resinsurance will depend on the views of the statutory body. In the United States a reinsuring company will be allowed to take credit for licensed Reinsurers in respect of both premium reserves and outstanding liability reserves. Unlicensed Reinsurers will usually deposit their share of both premium reserves and outstanding liability reserves with the Ceding Company. It is common practice particularly in the USA for unlicensed Reinsurers to provide 'Letters of Credit' LOCs for the premium and loss reserves which can be drawn down when needed.

In France, where gross reserving is followed, i.e., where no allowance is made for reinsurance, Reinsurers will normally deposit both premium reserves and outstanding liability reserves with the Ceding Company and the Ceding Company can count the reserves actually deposited as an *asset* to offset the gross reserves.

In the United Kingdom the authorities normally permit full credit for all reinsurances, i.e. all reinsurance is treated as "licensed". Reinsurers do not have to make deposits with the Ceding Company. Of course, a Ceding Company may desire, or required, such deposits for its own security and often does so.

Lloyd's adopts a similar view to the United Kingdom authorities. However, a limit is placed on the amount of outwards reinsurance that may be given credit, so that full credit may not be given for reinsurance in the calculation of technical (audit) reserves.

Technical reserves are usually held in the countries where the liabilities will be paid, i.e. such funds are localised and should not be usuable by the company concerned as they are earmarked for specific liabilities.

Note written in 2000

The continued development and expansion of the EEC is leading to a greater uniformity of regulation therein. The main rules of the EEC are to allow the free movement of goods and persons, services and capital throughout all countries of the community. The aim is to have the freedom of establishment of insurance companies or in fact any companies in the home country of the EEC and to allow the companies then to have a licence to trade throughout the rest of the EEC. The legal mechanisms are that the EEC publishes Directives and then subject to approval of these, the individual countries then pass the appropriate laws in their own countries. The speed in the various countries of drafting and approval of the laws varies considerably from country to country but more importantly, each country's interpretation of the Directives can vary also. The 3rd EEC Directive published in 1994 set out a framework of what was required of insurance companies and regulators within the EEC. This set out that the home country would to be responsible for the regulation of insurance companies based in their country. The various Directives set out the minimum solvency margins required for all insurance companies and the third set a minimum guarantee fund required for each company (of one third of the required solvency margin) amongst many other requirements.

In the UK following the 3rd non-life directive in 1994, the changes required in UK insurance regulations necessary were published in 1996. However because of the large differences in regulation between the countries in the past and the mutual suspicion of each other's regulators the process has been slow. The UK and I believe Denmark and Spain regulate reinsurance companies similar to insurance companies, whereas the rest of the EEC does not regulate them at all other than them coming under normal company law but it is likely some other countries will soon follow the UK method. The maximum credit for reinsurance allowable in the solvency margin is 50% however each country can set its own minimum thus allowing no credit for reinsurance.

One feature of the EEC has been the breaking down of monopolies and Insurance Pools which were common in Italy and tariff markets (that agreed insurance rates and conditions) which existed particularly in Germany, have now largely disappeared leading to much more price competition. In the USA most insurance regulation is at the state level and therefore there are 51 Regulators (the individual states plus Washington) although some states i.e. New York have considerable more influence than others.

(b) Solvency margins

Solvency margins or premium income limits are to make sure that an Insurer has sufficient free funds over and above the technical reserves to support future writings. Again, these are often required to be held in the country concerned but are normally part of a company's usuable assets as they are not earmarked for specific liabilities.

The solvency margin is measured as the ratio of free assets of the company divided by the premium income. The EEC sets minimum solvency margins for life and non-life companies and for non-life companies they are 16% of premium (but 18% for small companies below a certain premium volume) or 23% of annual claims costs (26% for small companies) whichever greater. Credit is given to this figure for reinsurance with a maximum credit of 50%. The solvency margin is also worked out on the net premium, so effectively therefore a further credit is given for reinsurance. The directives and the regulations set the rules for the valuation of assets. If the experience is much worse than average the minimum solvency margin will be increased by the claims cost factor and the Regulators have the right to insist on even higher solvency margins for start-ups or where recent experience is concerning.

This position in Lloyd's has changed. Previously a Name's solvency margin, i.e. the ratio of his deposit and assets, were related to his premium income net of reinsurance and net of commissions and brokerage. That has now changed and the ratios are now calculated on gross income net of commissions and brokerage but before reinsurance.

Lloyd's since 1994 has allowed corporate capital and in order to calculate how much capital is required for a corporate syndicate or corporate name a risk weighting is applied to the type of business written. Therefore, if the syndicate was writing just property catastrophe business it would have a high risk-weighting and thus a large amount of capital would be required but for a motor syndicate a much lower risk-weighting and thus lower capital would be needed.

Therefore, Reinsurers' position is:

Technical reserves: In France and other areas, e.g. U.S.A., with unlicensed reinsurance, Reinsurers may be forced to deposit their share of technical reserves with the Ceding Company.

For licensed Reinsurers in the U.S.A. for all Reinsurers in the United Kingdom and some other areas there is no statutory necessity for Reinsurers to make deposits for technical reserves.

Solvency margins: There is no necessity for Reinsurers to contribute to a direct writer's solvency margin as those solvency margins are normally calculated net of reinsurance ceded except for Lloyd's Syndicates.

(c) Valuation of assets

Please see Section C under "evaluating a Reinsurer's solvency" later in the chapter as the same rules apply.

Supervision of Reinsurance Operations

Reinsurers do not deal with the public and a financial failure of a Reinsurer can only affect the public if that Reinsurer's failure causes a failure of a direct writing company. Some supervisory authorities, notably the French, deal with this problem by requiring their direct writing companies to show technical reserves on a gross basis, i.e. ignoring the existence of reinsurance: they do not then need to regulate the solvency of Reinsurers. Other authorities give credit for reinsurance and allow direct writing companies to calculate technical reserves and solvency margins on a net basis. In this case a solvency test of Reinsurers is logical.

In the United States most authorities require reinsurance operations within their jurisdiction to show technical reserves on the same basis as direct writers. In Lloyd's there is no clear distinction between Insurers and Reinsurers and Lloyd's Reinsurers are treated on the same basis as direct Insurers.

In some areas, for example Switzerland and Germany, supervision of companies writing reinsurance only is less than that for direct Insurers. In the U.K. solvency margins introduced in 1971 do not apply to reinsurance companies. Therefore statutory control over Reinsurers is very varied.

The French approach is logical as it would mean that no supervisory solvency controls need to be exercised over reinsurance operations, the whole control on behalf of the public being exercised over the direct Insurer.

However, it is argued that if this were generally adopted it would create major problems for Reinsurers. It would mean, in practice, that Reinsurers would have to fund their share of technical reserves. This would require Reinsurers to localise cash, and localised cash is not available to meet urgent claims somewhere else in the world. (However, it should be noted that a technical reserve is made for specific liabilities and they should not be earmarked or disbursed for other purposes.) It would deprive Reinsurers of freedom of investment and could mean less interest earned by Reinsurers. Out of sheer necessity Reinsurers might require to employ greater resources of assets and capital in the business for a smaller return. However, the system of gross reserving, and its corollary — no control over Reinsurers' technical reserves — has much to commend it. For example, provided the authorities permitted the use of Letters of Credit or Bank Guarantees in lieu of physical deposits, the problem of interest earnings, investment freedom and cash availability would be mitigated to a large extent.

It would be interesting to see an objective statistical analysis done for one or two of the major international Reinsurers to see what effect gross reserving would have on their cash and investment, using Letters of Credit and without using them.

If gross reserving for direct Insurers could be adopted without too much dislocation of the reinsurance world then reinsurance operations could get the regulators off their backs and their financial viability would be judged by their own clients and their own directors and shareholders.

Presuming that gross reserving for technical reserves is not adopted internationally, then these alternatives present themselves:

> The first would entail an accepted common method of calculating Reinsurers' technical reserves and solvency margins. Each authority could then give credit for reinsurance placed by its own direct writers with those Reinsurers in other territories who had passed these tests.
>
> The second alternative is to attempt no statutory control but to trust direct writers to select their Reinsurers, the adage of "*caveat emptor*" being applied. Insurance companies, on the whole, are professionals and in the main perfectly capable of selecting sound

Reinsurers. It is in their interest, as well as in the interest of their policyholders, so to do. This is what has always happened and failures in the reinsurance field have been comparatively few.

One wonders whether the employment of large Government supervisory staff and the cost and trauma involved, which increased supervision would entail, would be worth it. The public would end up by paying for it by taxes and increased premiums, and would they get value for money? One doubts it. Some moves by Reinsurers themselves, either in national markets or internationally, to form associations which guarantee the reinsurance debts of any association member, could be the best answer. This self-regulation would immediately entail such an association applying some form of audit of technical reserves and solvency control over its members and some form of contingency fund. Lloyd's already does this.

The problem is to deal with the "cowboys" — those Reinsurers who come into the business for the ride and who can unhorse quite a few others, until they are corralled and put out to grass. It is my firm opinion that self-regulation could be a better method than State regulation. The reinsurance industry, nationally and internationally, ought to consider self-regulation seriously if it wishes to avoid gross reserving and if it is to avoid more State regulation.

The first step in self-regulation might be to introduce a common code of presentation of reinsurance accounts which would show how technical reserves have been calculated and would provide sufficiently clear evidence to allow others to see that technical reserves and solvency margins conform to certain minimum standards. Such a suggestion is contained later in this chapter.

2000 comment

Self-regulation has been very effective for many years at Lloyd's and has worked well in many other industries. However self-regulation is becoming increasing difficult to police as often the regulators are in competition with those they are regulating creating a conflict of interest. It was not a problem in the old days when Lloyd's was more like a club and everyone knew everyone else. In these days of computerisation and globalisation things move too fast for the market to know everything that is going on. So, I believe external independent regulation is the best. I think it is essential that the regulators do talk to the market, do pick up the gossip, do receive emails so they hear of any problems early enabling them can react quickly if necessary as the self-regulation would do. This is because by the time that the rating agencies come up with the warnings, it may be too late.

As we said earlier there is no one regulator in the USA, there are fifty-one one for each state plus the Federal Government. In the EEC, one for each country like the rest of the world. Therefore it is important there is some consistency between all regulators. I like the way the committee of insurance commissioners of the individual States in the USA produced the IRIS tests. They perform eleven different tests on the data produced by each company. If the result of these tests is either greater or less than a set figure it may show an early warning of problems ahead. Some of these tests are as follows:

1. Premium to Surplus Ratio.

The Net Premium Written should be less than 300% Policyholder's Surplus

The policyholder's surplus is the addition of the paid-up capital of an insurance company and any additional free reserves the company has after all liabilities have been deducted. It gives comfort to the policyholder if there is plenty of free cash to pay for any sudden deterioration in claims experience. If the company is writing a premium of more than three times the surplus it is over-trading i.e. writing too much business.

2. Change in Premium

If there is an increase or decrease in premium of more than 33%, it may indicate financial difficulties. A large increase may be healthy, indicating price increases, but it may also indicate a rapid expansion and thus instability or a large reduction in rates thus attracting many more policyholders. The large decrease may also be healthy indicating a cut-back on unprofitable lines or else unwarranted rate reductions.

3. Loss Ratio or Profitability Ratio

What are the historical loss ratios or profitability ratios of the company?
Loss ratio is calculated by dividing the incurred claims into the gross premium including commissions etc. The profitability ratio is the percentage of profit relative to gross premium after taking into account investment income, expenses and loans. Is the company making a profit or not?

4. Change in Surplus

What is the change in surplus from last year?
If the surplus has dropped by more than 10% then that is a concern also if it has increased by more than 50% (though not always) that can also be a concern.

A number of companies had large increases in surpluses before they failed, possibly caused by last minute capital infusions or changes of reinsurances etc.

5. Increase in reserves since last year

The companies increase in reserves in one year should be less than 25% of the prior years surplus

If there is a movement of loss reserves (these include IBNR) of more than 25% of the prior years surplus, it probably indicates a large deterioration in reserves. Where do current reserves end up? At this rate the company might go insolvent!

There are other tests that measure investment performance, liquidity ratios (how much real cash do they have available) and other reserve tests. These are quick ways of testing the strength or an insurance company or Reinsurer and are often performed by the various rating agencies.

Main reasons for insolvency are:

(1) Bad results.

(2) Bad asset management: — Too much in property or equities at the wrong time.

(3) Overwhelming liabilities — Asbestos or pollution or LMX.

(4) Undercapitalised

(5) Weak regulation. — Where are they based?

(6) Hostile environment — Motor, WCA only and unable to get rate increases needed.

Ways to spot problems early in insurance or reinsurance companies:

(1) Rating agency warnings or failure to pass key tests shown above.

(2) Delays in paying claims.

(3) Reduction in underwriting.

(4) Grapevine and gossip.

(5) Press comment.

Read and listen and you'll save money.

Controls for the Protection of Local Insurance and Reinsurance Markets

Insurance and reinsurance need the freedom to trade internationally if they are to give the best service to industry and the public. They need the broadest possible base to acquire a spread of business in order to assimilate the very large exposures, both on single risks or catastrophic accumulations, now common to all countries.

On the other hand, national interests are increasingly concerned with the protection of their own economies, for example, to use insurance funds for local investment and to localise technical reserves for the protection of their citizens.

It is important to reconcile these two conflicting points of view. Too much local control denies the public and the industry of that country the most efficient insurance and reinsurance protection. Total local control in the form of one compulsory State insurance company has always led to inflexible and inefficient insurance cover being provided to the public of that particular country. One compulsory reinsurance company has a similar effect.

On the other hand, concentration of the world's reinsurance industry in the hands of a few of the more developed countries is equally unacceptable. We have to emphasise continually that too much localisation can be a very bad thing for the country concerned and we must work towards an international reinsurance industry in which many can participate.

Undoubtedly notional controls limiting the placing of insurance outside national boundaries has led to a great increase in reinsurance business. This process of localisation has grown, particularly in the 1960s and 1970s, and has meant that a considerable volume of business which was formerly written direct across national boundaries, is now written by way of facultative or treaty reinsurance. In that it limits the Insured to a restricted and possibly uncompetitive market, it can be very inimical to the efficiency of that country. It also has the effect that a direct writer may have little expertise in handling large and difficult risks and, being limited to his own country's business, may have no "book" of such risks. Perforce, therefore, he turns to his Reinsurers for technical help and not, as in the past, to the large international direct writers who co-insured with him. International Reinsurers have, and must, become technically efficient in the inspection, servicing, rating and underwriting of these large or technically difficult risks.

Therefore, one effect has been the increasing involvement of large Reinsurers in giving service and advice to national companies and a larger volume of facultative reinsurance on such large or technical risks.

Controls exercised over direct insurance policies, e.g. controls over policy forms or rates, are often done with the intention of protecting the policyholder. Usually they have an opposite effect. Should controls mean that policy forms are restrictive and rates are high, then the local insurance companies may enjoy an unnaturally large profit at the expense of their national policyholders. Their Reinsurers, who are competitive, will unavoidably have to pay high ceding commissions and considerable overriders to these direct writers, thus augmenting the direct writers' profits. The effect is one of poor service to the public with benefit going by way of enhanced commission either to direct Insurers or their agents.

On the other hand, should State control mean that rates are too low, then Insurers will inevitably lose money and may have to reinsure at less than cost, thus increasing their net loss. The result can only mean that before long no markets will exist for such business and the public will suffer by not being able to purchase insurance on that class at all.

There is no better way of providing the public with the protection it needs and desires than the widest based free market. Government supervision over rating and policy forms should be minimal but strong and effective solvency controls are essential.

As we shall see, solvency controls are exercised by control of premium income. This is used as a yardstick to judge exposure.

Therefore, it is logical that the level of premium rates is either controlled or shown to be properly based. A company or Underwriter who consistently undercuts proper rating either deliberately or in ignorance, represents a future insolvency risk. This has been clearly demonstrated in the decade 1975-1984.

Consumer pressures in nearly all countries resulted in the demise of most tariff rating systems. Japan being a notable exception until recently. Direct Underwriters were left without a "yardstick" and severe competition created underwriting at unsound rates. The effect, despite high interest rates, has led and will lead to insolvencies of Insurers and Reinsurers.

Although I am an advocate of a free market and competition, such competition does need a statistical framework within which to work if it is to provide stability. There is need for national and international evidence to support recommended rates for those classes of insurance business where the spread is wide enough to produce viable experience.

An obligatory tariff may be against the public's interest but some form of rating standards could be beneficial and regulating authorities could take action against those clearly and consistently writing at variance with it.

Controls exercised over remittance of money strike very deeply at the whole basis of international reinsurance. Reinsurance, like insurance, needs the money of the many to discharge the claims of the few. Any hold up of premiums must mean that in times of stress it may not be possible to fund large claims quickly. The ability of the world-wide reinsurance market to respond quickly to one country which has suffered a catastrophic loss depends on all countries permitting free flow of premiums across frontiers. It is not always realised that when a disaster strikes one country then prompt payment by Reinsurers may not only save the original national companies from going bankrupt but may save that country's economy from a severe strain. In my short life-time certainly the Managua earthquake of 1972 and the disastrous Darwin cyclone Tracey in 1974 illustrated this point. Therefore, countries which do not permit free passage of premiums should not complain if, when things go wrong, they have to wait to receive losses.

PART 2

Evaluating a Reinsurer's Solvency

Whether we accept that State supervision of reinsurance operations is desirable or not, there is a need to consider how a Reinsurer's solvency can be assessed. If this is not done by State supervision it must be done by the Reinsurer's clients and should be done by the Reinsurer's owners, directors and auditors, and may need to be done by buyers or sellers of reinsurance operations.

The course we advocate follows the methods used in assessing the solvency of direct Insurers and consists of these elements:

(A) the quality and reputation of the people who own and operate the reinsurance concerned.

(B) the past record of the operation.

(C) that the assets backing the operation are readily realisable and properly valued.

(D) that technical reserves in respect of business on the books are sufficient to discharge all known and unknown future liabilities.

(E) that sufficient solvency margins remain to support future writings.

(A) People

Unless the reinsurance operation is conducted by people of honesty and integrity there is no point in going any further. Reinsurance depends on trust and untrustworthy people should not be a part of it. Given integrity, then the experience and past record of people is vital. Reinsurance is a long term relationship of trust and judgement. Experience in the business is essential. It simply does not compare with, say, selling computer goods. For example, the very long tail business involved in some classes of reinsurance means that an Underwriter's record, over a long period, must be proven before true faith can be accorded to him. In essence, an assessment of the character, intelligence and experience of Owners, Directors, Underwriters and Managers is the first test of the solvency of any reinsurance operation and can be more important than figures.

(B) The past record of the operation

Reinsurers are judged often on their ability to produce the cheapest terms. In a competitive world, such as reinsurance, the ability to produce a rate consistently below one's competitors can only stem from either greater efficiency or eventual insolvency due to consistent loss of money. A Reinsurer with a bad underwriting track record is a potential insolvent for the very reason that if the known back record is poor, then the unknown future on the business he already has on his books is likely to be even worse. The best and safest Reinsurer is one whose past record on underwriting is consistently profitable.

The words ... "record on underwriting" ... are vital. Firstly, a Reinsurer whose underwriting is consistently unprofitable, but who relies upon investment gain to save him, can be a candidate for insolvency. Inevitably a day dawns when the underwriting losses increase to overwhelm the investment gain or the investment gain reduces to produce the same ultimate result — not enough "lolly" to pay the cleaning bill!

Secondly, in judging this record his gross results before benefit of outwards reinsurance is the best yardstick.

This is very important because I write these words in 1985 and many Underwriters' track record in the past ten years has been saved by the use of reinsurance. An Underwriter's record should be judged on his gross experience as well as his net.

(C) Assets

It is then essential to verify whether the assets shown have been valued properly and are assets suitable to be held in trust for insurance policy holders. Obviously cash holdings, government securities and certain municipal and local authority investments are all acceptable. A reasonable amount of well-spread quoted equities are normally acceptable, but one must investigate thoroughly the real value of:

(a) large loans or mortgages and loans or mortgages to related companies or individuals.

(b) debts — particularly to related bodies.

(c) unquoted equities.

(d) a single large equity investment.

(e) large property holdings.

(f) property leased by related bodies or occupied by the insurance company.

Of course, an experienced auditor or accountant would have taken very special care to ascertain the true value of such assets and would have made special reference in his report to any material asset falling in these categories. However, we need an agreed practice by reinsurance companies and their accountants or auditors as to what are suitable assets to cover technical reserves and a wider list to cover solvency margins, with limitations on the size of certain types of assets.

(D) Technical reserves

Technical reserves result from the audit of existing business to make sure that it will be solvent on finality. Firstly, at any given point of time, a reinsurance portfolio will have an unearned portfolio of business, that is to say, the unearned premiums in respect of business in force at that date. No exposure has yet been incurred on that business and the unearned premium relating to it should be fully reserved, less any commission, premium taxes which are returnable.

Thus, technical reserve No. 1 is the gross unearned premium reserve less those acquisition costs which are recoverable if the policy is cancelled.

Technical reserve No. 2 is the estimate of all losses and other liabilities which have already occurred and consists of the following:

(a) losses already reported but not paid, i.e. known outstandings.

(b) this is generally known as I.B.N.R. which stands for "Incurred but not reported". It embraces a number of factors, all of which are very difficult to estimate, such as the possible unforeseeable deterioration in the known outstanding loss reserves which may occur, e.g. currency fluctuations or future inflation at an unforeseen rate, reserves for losses which have not yet been reported and reserves for other liabilities which have not been reported, for example, a return premium.

(c) the reserve for the company's own future expenses which cannot be cancelled, particularly the cost associated with the recording and settlement of all outstanding and unknown or I.B.N.R. claims which must include the continuing expenses of running the company's own claims department for the entire period of the run-off which may be for 20 years or more! These costs will have to be inflated for future increases in wages, computer costs and office rents and will be a very considerable extra addition to the reserve.

To reiterate, an operating reinsurance company should show, at any one moment of time, that it is technically solvent, i.e. that it holds sufficient free assets (properly valued) to discharge all its liabilities on the business it has on its books, without taking into account any future earnings on those assets. These technical reserves will consist of two parts:

(1) Unearned premium reserves.

(2) Outstanding liability reserves, including future loss expenses, future claims handling expenses, and I.B.N.R.

If the company is not technically solvent then it is unlikely to be able to meet its present commitments to its policy holders and is thus technically insolvent. It may not actually become insolvent for some years. In addition, if it is to continue to operate, i.e. take on new commitments to policy holders, it must show a margin of solvency so that the assets held exceed the technical reserves. This margin of solvency should vary with the volume and type of future business to be written and I will discuss it later in this chapter.

A new company will have no past business and no technical reserves and its margin of solvency will be its paid-up capital, which can be regarded as a minimum guarantee of solvency.

(D1) Unearned premium reserves on a reinsurance account

This is not applicable to Lloyd's or those companies adopting a three-year method of account. The methods of accounting unearned premium for direct writing companies are well known. However, with a reinsurance operation, certain reservations have to be made:

(i) Excess of loss premiums may be very nearly fully earned in any year. An excess of loss policy commencing early in the year with a large deposit premium may well result in a small unearned premium reserve.

(ii) Pro rata treaties accounted on an earned basis should have little or no unearned premium reserve provided the accounts are up to date.

(iii) Pro rata treaties accounted on a written basis will have a reserve similar to direct business but accounts will be late. Once a premium portfolio has been transferred there will be no unearned premium.

(iv) On a facultative reinsurance unearned premiums should equate to those on a direct operation.

To arrive at some idea of a reasonable reserve, one needs to realise that reinsurance accounts, comprising excess of loss business and/or a volume of U.S.A. and Canadian pro rata treaties accounted on an earned basis, may have a reserve less than that required for a direct account.

(D2) Loss reserves

I am starting this section with suggested proformas for the setting out of the calculation of a reasonable reserve. It is in two parts. The first will be a loss reserve for each class of business and the second a reserve for the whole account. I will comment on each in turn. Many items will be supported by schedules or calculations to show how they are calculated.

Reserve Statement (One for each class of business). See below.

Table 1

1. Noted gross outstanding losses (before any reinsurance collections).
2. Gross reserves for special cases or for known loss situations where there are few or no noted outstandings.
3. Extra amounts on 1 and 2 for inflation to estimated settlement dates (including fees).
4. Total gross outstanding loss reserves (1) + (2) + (3).
5. Reinsurance recoveries on above.
6. Estimated uncollectable reinsurance recoveries.
7. Anticipated reinsurance recoveries (5-6).
8. Net known outstanding reserve (4-7).
9. I.B.N.R. net or reinsurance.
10. Contingent or fluctuation reserve on I.B.N.R.
11. Future I.B.N.R. movement (9+10).
12. Total of unknown outstandings and I.B.N.R. for that class of our business (8+12).

Table 1 Notes to items numerated above:

(1) Noted gross outstanding losses. These will normally follow the estimates of Reassureds but many large or disputable losses will be reassessed by the Reinsurer himself.

(2) Reserves for special cases. These could be included in the known outstandings and I.B.N.R. but in my view certain loss situations where there is little or no pattern of past settlements, do not lend themselves to normal statistical I.B.N.R. calculations and there may not even be noted advices against specific policies.

If we take three examples:

(a) a major physical catastrophe and its effect upon a retrocessional account.

(b) asbestos in the 1980s.

(c) pollution in the 1990s.

In all these cases a loss situation has developed which must be reserved. The eventual loss which we have to reserve cannot be calculated by reference to our known specific advised losses, neither can it be related to past developments nor to our premium income.

The only basis I can probably use is (1) to use our total exposures and to estimate what percentage of those are likely to be involved.

Alternatively (2) to use an estimated total market loss and to estimate our likely share. Or (3) to estimate our involvement with reference to similar past disasters of the same or similar magnitude.

(3) Where noted reserves are indexed for future inflation this may not be necessary, but if not, it is vital and must include inflation of fees or loss expenses.

(6) This must include not only those Reinsurers who are in trouble, but some factor for those who *may* not pay.

(9) *I.B.N.R.* This really needs a book on its own. I.B.N.R. varies so enormously on any reinsurance account. Let us consider two examples.

Firstly, a personal accident quota share; Shortly after the close of any year the outstanding losses will be known and reinsurance recoveries on them will be known. I.B.N.R. losses should be minimal.

Secondly, a products liability excess account; At the close of any year it is likely that no losses will have been paid and that known outstanding losses will be minimal. In fact, on this type of very long-tail business, it may be many years before any losses are paid and several years before the majority of eventual losses are advised or are capable of assessment. It will be impossible to ascertain whether the business is going to be profitable or not.

Very long-tail business has become as long as life business and in some cases longer than life business. No regulatory authority has yet treated such long-tail non-life business in a similar way to life. In fact, very long-tail non-life business is more dangerous than life business as the eventual liabilities, i.e. claims, do not have a stipulated limit as they do on life business.

We must ensure, at any time, that reserves are enough to pay future liabilities and also to ensure at any time, that reserves are enough to pay future liabilities and also to ensure that no so-called "profits" are available until these liabilities can be ascertained. In order to do this I would suggest the division of reinsurance writings into five classes. Of course, these suggestions are mine and the allocation to a particular class is, again, only a suggestion and does not include all types of reinsurance business.

(See Table on the following page.)

Some Methods of Evaluation of Technical Reserves Including I.B.N.R.

(a) Tabular approach using past statistics

We need to keep statistics on a year of account basis for each class, for the results as they develop for all policies written in that year of account. That is premium as it is earned (after two years it should be fully earned), paid losses and estimated outstanding losses at the end of each development year.

These statistics being kept for five years for Classes I and II, ten years for Class III and fifty years for Classes IV and V. They will form the basis of making I.B.N.R. reserves in the future.

I will use typical figures for Class I and Class V to illustrate. The Class V figures exclude Asbestos and Pollution claims:

CLASS I 1985 — Year of account statistics			
Position at close of development	*Settled loss to date as percentage of premium*	*Estimate of known o/s losses at given date*	*Total known losses*
Year 1 (1985)	50%	35%	85%
Year 2	80%	12%	92%
Year 3	90%	3%	93%
Year 4	92%	1%	94%
Year 5	93%	0%	93%

If statistics for 1986, 1987 and 1988 should show a similar pattern it will reveal that the eventual settlement of the business is known pretty accurately by the end of Year 3 or even Year 2, and that the I.B.N.R. to be added to Year 2 known losses is small in this case 1% of the premium income, or approximately 1½% of paid loss.

CLASS (I) Very Short	CLASS (II) Short	CLASS (III) Medium	CLASS (IV) Long	CLASS (V) Very Long
Pro rata R/I of:		Pro rata Reinsurance of:	Pro rata Reinsurance of:	Excess of Loss R/I and Stop Loss R/I of Class (4)
Personal Accident	Excess Loss and Stop Loss Reinsurance of Class (1)	Motor T.P.		
Crop Hail Livestock		Professonal Indemnity and Third Party on a "claims made" basis	Professional Indemnity on a loss occuring basis	
Voyage and Transits Property		Third Party Excl. U.S.A. where neither products nor pollution coverage is a hazard	Marine Liability	
HCP Aviation Hulls War		Marine Hulls	U.S.A. Third Party and Casualty	
Motor Fire Theft and Collision		Aviation Passenger Liability	(b) Excess of Loss and Stop Loss Reinsurance of Class (iii)	
		W.C.A. and EL (excl. U.S.A.)		
		Builders risks		

N.B. (1) These classifications are not complete.
(2) It may be felt that a greater number of classes are needed.

CLASS V 1985 — Year of account statistics excluding Asbestos and Pollution

Position at close of development	*Settled loss to date as percentage of premium*	*Estimate o/s at close of year*	*Total known loss at close of year*
Year 1 (1985)	0%	10%	10%
Year 2	5%	15%	20%
Year 3	20%	20%	40%
Year 4	40%	30%	70%
Year 5	60%	40%	100%
Year 6	70%	35%	105%
Year 7	90%	30%	120%
Year 8	100%	20%	120%
Year 9	110%	20%	130%
Year 10 (1995)	115%	15%	130%
Year 11	120%	15%	135%
Year 12	125%	15%	140%
Year 13	130%	15%	145%
Year 14	133%	15%	148%
Year 15	135%	15%	150%
Year 16	138%	12%	150%
Year 17	140%	10%	150%
Year 18	143%	10%	153%
Year 19	145%	10%	155%
Year 20 (2005)	147%	8%	155%
Year 30	Estimated L.R.		160%

Once again, as statistics build up for 1986, 1987 and 1988, a pattern of settlement emerges and, assuming that 1985 Year's figures are typical, these show that eventual results become fairly clear between Year 12 and Year 20. However, the I.B.N.R. *reserves* at the end of:

Year 1	should be 150% of the premium	150%
Year 2	" " 140% " " "	140%
Year 3	" " 120% " " "	120%
Year 4	" " 90% " " "	90%
Year 5	" " 60% " " "	60%
Year 6	" " 55% " " "	55%

To move on to a second stage we need to incorporate into these statistics two further columns — the estimated I.B.N.R. made at the close of Year 1, Year 2, etc., and thus the estimated final settlement made at the close of Year 1, Year 2, etc., viz:

(These will clearly show whether past estimates were accurate and will indicate past mistakes which can be rectified in the future.)

(See Table on page 406.)

In the early years these statistics reveal an under-estimation of the final outcome and an under-reserving. This is very usual, particularly as few Underwriters are prepared to admit that the business they are currently writing will produce an underwriting loss. It is not necessarily too serious if the investment earnings offset it. In our example, an interest rate of 15% simple per annum will produce an investment return by the end of Year 7 of some 60% of the premium. The under-estimation at the close of Year 1 of 75% (160% — 85%) is reduced to 15% if this interest earning is offset.

These statistics on long-tail business, once they are collected for a number of years, can be used in various ways for future estimates of I.B.N.R. or the final outcome of an account.

Before we discuss this further we should issue some words of warning. Any predictions for the future, derived from past statistics, will be invalid unless allowance is made for future changes, as for example in:

(a) exchange rates.

(b) future level of inflation.

(c) future level of social inflation.

(d) change in the original premium rates.

(e) changes in underwriting practices.

(f) changes in reinsurance protection.

(g) unknown hiccups, e.g. asbestosis.

However, with these caveats in mind, we could suggest that the final outcome of future years might be predictable. One thing is obvious; for the first five years, at least, no real prediction is possible as the account has not had time to develop. During these years the loss reserving of a long-tail account should at least be such as to retain all premium as a minimum loss reserve, using interest earnings to pay losses. After five years, provided enough statistics were available to be valid, a relationship is made between losses paid, after five years, to the final result — or losses paid and known o/s to the final result, could be established.

CLASS IV 1985 Year of account

Col. 1	Col. 2	Col. 3	Col. 4	Col. 5	
Position at close of development	Settled losses to date as per cent of premium	known o/s at close of Year	Total known losses at close of Year	Total losses estimated Est. made at close of Year for I.B.N.R.	close of Year i.e. estimate of final result
Year 1	0%	10%	10%	75%	85%
Year 2	5%	15%	20%	70%	90%
Year 3	20%	20%	40%	50%	90%
Year 4	40%	30%	70%	30%	100%
Year 5	60%	40%	100%	20%	120%
Year 6	70%	35%	105%	20%	125%
Year 7	90%	30%	120%	10%	130%
Year 8	100%	20%	120%	10%	130%
Year 9	110%	20%	130%	10%	140%
Year 10	115%	15%	130%	10%	140%
Year 11	120%	15%	135%	10%	145%
Year 12	125%	15%	140%	20%	160%
Year 13	130%	15%	145%	15%	160%
Year 14	133%	15%	148%	10%	158%
Year 15	135%	15%	150%	5%	155%
Year 16	138%	12%	150%	5%	155%
Year 17	140%	10%	150%	2%	152%
Year 18	143%	10%	153%	1%	154%
Year 19	145%	10%	155%	nil	155%
Year 20	147%	8%	155%	nil	155%
to 00	160%	0%	160%	nil	160%

In our example the final estimated outcome of 160% is approximately 270% of the settlement after five years; and minimum o/s and I.B.N.R. reserves of the following could be deduced:

After	5 Years	170%	of paid	losses	after	5 years
"	6 "	130%	"	"	"	6 years
"	7 "	80%	"	"	"	7 years
"	8 "	60%	"	"	"	8 years
"	13 "	25%	"	"	"	13 years

Or the relationship could be worked using Col. 4 – the total known losses plus o/s.

I would emphasize that I have used a long-tail account excluding asbestos and pollution as there are special situations and could not in 1985 be predicted from any past statistics. These statistics are conservative and some accounts might have needed a much greater I.B.N.R.

Before leaving this section, one must deal with one further point. In preparing statistics, should one use gross figures, i.e. figures before deduction of reinsurance recoveries or net figures, i.e. after deduction of reinsurance recoveries and anticipated future reinsurances recoveries on known outstandings and I.B.N.R.?

One can argue the case either way. Net figures can be a snare and delusion for the future, if reinsurance recoveries are doubtful due to failure to pay or are subject to dispute and delays. Also, they are a snare if reinsurance arrangements have materially changed. My belief is that gross figures should be used or that gross and net should be used. If net are used by themselves, allowance must be made for any failure to collect, delays in collection and changes in reinsurance and these cannot be assessed without having the gross figures.

(b) The graphical approach using past statistics

Tables are all very well but the progression of settlements is much better seen graphically. If one plots for each year of account the settlements to the close of any development year on the vertical axis against the years of development on the horizontal axis. The pattern will produce an exponential curve. I show on page 408 a typical long-tail settlement curve for 25 years of loss development.

One needs to plot such curves for all the past years of account, yours and any other people's available or any market statistic available. The

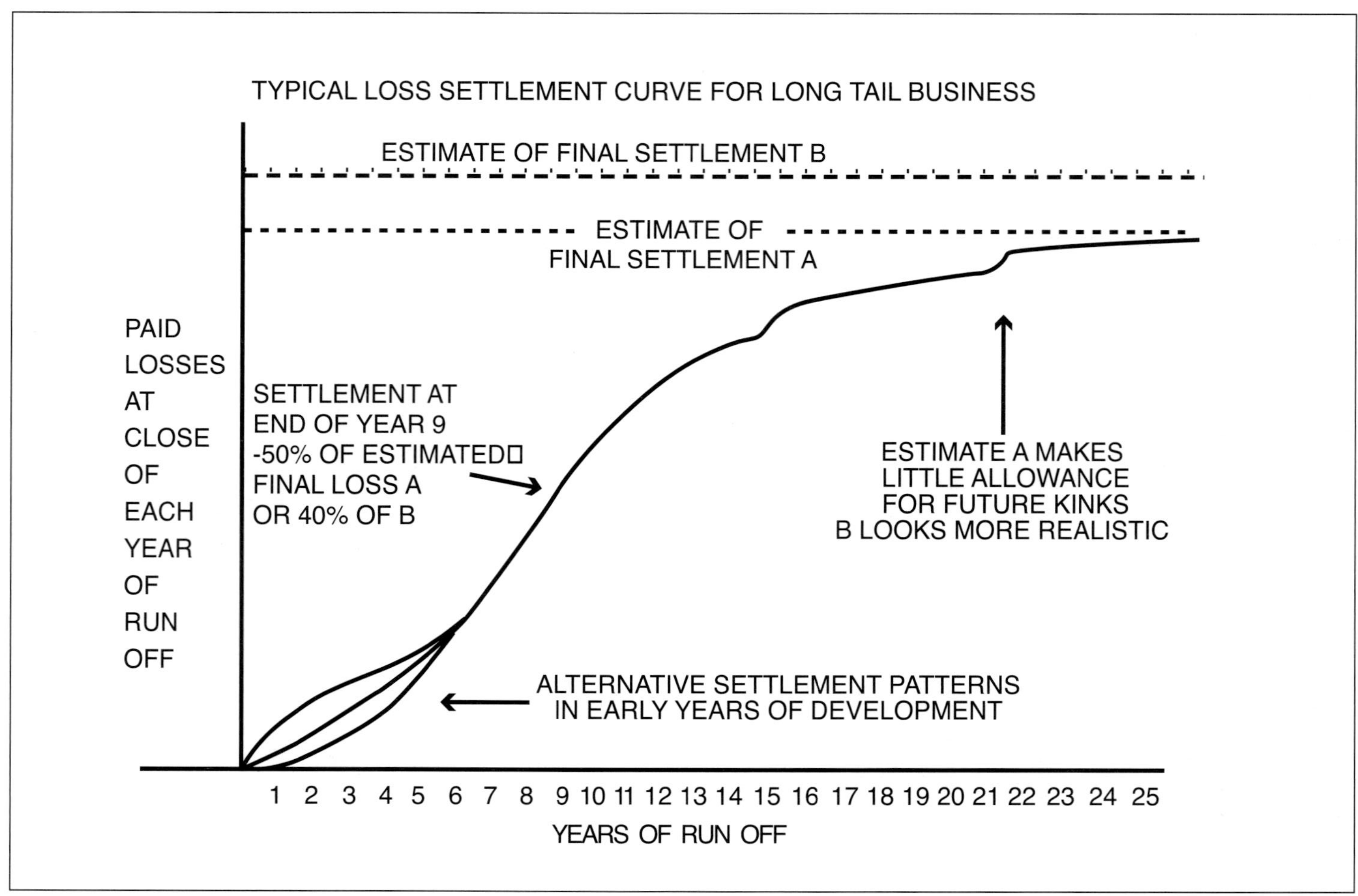
TYPICAL LOSS SETTLEMENT CURVE FOR LONG TAIL BUSINESS
ESTIMATE OF FINAL SETTLEMENT B
ESTIMATE OF FINAL SETTLEMENT A
PAID LOSSES AT CLOSE OF EACH YEAR OF RUN OFF
SETTLEMENT AT END OF YEAR 9 -50% OF ESTIMATED FINAL LOSS A OR 40% OF B
ESTIMATE A MAKES LITTLE ALLOWANCE FOR FUTURE KINKS B LOOKS MORE REALISTIC
ALTERNATIVE SETTLEMENT PATTERNS IN EARLY YEARS OF DEVELOPMENT
1 2 3 4 5 6 7 8 9 10 11 12 13 14 15 16 17 18 19 20 21 22 23 24 25
YEARS OF RUN OFF

more the better and as stated above, gross statistics may be more reliable than net and a single currency such as U.S. dollars will eliminate variations in currencies.

Having plotted lots of curves one can arrive at a typical curve and use it to predicate the results of years which are developing. This will only become valid once the developing year assumes a shape or once the settlement pattern levels off. To test this validity a second series of graphs are needed.

On this graph one plots the loss ratio settlement at the end of a development year against the final loss ratio for that year of account. On this graph are plotted as many years of account as are available. The final loss ratio being plotted on the vertical axis and the loss ratio at the close of the development year on the horizontal axis. The graph on this page shows a graph for six sets of statistics, 1960-1965 years of account at the close of development Year 10.

Now if there is a valid relationship between Year 10 and infinity these points will form a line. Draw the line of "best fit" through them (you need to be a better mathematician than me to discuss the validity of

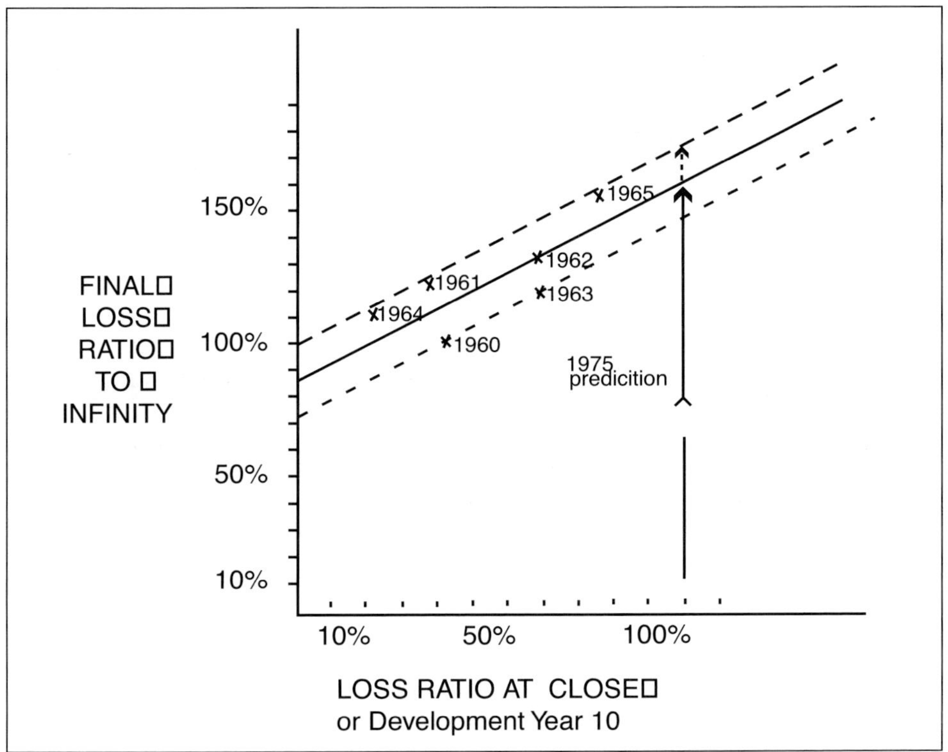

this line of best fit). Now you have a predictor! You hope! If there is no line, just a splodge, then no valid relationship exists. If the line does not proceed nicely upwards but plunges downwards you have a problem. However, I have a nice upward line and I want to predict my 1975 result which has a settlement of 110% at close of Year 10. I simply read off a final loss ratio of 160% *but* this is only a probability. The corridor of dotted lines encloses all plotted past loss ratios and using these the 1975 loss ratio can be predicted as between 153% and 175%.

For those who wish to delve deeper, talk to a good actuary.

(c) The assumed loss ratio approach

The problem of the predictions are that they may not help in the early years of development and, of course, viable statistics over 25 years take time to develop and may not be available. A very simple, and I think effective, method is to assume what you feel is a realistic final loss ratio for any year of account, then deduct your paid losses to the end of that development year from the assumed loss ratio; you then have your outstandings and I.B.N.R. reserve.

For example, at the end of 1985 you as a Lloyd's Syndicate have a book of U.S. Casualty long-tail business, my Class V, you want to evaluate your 1980 year of account. Being an honest man and knowing the competition in 1980 and the general market conditions, you reckon that a loss ratio of 160% is reasonable and, although this sounds high, you may well make an overall profit at this level when investment earnings are taken into account. Your settlement at the end of 1985 on the 1980 account is 25%. Therefore, your reserve is 135%.

(d) The assumed 100% loss ratio approach and interest accrued

A refinement of the above is to assume a loss ratio of 100% and add to it the interest you have earned (or an estimate) and from the total, deduct the paid to date, viz 1980 account at close of 1985 100% plus interest earned during 1980 — 1985, say 50% less 30% equal reserve 120%.

(e) A reserve based on a minimum % of premium income, e.g. Lloyd's minimum audit percentages

Here one uses past settlement tables to calculate a pattern of settlement. From this one deduces a final settlement loss ratio and calculates the percentage of premium income required on each year of account to achieve that settlement. It is similar to the tabular approach above. The problem is that a reserve greater than 100% is difficult to sell in the early years and thus Lloyd's minimum percentages are inadequate as a non-discounted reserve. Secondly, in older years the reserve necessary bears little relation to the original year of accounts premium income.

After 15 years you may still need a reserve equal to 100% of your original premium! As a discounted reserve, this method may have some merit but it should be used with extreme caution.

(f) Known outstanding losses plus I.B.N.R. factor

This test must always be used either in addition to others or by itself. For short-tail classes, my Classes I and II, it will give accurate enough figures on its own. It is vitally important that the known outstanding losses are assessed on a consistent basis and that basis is stipulated, viz:

(a) today's value of the loss plus, loss expenses

or

(b) increased by an inflation of 10% compound to estimated date of settlement subject to a maximum of the policy limit.

For long-tail and very long-tail losses, known outstandings will in the early years be of little help in establishing the I.B.N.R. and thus a proper reserve and other methods will have to be used. The loading necessary for I.B.N.R. will vary with the accuracy of the claims reserving, i.e. the case-by-case reserving. However, late reported losses must never be underestimated even if you consistently acheived a saving on your known outstanding settlements.

Whatever reserve you produce by other methods, your reserve should never be less than your case-by-case total plus an I.B.N.R. loading.

(g) Link ratio method

The link ratio method requires that the claims data is triangulated either quarterly of at least annually. It works well with incurred and paid claims but paid claims are more consistent and we will use them below.

Let us suppose that we have the total paid claims at the end of every calendar year for various underwriting years. We will show just the first three years overleaf:

year	paid claims end yr 1	ratio 2:1	paid claims end yr 2	ratio 3:2	paid claims end yr 3
1985	351	2.29	805	1.51	1216
1986	307	2.41	740	1.62	1199
1987	476	2.53	1205	1.45	1747
1988	549	2.46	1350	1.49	2005
1989	582	2.51	1460	1.51	2206
	average	2.44		1.52	
	last 2 avg	2.49		1.50	

If the paid claims at the end of the second year is divided by the total claims at the end of the first year a ratio is obtained, this is called a link ratio. It is very often similar for the same class of business unless something unusual happens. The link ratios can be worked out for different underwriting years and an average taken. One can also work out the link ratio between the 2nd and 3rd year, in this case the average is 1.52 or 152%. We may have the data for the later years and we could obtain other link ratios. Let us suppose there is very little claims movement after the end of the 6th year, then we could work out the development from the 6th year to infinity or ultimate. Let us look at the table below:

years	link ratios
1 to 2	2.44
2 to 3	1.52
3 to 4	1.24
4 to 5	1.12
5 to 6	1.05
6 to ult	1.25

If you knew what your paid claims were at the end of the 2nd year you could multiply the link ratios together and estimate what the ultimate claims would be. i.e. $(1.52 \times 1.24 \times 1.12 \times 1.05 \times 1.25) = 2.77$ or 277%. The paid claims after 2 years multiplied by 277% should approximate to the ultimate claims.

This method only works if you have the data over many years and would not work on long-tail business if the claims are still developing. It will not work therefore on a new account. The link ratios used could be the averages over all years or the average for more recent years as they probably have more in common with the current account. To be conservative you could use the highest link ratio between each year but beware there can be catastrophic years where losses are paid very early and upset the normal payment pattern.

Where your account is new you can either use methods (c) the assumed loss ratio and (d) the 100 % loss ratio plus interest until the pattern develops. Alternatively you could use external data on a similar account and use the link ratio method.

I.B.N.R. on Special Cases

Before leaving these suggestions on I.B.N.R. calculations, we should make some further comments on special cases such as asbestos, pollution and possibly professional indemnity. As time goes by these special cases will develop past statistics which can be used on a tabular or graphical basis. In 1997 this may be true of asbestos and possibly professional indemnity, but not yet in our view with pollution.

Leaving I.B.N.R. which is a long subject and was Item 9 on our Table 1 way back on page 400, we now move on to Item 10 on the same Table.

Contingent or fluctuation reverves on I.B.N.R. (Item 10)

We will need a contingent or fluctuation reserve on our I.B.N.R. estimates for unforeseen hiccups and in particular for failure of our Reinsurers in the future. This could be quite large!

Item 11 is a total.

Item 12 is the total of all the reverves needed for that class. The next stage is to add together all of these totals for all the classes including reserves for I.B.N.R. on special cases and proceed onto Table 2 below to produce our final reserve.

Table 2

1. Total of loss reserves by class (sum of Item 12 from Class Table 1 Page 400).
2. Estimated future cost of claims administration and settlement to finality.
3. Total non discounted reserve (1) plus (2).
4. Discount for future earnings on (3).
5. Total discounted reserves (3) - (4).
6. Credit for any indemnity provided (a) Time and Distance, (b) Quota share, excess aggregate or other reinsurances, to reduce the reserve.
7. Final reserve.

Table 2 Notes to items numerated on page 413:

(2) This should be a vital part of any loss reserve and will have to be substantial on long-tail business and must be indexed for future inflation of rents, salaries and computers.

(4) In the past, reserves have not been discounted and this went some way to preserving adequate reserves. There is no question that any Lloyd's Syndicate or Reinsurance Company that has become insolvent has always been under reserved even when not discounting.

The use of disguised discounting by Time and Distance has been a major cause of under reserving in the 1980s and 1990s. However, I feel that there is an argument for some limited discounting provided all other reserves are properly calculated and Time and Distance recoveries are properly credited. In my view, discounting should never be more than 4% nor more than 50% of going interest rates and there must be a maximum period of discounting, say, seven years.

Credit for the full indemnity may only be taken where the full indemnity is available from the reserving date. Where there is any structured settlement or delay imposed on collection under such policies, then the indemnity shall be discounted backwards from the stated settlement date or dates at an interest rate of 10% compound per annum, e.g. A policy with an indemnity of $1,000,000 with a condition that no loss can be collected for three years after the date the reserve is calculated, credit is taken for $751,351 only. Credit shall only be given provided the security of Reinsurers is approved by the regulatory authority or is covered by an unlimited and unconditional letter of credit.

We have now arrived at our final reserve Table 2 Item 7. Phew!

Now, having put up a reserve for your policy holders, what do you do with it?

(A) Pay as little tax as possible on it.

(B) Keep it in currency of your liabilities.

(C) Do not speculate with it.

Checking on Other People's Reserves

If you are a regulatory body or a major shareholder or a name at Lloyd's or a director of a company or an underwriting agent, then you can make sure that the operation you control or own is properly reserved by applying the methods used above, or making sure they are applied.

If you wish to evaluate other people's reserves, you may have very little information to go upon. I will now go out on a limb and suggest that rough checks can be made to give some guidance. You need to know:

A breakdown of premium income between my five classes or at least with I and II together. III and IV will be non-U.S. excess third party. V will be U.S. $ excess casualty. And you need to know that premium income for each of the past 10 years with the breakdown. If this is not available, the past two or three years will allow you to make a reasonable estimate of the earlier years.

The following will produce for you an idea of the *discounted* reserve needed for an operation that has been going for 10 years. If less than 10, minus a bit, over 10 years add a *chunk* and you must add for asbestos and pollution by specific investigation.

CLASSES I and II
known outstandings plus 20%

CLASS III
known outstandings plus 50%
or 150% of a year's income

CLASS IV
known outstandings plus 100%
or 300% of a year's income

CLASS V
known outstandings plus 150%
or 700% of a year's income

But one word of warning!

Statistics based on a premium income can be a source of delusion for a reinsurance operation which is reducing its rates or when the whole industry is reducing rates. People and their rating policy are more often a greater guide to solvency than statistics based on past premium incomes.

If your mind has stayed with me during the past pages you should now have some ideas on estimating the amount of money any reinsurance operation needs to meet its liabilities on its past underwriting. It will be technically solvent if that money is available in unencumbered assets.

We can now proceed to the second test which is to see if it has sufficient extra resources (i.e. a solvency margin) to justify writing business in the future.

(E) A suggested evaluation of a Reinsurer's solvency margin

Solvency margins should vary according to fluctuations expected on the business to be written. These fluctuations will be smallest where:

(a) the size of the individual policy is small in relation to the total premium income;

(b) there are little or no accumulation exposures or catastrophic exposures;

(c) the liabilities will be paid quickly and are not therefore subject to unknown future inflation;

(d) past statistics are available to demonstrate that the premium charged is sufficient.

It follows, therefore:

(1) That a large volume of short-tail small-risk portfolio without catastrophic hazard, and where premiums charged are statistically supported by past experience, can be written safely with a small margin of solvency.

(2) On the contrary, a small portfolio of long-tail or large risks, or with accumulation hazards, or a new type of insurance require a very substantial margin of solvency.

Solvency margins are set at a percentage of overall non-life premium income for direct writing companies. However, I would argue that different margins of solvency should be used for different types of business, and certainly this is necessary with a reinsurance operation.

We are discussing solvency margins for *future* writings by Reinsurers and we have to set these as a factor of estimated future premium income. Should this estimated premium be exceeded in practice, very quick action must be taken to restore the required margin.

In calculating this premium income, do we use written or earned income? Clearly the answer is written income because this is the measure of liability taken on. Should these margins be calculated on premiums net or gross of expense? We are requiring a margin of solvency against the future business losing money. This can happen because losses turn out to be greater than anticipated or because expenses are too great. Therefore, to base solvency margins on net income confounds the problem. Future solvency margins should be based on gross incomes before expenses. We therefore use gross written income. Will it be net or gross of outwards reinsurance? A reinsurance portfolio can use reinsurance to eliminate large risk exposures to protect against catastrophe exposure or to reduce the effect of future inflation on long tail business. In other words, an account with potentially large fluctuations can be turned by sound reinsurance into a steadier account requiring smaller solvency requirements. Therefore proper reinsurance, taken out to balance an account, should be welcomed provided, of course, the Reinsurers are reliable.

As regards direct writing companies, the approach in the U.S.A. is to permit licensed reinsurance to be deducted, and licensed Reinsurers are required to meet solvency margins on the reinsurance they write. The E.E.C. approach might be one of using net income with a reinsurance limit of 50%. Lloyd's operate on a gross basis. The E.E.C. method produces two margins of solvency, neither of which must be exceeded; one on the written premium net of reinsurance and one on the gross written premium.

Using gross written incomes solvency margins, or in Lloyd's premium income limits, might be set as follows for a reinsurance account.

Class A Pro rata reinsurance of (low fluctuating) property, personal accident, motor, aviation hulls, transit, cargoes and similar short-tail accounts.

Class B Excess of loss physical damage risk excesses. Pro rata (medium fluctuations) reinsurance of third party, marine hulls, aviation liability, oil rigs.

Class C Excess of loss catastrophe (high fluctuation) and all third party, marine, rigs and aviation excess of loss and all excess aggregate reinsurance.

Class A	25%
Class B	50%
Class C	100%

arbitrator. I do not want my views to be considered as a criticism, but lessons should be learned from the past. Both Reinsurers and Reassureds have to live within the law and must therefore conduct their business with that in mind and must remember that the law changes.

One should touch briefly on the USA.

The experience on asbestos shows above all that Courts in many States are influenced by public opinion and that where possible awards will be made or interpretations given that favour members of the public. That lawyers representing claimants will select those jurisdictions that favour the claimant. That once an award is made, however outrageous, it is not easy to reverse it. That the law is adversary in the extreme and immensely costly.

The only way that this will change is if public opinion changes or is changed. The only time I can recall this happening was in a few areas in the USA the local doctors were literally forced out of business and the public reacted by condemning those who sued them. This, in my view, is unlikely to happen to any wide extent, as most defendants are corporations and Insurers who have little public sympathy and virtually none if they are not American.

Much has been made of the fee system in use in the USA. My own view is that although it certainly adds to the problem it is not in itself the cause of the problem.

The worrying aspect is that contracts of insurance made many years ago in good faith have been completely rewritten to benefit claimants and this will undoubtedly continue, particularly with local juries and judges and the use of punitive damages.

So what advice can one suggest? Make your contracts as short as possible and as clear as possible and never write a USA Reinsurance contract without a clearly stated absolute aggregate limit of liability, including costs.

I am not qualified to comment elsewhere in the world and will confine the rest of this chapter to the English decisions. English Law and its effects have importance far beyond England. London has been and is still a major, if not the major, centre of international reinsurance. Thus English Court decisions should reflect the international nature of much reinsurance and past decisions relating to domestic insurances may have little relation to or bearing on large and complicated international reinsurance contracts.

I said earlier that many English Court decisions made in the past twenty years make little sense commercially. I am not alone in this view. Since originally writing these words, in 1996, I have read a small booklet entitled *"Modest Proposals for Bringing English Law up to Date"* dated October 1996 and written by Kenneth Louw and Hugh Thompson. I am delighted that they agree with me on many of the problems discussed in this chapter.

I quote from their Introduction:

> "We feel that the reinsurance industry is not being served by the legal process as well as it should expect. The industry, as with all forms of commercial activity, needs a set of rules upon which it can rely so that the understanding of contracting parties at the time an agreement is entered into is not undermined at some future date by the changing attitudes of the judiciary. Case law is not always a "good thing" since it develops *ad hoc* according to immediate needs and does not always take the overall picture into account. It is expensive, long-delayed and inclined at times to produce unwise precedents, which may be simply due to the relevant judge's inexperience of reinsurance practice and lack of understanding of technical principles.
>
> Arbitration also has some of these defects, in addition to which the confidential nature of the process precludes the market from having the opportunity to make use of precepts suggested by reasoned awards.
>
> Judgements and awards under English Law should also be considered in the light of the expectations of the international reinsurance markets."

It is worth spending a little time in considering what went wrong and why? I list here some of these problems.

1. Many of the cases which went before the Courts in the 1970's and early 1980's were between what the market would call "the bucket shop market" consisting often of those who themselves had little knowledge or experience in reinsurance and who sometimes appeared not to operate on the basis of good faith.

   Disputes between respectable Reinsurers and Reassureds rarely reached the Courts and often never reached adversarial arbitration.

Lawyers and judges therefore only saw "the bottom end of the market" and not unnaturally assumed that the reinsurance market was not only incompetent but was pretty dishonest as well.

2. Judges have reversed sensible commercial arbitration awards on the reasoning that they were "wrong in law". Thus now as a result arbitration must be done by lawyers or at least with a highly paid QC or ex-Judge as chairman so that they comply with the letter of the law.

   The result is that the legal profession has effectively developed a new area of business and commercial arbitrations have merely become another step in the legal process.

   The old arbitration clauses contained in so many reinsurances were designed and intended as a cheap and efficient alternative. That concept has been killed off by the law and really such clauses are now obsolete.

3. The adversarial nature of the English legal system can lead, if either or both of the parties is so inclined, to a reaction against conciliation and good sense. I am shocked when reading exchanges of correspondence between solicitors. They sometimes reflect a state of war and intransigence which has no relation to the merits or demerits of the dispute concerned and prevents a sensible compromise

   Some barristers are no better as they adopt an adversarial attitude even at arbitrations.

4. The inability or inclination of our commercial courts to apportion blame between two parties is another problem. So many reinsurance disputes arise because both sides have been stupid or negligent. In a traffic accident our courts seem able to say that although a driver was wronged, he was 30% to blame. Why cannot reinsurance cases be judged in the same manner? At the moment, however apportionment is not possible in a purely contractual dispute.

5. The ignorance of the law. The difficulties of the law in entering a new field of international reinsurance disputes with little or no previous knowledge or precedents are understandable. Just as those in our market need knowledge of the law, so the lawyers should have some education in our market. If QC's and Judges have no time for reinsurance education, then they need expert help on technical and market matters during court procedures. An

independent technical expert and an independent market practitioner should be available to a judge to guide and help him.

The two barristers are usually unable themselves to advise. How often have I and others stood by helpless when barristers pretend to a judge that they know an answer to a technical problem, when they do not? The use of expert witnesses is no substitute. The honest expert who will not support the case will obviously not be used by a solicitor. Therefore, unless the client can be persuaded that his case is hopeless and that he should settle (because no expert of quality will support his position), the quality of experts descends to those who can be persuaded to alter their views to suit a case or to those who had no real experience in the first place.

Experts should not be paid by the clients, the lure of fees is too great. Rather an expert or experts should be truly independent and paid for by the court and fail to give judges real disinterested expert advice and help. The new Civil Procedures Rules provide that an expert witness's overriding duty is to the Court rather than to the party who appointed him (unless the expert is instructed only to advise and not to testify in Court), but the parties remain liable for the expert's fees. Is this giving the market the worst of both worlds?

6. The difference between a genuine dispute and the "try on". In my view the Courts have found difficulty in distinguishing a real dispute from the dispute which arises because one party is seeking to avoid cover, often after many years, on specious arguments or is seeking to obtain cover for which he never paid a proper premium.

Unfortunately some "try ons" have succeeded and encouraged others. Even where the "try on" has not succeeded, the penalty against the loser has not been enough to deter others. I wish in a way that in such cases arbitrators and judges could award punitive damages or at least 200% of the costs of the aggrieved party, although I would not wish to be understood as encouraging outrageous punitive awards of the type or amount sometimes made by US juries!

I am sure that much time and money would have been saved if the judge had access to, say a small panel of independent market experts and arbitrators had greater power of penalising the "tryers on."

7. The fallibility of case law in a changing market. English law builds up by case law. Past judgements are used to decide new cases. This

makes sense if the cases are similar. It fails when they are not. Modern reinsurance has developed so far and so fast that it bears little resemblance to traditional reinsurance and yet past case law is still used when it has little or no relevance.

8. The different functions of reinsurance.

At the start of the book's first edition published in 1981which was mainly written in the late 1970's, the two fundamental functions of reinsurance were set out on page 1.

(a) The "passing on" of liability on an insurance
and
(b) The protection of an insurance account.

The passing on function is done mainly by contributing or pro rata reinsurance where the Reinsurer is linked and tied in to the original insurance.

The protection of an account is done mainly by non-proportional reinsurance and is not linked or tied to the original insurance. It is a contingency insurance and when that contingency happens i.e. an earthquake it is the effect that contingency has on the business reinsured that is being protected. This type of reinsurance should have no connection with the original policies or even with their terms or liability under them. It stands alone as an individual insurance.

The Courts have seemed unable at times to distinguish between the two functions and types of reinsurance. The remarks of Hobhouse in the Court of Appeal in the case of *Toomey v Eagle Star* are very enlightening. The contract between Toomey, a Lloyd's Syndicate, and the Eagle Star was a typical excess aggregate policy covering the movements on a run-off account. "The contract in this case although described as a reinsurance is not in my judgement correctly described. It is a contract which relates not to individual risks but to the totality of the relevant accounts."

Of course Hobhouse in a way was quite right if you ignore the developments of non-proportional reinsurance over the past eighty years and think of reinsurance as being limited to the function of passing on liability.

Let us then turn to some of the problems.

(1) Disclosure

The Oceanus decision given in 1982 required disclosure of all information on the basis of what would influence a "prudent Underwriter". Since then subsequent cases have modified this. In particular, *Pan Atlantic v. Pine Top (House of Lords, 1994)* requires the Reinsurer wishing to avoid to show that the Underwriter who actually wrote the risk relied on the non-disclosure in question. But has real clarity been obtained? The force of Pan Atlantic v. Pine Top has been rather watered down in subsequent cases, where, once objective materiality is shown, the court fairly readily infers that the actual Underwriter would have been influenced, even if he does not give evidence to this effect.

What we need is a realisation that although complete, once and for all a disclosure may be possible on a simple reinsurance. However, when applied to a complicated reinsurance programme it makes little sense and bears little relation to the way the market works. A Reassured or his Broker approaches a Reinsurer or several Reinsurers with a request for a quotation on his programme and provides basic information. The quoting Underwriters then ask for clarification and for further information and the client anticipates this

Questions and answers continue until the potential Reinsurer feels that he has all the information he needs to quote. If more than one Reinsurer is quoting then two different sets of materials may be produced.

The point is that this is and always has been a two way process. Of course, non-disclosure of matters that the Reassured knows or should know to be relevant is negligent but the decision of the potential Reinsurer to quote or to accept the business without having the information he needs to make, a proper decision is also equally negligent. To my mind there must be the concept of contributory negligence applied to future cases.

Secondly, surely the punishment should fit the crime. The only remedy to non-disclosure appears to be repudiation of the contract. Surely where the contract would have been accepted in any case with perhaps an alteration in premium or an exclusion (if the non-disclosed facts were known at the time) then a repudiation of the contract is far too draconian. The penalty should relate to the damage suffered from the non-disclosure.

(2) **Underwriting standards**

The judgement in the Merrett case in 1995 instead of using "prudent" (as in the *CTI v. Oceanus* thirteen years earlier) now speaks of Underwriters who are "competent." One standard required is "that reasonably expected of a competent Underwriter specialising in the type of business underwritten". An Underwriter should be aware of risk "to the extent that other ordinarily competent members of his profession would be alert". However the law does not impose liability or damage resulting from an error of judgement which a reasonably well-informed and competent Underwriter could have made. (My emphasis).

I just wonder where this judgement will lead and the effect it will have on innovation and flair in our markets. Cuthbert Heath, Roy Merrett, Robert Kiln, Matthew Drysdale, and so many others, who pioneered areas of business, were judged in their time to be reckless by their peers and there were often no others in their field of business. How long will it be before Reinsurers have yet another reason to repudiate contracts on "the grounds of reckless or say incompetent underwriting."

Future Reassureds are warned not to reinsure difficult or innovative types of business or if they do, get an actuarial certificate first! I hope I am wrong, but I fear that this Merrett decision sows the seeds for many more disputes in the future.

(3) **Warranties and Conditions.**

There needs to be a meeting of minds between reinsurance and the law both as to what these two terms mean and the penalties exacted if a warranty or condition is breached. I say no more!

(4) Insolvency and the ultimate loss clause (see also Chapter VIII under ultimate net loss clause)

The standard ultimate net loss clause contains these words "the term 'ultimate net loss' shall mean the sum actually paid by the Company" (My emphasis). These words on their own are crystal clear; the Company must have actually paid before he can collect. Yet for sixty years at least, Reinsurers have always paid their losses to a Reassured who cannot pay his Insureds due to insolvency. Why?

(a) Because a premium was paid for the cover.

(b) Not to pay could be a means of making a Reassured insolvent and thus avoiding liability.

(c) Insolvency laws (in the public interest) prevent payment being used to refund specific losses, as opposed to increasing the fund available to meet (at least pro rata) the claims of all creditors.

(d) The reinsurance contract is distinct from the original insurance.

It would be a breach of good faith for such a payment to be refused. This honest and established market practice was challenged by Reinsurers wishing to escape their liabilities. It was the subject of arbitration, then three levels of courts finalising in the House of Lords who upheld the market practice (*Charter Re v. Fagan*, 1996). But what was so disturbing about this whole procedure was that from the first arbitration, Market practice and good faith had to be ignored and the whole arguments turned on the literal meaning of those words in the context of the rest of the contract wording.

To put a seal on the effect of the *Charter Re* case, the London market has devised an insolvency clause, LIRMA G86, which provides that a Reinsurer's indemnity obligation is triggered by ascertainment of the Reinsured's liability and not the discharge of that liability. Further, the fact that the Reassured will eventually pay only a dividend on inwards claims does not mean that the Reinsurer's liability is reduced in proportion. LIRMA G86 is shown in Chapter VIII in full under net retained lines clause.

The matter is settled in England, what about the rest of the World?

My view remains that regulatory advisers everywhere should follow the USA lead and insist on an insolvency clause.

(5) **Claims and Losses**

So far the difference between a "claim" and a "loss" does not seem to have been made by the Courts. There is need for the market to be distinct in its wordings. On a facultative pro rata reinsurance the Reinsurer follows the settlements of losses, i.e. where liability exists. I suggest that on most large treaties Reinsurers should follow the settlement of claims (whether liability is admitted or not); provided only that the Reassured has not acted negligently or for extraneous business reasons in settling a claim where liability clearly does not exist.

On excess of loss and other non proportional reinsurances, a Reassured desiring protection for his settlement of a claim, not just a loss, should make sure that his ultimate loss clause refers to claim rather than loss and any loss settlement clause becomes a claims settlement clause.

(6) **Claims expenses.**

Here we have yet another example of legal arbitrators and judges looking at a literal meaning of words and ignoring market practice. Since reinsurance was first practised, good faith required that a Reassured acted as if he was unreinsured. In other words, he acted in good faith in the interest of his Reinsurer as well as his own interest. If he was faced with a claim he would take such action as was necessary to either prevent that claim becoming a loss or if it became a loss, to reduce that loss. Naturally in so doing, the Reassured would incur expenses or pay out sums to alleviate the loss. Such payments could take many forms and often did.

I recall a case I once had in Paris in the 1950's. I underwrote in London a Parisian motor cover. The cover holder, Michel, was a past master at settling claims. Robert would visit Paris twice a year and one of his jobs was to check on outstanding claims. I noticed one for De la Rue which had settled for quite a considerable expense.

Michel explains "Oui Madame De la Rue she was injured so I go to see her with some flowers and some Chanel and then another visit with some Armagnac. Then I take her away for a week in my car to a Swiss Spa. We had a very happy week together and she is now well and recovered. No loss to you. The loss expense was high but we had the best suite and take the waters for a week. It is expensive but much less than the claim". A legitimate "loss expense".

Later I mentioned this in passing to my quota share Reinsurer, also a distinguished Frenchman as an example of how claims should be settled. He was delighted to pay his share.

Whatever form they took, provided they were made in good faith and to protect the Reassured, he in good faith paid them as "loss expenses" i.e. it was not necessary to call them "claims expenses" as they were expenses or payments made to eliminate or reduce potential losses.

Along comes Asbestosis (Appendix) and the Wellington Agreement. An agreement made in good faith to mitigate the effect of asbestos losses on the Reassured *and his Reinsurers*. Part of the Wellington payments were for fees, the cost of administration of the facility and part of the whole package was to pool losses between Insurers. Insurers paid part of the losses of others and others paid part of theirs. The agreement was a package and the payments under that package were paid out to reduce the cost of asbestos losses.

The Market, in good sense and good faith, entered into the agreement and regarded all Wellington payments as proper loss expenses, except for some Reinsurers who ratted. Not so, said the law, your wording does not allow you to pay losses for which you have no liability, you must redo your claims to eliminate other people's losses. In itself a virtually impossible task!

Surely we need either to establish that loss expenses means all payments of whatever nature made (in good faith) to avoid losses or to mitigate their effect?. In view of recent court decisions, notably *Baker v. Black Sea and Baltic*, it is obvious that this will not be achieved. There is therefore an urgent need for wordings to make clear that " all expenses in handling losses or claims whether valid or not" are covered.

(7) **One event. One loss occurrence. One common cause.**

When a Reassured wishes to protect his insurance account or his reinsurance account, he has basically three options:

(a) to take out a quota share reinsurance on his business. To do this he pays a pro rata share of his premiums and receives a pro rata share of all claims and expenses.

(b) to take out an aggregate reinsurance to protect his business from a series of losses, This costs much less premium.

(c) to take out an excess of loss contract to pay him if he suffers either a large individual loss or a series of losses arising out of some contingency. The contingency being a catastrophe, an accident, an event or whatever. For this the premium he pays is much less than the quota share and much less than the aggregate premium (for a comparable limit and deductible). The Reassured has a choice and he gets what he pays for.

The definitions of the contingency is contained in the reinsurance contract and even if "an event" for example is defined in the original contract of insurance, it clearly could have an entirely different meaning in the context of the reinsurance contract.

In Chapter VIII we have set out an example of the contingency defined as "a loss occurrence" and defined in the "Hours clause". So far I believe that there has not been a major dispute over this clause. When it comes I hope my explanations in Chapter VIII may help in its resolution.

The Courts have, however, been involved with the "one event" definition or the variants used in third party contracts (see Chapter XI). I feel that if a Reassured eschews the quota share and the aggregate reinsurance methods and chooses an excess of loss at a cheaper premium, then he should not seek to turn that protection into an aggregate cover by extending the meaning of "event" beyond common-sense meanings or manufacturing an "event" to obtain aggregate protection at a cheap price. An "event" surely must mean something unusual that happens in a limited time and space.

The recent Appeal Court decision in *Caudle v Sharp (1995)* is to be welcomed in this context. Here the Court decided that the Underwriter's state of mind was not an event. Quite right in my view, but this case is disquieting in that an arbitration panel and a lower Court took an opposite view and it still leaves open the question of what was "one event". Some have suggested that the writing of a slip could be "an event" as was indicated in this case. This further debases the worth of using the word "event" in these wordings (see the Liability Chapter XI under occurrence definition). Market commonsense would probably say that there was no event, as it happens hundreds of times in a working day, but as a matter of law it probably is an event.

The Reassured in this case purchased an "event" cover on a class of business (professional indemnity), where such a cover was quite inappropriate. He needed to pay more premium and take out a quota share or aggregate protection. If he was concerned with this exposure on individual risks, he could have also purchased a simple excess of loss contract to pay on an each and every loss basis. We should not expect Courts to have to search for "an event" just because there is a contract with that definition in it and the Reassured has bought the wrong protection.

These remarks too have a wider relevance in considering other third party classes, for example, pollution, products liability, industrial disease as well as physical damage perils such as hail, freeze and forest fires.

To conclude this chapter, what of the future?

(a) The Arbitration Act 1996 (in force from 1 January 1997) may resuscitate arbitrations as an alternative to the Courts. One sincerely hopes so, but it will only so happen if the Legal profession helps and assists non-legal arbitrators rather than shooting them down. Solicitors and barristers should be kept out of arbitrations or help the arbitrators.

(b) Alternative Dispute Resolution (ADR)

In June 1996 the Commercial Court issued a statement on ADR which accepts ADR as an alternative to the courts as a means of resolving disputes. The new Civil Procedure Rules take this process a stage further; In effect, the Court will only hear the parties' dispute only if ADR is not appropriate or if ADR has been tried and has failed. Nevertheless, the effectiveness of ADR will depend greatly on the attitude of judges, barristers and solicitors to it. This will in turn depend on the quality of its practitioners. To date, ADR appears not to have been as successful in the area of reinsurance disputes as in other areas, perhaps because of a fundamental lack of knowledge among some mediators about the way that the market works.

That is not to say that mediators should be reinsurance experts but a mediator who cannot understand the expectations or grievances of a Reassured or Reinsurer is less likely to gain respect of the parties and bring them together.

The problem as I see it is basically simple. Where two parties are genuinely concerned to resolve a dispute amicably, then they will do so by ADR or by use of a mediator or market arbitration and only use the Courts to resolve any important legal principles. If, on the other hand, one of the parties is determined to avoid his obligations or determined to fight to obtain dubious coverage, then any form of ADR or mediation or arbitration is doomed to failure. I take heart from recent statements.

(A) The Commercial Court on ADR; and the acceptance of the new Arbitration Act for example.

(B) Lord Ackner's speech of 5th November 1996 in the House of Lords on the Second Reading of the Civil Procedures Bill.

"…. Because of the adversarial culture, it takes quite unnecessary length of time for the idea of settlement to become the focus of the advisers to the parties and the parties themselves."

If the culture changed so that the advisers basically said to the litigants on each side, "Look, usually the best solution to disputes is to achieve a sensible settlement. The best way of achieving a sensible settlement is for me to write a sensible letter to the other side, not full of aggressiveness but full of reason, and to encourage the other side to so respond. So don't be disappointed if you see a letter of sweet reason. It does not mean that I am not ready to fight with enthusiasm if we come to Court. But until that event occurs, let me make the best possible attempts to settle your case."

(C) A judge's comments on discussing an application to remove an arbitrator.

"It would be better If Solicitors and Counsel who are taking part in an arbitration before a single arbitrator (who has no legal qualifications) if they sought to give him assistance in every stage in formulating questions which he might need to put to a legal advisor, rather than making adverse comments about the way he initially thought of deciding to deal with the matter. He is entitled to look to the parties for more assistance than in my judgement, he was getting in this case. I have nothing but sympathy for the predicament in which he found himself."

In addition some recent court decisions are encouraging.

(a) The House of Lords ruling in *Charter Re v Fagan* commented on above.

(b) Commercial Court In *American Centennial v. Insco rejecting* that acts of directors of a savings and loan association in carrying out its business constituted " a series of events … Originating from one cause."

(c) The House of Lords in *AXA Re v Field* held that, in the context of a treaty excess of loss reinsurance of a liability account, it is wrong to assume that where the underlying insurance contract and the reinsurance contract both contain provisions which allow losses to be aggregated, the parties are likely to have intended the effect of those provisions to be much the same. An excess of loss treaty

> covering a direct Insurer's whole account is not in any real sense back-to-back with the underlying insurance policies (although the position might be different with proportional or facultative reinsurance).

I will end this chapter by quoting from Louw and Thompson's booklet.

The Insurance Act 2006?

"Few would argue with the opinion that the Marine Insurance Act 1906 has been an outstanding success and an object of admiration. Not only is it the only codification of insurance in this country but it is written so clearly it has probably scotched the need for countless cases of litigation (despite causing some litigation arising from inappropriate provisions of the 19th Century origin). It is unsurprising that the Courts have tended to extend its provisions to other classes of business, and to reinsurance."

"We suggest that MIA needs to be overhauled, whether by amendment or by entire replacement with a new Act. If the latter course were adopted, advantage could be taken perhaps to incorporate provisions of application to other classes and types of insurance (except life and personal lines business which might need separate consideration), and of course including reinsurance. The objects should be:

(a) to codify the present state of the law, whilst rejecting any anomalies which have arisen from the *ad hoc* nature of case law;

(b) to update the provisions of the MIA and amend such provisions as do not now appear to conform with market practice;

(c) To develop the law with an eye to the international nature of the business and the development of new products (e.g. financial reinsurance) and trading procedures."

"Whether or not additional legislation is the ultimate or best solution to the drawbacks of the present state of the law affecting reinsurance, there is also a responsibility which should be accepted by the reinsurance community to try to place its own house in order — the lawyers cannot be blamed for everything!"

"We wonder why so little has been done by the market in raising standards of procedure by encouraging uniform practice, standardising wordings (and having all clauses examined by lawyers), or even introducing codes of conduct to be followed by the members of market associations".

"It would be a great advance, for instance, if the complete wording of a contract were established and made known to prospective Reinsurers at the time a contract was first offered in the market, rather than, as has been the case, where the wording has been often drafted years after slip placement, or is never issued."

"We quote a source from the legal fraternity: "You are not going to be able to legislate for incomprehensible wording, bad draughtsmanship, lack of understanding of agency obligations of Brokers, and Underwriters who speak a difference language from the Brokers." Are we wrong in suggesting that the market associations have been and possibly still are, too tentative in tackling the ills that have beset the market?"

"Would that we could return to the good old days when disputes were settled over a cup of tea and a favour granted, would be reciprocated in the future!"

"That is not to be since margins are too tight, the reinsurance stage is too large, and personal contact has become too remote. A casualty arising from these developments has been a breakdown of the level of trust within the market. Although this country has been proud to conduct insurance with the minimum of regulation, it is now time to rely upon more formally defined legal codes such as some of those now developing in other jurisdictions. There is no need to stress the recent history of the London insurance and reinsurance market to justify this assertion."

"We recommend that the legal profession and the insurance institutions should in concert consider means by which this laudable aim could be achieved and, if needs be, press the Government into drafting and passing new legislation before the MIA reaches its centenary."

CHAPTER XVII

PHILOSOPHY ... PROGRAMMES ... PEOPLE

How does one conclude? Perhaps we might finish with a few general thoughts.

Robert is reminded of an old friend from Philadelphia — a tough, dry-humoured, forceful and resourceful Broker whom I have admired for many years. He once said to me, "Robert, I always think that a Reassured is like a tree. A new insurance company must be properly planted with the right capital in fertile soil. To survive it will need the firm stake of a good catastrophe contract to withstand the storms. It will need cultivation and the 'manure' of a pro rata treaty to enable it to grow. It will need a guard of an aggregate to stop the deer nibbling it away. It will need the propping up of a limb if it gets too top heavy by facultative treatment. It needs to be left before the fruit of dividends is picked so that it husbands its reserves and retains its vigour for future sound growth. As it grows it can discard the netting of an aggregate, the treaty cultivation becomes unnecessary and even the stake is outgrown."

Luckily even large mature trees can still be blown over and need protection of some sort. The Reassured, then, uses reinsurance to help him grow and prosper and, of course, in the long run, he pays for his protection. Like any other protection, the more he pays the better the protection. The cheapest price may not be the best. A large volume treaty may cost more than a risk excess but it will provide more protection.

A well-established Reinsurer may be more expensive than a cut-price one but the former provides the best protection. The programme you buy should suit you and your pattern of development at that particular time. Reinsurance provides not only protection to grow and prosper but security and peace of mind to the people who conduct the business.

Insurance Underwriters must never be forced by management into discarding protection which they consider necessary for their peace of mind, otherwise they will not have the confidence to expand their business.

Reinsurance also provides an efficient way of giving the public the capacity it needs at a minimum cost. If all direct writers had to accept only net lines, think of the extra time and trouble that would cause the public and Insurers alike. Therefore, it is an essential service in any free society.

Some Thoughts on Reinsurance Programmes

On property business there is no real alternative for the smaller and medium-sized company to the surplus treaty supplemented by facultative reinsurance. However, a surplus in the form of a graded quota share is a viable alternative to consider. It reduces the paperwork. Once established, a small limit excess risk contract to increase the retention before cessions are made to the suplus treaty, is worth considering. It will save costs and increase the net retained income. However, a pure excess approach on property business is best left, until the account is large and balanced, with very experienced Underwriters.

We have discussed net retentions; we think the tendency of most companies is to be too cautious in determining net retentions and to be too complicated. The first thing is to decide what is a proper normal-sized loss exposure in relation to three things:

(1) The Reassured's estimated net premium income.

(2) The Reassured's estimated gross profit.

(3) The Reassured's net assets or surplus.

A net retention of between 1% and 3% of a Reassured's premium income is a fair minimum; on a gross profit, including investment profit, a loss of between 7½% and 15%; on assets and surplus a figure of between 3% and 6%.

Citing an example using the lower figures:

A company with assets and surplus, including capital of, say, 6,000,000, writing a net income of 15,000,000 with estimated gross profit of, say, 500,000 from investment and 750,000 from underwriting, might keep a minimum normal net retention of:

1% of premium income	=	150,000
7.5% of profit	=	90,000
3% of assets	=	180,000

The company should be able to lose 150,000 or 200,000 as a normal loss on ordinary total losses on single exposures. The catastrophic loss — the one which happens once in several years — needs different thought and we have discussed this in an earlier chapter. A retention equal to 5% or even 10% of assets would produce a loss of the order of 750,000.

Applying these thoughts to our company, then, if the business is property, we are envisaging a maximum net retention of, say, 150,000 on a single exposure and a net loss retention of 750,000 on one catastrophe.

With a surplus treaty the tendency will be to set a scale of net retentions graded down from 150,000 on an office to, say, 1,000 on a haystack. Is there really any sense in this? If the office is rated at .10% per annum and haystacks at 10% per annum, and these rates *correctly estimate the exposure losses*, why not keep the same retention on both classes? Say one keeps a net retention of 150,000 on ten thousand offices at .10% to produce a premium of 1,500,000 and 150,000 on a thousand haystacks at 10% to produce a premium of 1,500,000, and assume that the rates are fixed at 200% of anticipated cost of losses, then the results on the two accounts will look as follows (assuming all losses are total losses):

Offices:	10,000 risks with 5 total losses
Haystacks:	100 risks with 5 total losses

If the gross underwriting is correct, and the original rating is correct, then a fixed net retention to loss should be logical. Of course, if all the offices are 50% subject to loss, i.e. only a 50% loss to value is possible, then the net retention can be doubled for the offices.

In practice, of course, one can never be sure that the original rates are correct and the natural tendency is to grade retentions according to the exposure to loss of each risk which the original rates reflect. It is my view that this is often overdone and Ceding Companies produce net line sheets with over large variations and great complications.

Where the account is a motor one the protection will be excess of, say, 150,000 per loss regardless of whether the loss is produced by a pop star with a souped-up Mercedes with a rate of 10% or a sober person — like me — with a rate of .50%. Why do not the property Underwriters use a similar attitude? Of course, large property Underwriters, whose reinsurance is on an excess of loss basis, often do so and keep a single deductible on all types of risk losses.

The psychology is also vital in fixing net retentions. If an Underwriter is nervous and unhappy with the same retention on all types then he must have a reinsurance protection with varied net retentions to suit his character.

In order to achieve balance between net retained premium income and net retention, the limited use of a risk excess can help. Assume an insurance company keeps net retentions varying from:

100,000	Class 1
5,000	Class 8

with a 10-line 1st surplus. The gross premium income is 5,000,000, of which 3,000,000 is ceded to the 1st surplus, leaving 2,000,000 income retained. This means that the top net retention of 100,000 is 5% of the net income and this is a higher figure than many might regard as prudent. Say, by multiplying all retentions by 250% to:

250,000	Class 1
15,000	Class 8

the net income can be increased to 3,050,000, then a risk excess is bought for 150,000 × 100,000 each and every loss each and every risk, at a reinsurance premium of 50,000 — the net income is 3,000,000 against a net retention of 100,000. The net retention now represents 3⅓% of net income, not 5%, and achieves a reasonable balance.

With large established companies, operating with a broad territorial spread, the tendency is to have one treaty for a small number of lines to take care of the really large risk exposures but to keep very sizeable net retentions, these large net retentions being protected by an excess of loss contract.

Reinsurance Operations

Turning to Reinsurers themselves, what makes a successful reinsurance operation? It must be the integrity of those involved. In spite of the problems of the late '70s and 1980s, we are fortunate in that the quality of people in reinsurance remains high. This has to be so because our Reassureds are themselves professionals and a fool or knave is not tolerated for long.

A Reinsurer must underwrite each piece of business to make a profit in the long term. An underwriting profit *per se* must be the prime criteria. Reliance upon investment gain to offset underwriting losses continually will be suicidal. Spread is essential — spread by classes, geographically and by reinsurance to achieve spread by time, but never take on unprofitable business to achieve spread. Expenses must be watched; here a Broker often may be much cheaper than a direct reinsurance account. Again, never increase volume on unprofitable business to reduce expense ratios except for a very short period.

Reserving has become of major importance and, with the growth of long-tail and longer and longer tails, this aspect of a Reinsurer's life needs constant reviewing.

Lastly, investment — no Reinsurer can survive today without a first-class investment team.

We are often asked by the young, "What qualities do you need to be a reinsurance Underwriter?" Our answer varies before and after a bad loss, but we usually answer on these lines …

"You need five qualities:

Firstly. A quick mathematical mind; the ability to do mental arithmetic fast — a cross between a barrow boy and an actuary!

Secondly. Ability to foresee future trends and calculate probabilities — a cross between a bookie and a gyspy!

Thirdly. The ability to regard it all as a game and the personality to enjoy taking decisions and move on to the next without worrying — a good bridge or poker player.

Fourthly. A good factual memory, patience and the ability to assess people's integrity — a psychological computer.

Fifthly. Integrity.

If you have those qualities go ahead. It is a fascinating profession and well rewarded but never forget the difference between success and failure in underwriting is only 10%, so if you want a quiet secure life join the Civil Service or a life company or a large direct Insurer".

Our best wishes to all those starting on the reinsurance road.

We hope this book may improve the visibility for you so that you need not cut corners and can avoid some of the potholes.

APPENDIX

ASBESTOS AND POLLUTION

The problems presented to Reinsurers particularly on USA Casualty business have been with us for the last 50 years and are referred to in a number of places in this book. However, the huge escalation of asbestos-related claims during the 1980s have created a new dimension of problems both for direct Insurers and their Reinsurers, primarily on the liability (casualty) side but also on property business. There is no doubt that asbestos-related claims represented the major challenge of the 1980s and 1990s and will continue well into the next century .Who knows what other products and or industrial diseases may not follow in the wake of asbestos.

Fourth Edition

This section in the third edition was included as a chapter in its own right with pollution. However we have decided, as it was largely a historic problem that arose out of writing largely USA casualty business from the 1930s to the early 1980s it is more appropriate now as an appendix. From the 1960s to the mid 1980s it was common for Reinsurers world-wide to write so called “global “ excess of loss catastrophe layers that included both property and casualty lines. This resulted in property Underwriters who participated on these “global “ programmes exposing their backers to a host of potential asbestos and pollution and other claims. These policies are no longer obtainable and therefore we have also excluded that section.

For the third edition Chris Ventiroso of the Harvey Bowring syndicate at Lloyd’s (now part of Amlin) did a very full and erudite explanation of the development of the aggregate extension clause. The inclusion of this extension clause was one of the main reasons for Reinsurers to be exposed to asbestos claims. We have mutually decided due to legal developments since then not to include that paper in this edition. Readers who wish to follow this up should get hold from a library copy of the third edition.

We are pleased to include in this chapter help from three experts in this field. The first is Charles Skey, who is a well known both in London and the Reinsurance Industry world wide for his charm and expertise. He is in every sense "a leader" and his views based on lifetime experiences are always cogent and sensible. Charles allowed the author to use the explanations of the asbestos-related problems and pollution from his underwriting report sent to his names in 1990. It summarises both these problems in an understandable way and We are grateful to him and to the R.A.Edwards Syndicate (now part of Ace) to use them.

Secondly we are indebted to Thomas J Quinn, a partner in Mendes and Mount of New York, who has helped us trace the history of the asbestos problem. Including the setting up of the Wellington agreement. It is one of the clearest statements of how the asbestos problem developed.

Thirdly May I thank Valerie Fogleman, a partner at Barlow Lyde and Gilbert of London for her short history of the pollution problem so far.

ASBESTOS

Mr Charles Skey's addendum to his report to members of the R.A.Edward's syndicate 1990.

Asbestos, once widely regarded as the "wonder-fibre", has in recent years given rise to "fibre phobia" and an onslaught of litigation. A group of fibrous inorganic materials that share specific properties, asbestos has been considered since ancient times as one of man's most useful natural resources due to its ability to withstand searing temperatures yet remain soft and pliable. Today, utilised primarily for its insulating and fire-retardant properties, asbestos is contained in over 3,000 products of note. Ironically, however, its usefulness and widespread production have spawned a volume of litigation targeted at those responsible for its manufacture. Accurate evaluation of the eventual size of the problem of asbestos-related bodily injury claims is precluded by the long latency period, sometimes up to 20 to 30 years, between a claimant's exposure to asbestos fibres and and the clinical manifestation of asbestos-related disease.

In 1985, under the terms of the Wellington Agreement, the Asbestos Claims Facility (Facility) was established between certain subscribing asbestos producers and Insurers to respond to personal injury claims. Although the Facility achieved a reduction in litigation and an acceleration of claims payments to injured parties, internal dissention led to its dissolution in October 1988.

Following the demise of the Facility, the Centre for Claims Resolution (CCR) was formed to allow an alternative to court resolution of asbestos-related bodily injury and coverage issues. The CCR, although producer-driven, is supported by Insurers. It is guided by the philosophy of, where prudent, settling meritorious claims early through group settlement, thereby reducing indemnity and defence costs. In its first full year of operation, the CCR has achieved a significant increase in the rate of the settlements over prior years administered through the old Facility.

Unfortunately, new cases continue to be advised to the CCR at a monthly average of 2,100 for 1989, souring hopes that the problem of asbestos-related bodily injury had peaked. The CCR began 1989 with roughly 69,000 claims pending to its members. Although it closed approximately 24,400 claims in 1989, approximately 24,600 new claims were filed. It is gratifying that the average settlement amount has remained fairly consistent over time, indicating that the seriousness of the claims may be declining. Notably, a large percentage of the cases, over 80%, stem from traditional occupations, i.e. construction, shipyard and insulation. The balance of the claims emanate from non-traditional occupations, basically workers in the steel and tyre manufacturing industries.

Property damage claims arising from asbestos containing materials (ACM) in buildings were not considered by the old Facility, nor are they part of the CCR. Initially, concern over the potential hazards of ACM focused upon schools in the form of legal actions for the "Rip Out and Replacement" in school buildings. In 1986, Congress enacted the Asbestos Hazard Emergency Response Act (AHERA) which required the United State Environmental Protection Agency (USEPA) to establish a comprehensive regulatory framework of inspection, planning, maintenance and abatement of ACM in the nation's schools. While ACM in school litigation is ongoing, the recent thrust of legal activity appears to have shifted to the arena of public and commercial buildings. The estimated cost of removing ACM from all public and commercial buildings would clearly be very substantial.

On 30th January 1990, a multi-state lawsuit was filed in the United States Supreme Court by the Attorneys General of 29 states seeking a resolution of the ACM in public buildings issue. There is reason for suspicion that the lawsuit is politically motivated and although it is too early to hypothesise on the merits of the case, it has been described by one commentator as "pure hokem". Nevertheless, the action may signal additional suits in the future.

Whether Insurers of asbestos producers and manufacturers ultimately will be required to pay for the cost of removal and remediation will depend on the judicial resolution of several key issues, including whether the presence alone of asbestos constitutes property damage under Comprehensive General Liability policies, and if so, which policies are triggered.

Unfortunately, the weight of decisions to date suggests that ACM in building does constitute property damage. On a positive note, however, one influential California State Court recently withdrew an earlier pro-insured ruling on the trigger of coverage issue. Originally it ruled that ll policies between the time ACM were installed through removal are jointly and severally liable for the cost of removal and remediation. Under the revised ruling, uniformly considered as pro-Insurer, coverage is triggered either upon installation of the ACM or when asbestos fibres enter the air. There is reason for optimism that the revised ruling will set precedent in asbestos property damage coverage litigation nationwide. Another positive note for Insurers is the seemingly increased recognition that removal itself is not without risk and indeed, recent scientific data questions whether removal and remediation efforts actually increase health risk. This may mean a move by the USEPA away from removal toward asbestos air monitoring and regular air sampling. However, this would not eliminate claims for diminution of the value of buildings containing ACM.

Thomas J Quinn's abridged description of the developments of Asbestos as a Products liability problem

ASBESTOS BODILY INJURY LITIGATION

While isolated claims for asbestos bodily injury were first filed many years ago, the deluge of litigation over approximately the past 16 years is generally traced to the case of *Borel v. Fibreboard* a 1973 decision from the U.S. Court of Appeals for the Fifth Circuit. The Court of Appeals affirmed a judgement from the U.S. District Court for the Eastern District of Texas in favor of Borel, an insulation worker, against Fibreboard and other manufacturers of asbestos products. *Borel* was the first appellate level case to rule in favour of a plaintiff with an asbestos-related disease on the basis of products liability theories. The Fifth Circuit in *Borel* ruled that the asbestos injury to the plaintiff had been continuous in nature, and that each of the defendants which manufactured products to which *Borel* was exposed was jointly and severally liable for the damages.

Following *Borel*, additional suits began to be filed, starting in the Beaumont, Texas area, the site of the original *Borel* verdict, and gradually spreading across the entire United States. Within ten years after *Borel*, there were approximately 25,000 cases pending, and, at the present time (2000) the number of open and close cases is over 400,000 up from 220,000 only as far back as 1994.

In the years following the *Borel* decision, policyholders, the producers of asbestos-containing products, were under tremendous financial pressure. They were faced with an obligation to defend an ever-growing number of individual asbestos bodily injury claims. Suits would invariably name multiple defendants, 30 or more in some cases, each of which was required to retain counsel to defend its interests. Defense counsel were required to respond to the Complaint, conduct discovery, including interrogatories to the plaintiff, depositions of the plaintiff, his family, and co-workers, as well as conduct extensive medical discovery, which involved examination of the plaintiff's complete medical history, and despositions of physicians retained by the plaintiff and by the defendants. Complete discovery into the plaintiff's work and exposure history was required to ascertain the products to which the plaintiff was exposed. It would thus not be uncommon for 20 to 30 lawyers to attend the deposition of a single plaintiff, questioning him about his personal, medical and work history, with substantial defense costs being incurred by the defendants.

The Insurers as well were under significant pressure. The primary policies generally provide that the Insurer is obligated to defend the policyholder and to pay any claims on behalf of the policyholder. In view of the disputes regarding trigger of coverage, and other coverage issures which will be discussed subsequently, policyholders were generally incurring the defense and indemnity expenses for their own account, without contribution by the Insurers. Many jurisdictions in the United States will permit a policyholder which successfully establishes coverage to obtain bad faith punitive damages against an Insurer which wrongfully refused to defend or pay claims. Policyholders in the coverage litigation generally sought substantial punitive damages against their Insurers. At the same time, the declaratory litigation costs to the Insurers were also quite significant, a situation which was exacerbated by the fact that the Insurers were generally not having any success in litigating the coverage issues. To further increase the Insurers' exposure, some jurisdictions permit a policyholder which successfully establishes its right to coverage to recover its own attorney fees and costs. This is an exception to the usual rule in U.S. litigation, which requires each party to bear its own legal fees, and it obviously increases the potential exposure to the Insurers.

The existing United States tort system, which required the finding of fault through an adversary procedure, was clearly incapable of efficiently delivering funds to victims of asbestos disease. It was estimated by the Rand Corporation in 1983 that the contingent fee system and extensive defense costs, as well as other transactional costs, were consuming approximately 63% of the funds spent on the asbestos bodily injury problem, leaving only approximately $.37 of each dollar to compensate the plaintiff. In view of the rising number of claims, it appeared likely that the transactional costs would erode or consume the assets, including the insurance assets, of the major defendants, leaving many of the plaintiffs uncompensated.

Commencing in the mid-1970s, policyholders, frustrated in their efforts to obtain either defense or indemnity against loss from their Insurers, began to initiate declaratory coverage litigation. The liability policies generally provided coverage for bodily injury which occurs during the policy period. Two major "trigger" theories emerged from this dispute, the "exposure" theory and the "manifestation" theory.

Appellate level decisions on these issues began to emerge in the early 1980s. In 1980, the United States Court of Appeals for the Sixth Circuit affirmed a District Court ruling adopting an injurious exposure trigger in *Insurance Company of North America v. Forty-Eight Insulations* which was the first Federal appellate court decision on the trigger of coverage issue with respect to asbestos claims. The Sixth Court agreed with the District Court that general liability policies are triggered by "exposure" and that each Insurer during the period of such exposure was obligated to pay a pro rata share of defense and indemnity costs.

In a decision which was to have a far-reaching impact on the insurance industry, the Court of Appeals for the District of Columbia Circuit in 1981 handed down its decision in *Keene Corporation v. Insurance Company of North America*. The Court of Appeals adopted what came to be known as the "triple trigger", "comprehensive trigger", or "continuous trigger" decision, finding that the Insurers were obigated if they provided coverage during the period of injurious exposure, at the time of manifestation, or at any point in time from last exposure to manifestation, known as the "exposure in residence" time. The Court reasoned that the asbestos disease process continues to produce new injury even when injurious exposure has ceased, so that the policies from the date of last exposure to date of manifestation are also triggered. Thus, all policies providing coverage from first exposure to manifestation were held to be obligated pursuant to the *Keene* decision.

The United States Supreme Court, despite requests by the parties, refused to review any of the Federal asbestos trigger decisions, i.e., *Forty-Eight Insulations*, *Eagle Picher* or *Keene*.

The most aggressively litigated asbestos coverage case, the *Asbestos Insurance Coverage Cases*, also known as the *Co-ordinated Case*, tried by Judge Brown of the San Francisco Superior Court in California, was a consolidation of cases filed by five separate asbestos manufacturers (GAF, Manville, Armstrong, Fibreboard, and Nicolet). The case involved many years of discovery and trial, with hundreds of depositions having been taken and literally millions of documents produced. The issues were so complex, and so closely contested that the actual trial was separated into various phases, which were separately tried by Judge Brown, with some issues being tried by a jury as well, over the course of approximately two years. This case, clearly the most expensive coverage case ever to be litigated in the United States, required the modification of an auditorium in San Francisco to accommodate all of the parties, as the courtroom was not sufficiently large. Fifty law firms, involving 250 attorneys, participated in the case. Pursuant to Judge Brown's broad discovery order, over 100 million documents were produced, and approximately 1200 depositions were taken. The result of this significant expenditure of time and money was a judgement even more expansive than *Keene*. Judge Brown ruled that all policies in effect from first exposure until date of claim or date of death are triggered for coverage purposes. Judge Brown's rulings were eventually upheld by the California appellate court.

Scope of Coverage

In addition to the "trigger of coverage" problem, a second issue which arises in coverage litigation is referred to as the "scope of coverage" issue. This issue involves the extent of the obligation of an Insurer once its policy is triggered. Insurers generally argue that, in accord with the *INA v. Forty-Eight Insulations* case, each policy is only obligated to respond for a pro rata share of defense and indemnity amounts. To the extent that a policyholder is uninsured, or has insolvent Insurers, the policyholder must itself bear the burden of amounts allocated to said years. The policyholders, supported by *Keene*, *Lac D'Amiante du Quebec*, the *Asbestos Insurance Coverage Cases*, *J. H. France* and *Owens Illinois* case argue that the policies require the Insured to pay "all sums" which the policyholder is obligated to pay. Thus, the argument continues, each Insurer is jointly and severally obligated to pay all defense and indemnity amounts, and the policyholder is free to select the policy and year which initially must pay for defense and indemnification.

The Insurers selected by the policyholder preserve their rights to obtain contribution from other triggered policies, either on equitable subrogation grounds or pursuant to "other insurance" causes. However, this joint and several scope of coverage theory places the burden, and the resultant expense and uncertainty, on the selected Insurer to pursue other triggered Insurers. Should the Insurers in the other triggered years be insolvent, or should they be unwilling to contribute, any recovery would be speculative and expensive to obtain.

Cases such as *Keene* also express the view that a policyholder is not required to contribute if it is self-insured, uninsured, or if its policies are in excess of substantial deductibles. Self-insurance is not considered by some Courts to be insurance for the purposes of contribution under "other insurance" clauses. Accordingly, an Insurer whose policy was "triggered" may be unable to obtain contribution from the policyholder itself, and could thus be forced to bear an inequitable share of the loss.

Summary

There is no doubt that the Courts in the United States, both State and Federal, have viewed insurance as a solution to the overwhelming social problem presented by asbestos claimants. I am not personally aware of any case where a court has found no coverage for asbestos bodily injury claims in the absence of specific asbestos exclusions, which were first utilized by London Insurers for known asbestos product manufacturers in the late 1970s. In fact, the Courts almost invariably adopt the coverage position requested by the policyholder, the position which maximizes the available coverage limits.

Background of the Agreement Concerning Asbestos-related Claims

It was against the above background that an *ad hoc* group of policy-holders and Insurers began to meet in the early 1980s to attempt to negotiate a resolution of the various problems caused by the asbestos litigation, both the underlying litigation and the declaratory litigation.

The policyholders and their Insurers which formed the initial negotiating group sought a solution which would:

– *Minimize defense costs in the underlying cases through prompt settlement of meritorious claims and aggressive defense, through one attorney, of disputed claims.*

– *Resolve contribution and indemnity cross-claims among policyholders, which would have the effect of allowing the defendants to unite in their opposition to the plaintiff and which would permit the representation of the group of policyholders by common counsel, a situation which could not exist if the parties were adverse through cross-claims.*

– *Resolve the major coverage disputes between policyholders and Insurers, in order to eliminate the expense of declaratory coverage litigation.*

– *Establish a procedure for Alternate Dispute Resolution, so that remaining disputes between or among policyholders and Insurers could be expeditiously resolved in a cost-efficient manner.*

These objectives were essentially met by the terms of the "Agreement Concerning Asbestos-related Claims", which was signed by 32 policyholders and 15 Insurers on June 19, 1985, and which was subsequently executed by other policyholders, including GAF Corporation in January of 1987. The Agreement was negotiated under the auspices of the Center for Public Resources, a non-profit organization whose purpose is the resolution of disputes outside of the litigation system, under the direction of Dean Harry Wellington as the Mediator. The agreement thereafter became known as the "Wellington Agreement".

POLLUTION

This is a short history of the pollution situation written by Valerie Fogleman a partner of Barlow Lyde and Gilbert.

In 1980, the US government enacted legislation to establish strict, retroactive, joint and several liability for cleaning up historic pollution. Congress drafted the legislation, officially called the Comprehensive Environmental Response, Compensation and Liability Act but generally known as Superfund, broadly in order to impose liability on a wide range of "potentially responsible parties" (PRPs). PRPs include current and former owners and operators of contaminated sites as well as any person who "arranged for" hazardous substances to be dumped at a contaminated site.

Congress considered that the Superfund programme would lead to an estimated 400 to 2,000 seriously contaminated sites in the US being cleaned up at an average cost of between $3 and $4 million per site. Its estimates of both the number of contaminated sites and the cost of cleaning them up were seriously flawed, however. Since 1980, tens of thousands of contaminated sites have been discovered, and the cost of cleaning up the worst sites has risen to an average of $50 million per site. As a result, Congress increased the annual amount, which it appropriated to the US Environmental Protection Agency (EPA) for the programme from £0.32 billion from 1980 to 1985 to £1.7 billion from 1986 to 1993. Since 1994, annual appropriations have averaged $1.3 billion.

Claims arising from Superfund and similar state legislation began to have a significant effect on primary and excess general liability Insurers in the mid-1980s. Since that time, US, London market, continental and other Insurers and their Reinsurers have paid many hundreds of millions of dollars in claims under general liability policies, many of which were issued prior to 1980. The key issues, which have arisen, include:

(1) Whether government-mandated clean-up costs constitute "damages" under standard comprehensive/commercial general liability ("CGL") policies;

(2) whether the insured expected or intended property damage to result from its conduct;

(3) whether proceedings issued by a governmental agency are a "suit" under CGL policies;

(4) determining which policies are triggered when the resulting damage spans many policy periods;

(5) allocating the costs of progressive environmental damage between the various primary and excess policies on risk during an occurrence;

(6) whether pollution exclusions with a sudden and accidental exception bar cover for gradual pollution;

(7) whether absolute pollution exclusions bar cover for environmental and other pollution;

(8) whether the owned property exclusion bars cover for cleaning up groundwater and subsoil on the insured's property to prevent further environmental harm to groundwater or nearby property; and

(9) whether cover exists for pollution-related claims under the personal injury section of CGL policies.

Results of litigation on these issues continue to be mixed. Although Insurers have had notable successes, many courts have ruled in favour of insureds, finding that clean-up costs and associated expenses are recoverable damages under CGL and excess policies.

As pollution insurance coverage disputes have been litigated or have settled and as reinsureds have presented claims to their Reinsurers, reinsurance issues have arisen. Key reinsurance issues include:

(1) the allocation of costs between reinsurance agreements;

(2) whether costs incurred by reinsureds in disputing insurance cover with insureds are covered by reinsurance agreements; and

(3) the effect of follow the settlements clauses.

It is impossible to predict accurately how long reinsurance disputes arising from claims under Superfund, similar state legislation and associated personal injury, property damage and natural resource damage claims will continue or to quantify the cost of such disputes to Reinsurers. Although clean ups at many of the more complex and costly sites under the Superfund programme are nearing completion or have been completed, further contaminated sites continue to be discovered and associated claims continue to be made.

In November 1995, Standard & Poor's Insurance Rating Services considered that pollution-related liabilities would cost Reinsurers at least $125 billion between 1996 and 2024. In January 1996, A.M. Best estimated that such claims would cost Insurers approximately $73 billion, with approximately half of the costs arising from state Superfund programmes.

Claims against insureds, Insurers and Reinsurers from pollution are not limited to incidents in the US. The UK has introduced a regime to remediate contamination caused by historic pollution incidents as have many other countries. In addition, the European Commission's proposed regime to impose strict, prospective, joint and several liability for clean-up costs, biodiversity damages (that is, damage to natural resources which affect biodiversity), property damage and personal injuries for specified pollution incidents has gathered pace during recent years. As with US pollution legislation, the introduction of these regimes has resulted and will continue to result in claims against reinsurance agreements.

Conclusion

There will be many further developments on Asbestos and Pollution and other industrial diseases etc. in the next century. However relating to Lloyd's syndicates now are all reinsured by Equitas the company formed to take all the run off from 1992 and prior years and therefore claims no longer affect individual syndicates. In 2000 Equitas had to "make further provisions for asbestos litigation". Haven't we heard that before, will it ever end!

I understand that the Year 2000 date change which began the new century has been a non-event but some Insureds are looking to recover the cost of their remediation programme put into place before , nothing ever changes!

GLOSSARY OF SOME REINSURANCE TERMS

A

Accounted Income — The premium income of an Insurer accounted in his books for any year.

Acquisition Costs — Costs incurred specifically in writing or issuing an insurance policy, e.g. commission to a Broker as opposed to the company's general overheads.

Additional Perils — Perils added to the main peril covered under a policy, e.g. flood included under a fire policy.

Adjustable Policy — An insurance or reinsurance where a provisional premium is payable at inception and adjusted after expiry.

Aggregate Excess Reinsurance — A reinsurance, which covers the aggregation of all losses that occur during a period excess of the deductible.

Allied Perils — Perils additional and similar or allied to the main perils covered under a policy, e.g. explosion or sprinkler leakage included in a fire policy.

Arbitration Clause — A clause in reinsurance policies under which both parties agree to submit disputes to arbitration.

Assigned Risks — Risks (usually those which are hard to insure) which are assigned to be written by certain Insurers or pools of Insurers.

B

Back up — Reinsurance that responds once the "upfront cover is exhausted". It is sometimes called a reinstatement cover.

Bank Guarantee — A guarantee by the Bank made instead of depositing a physical asset or cash, e.g. for a loss reserve.

Banker — A "reinsurance" contract where premiums are "banked" with a Reinsurer with the intention that they will return the premium in the future with interest.

Binding Cover — An authority issued by an Insurer to another party to accept insurances on his behalf.

Books and Records clause (access to records clause) — Authority in a treaty for Reinsurers to have the right to enter a Reassured's office and inspect his books and records.

Bordereaux Advices of cessions to a treaty, giving details of each cession.

Broker of Record A clause in a treaty or contract wording recognising the Broker of that reinsurance.

Burning Cost (1) The cost of past losses.
(2) A rating method where the rate is a function of past loss experience.

C

Captive Company An insurance company owned by a "parent" company and writing its owner's insurance.

Casualty (1) Liability or third party business.
(2) A loss; notably a marine sinking.

Catastrophe A disastrous loss.

Catastrophe Reinsurance A reinsurance contract to protect against single serious loss or losses.

Caveat Emptor Where the onus is on the buyer to beware.

Cession The reinsurance of part of an original insurance.

Ceding Making a reinsurance cession.

Ceding Company One who cedes.

Claims Co-operation Clause Where the Reassured agrees to consult and co-operate with Reinsurers on claims handling and settlement.

Claims made Basis An insurance contract which covers only losses which are first advised to the Insurer during the contract period.

Closing Reinsurance Reinsurances of an entire portfolio of outstanding liabilities and o/s claims to close down an insurance operation.

Co-insurance (1) In the U.S.A. direct insurance stipulation of insurance to value
(2) A number of direct Insurers insuring the same policy.
(3) Retention by the Reassured in his own reinsurance (c.f. Co-reinsurance).

Commutation The finalization of an outstanding loss by payment of an agreed figure in settlement. This can also be applied to unknown losses i.e. I.B.N.R. and thus the contract becomes "commuted" and no further claims can be paid.

Consequential Loss Insurance of loss following direct damage, e.g. loss of profits; loss of use insurance. Business interruption.

Contingency Insurance Insurance of loss due to a contingency, e.g. non-performance, cancellation of event.

Contingent Commission Profit commission or share of profits on a reinsurance.

Commutation The finalisation of an outstanding loss by payment of an agreed figure in settlement.

Contract Specifically a reinsurance contract where a premium is paid to cover certain eventualities.

Contributing Business Where Reinsurers' liability for claims is proportional to premium ceded.

Costs in Addition An insurance or reinsurance contract that pays all legal fees associated with the claim in addition to the claim itself. The costs are usually split between the retention and the excess layer in proportion to the loss.

Costs Inclusive An insurance or reinsurance contract that pays all legal fees associated with the claim within the policy limit. Either the costs or the claim can exhaust the limit.

Cover Note A piece of paper giving or confirming insurance or reinsurance cover.

Co-reinsurance (1) Retention by a Reassured in his own reinsurance.
(2) Several Reinsurers on the same reinsurance.

Cut Through Clause A clause making a Reinsurer directly liable to a direct Assured in lieu of the Reassured.

D

Debited Income The premium income debited by an Insurer during any period.

Deductible
(1) On direct insurance the first part of an insured loss paid by the Assured and thus not insured. (Also called an Excess.)
(2) On excess or aggregate reinsurance, the first part of a loss or aggregate retained by the Reassured. The point at which a Reinsurer becomes liable to pay.

Deposit Premium A premium or part premium paid at inception of an insurance or reinsurance.

Direct Liability Clause c.f. cut through clause: making a Reinsurer directly liable to an Assured, by-passing the Reassured.

Discounting The reduction of loss reserves to take into account future projected investment income.

E

Earned Income in a Period The proportion of total premium that would have been charged for a particular period on a policy. i.e. the earned premium for 6 months would be 50% of the annual premium.

Earned Premium Income The sum of all the individual earned premiums on all policies making up a block of business.

Excess Aggregate Reinsurance A reinsurance, which covers the aggregation of all losses that, occur during a period excess of the deductible.

Excess Cession A reinsurance contract that only pays claims that are in excess of the excess point and for which a premium has been ceded or paid.

Excess of Loss Insurance An insurance where the Insurer's liability only attaches when a loss exceeds a certain figure(this is often called the excess point or deductible). Compare with franchise.

Excess of Loss R/I Clause A clause in a reinsurance contract excluding from that contract excess of loss reinsurance accepted by the Reassured.

Excess Line Excess Risk An excess of loss reinsurance where the limit and deductible are expressed as a percentage of premium income.

Excess Loss Ratio An excess aggregate reinsurance contract where the deductible is expressed as a percentage of premium income. Often called a stop loss.

Ex Gratia A claim settlement made without admission of liability or where liability clearly does not exist.

F

Facultative Reinsurance	An individual reinsurance negotiated and placed individually.
Facultative Obligatory Treaty	A treaty where reinsurances are ceded optionally by a Reassured but where Reinsurers are obliged to accept all such cessions.
Fair Plan	Schemes in the U.S.A. under which certain risks can be insured by insurance pools at controlled rates.
First Loss	The first part of an insured loss — often the deductible of an insurance or reinsurance.
First Surplus Treaty	An arrangement to cede amounts above a Reassured's net retention on any insured policy.
Flat Rate	Where a contract is rated at a fixed rate rather than an adjustable rate.
Franchise Deductible	Where an insurance or reinsurance only covers losses exceeding a certain size but then it pays the whole of the loss including the deductible.

G

Generic Losses	Losses that arise out of a common cause but not necessarily one event, i.e. asbestos, savings and loans, under-valuation of property by surveyors etc.
Global Excess	An excess of loss contract covering all classes including property and casualty (cover now rarely given this way because of asbestosis).
Gross Premium	The full amount of premium before deduction of any costs.
Gross Premium Income	The total of all gross premiums without deduction of any premiums paid for reinsurance.
Gross Net Premium Income	The total of all gross premiums before deductions of any commissions or costs but after deduction of premiums paid for reinsurance outwards.
Gross Net Written Premium Income	The total of all gross premiums written during a period before deduction of any commissions or costs but after deduction of premiums paid for reinsurances commencing during the same period.

Gross Net Earned Premium Income — The total of all gross premiums earned during a period less the earned portion of premiums for outwards reinsurances.

I

(I.B.N.R.) Incurred But Not Reported — A loss that has happened but has not been notified yet. Also used for known losses that have happened and known reserves where the quantum of the loss may increase in the future.

Indemnity —
(1) The principle of indemnity, i.e. the reimbursement by insurance of a financial loss actually suffered. No more, no less.

(2) The amount of an insurance policy or amount of claim paid to indemnify an Insured.

Indexation — Indexed Deductible — A method of varying the deductible and the indemnity of an excess loss reinsurance according to prices, cost of living, wages or some similar index.

Insurable Interest — The principle that an Insured must suffer financial loss or injury before having the right to an insurance recovery.

Interlocking Clause — A clause on a risks attaching layer that allows the Reassured to retain only one retention for losses that affect different risks attaching years. The loss is paid proportionally by Reinsurers on the different years with the deductible and limit also reducing proportionately.

L

Legal Expenses — Specifically legal expenses in relation to a claim.

Letter of Credit (LOC) — A line of credit issued normally by a Bank to a Reassured, which can be drawn down to cover a liability, e.g. to cover the reserve for a loss in lieu of cash deposit.

Liability —
(1) The liability of a Reinsurer to a Reassured.
(2) In the U.S.A., third party liability is a class of business.

Loading — A loading applied to losses or loss experience to produce a rate or premium for a contract.

Long-Tail Business — Classes of business where claims take a long time to be advised or to be settled.

Loss
(1) An individual settled claim.
(2) A number of individual settled claims from one incident.
(3) Where the balance between premiums and claims is negative i.e. an underwriting loss or technical loss.
(4) Balance on a year's trading.

Loss Cost A rating method where the rate is a function of the losses under a contract.

Loss Expenses Those expenses incurred in settling claims or losses, c.f. claims expenses.
Technically "loss expenses" does not include expenses incurred in successfully rejecting a claim.

Loss Occurrence
(1) An occurrence of a single loss.
(2) An occurrence of several losses in the same incident or catastrophe or disaster.

Loss Occurring A reinsurance policy that is "losses occurring" covers all losses that occur during the specified period usually 12 months.

Loss Portfolio The transfer from one Reinsurer to another of liability for outstanding losses for a consideration.

Loss Prevention Steps taken to prevent or lessen losses occurring or to lessen their effect.

Loss Reserve
(1) The setting up of a reserve for outstanding losses.
(2) The setting up and the depositing by a Reinsurer with the Reassured of such a reserve.

Loss Warranty Often called a market franchise. A policy that responds to the size of a market insured loss, e.g. if the hurricane is over say $5billion.

M

Manual Increase The premium as set out in a "manual" in the U.S.A. for an increase in the limit of an insurance policy.

Margin of Solvency The difference between the assets and liabilities of an insurance company particularly related to the volume of business written.

Market Franchise See loss warranty.

N

Name — Historically only individuals but now it can be companies who back particular syndicates at Lloyd's.

Natural Expiry — The normal expiry date of a policy of insurance.

Net Loss — A loss after deduction of recoveries, salvage and reinsurance.

Net Premium —
(1) A premium net of brokerage, agents' costs or ceding commission.
(2) A premium net of reinsurance cost.

Net Retention — The amount of liability retained by a Reassured for himself on a risk or policy.

Net Retained Lines Clause — A clause in an excess loss contract stating that the contract covers liability on net retentions only.

Non Proportional Business — Reinsurance where a Reinsurer's share of loss is not proportional to his share or original premiums, e.g. excess loss reinsurance or excess aggregate reinsurance.

O

Obligatory Treaty — A treaty where a Reassured is obliged to cede and a Reinsurer is obliged to accept.

Occurrence — Loss occurrence — an event, disaster or catastrophe which gives rise to many individual policy losses.

Open Year — An insurance or reinsurance year of account which is not closed or finalised. Common with Lloyd's and companies which may keep a year of account open until the 36th month.

Original Net Rate — The rate charged on an original insurance less acquisition costs.

Original Gross Rate — The rate charged on an orginal insurance without any deductions.

Outstanding Claim — A claim not paid yet.

Outstanding Claims Advance (OCA) — An advance payment by Reinsurers to a Reassured to cover the Reassured's outstanding claims — often made in trust.

Outstanding Claim Reserve A deposit made by Reinsurers with the Reassured to cover outstanding claims.

Overriding Commission (Overrider)
(1) A commission paid to a Reassured by a Reinsurer in excess of the Reassured's expenses or acquisition costs.
(2) A percentage of premium paid on a proportional treaty in addition to acquisition costs to cover the reinsureds costs.

P

Physical Damage Notably a peril causing destruction of property rather than third party or contingent loss.

Policies Issued Basis A treaty protecting original insurances commencing within a period.

Portfolio Reinsurance A reinsurance of an entire book of business.

Premium Income The sum total of premium in a certain period.

Premium Reserve A sum deposited by a Reinsurer with the Reassured to cover business in force at a given moment.

Primary A primary policy pays all the losses below an excess policy or programme it is the most exposed part of the programme with usually a large loss frequency.

Proportional Specifically reinsurance where the Reinsurer receives a proportion of premiums and pays the same premium of any claim on that risk.

Pro Rata In proportion.

Pro Rata Temporis In proportion to time.

Q

Quota Share A proportional treaty where the same proportion is ceded on all cessions.

R

Rate On Line (ROL) A commonly used term on an excess of loss layer by dividing the premium received by the limit worked out as a percentage, i.e. with a rate on line of 10% one would expect a total loss every ten years.

Reassured **Reinsured**	One who is reinsured.
Reciprocity	The mutual exhange of reinsurance.
Reinstatement	If a catastrophe programme has a loss. The Reassured can reinstate the limit covered to protect against a further loss, a reinstatement premium is paid. All excess of loss programmes can have limited reinstatements and sometimes they are free.
Reinsurance to Close	Reinsurance of an entire operation to close it down. Particularly a Lloyd's Syndicate closing and paying out at 36 months of a year's account.
Reinsurer	One who accepts a reinsurance.
Retrocession	Used to mean a proportional reinsurance of a reinsurance account now used mainly for non-proportional or excess of loss contracts.
Retrosurance	Archaic word for excess of loss retrocession, use retrocession instead.
Risk	(A) An individual exposure. (B) A peril insured. (C) An insurance or reinsurance transaction, e.g. a "good risk".
Risks Attaching	A risks attaching reinsurance covers all losses that occur on policies that attach or incept during the period of reinsurance, usually 12 months, whenever the losses occur. Compare with losses occurring and claims made.
Risk Excess	An excess of loss reinsurance where the contract is expressed: "excess of each and every loss each and every risk". (N.B. Risk being an individual exposure.)
Risk Exposure	The aggregation of risk values over a certain level or deductible.
Risk Management	The art or craft of assessing an Assured's exposure to loss and taking steps to mitigate that exposure.
Risk Profile	A table that shows the size of individual risks written in bands.
Roller	A "reinsurance" where premium each year, paid each year net of recoveries, is rolled forward to next year's contract and added to the indemnity thereunder.

S

Second Surplus The amount on a risk surplus to the Reassured's net retention and cession to any first surplus.

Self-Rated A contract rated as a function of its own loss experience.

Short-Tail Business on which claims are known and settled quickly.

Signed Risks A Lloyd's term for risks signed by their Central Office, signing often taking place after the date business is accepted. This has changed since 1995 all policies now attach to the year of account to which they incept not to that which they sign.

Sliding Scale Where a treaty ceding commission fluctuates according to treaty results.

Spiral A term used when Reinsurers of a reinsurance account reinsured themselves, therefore the reinsurance was useless. Once losses reached the so-called spiral market all layers would be exhausted very quickly. The PMLs ARE 100%!

Spread Loss A type of financial reinsurance that spreads a loss over many years.

Stop Loss An excess aggregate insurance or reinsurance, i.e. a contract that stops aggregate losses at a certain point.

T

Technical Reserves Reserves made for future underwriting liabilities on an insurance or reinsurance account.

Time and Distance A financial reinsurance where the contract will pay out specified payments in the future. The limits paid out will be greater than the premium, due to the delay of settlement, this difference is intended by the seller to be made up by investment income.

Treaty An agreement between a Ceding Company and Reinsurers to cede individual reinsurances.

Twenty-fourth System A method of calculation of earned premium from written premiums.

U

Uberrimae Fides — Utmost good faith (almost archaic).

Underwriting Agent/Agency — A firm carrying out underwriting for a group of insurance companies or Lloyd's names.

Ultimate Net Loss — The loss to a Reassured after deduction is made for all recoveries and salvages.

Unearned Premium — (1) At any date the amount of premium on a policy representing the period that that policy has to run.

(2) The total of the above on a reinsurance portfolio.

Unearned Premium Reserve — The amount deposited by a Reinsurer with his Reassured representing the unearned premiums at the close of a year.

Unexpired Liability — The proportion of a policy which has to run at any date.

Use and Occupancy — Insurance of loss of use of a plant or machinery or occupancy of a building.

W

Written Premium — Premiums received for policies attaching during a period.

SOME ABBREVIATIONS

a/c	Year of Account, e.g. 1985 A/C
A.P.	Additional premium
Adj.	To be adjusted at
a.o.l.	Any one loss
ART	Alternate risk transfer
B.C.	Burning cost
C.C.	Ceding commission
C/F	Carried forward or carry forward
C.G.L.	Comprehensive/commercial general liability
C.N.	Cover note
C.L.	Consequential loss
Con. Loss	Consequential loss
Coins.	Co-insurance
D. & O.	Directors and Officers Liability
Dep.	Deposit, e.g. Dep. prem.
e.e.l.	Each and every loss
e.e.r.	Each and every risk
E & O	Errors & omissions
Ex R/I	Excess of loss reinsurance
Ex. Agg.	Excess aggregate reinsurance
Excl.	Exclusion
E.P.I.	Earned or Estimated premium income
E.M.L.	Estimated maximum loss
Fac.	Facultative
Fac/Oblig.	Facultative obligatory treaty
F.G.U.	(Loss) from the ground up
I.B.N.R.	Incurred but not reported
1st S.	First surplus treaty
G.N.P.I.	Gross net premium income
G.N.E.P.I.	Gross net earned premium income
G.N.W.P.I.	Gross net written premium income
H.P.R.	Highly protected risk
L.M.X.	London market excess (includes retrocession)
L.O.C.	Letter of Credit
L.R.	Loss ratio
M.I.	Manual increase
M.F.L.	Maximum foreseeable loss
M & D	Minimum & deposit premium
Min.	Minimum
N.C.A.D.	Notice of cancellation (given) to anniversary date
N.P.I.	Net premium income
N.R.L.	Net retained line
O.D.	Occupational disease

O.R.	Overrider
O.N.R.	Original net rate
O.G.R.	Original gross rate
O/S	Outstanding
	Outstanding loss or claim
O.C.A.	Outstanding claims advance
P.M.L.	Probable maximum loss
P.D.	Property damage (third party)
P.I.	Professional Indemnity
P.L.	Public liability
p.r.	Pro rata
Q.S.	Quota share
R/I	Reinsurance
R/Id	Reassured/Reinsured
R/Irs	Reinsurers
Retro.	Retrospective rating or retrocession
Reinst.	Reinstatement
R.P.	Return premium
S.L.	Stop loss
s.r.	Short rate
2nd S.	Second surplus treaty
T.P.	Third party
3rd S.	Third surplus treaty
U/O	Use & occupancy insurance
U.N.L.	Ultimate net loss
W.C.A.	Workers compensation act
W.P.I.	Written premium income
Wty.	Warranty

BIBLIOGRAPHY

1. *Alternative Risk Financing.* Published by Jim Bannister Developments Limited in association with Aon Group and Zurich International.

2. *Reinsurance Underwriting 2nd Edition* written by Robert Kiln and Stephen Kiln published by LLP.

3. *Predictions on Lloyd's and Reinsurance* by Robert Kiln published by LLP.

4. *Modest Proposals for Bringing Reinsurance Law up to Date.* By Ken Louw and Hugh Thompson.
Reinsurance Evaluations www.re-eval.co.uk

INDEX